D0758795

The Economic North–South Divide

Six Decades of Unequal Development

Kunibert Raffer
Department of Economics,
University of Vienna, Austria

H.W. Singer
Institute of Development Studies,
University of Sussex, UK

Edward Elgar
Cheltenham, UK • Northampton MA, USA

© Kunibert Raffer and Hans Singer 2001

All rights reserved. No part of this publication may be reproduced, stored in a retrieval system or transmitted in any form or by any means, electronic, mechanical or photocopying, recording, or otherwise without the prior permission of the publisher.

Published by
Edward Elgar Publishing Limited
Glensanda House
Montpellier Parade
Cheltenham
Glos GL50 1UA
UK

Edward Elgar Publishing, Inc.
136 West Street
Suite 202
Northampton
Massachusetts 01060
USA

A catalogue record for this book
is available from the British Library

Library of Congress Cataloguing in Publication Data
Raffer, Kunibert, 1951–
    The economic North–South divide : six decades of unequal development / Kunibert
    Raffer, H.W. Singer
        p. cm.
    Includes bibliographical references and index.
    1. Debts, External – Developing countries. 2. Economic assistance – Developing countries. 3. International economic relations. 4. Economic history – 1945–
I. Singer, Hans Wolfgang, 1910– II. Title.

HJ8899.R338 2001
338.9 – dc21

                                                                                          2001023134

ISBN 1 84064 152 5

Printed and bound in Great Britain by Biddles Ltd, *www.biddles.co.uk*

Contents

Figures

Tables

Preface

The unequal relationship between North and South, or the centre and periphery of the world economy, which is the subject of this book, has many dimensions. We had to be selective in dealing with what we believe to be the most important of these dimensions. Other authors might legitimately make different choices. But underlying our whole book is a conviction that the present structure of the world economy makes for unequal relations – what has been called a 'structuralist' viewpoint. Few would deny that there is at present a very unequal distribution of economic power; and most would agree that it would be desirable to reduce this inequality. It is to this purpose that the arguments and proposals of this book are addressed and it is from this perspective that they should be judged. It seems to us an inevitable component of the now universally agreed goal of development: the reduction of poverty. After setting out the evolution of the present unequal global governance (Chapter 1) and the much debated question of terms of trade (Chapter 2), Chapters 3 and 4 survey the evolution of development thinking and policies with our perspective in mind. We then turn to the basic subjects of trade, aid and debts, with special emphasis on Lomé (EU/ACP relations), the currently (September 2000) particularly topical case of oil and OPEC, and the case of the Asian tigers. In a concluding chapter we present what we hope are positive proposals for a more equal world order, where people seem to matter again.

In writing this book we have repeatedly received valuable help from friends and colleagues drawing our attention to a special publication, providing useful information or valuable suggestions. We are thus able to sharpen our points. We are indebted to Ruthanne Cecil, Raphie Kaplinsky, Roddy McKinnon, Alex C. Michalos, Bruce Rich, John Toye and Adrian Wood. We are grateful to Kim Collins for her assistance, going well beyond normal secretarial support.

Chapter 1, though revised, draws on the paper 'Half a Century of Economic and Social Development Policies of the UN and Bretton Woods Institutions' by H.W. Singer in *The Pakistan Development Review* (Winter 1995, **34**(4), pp.375ff). Chapter 2 is based on Singer's 'Beyond Terms of Trade: Convergence/Divergence and Creative/Uncreative Destruction', published by the *Zagreb International Review of Economics and Business* (**1**(1) May 1998, pp.13ff). We gratefully acknowledge permission to use these papers.

K.R.
H.W.S.

Abbreviations

ACP	African, Caribbean, Pacific (countries)
ADB	Asian Development Bank
AID	(US) Agency for International Development
APEC	Asian Pacific Economic Co-operation
ATC	Agreement on Textiles and Clothing
BIS	Bank for International Settlements
BWIs	Bretton Woods institutions
CE	Commercial Element
CEECs	Central and Eastern European Countries
CFF	Compensatory Finance Facility
cif	cost, insurance and freight
CIS	Commonwealth of Independent States
CMEA	Council of Mutual Economic Assistance
CTTs	countries and territories in transition
DAC	Development Assistance Committee
DFToT	Double Factoral Terms of Trade
DSR	Debt Service Ratio
ECA	Economic Commission for Africa (of UN)
ECLA(C)	UN Economic Commission for Latin America (and the Caribbean)
ECOSOC	Economic and Social Council (of UN)
E(E)C	European (Economic) Community
EDC	Export Development Corporation (of Canada)
EDF	European Development Fund
EIA(US)	Energy Information Administration
EIB	European Investment Bank
ERP	European Recovery Program(me)
ESAF	Enhanced Structural Adjustment Facility
EU	European Union
FAO	Food and Agricultural Organization of the UN
FDI	foreign direct investment
fob	free on board
FTA	Free Trade Areas
GATS	General Agreement on Trade in Services
GATT	General Agreement on Tariffs and Trade

GDP	gross domestic product
GNP	gross national product
GPG	global public good
GSP	gross social product
HIC	Highly Indebted Country
HIPC	Highly Indebted Poor Country (Initiative)
IBRD	International Bank for Reconstruction and Development
IC	Industrial Country
ICOR	incremental capital-output ratio
IDA	International Development Association
IDB	Inter-American Development Bank
IFC	International Finance Corporation
IFI	international financial institutions
ILO	International Labour Organization
IMF	International Monetary Fund
ISEW	Index of Sustainable Economic Welfare
ITO	International Trade Organization
LLDC	least developed country
LTCM	Long Term Capital Management
MAI	Multilateral Agreement on Investment
MFA	Multi-Fibre Arrangement
NAFTA	North American Free Trade Agreement
NBToT	net barter terms of trade
NEF	New Economics Foundation
NFIDCs	net food-importing developing countries
NGO	non-governmental organization
NI	Net Importers
NIC	newly industrializing country
NIEO	New International Economic Order
NIS	newly independent states
NPL	Non-Performing Loans
NPV	net present value
NTB	Non-Tariff Trade Barrier
OA	Official Aid
ODA	official development assistance
ODF	Official Development Finance
OECD	Organization for Economic Cooperation and Development
OED	Operations Evaluation Department (of the IBRD)
OEEC	Organization for European Economic Co-operation
OOF	other official flows
OPEC	Organization of Petroleum Exporting Countries
PRGF	Poverty Reduction and Growth Facility

PSI	Preshipment Inspection
PST	Prebisch–Singer thesis
RTA	Retroactive Terms Adjustment
SADC	Southern African Development Community
SA(L)	structural adjustment (loan)
SC	southern country
SDA	Social Dimensions of Adjustment
SDR	special drawing right
SILIC	Severely Indebted Low Income Country
SPR	Strategic Petroleum Reserve
SSA	Sub-Sahara Africa
(S)UNFED	(Special) UN Fund for Economic Development
TMB	Textiles Monitoring Body
TNC	Transnational Corporation
ToT	terms of trade
TRIMS	Trade Related Investment Measures
TRIPS	Trade Related Intellectual Property-Rights
UN	United Nations
UNCTAD	United Nations Conference on Trade and Development
UNDP	United Nations Development Programme
UNEDA	United Nations Economic Development Administration
UNICEF	United Nations International Children's Emergency Fund
UNRRA	UN Relief and Rehabilitation Administration
WEP	World Employment Programme
WTO	World Trade Organization
WTO	World Tourism Organization

1. Six decades of economic and social development policies

THE SYSTEM ORIGINALLY ENVISAGED AT BRETTON WOODS AND SAN FRANCISCO

It is customary to date the origin of the Bretton Woods system back to 1942 when Keynes, and his associates in London, prepared the three famous memoranda on the International Clearing Union, on commodity buffer stocks and on a Fund for Relief and Reconstruction. To these three memoranda we may add the Beveridge Report which appeared in the same year, 1942. Keynes had taken a great interest in the Beveridge Report and this model of a national social welfare state was readily capable of international extension and application.

However, in this historical perspective we may well go a little further back. The Great Depression of the 1930s had shown that in the absence of multilateral agreements and multilateral institutions the economic system was in danger of degenerating into beggar-my-neighbour policies leading to general immiserization. The World Economic Conference of 1931 had been a first attempt to create an international economic order to prevent this from continuing. Although this attempt ended in failure the ideas then brought forward had continued to reverberate in Keynes's mind. His vision underlying the 1942 documents was governed by the overarching principle of 'never again!' – never again back to the conditions of the 1930s which were seen as having brought about not only mass misery and mass unemployment but also Hitlerism and war. Also never again a failure like that of the 1931 World Economic Conference.

We may then move forward to 1940. Hitler was triumphant and his minister of economics and president of the Reichsbank, Walter Funk, proclaimed in Berlin a 'new order' under which Europe with its colonies and indeed the world would be unified under German leadership. It might be interesting to note in passing that Nazi plans of a new order included a European Economic Community with an Economic Council composed of representatives of member states, and committees for trade, agriculture and so on, very similar to present EU structures, even the prospect of a European currency union, though no European Parliament, not even one without real parliamentary powers (Laughland, 1997, p.35).

This new order was treated as a big propaganda item by the Germans and the British minister of information, worried about the propaganda effect of Funk's new order, asked Keynes to prepare a broadcast to counteract and discredit the German propaganda. At that point Keynes became convinced that the most effective counter-move would be to prepare a valid counter-proposal rather than attack Funk's 'fraudulent offer,' as he called it. From then on Keynes's mind turned to such a constructive counter-proposal, namely to counter Funk's fraudulent new order with a genuine new international system. In that sense Keynes's idea of the Bretton Woods system can be considered as a case of good coming out of evil.

The structure envisaged by Keynes, arising from his belief in the possibility and sustainability of full employment through active government policy – later expanded by Harrod and Domar to full employment growth – and embodied in the 1942 memoranda rested on four pillars. The first pillar was that of global macroeconomic monetary and financial management. The original bold idea was of a world central bank which would maintain full employment equilibrium and provide the liquidity required for this purpose by expanding the supply of 'bancor' (his proposed world currency). This would mainly serve to finance the balance of payments deficit countries: quite logically, the balance of payments deficit countries were to be supported; they were the 'good boys' who created additional net employment in the rest of the world. By contrast, the balance of payments surplus countries were the 'bad boys' exporting unemployment to the rest of the world. In fact, at one stage Keynes proposed an international tax on balance of payments surpluses at the rate of 1 per cent a month, partly to finance the deficits, partly to finance international commodity buffer stocks and partly to give an incentive to balance of payments surplus countries to reduce their surpluses by following more expansive policies. While this is an over-simplified picture of 1942 thinking, there is sufficient truth in it to bring home to us the startling contrast to the current orthodoxy when balance of payments equilibrium or surpluses are considered to be the result of virtue and deficits are a symptom of vice.

Even in 1942, in his 'Proposals for an International Clearing Union', when ideas of a world currency and world central bank were beginning to recede, Keynes had written: 'We need a system possessed of an internal stabilising mechanism, by which pressure is exercised on any country whose balance of payments with the rest of the world is departing from equilibrium *in either direction*, so as to prevent movements which must create for its neighbours an equal but opposite want of balance' (quoted from Harrod, 1951, p.527, note that the emphasis is in Keynes's own 'Proposals'; Keynes 1980, p.169, emphasis missing in the Moggridge edition). Some traces of this original vision are still visible today in the somewhat shadowy so-called 'surveillance' of industrial countries by the IMF, as well as demands that structural adjustment enforced by the Bretton Woods institutions should be more 'symmetrical'. In essence, however, the task of global macroeconomic management has been removed from the multilateral system and is now undertaken – in theory at least – by the G5 and G7, in combination with the 'privatized liquidity creation' through the commercial banks.

Keynes had already given a great deal of thought to what emerged as one of the key controversies surrounding the IMF, which is the question of conditionality. He objected to a 'grandmotherly' fund. (Today the IMF as well as the World Bank have become worse than grandmotherly – grandmothers are supposed to have a human face!) When he had to accept the idea of conditionality, he did so on the basis and assumption of a very large Fund. He proposed a Fund equal to half of annual world imports and on that basis was willing to concede conditionality. The American side (Harry Dexter White) proposed a much smaller Fund – one-sixth of annual world imports – and on that basis was ready to relax the criteria for conditionality. What we got instead of a trade-off between size of the Fund and degree of conditionality was the worst of all possible worlds: a small Fund with tough conditionality. Conditionality did not exist in the original IMF Articles of Agreement. The Fund started applying it from 1952 as a matter of a board policy decision (Avramovic, 1987). It was as late as 1969 that conditionality became explicitly enshrined in the Articles of Agreement (Spraos, 1986). Today's strictly conditional Fund is only 2 per cent of annual world imports. Perhaps the difference between Keynes's originally proposed 50 per cent and the actual 2 per cent is a measure of the degree to which our vision of international economic management has shrunk.

The second pillar was what ultimately emerged as the International Bank for Reconstruction and Development, or the 'World Bank'. Its historical origin lies in the proposed European Reconstruction Fund – a natural answer to Funk. In the 1942 relevant memorandum this had developed into an investment fund for relief and reconstruction: hence the often-quoted statement that originally the IMF was supposed to be a bank (in the sense of a world central bank), while the 'World Bank' was supposed to be a fund (namely the investment fund proposed in 1942). The reconstruction task proved to be less important for the new institution than was visualized in 1942, partly because of the Marshall Plan and the large US loan to the UK negotiated by Keynes towards the end of his life, and partly because some of the intended functions were taken over by the newly created UN Relief and Rehabilitation Administration (UNRRA). On the other hand, the development function for poor countries was given additional emphasis at Bretton Woods as a result of the presence of delegations from these countries (mainly Latin American but also including an Indian delegation, pro forma led by British officials as India was in the transition to independence). Originally in 1942 not much attention had been paid to development problems. Most of the countries involved, especially the Latin American countries, were assumed to do quite well during the war as a result of high prices and high demand for their raw materials, and also the protection afforded to their nascent industries as a result of reduced competition from the belligerent industrial countries. In fact Argentina emerged at the end of the war as one of the richest countries in the world in terms of per capita GNP. Most of the rest of the Third World had not yet emerged into independence and was not considered to be in urgent need of external support. Many, like India, were accumulating large external surpluses – the sterling balances – and the problem seemed to be more one of help for the UK in clearing these sterling balances than of external aid to India.

It is fair to say that originally the British side – in other words Keynes – was much more interested in the Fund than in the Bank. By contrast, the preparatory moves on the US side had been much more centred on what became the World Bank. The first major move in US thinking about the post-war international order was the commissioned report of a study group of the US Council of Foreign Relations (led by Jacob Viner and Alvin Hansen). This proposed an International Development Board to study and prepare development projects throughout the world. The shape of a future project-oriented IBRD can be clearly seen to emerge from this report. Given this initial concentration of the British side on the Fund or International Clearing Union and the US initial concentration on the Bank, it is somewhat ironic that at Bretton Woods itself it was the American (in the person of Harry Dexter White) who chaired and organized the discussions of the Fund in Commission I, while the British (in the person of Keynes) chaired the discussions on the Bank in Commission II. By that time, in 1944, the work in the US Treasury on the Fund had, of course, strongly developed, while Keynes's interest in the Bank had steadily increased. However, perhaps even more important in his thinking was the establishment of an international organization to stabilize primary commodity prices. That was the third pillar of the system he envisaged.

The third pillar was the International Trade Organization (ITO). Keynes had been a long-term advocate of stabilizing primary commodity prices, particularly in his article on 'The Policy of Government Storage of Food-Stuffs and Raw Materials ' in *The Economic Journal* in 1938. Predictably, he incorporated this idea in his proposals for Bretton Woods, linking it in an early version with his proposed International Clearing Union by suggesting a world currency based not on the dollar, gold, bancor or SDRs, but on the average price of 30 primary commodities (including gold and oil). This would automatically have stabilized the average price of these commodities without ruling out fluctuations of individual commodity prices. The main idea was to prevent the collapse of primary commodity prices which had been a marked feature – and in Keynes's view a contributory factor – of the Great Depression of the 1930s.

Such bold ideas cut little ice with Henry Morgenthau, the secretary of the US Treasury, and in fact were quickly subdued even in the London preparatory group. What remained was the proposal to set up an ITO which would have among other objectives that of stabilizing primary commodity prices by using buffer stocks, commodity agreements and direct intervention. The establishment of the ITO was firmly decided at Bretton Woods and when Keynes left the conference with everybody standing up in his honour and singing 'For he's a jolly good fellow', it was the firm belief that the achievements of Bretton Woods included the creation of this favourite brain-child of his.

Alas, the ITO was never created. Although it was quite smoothly negotiated in Havana and accepted there by all concerned, the mood in the US Congress by the time it was presented for ratification had begun to swing against the UN and international institutions. The internationalist Roosevelt/Truman era was coming to an end and the McCarthy era was beginning to cast its shadows. The ITO charter was not brought to the US Congress in time to catch the favourable tide. By the time it was brought to the US Congress, ratification had become hopeless and the ITO was abandoned even without a vote. The other countries were all set to ratify but had waited for the US Congress to ratify first. Thus the Bretton Woods system was incomplete from the beginning, lacking its intended third pillar. GATT did not fill the gap, since it had no functions relating to the stabilization of commodity prices or regulation of commodity markets.

One can engage in a number of counter-factual speculations. If Keynes had suspected that the ITO would not be created, would he still have advocated acceptance of the agreement concerning the Bank and the Fund? We do not know: by the time it was clear that the ITO would not be established, Keynes was dead. Our own guess is to answer this hypothetical question with a 'no' – but there is no way of proving it (or for that matter of disproving it). Another counter-factual speculation is this: if the real price of oil, together with practically all other primary commodities, had not deteriorated from the 1950s to 1973, would the OPEC countries still have engaged in their dramatic quadrupling of oil prices in 1973 and then again multiplied it in 1979? It is often forgotten that the 1973 action did little more than restore the real price of oil in terms of manufactures to what it had been before.

Without OPEC's action in 1973, the Bretton Woods system might not have collapsed and might have recovered from the abandonment of the fixed exchange rate between gold and dollar by President Nixon in 1971. Also, if non-oil primary commodity prices had been maintained and stabilized between the 1950s and 1973, the rise in oil prices, which was important but by no means the main or the only factor responsible for these evolutions (Raffer & Singer, 1996, p.133), would not have contributed to the balance of payments crisis and subsequent debt crisis among the countries in the South. Yet another speculation: if the Havana ITO Charter had been brought more speedily to Congress for ratification and had been more firmly supported by the US administration, the ITO might well have come into existence. History as it might have been is always a fascinating business.

The fourth pillar of the system was meant to be a soft aid programme linked more directly with the United Nations. It is noteworthy that the first draft proposal for the IBRD prepared at the US Treasury under the direction of Harry Dexter White was entitled 'A Bank for Reconstruction and Development of the United and Associated Nations'. At that time, of course, it was still visualized that the two Bretton Woods institutions would be a firm and integral part of the United Nations system which had still to be created during the year or two following upon Bretton Woods. Indeed, legally and technically, the Fund and Bank are specialized agencies of the United Nations and their guidance by the UN General Assembly and UN Economic and Social Council was intended – but we all know what the reality is. Today, the secretary-general of the United Nations is not even allowed to address the annual meetings of the Fund and Bank! All that is left from the original intention is a note on the IMF's homepage that its Articles of Agreement were adopted 'at the UN Monetary and Financial Conference, Bretton Woods, New Hampshire, July 22, 1944'.

The aid programme within the United Nations was meant to be different from IBRD lending in being on a grant or highly concessional basis, and also not limited to a project basis. The attempt to create such a mechanism with the United Nations centred upon the proposal for UNEDA (United Nations Economic Development Administration). This was originally proposed by V.K.R.V. Rao in his capacity as chairman of the UN Sub-Commission for Economic Development and in a simultaneous UN Secretariat (1949) Report on *Methods of Financing Economic Development in Underdeveloped Countries*. This was then continued in the negotiations for SUNFED (Special United Nations Fund for Economic Development). In the uncongenial climate for the UN of the early and mid-1950s, this – like the ITO – was doomed to failure. SUNFED remained UNFED – its original and unfortunate acronym (for further details, see Singer, 1984). However, in the happier climate of the late 1950s and early 1960s (the Kennedy era), there was at least a partially satisfactory outcome. The soft aid fund was created, but it was attached to the Bank rather than to the United Nations, in the form of IDA. The United Nations obtained two valuable consolation prizes: the UNDP (technical assistance had always been a strong feature of UNEDA and SUNFED) and the World Food Programme.

While this 'Grand Compromise' of 1959-61 was more satisfactory than could have been hoped for some years earlier, it laid the foundation for an unfortunate division between financial aid on the one hand and food aid and technical assistance on the other. It also helped to confirm an even broader cleavage: the UN was not to be trusted with the 'hard' instruments of development such as finance and macroeconomic policy making; that was to be the preserve of the Bretton Woods institutions with their system of weighted voting and firm control by the Western industrial countries. The UN was to be put in charge of the 'soft' instruments, such as food aid, technical assistance, children, women, social policy and, more recently, the environment. We will not here discuss the justification and viability of such a division of functions (see Streeten *et al.*, 1992). All this would not matter too much if there were really a unified UN system. This remains a hope for the future.

Thus in overview the original vision of a system resting on four pillars has remained unfulfilled. Some pillars are missing altogether, and some are constructed in a way quite different from the original plans. All the same, the system proved an immense benefit to the world for the 25 years or so until its collapse in 1971 and 1973. Our task is to recreate a genuine system with the same vision as that shown in 1942. It would not of course be the same system: times have changed and we should have learnt some lessons from past experience, but, all the same, the original ideas still have still much to teach us if we can only recapture the spirit of 1942.

GAPS IN THE BRETTON WOODS SYSTEM

The important gaps in the system created at Bretton Woods and San Francisco have to be filled. As political changes usually take time, we propose to think ahead for perhaps 25-30 years - a period long enough to permit significant and major changes, beyond tinkering with minor detail, yet short enough to rule out Utopian dreaming, such as world government, equal sharing of all food produced, equal sharing of incomes and so on. Over this medium period, if the political will exists, we can hope to do three things: (a) fill the gaps which were left when the present system of international organizations was created some 60 years ago, (b) improve the present working of the system, and (c) cope with new problems which were not thought of 60 years ago.

Filling the Gaps

(1) The chief gap to be discussed here centres upon the problems of commodities, deriving from the failure to implement the ITO. This was to

have commodity price stabilization as one of its central functions by means both of action on individual commodities and of multi-commodity action. The latter, in the original vision, was to be closely linked with the new international monetary system operated by what became the IMF. Keynes's world currency based not on gold, dollars or SDRs, but on a basket of 30 commodities (including gold and oil) was much too radical for its time. It had to be dropped when the 'serious' discussions started at Bretton Woods. But it was later revived, in 1964 when UNCTAD was established, in a proposal by three leading economists of the day (J. Tinbergen, N. Kaldor and A.G. Hart) to UNCTAD I for a multi-commodity reserve currency. These proposals would have automatically stabilized the average price in terms of world currency of the 30 commodities and thus removed the more general swings, volatility and declining trend of commodity prices (their so-called 'co-movement') while leaving individual commodity prices free to fluctuate in relation to the average, in the light of specific conditions. Keynes and the three economists were firm believers in the benefits of commodity price stabilization for the world economy, in line with prevailing professional opinion among economists dating back to Jevons and both Grahams (Benjamin and Frank).

The advantages of a commodity reserve currency, as set out by Keynes and the three economists in their 1964 proposal, were threefold:

1. to provide additional liquidity for an expanding full-employment world economy by supplementing such other sources of liquidity as gold, supply of dollars via US balance of payments deficits, SDRs or other forms of specially created international liquidity. The need for this and the wisdom of the proposal have been amply demonstrated in the slowdown of world growth following the breakdown of the dollar exchange system in 1971 and the rise in oil prices in 1973;
2. to provide an anti-cyclical regulator for the world economy using commodity prices as an automatic trigger. Rising commodity prices would indicate inflationary pressure and lead to contractionary action by releasing commodities from international buffer stocks and thus absorbing money out of circulation, and vice versa in the case of falling commodity prices;
3. by stabilizing and maintaining prices it would promote investment and transfer income to the poorer primary commodity-producing countries and thus help towards a more equal distribution of world income as well as maintain exports from industrial to primary-producing countries.

Such schemes proved to be too ingenious and clever to be acceptable in 1944 or 1964 – or indeed today. But in their absence, the terms of trade of Southern Countries (SCs) have shown a consistent tendency to deteriorate (as forecast by the 'Prebisch–Singer thesis') and to be highly volatile (highly detrimental to rational planning and policy formulation). All this makes the value of international integration of primary product exporters into the world economy quite doubtful. It also means a constant tendency to transfer income from poorer to richer countries and thus contributes to divergence rather than convergence. It has offset much of the flow of aid and investment into poorer countries; it is an irrational way to run the world economy to give with one hand and take away with the other. As explained later, the deterioration in terms of trade has been further added to by the enforced country-by-country stabilization and structural adjustment programmes of the Bretton Woods Institutions (BWIs).

In some other respects, the gap created by the missing ITO has now been filled by the creation of the World Trade Organization (WTO) to take the place of GATT. However, the functions in the commodity field assigned to the ITO are missing from the mandate of the WTO, so the gap remains. The establishment of the WTO could have made it easier to add this later to its functions, but this was not done. It is more likely that action in this field will start by breathing life into the (currently largely inoperative) IMF Compensatory Financing Facility. Avoiding the destructive approach of structural adjustment programmes that does not take into account the fallacy of composition is also necessary.

Part of the explanation for the lack of international action in the commodity area is that for the industrial countries weak commodity prices may look like a good thing in helping to control inflation. However, there must be better ways of controlling inflation than at the expense of poorer exporting countries. Our gain in inflation control will also be at the expense of our own employment as a result of reduced import capacity of primary producing countries.

(2) A less obvious, but perhaps even more important, gap is the absence of the overarching roof of global governance and coordination which the UN was supposed to represent in economic cooperation and development (as well as the political and military arena). The UN has been created and on paper the UN General Assembly and the UN Economic and Social Council (ECOSOC) have been given the necessary mandates; the BWIs on paper are specialized agencies of the UN. But in fact the unified UN system has disintegrated into two separate systems. The 'Bretton Woods' system has not only become separate and independent, but also immensely more powerful in the development field than the UN system. The main reason lies in the different systems of voting and decision making. The UN is governed, at least in the economic area, by a rule of a-country-a-vote, while the Bretton Woods system is an a-dollar-a-vote system. This gives the financially powerful countries firm control of the Bretton Woods institutions and has led them to concentrate their

support and resources on the World Bank and IMF, while withholding them from the UN system where, since the independence of many new countries, they are in a voting minority.

This has set up a vicious circle for the UN system. By withholding resources, the system has become crippled and incapable of playing its assigned role in development. This is then interpreted as failure and incompetence and becomes a reason, or pretext, for further withholding of resources. The present division of labour between the two systems is that the 'hard' aspects of development relating to monetary policy, trade, aid, development strategies and so on have been removed from the UN system which is left with the 'soft 'aspects, such as social security, employment, vulnerable groups such as women and children, health, education, development, refugees, emergencies and so on. Unsatisfactory as such a division of development into 'hard' and 'soft' issues is (especially in the light of recent redefinitions of the purposes of development and the importance of human factors), it might be workable if the two aspects were equally supported. But this is not the case. The 'soft' issues wither away, or else are taken over in the Bretton Woods system as subordinate items in a 'hard' system.

To restore a better balance and a unified system it may be necessary to create a unified voting system. Neither a-country-a-vote nor a-dollar-a-vote can claim to be fully democratic. An ideal voting system would move the present UN system closer to the Bretton Woods system and vice versa, and would also pay attention to population size and human/cultural achievements. If the political will exists, such a more satisfactory and democratic system of decision making will not be difficult to devise (see Chapter 14); there are already elements of such systems in existence, the tripartite system obtaining in the International Labour Organization (ILO).

Apart from resulting in a divided system and an imbalance of support and resources, the gap created by the absence of overarching global governance and coordination by the UN has also led to a shift of these functions out of the multilateral system into the G5, G7 and finally G8, the group of the five, seven or eight financially most powerful countries. This is, however, a clearly undemocratic forum representing less than 20 per cent of the world's population (of 'We the People' in the opening words of the UN Charter). There is also a general dissatisfaction with the quality of governance and coordination achieved in this forum. Some improvement could be made by enlarging the G8 (countries like China, India, South Africa or Brazil could become members) and giving the secretary-general of the UN and the UN agencies an active secretariat role in the G8. Another suggestion that has been made is to create an Economic Security Council (without a veto) but with a balanced distribution of voting power and with the power of the present

Security Council to make decisions binding on all member countries. Or else the present mandate of the Security Council could be broadened to deal with economic and social as well as military 'threats to peace'.

There is still another approach to the urgent problem of securing financial resources for the UN system. That is to replace the present system of assessed contributions with its accumulating arrears and incentives simply to leave the organization with independent resources arising through international taxation. Several candidates for such international taxation have been proposed: the 'Tobin Tax' on foreign exchange transactions (discussed in greater detail in Chapter 14), taxes on pollution, air travel, use of common resources of the sea, and so on. We may here recall that Keynes in his original proposals for Bretton Woods (in 1942) proposed a tax on balance of trade or balance of payments surpluses (at the rate of 1 per cent a month) – such a tax would hit Japan hard! However, he wanted this recycled to deficit countries, not used to finance international organizations. The subject of international taxation is certainly on the agenda of 'Beyond Bretton Woods'. The proper collection of international taxation would require not only the approval but also the full cooperation of member countries. The 0·7 per cent UN aid target, accepted by nearly all OECD countries, could also be considered to incorporate the idea of an international tax on GNP, an international income tax which could be converted to a progressive rate, as often suggested by Jan Tinbergen.

(3) A third gap relates to food security, perhaps the most elementary of human rights. The idea of international food reserves prepositioned in vulnerable areas to provide survival diets in 'normal times' as well as in emergencies has never quite been achieved. We have a UN World Food Programme which plays a vigorous and essential part, coordinating as well as operational, in emergencies. We have an International Emergency Food Reserve, but it is never up to its target level (itself ridiculously low at 500 000 tons) and above all is never readily enough available, particularly for the preventive timely action which could be much cheaper and more effective than responding to emergencies after they have happened. Hunger and malnutrition have not been wiped out in the Brave New World as visualized at Dumbarton Oaks in 1944, where the FAO was established, the Food and Agricultural Organization which became a specialized agency of the UN.

Removing Distortions

The three gaps described above concern what has been described as the third and fourth pillars of the system and the projected roof overarching the structure. The remaining two pillars, the BWIs, have been successfully established, and indeed in some respects they have become more powerful than visualized. But only in some respects – and therein lies the distortion. Through their structural adjustment and stabilization programmes, backed by the full weight of all donor countries, they have exerted a powerful influence over SCs held within a debt trap and a foreign exchange shortage trap. Their influence, which was not reduced by the decisions of the Cologne Summit of 1999, is such as to bring the legal concept of national sovereignty into doubt, at least in economic policy making. Restricting national sovereignty is not in itself a bad thing; it is in fact inherent in the concept of the UN system and of global governance. The trouble is that countries have to comply under duress, without democratic control, and that pressure by the BWIs is not symmetrical – not equally applied to industrial countries and to surplus countries. It is not the kind of global governance envisaged over 50 years ago. The founders of the IMF, for example, wrote equal treatment of all member countries into its constitution, yet its 'surveillance' of industrial and surplus countries amounts to little more than a shadow, while its 'surveillance' of indebted and deficit SCs is often little less than rule from Washington. Restoring symmetry means either more effective pressure on the rich countries or relaxation of the pressures on deficit countries.

In the absence of such symmetry, the BWIs are driven to treat all the problems of foreign exchange deficits as internal to the policies of these countries and disregard all factors external to them, from debt pressures to deteriorating terms of trade, protectionist barriers to their trade and their access to technology. The deficit countries are treated by a 'grandmotherly IMF' as 'bad boys' who have to adjust to the 'facts of life'. Yet the BWIs were created to change the facts of life. Nor is it, in the context of an expanding full-employment world economy, quite clear whether it is not the surplus countries rather than the deficit countries which have to be 'disciplined' and 'restructured'. The underlying analogy with profligate and 'economical' individuals is one of the economic fallacies of composition, when moving from individuals to countries or from countries to regions or the world. What is good for country A is not necessarily good for the higher community of countries A,B,C,D... together. Yet the country-by-country approach of stabilization and structural adjustment programmes disregards such fallacies of composition.

This is best illustrated by the country-by-country pressure on deficit countries to expand exports and be more 'outward oriented'. If many countries exporting the same commodities are simultaneously pressed to expand their exports the predictable result is oversupply, collapse of prices and deterioration in terms of trade. To that extent, the deteriorating terms of trade are not an exogenous fact of life to which countries have to adjust but the result of the adjustment process itself – or rather the way adjustment is at present carried out country-by-country. In the particular example discussed here, it is the previously discussed gap in commodity policy which distorts the approach to adjustment and makes it a factor in immiserization rather than salvation.

There are other doubts concerning the IMF/World Bank approaches to stabilization and structural adjustment, revolving around their pronounced neoliberal ideology with heavy emphasis on government failures and little emphasis on market failures. Japan is not alone in pointing out that this does not agree with the development experience of East Asian countries. Many economists share these doubts on a wider basis, particularly so after the Asian crisis of 1997. They point out that each country has its own specific mixture of government failures and market failures, and its own specific way in which these failures had best been tackled. The universalist neoliberal recipe of 'getting prices right' and 'getting the government out of business' is by no means justified by actual results. A revision of the Washington Consensus must be part of the 'Beyond Bretton Woods'. Structural adjustment is itself in need of structural adjustment!

More could be said on this subject of removing distortions in the actual operation of the system created some 60 years ago, but we now turn to new problems created after the system started operating.

Coping with New Problems

There were problems which could not have been foreseen at Bretton Woods. There has been a tendency, in the absence of full international discussion and appropriate arrangements, to deal with these problems in an ad hoc and unsatisfactory manner. Here we can do no more than list some of these unforeseen problems.

First and foremost among these is the well-named 'debt trap' in which most SCs are now caught. One of its sources is the way the big financial oil surpluses were recycled through the commercial banks as debt-creating loans, after the big rises in oil prices in 1973 and again in 1979. This is not a glorious page in anybody's books, not OPEC's, not the commercial banks', not the BWIs', and not those of Southern governments. Nobody gave much thought to the unsustainable nature of plugging balance of payments deficits through the progressive piling up of debt service obligations. The problem has thus been with us for over 30 years, and in the form of an acute crisis since 1982, when Mexico suspended payments. It has been the subject of roll-overs and other temporary expedients rather than a clean solution. It is time that the problems were recognized as a joint responsibility, not that of the debtor countries alone. As late as 1980, shortly before the bubble burst, the BWIs welcomed the 'efficient' recycling of the oil surpluses through the commercial banks as signs of the strength of the international financial system. Even after August 1982, the BWIs felt that the money market functioned well, seeing no signs of liquidity bottlenecks, or of restrictions regarding the capital base of private banks limiting lending to the South, which was supposed to continue on a large scale (cf. Raffer, 1994a).

Many of the debts, especially of African countries, are multilateral debts owed to the IMF and the World Bank. Given the history of debt and the enormous financial strength of these institutions, there seems no strong case for their 'preferred creditor' status and no need for their AAA credit rating to suffer if they participate in the necessary clean solution – an international insolvency modelled on the US Chapter 9 of Title 11 (Bankruptcy). At the beginning of the 1990s, especially in Latin America, there was a revived inflow of new capital, which was again hailed as a sign of confidence and of the effectiveness of the world financial system, even though the BWIs' own data did not confirm their optimism (Raffer, 1996a). Although this flow adopted increasingly the form of direct and portfolio investment and was not legally debt creating, this is more a difference of form than of substance; the transfer of profits and payment of dividends also constitute future claims on the balance of payments – in effect a future tax on export earnings. These investments proved to be highly volatile. They can be and have been withdrawn or liquidated at short notice, as we have seen repeatedly since the case of Mexico in 1994–5. Those who forget the lessons of history are condemned to repeat them. Just as people said some 60 years ago, 'Never again!' to the dreadful conditions of the 1930s which led to the rise of Hitler and war, so we should today say 'Never again!' to the debt crisis. You cannot expect development when 20–30 per cent of export earnings are taxed away for debt service, on top of another 20–30 per cent taxed away in worsened terms of trade over the last 20 years.

There is also a need for a new relationship between the richer and poorer countries. The present relationship is thoroughly unhealthy. The richer countries feel like unwilling dispensers of favour imposing strict discipline as conditions for their favours, using the allegedly neutral Bretton Woods organizations to act as their instruments, overseers and debt collectors, while the poorer countries feel they do not really own the policies imposed on them but that they are beggars who cannot be choosers. The result is predictable: there is popular resistance and unrest in the poorer countries and the policies are poorly implemented. When results are negative, the countries blame the BWIs, while these two blame government failures – an unhealthy game of scapegoats. The right way forward is surely by way of development contracts, genuine contracts in which both sides make clearly defined and voluntarily entered commitments, and remain in continuing consultation to adjust the contract in the light of unforeseen new circumstances. Conditionality must become a two-way business. Unfortunately, the only system of North–South, relationships still emphasizing partnership, Lomé, is currently being dismantled (see Chapter 7).

One example is the 20/20 contract proposed in the UNDP *Human Development Report 1994*, and endorsed at the World Social Summit in Copenhagen. This would require SCs to devote at least 20 per cent of their government expenditure to health, education, sanitation, water supplies and other priorities for human resource development. Donor countries would commit themselves to devoting at least 20 per cent of their aid to these sectors. The logic of this contract also seems to require a commitment relating to the overall volume of aid such as the 0·7 per cent target.

The reunification of the UN system and more balanced distribution of support and resources also requires a unification of the two conflicting development paradigms: the UN paradigm of sustainable human development as expressed in the UNDP *Human Development Reports* and the paradigm of growth based on macroeconomic discipline and market orientation underlying the Washington Consensus of the Bretton Woods system. Both paradigms contain important elements of truth waiting to be reconciled and combined. This is an intellectual task for developing thinking in the days beyond Bretton Woods. A particular challenge now is the marginalization of Africa, which is assuming dramatic dimensions. To prevent a whole continent from becoming excluded from progress in the rest of the world is a major challenge requiring exceptional action on the dimensions of the Marshall Plan. Will the world community be willing and able to face this task and take the exceptional actions required? Within the limits of this introductory chapter, there is no room to outline the details of this task, which must include a Green Revolution in Africa.

The marginalization of Africa is but an extreme example of the polarization of the world economy. The general picture is one of divergence rather than convergence: the gap between the richest and the poorest quintile of countries is now much greater than 60 years ago when Keynes developed his ideas, and still increasing. The same is true of the richest 20 per cent of the world's people compared with the poorest 20 per cent. The UNDP (1992, p.1) found that 'the richest 20% of the world's population had incomes 30 times greater than the poorest 20%' in 1960. By 1990, this ratio had increased to 60; by 1995 it had increased to 82 (UNDP, 1998, p.29). Disparities within countries are 'just as stark' (ibid.). Wide disparities and sharply risen inequality can also be observed within industrial countries. Thus, contrary to the hopes of Bretton Woods in 1944, and also contrary to the expectations of classical economics, the paths of North and South have diverged, not converged.

2. Beyond terms of trade: convergence, divergence and (un)creative destruction

The purpose of this chapter is to set the theory of the long-run tendency for prices of primary products to decline in relation to manufactured products into the more general context for which it was originally intended.

The simplest version on which the discussion has perhaps unduly concentrated is the simple proposition regarding net barter terms of trade as quoted in the previous sentence. In this sense it has become known as the Prebisch–Singer Thesis (PST). With given and mutually agreed definitions of what constitutes primary commodities and what constitutes manufactures, this proposition can be statistically tested. This has been widely done, with the evidence generally pointing (especially when the analysis includes the recent period since 1980) to the thesis being verified and supported, or at least not refuted. For this it does not matter very much whether the data are interpreted as a persistent declining trend or as essentially stationary with intermittent downward breaks. The general policy conclusion would be to emphasize the importance for SCs of diversification of exports into manufactures as intensively and rapidly as possible – in other words, industrialization. In this the PST fitted into the mainstream of development thinking at the time of its publication and the period immediately afterwards. By showing that all available empirical evidence contradicted the orthodox view that net barter terms of trade would move in favour of SCs – a necessary condition for world markets to work as predicted by theory – it argued against the mainstream. Development and industrialization were treated as virtually synonymous. Significantly, the seminal paper by Rosenstein-Rodan in 1943 was entitled 'Problems of Industrialization of Eastern and South-Eastern Europe'.

The PST itself does not involve any view on whether the shift towards industrialization should be by way of export promotion for manufactures or by way of import substitution for previously imported manufactures. In the conditions of 1950s and 1960s, a tendency to give preference to import substitution was natural since (a) SCs had to build up a domestic production capacity in order to export manufactures, and (b) they would find it initially easier to produce for an existing and known domestic market than for an unknown global market.

A first and simple extension of the PST was to move from a proposition related to different kinds of commodities to a proposition related to different kinds of countries. As the share of manufactures in the exports of SCs increased it became increasingly necessary to break with the identification of the terms of trade between primary commodities and manufactures with the terms of trade of SCs with more industrialized and richer countries and to undertake separate studies of the manufacture–manufacture terms of trade. These studies suggested that diversification into manufactures - while it was recommended as part of industrialization, reduction of risks of price volatility, creation of employment, as well as future savings of imports – was not in itself an escape from deteriorating barter terms of trade (as distinct from income terms of trade). Research has tended to establish that manufacture–manufacture barter terms of trade of SCs have deteriorated as well as primary–manufactured barter terms of trade in recent years, perhaps even faster. The kinds of manufactures which SCs could export in the early stages of development were different from the kind of manufactures which they imported from developed countries. This also suggests a certain specificity of products with regard to their trade effects, as analysed by the new theory of Unequal Exchange (Raffer, 1987a). The manufactures exported by SCs tend to be technologically simpler than the manufactures imported from developed countries – hence the extension of the PST from commodities to countries also involved a shift from emphasis on industrialization and diversification to an emphasis on building up technological capacity, entrepreneurial skills and human capital in general. Without such a technological capacity, a shift into manufactures required foreign investment or aid.

The PST, taken by itself (and leaving aside the case of rich oil exporters), would create a presumption (although no certainty) of divergence within the world economy. Other things being equal, falling terms of trade for poorer countries and improving terms of trade for richer countries would mean greater international inequality between countries. Other things of course would not be equal. In particular, if the deteriorating barter terms of trade are accompanied by increased income terms of trade (which means if the volume of exports expanded so heavily as to outweigh the decline in barter terms of trade) while the opposite was the case for the countries which had improving terms of trade, the PST would be compatible with convergence rather than divergence. But even if income terms remained constant (export volume expansion maintains export revenue in the face of declining barter terms of trade) this would still amount to international divergence since the poorer countries would have to mobilize greater resources for the increase in export volume. Increased income terms of trade at falling net barter terms of trade mean that even more has to be exported; factor remuneration per unit declines as well, thus more has to be sold for the same amount of money earned. If –

as everyone assumes – technological progress is slower in SCs, falling prices are not compensated by increased productivity. Factors are remunerated increasingly unequally by the world market, in contrast to the assumptions of orthodox textbook theory.

These increased resources would have to be diverted from domestic consumption or investment, increasing divergence between countries in the world economy. In any case, if people in the poorer countries have to work harder and produce more (while this is not required in the richer countries) simply to maintain income terms of trade, that in itself represents an element of divergence.

The presumption of the PST was that this would not happen in reality. On the contrary, it was assumed that the income elasticity as well as the short-run price elasticity in the case of price reductions of primary commodities were lower than for manufactures; hence the income terms of trade would contribute even more to international divergence than the barter terms of trade. However, it deserves to be emphasized that the PST – although statistically mainly discussed in terms of barter terms of trade – was intended as a contribution to the analysis of double factoral terms of trade showing that unequalizing factors existed in international trade. Hence the emphasis on lower price elasticities and income elasticities for primary commodities in the early formulations of the PST. The fact of lower income elasticity compared with manufactures (for instance Engel's Law) is well established and largely uncontroversial.

The move from barter terms of trade to income terms of trade is a stepping stone to move towards factoral terms of trade (single or double). If productivity in SC exports, whether commodities or manufactures, improves sufficiently there could still be increases in welfare and factor incomes even in the face of declining income or barter terms of trade. However, to change divergence to convergence it would be necessary for technical progress to be faster in the poorer countries than in the export industries of the richer countries. Necessary but not sufficient. The PST argues that one must also include the possibility that the fruits of technical progress are differently distributed in different types of countries. Specifically, the PST argues that there is a tendency for the results of technical progress to be retained in the richer countries in the form of higher incomes, while the benefits of technical progress in the export industries of poorer countries result mainly in lower prices. While this differential way of distributing the fruits of technical progress would make no overall national difference (higher real incomes in both cases whether by way of higher incomes or of lower prices) internationally it does make a difference, leading to yet greater divergence between rich and poor countries.

If the assumptions of the PST are accepted, the richer countries benefit both ways: as producers of exports in the form of higher incomes and as consumers in the form of lower import prices. The argument is that, in the case of primary commodities and simple manufactures, there is more intense competitive pressure in world trade forcing exporters to pass on increases in productivity to consumers, whereas in the case of the higher-technology manufactures exported by richer countries stronger labour markets combined with a cost-plus marking up system of prices ensure that gains from productivity accrue more to the producer. Thus the shift from barter or income terms of trade to factoral terms of trade does not help to reduce the effect of the PST to point in the direction of international divergence between countries. Quite to the contrary, it shows its main point as presented by Singer (1950) and Prebisch (1949) – or 'core' (Raffer, 1986) – more clearly: within the PST falling NBToTs are a sufficient condition for the loss of productivity gains.

Here we have arrived at the real objective of the PST, which is to argue that international trade and investment have a tendency to contribute to international divergence rather than convergence. It is of course only one factor out of many. The PST leaves open the possibility that other forces making for convergence are stronger and overrule the tendency towards divergence. However, the PST, by pointing out this tendency towards divergence, served to modify the then prevailing optimistic view that there must be convergence, which means that SCs would grow faster than the richer industrial countries.

What were the arguments for this prevailing optimistic assumption of convergence? One argument was to assume a more favourable incremental capital–output ratio (ICOR) in the poorer countries. As capital was scarce in relation to labour and natural resources in the poorer countries, it would have a higher marginal productivity. Each unit of capital could be combined with more labour and natural resources, producing a more favourable ICOR. Arthur Lewis (1954), in his assumption of unlimited labour supplies arising from hidden unemployment in agriculture in the South, also contributed to this assumption of a low ICOR. Hence he often stated that it would be sufficient to increase investment from very low to still relatively low investment rates (such as 12 per cent of GDP). In the absence of reliable data, a constant and favourable ICOR of 3:1 was assumed. By contrast, in the rich countries capital was relatively abundant and would come up against diminishing returns. Also countries in the North have a higher level of existing capital assets: more of their savings are absorbed by *replacement* investment than in SCs.

Another argument for convergence was seen in the fact that SCs could use the existing technology ready made for them by the industrial countries without having to go to the cost and pains of Schumpeter's creative destruction. Instead, technology would be presented to them free on a silver plate. This would help them to catch up with richer countries.

A third argument was historical experience. History showed clear examples of catching up processes. Friedrich List had shown the way for Germany to catch up with England by way of infant industries initially protected. This was followed by other countries catching up until the OECD club, including Japan, was complete and at very similar per capita income levels. Post-war history also shows clear examples of catching up, such as the East Asian tigers. It seems clear that catching up is a possibility for individual countries and that examples of convergence occur in the world economy. In the cases of the East Asian tigers, for example, any initial tendencies towards divergence could be overruled or were non-existent. The latter possibility is supported by more recent research which tends to show the existence of stronger technological capacity, especially in human capital, in the tiger economies, enabling them to retain the fruits of technical progress and move rapidly into the more knowledge-intensive types of manufactured exports, thus avoiding too negative effects of deteriorating terms of trade. Their strong economic structures and human capital accumulated within these countries have enabled them to rebound from the Asian crisis with surprising speed.

One obvious way of measuring convergence or divergence over a given period of time is to compare the rates of economic growth or other improvements in human development for SCs as a whole with those of industrial countries (ICs) as a whole. For example, if we take the period from 1970 to 1997, we find that GDP per capita (in 1987 dollars) increased for SCs by a little over 51 per cent, but a little over 53 per cent for ICs. From this we would be justified in saying that for the selected period and the selected criterion there has been a mild tendency toward divergence. But the overwhelming conclusion from such figures would be that there has been such a big improvement in both groups that the divergence and the whole issue of convergence/divergence becomes almost irrelevant.

There is, however, a pitfall in this conclusion. Although for the two groups taken separately the improvement is 51 per cent and 53 per cent, respectively, for the world as a whole the improvement is only 25 per cent. This apparent paradox is, of course, explained by the increasing weight over the period of the poorer group (SCs) and the diminished weight of the richer group (industrial countries). This is due to their different rates of population increase: 2·0 per cent for SCs against 0·6 per cent for the North. Given the big difference in per capita GDP between the two groups (around 21:1), this shift in relative weights within the total world population was sufficient, over these years, to wipe out over half the improvement in each category taken separately when the concept of 'One World' is accepted. This would dampen our optimistic conclusion that the improvement overshadows the convergence/divergence issue. The SC average hides great disparities: the average GDP per head of LLDCs has shrunk by nearly 15 per cent, while it multiplied by 4·7 for East

Asia, and slightly more than quadrupled in the region 'East Asia (excluding China)', clearly reflecting the growth in tiger economies and China. In Latin America and the Caribbean, it grew only by 21 per cent over this period; in Eastern Europe and the CIS it shrunk by 31·7 per cent between 1990 and 1997, the only two years for which data are provided.

The figures of the above example are taken from the *Human Development Report 1999* (UNDP, 1999, p.154, Table 6) and in turn derived from the World Bank's *World Development Indicators 1999*. They are marred by the omission of the period 1975–85 for the 'Eastern Europe and the CIS' group of countries for which no data were provided. But this omission does not affect the point that, mathematically, differential rates of population increase are over any longer period a powerful force driving down those indicators conceived as global averages in relation to indicators for the poorer and richer countries taken separately, which underlies much of the convergence/divergence debate.

The apparent paradox is also confirmed for the slightly shorter period 1975–95 when annual GNP per capita growth rates are found to be 2·3 per cent for SCs, 1·9 per cent for ICs, but only 1·1 per cent for the world as a whole (UNDP, 1999, p.183, Table 11). For this shorter period, however, there is a limited convergence, at least in relative terms. As East Asia and East Asia minus China had rates of 7·3 and 6·8 per cent, respectively, during this period ending in 1995, while LLDCs (−0·2 per cent) and Sub-Saharan Africa (−0·9 per cent) had negative growth rates, these figures basically reflect the same diverging tendencies between regions. East Asian growth rates, and thus the rates of all SCs, were no doubt influenced by the 1997 crash, which is likely to explain part of the difference between the two time series.

The assumption of a tendency towards global convergence, implicit in the neoclassical production function, the theory of comparative advantages and the theorem of an equalization of factor prices, can be and has been statistically tested by a number of analysts. The general result is that, on a global scale, which means including all countries in North and South for which data are available, there is no visible tendency towards convergence. Convergence would require that initial per capita income levels of countries should be negatively correlated with subsequent growth rates; but no such firm negative correlation has been found. Naturally, much depends on the choice of initial and terminal dates but, generally speaking, the findings support divergence rather than convergence, particularly for very long time periods and also particularly for the period 1980–2000. What convergence has been found is among the limited group of industrial countries, for example among the OECD or EU countries. It is, however, questionable whether whatever catching up of the poorer EU countries (such as Greece, Portugal, Ireland and Spain) occurred has been due more to the various and often generous subsidies from wealthier EU countries, rather than to a natural tendency towards convergence. On a truly global scale, divergence rather than convergence seems the rule, and to that extent the PST is in line with empirical data.

Analysing annual GDP per capita growth rates from 1870 to 1990 – the terms of trade series on which the PST is based starts in 1873 – Pritchett (1997, p.12) concludes after comparing sources of historical data: 'Although there is not a great deal of historical evidence on GDP estimates in the very long run for the less developed countries, what there is confirms the finding of massive divergence.' There is a 'staggering' increase 'in absolute gaps in per capita income between rich and poor' (ibid.), and 'divergence in relative productivity levels and living standards is the dominant feature of modern economic history' (ibid., p.3), as 'growth rates between developed and developing countries show considerable divergence' (ibid., p.14). There is a clear distinction between North and South. While growth rates for the former converge, SCs show a variety of experiences, from spectacular cases of catching up to 'nosedives', such as Mozambique, with a negative growth rate of 2·2 per cent during 1960–90. A focus on India and China does not change Pritchett's conclusions: these countries diverged significantly relative to the leaders between 1870 and 1960.

Starting from research providing historical evidence that SCs were considerably richer in the past than previously believed, Pritchett points out, divergence would even be larger than his own results show. He quotes Bairoch's (1993) finding that there was almost no gap between North and South as late as 1800, which means before the heydays of colonialism, when many Southern economies were crippled. The Fijian coup forcing the EU and the ACP countries in 2000 to move the ceremony of signing their Convention to Cotonou shows that the effects of colonialism are long-lived. The root of Fiji's ethnic problem is that Indians were brought to the islands as 'indentured labour' (a less euphemistic expression would be 'temporary slaves') decades ago, to work on sugar plantations, causing a massive demographic change, and ethnic tensions after independence.

Conspicuous examples of catching up by initially very poor countries – such as South Korea or Taiwan (cf. Chapter 9) – are notable exceptions to the rule of divergence. Some evidence of conditional convergence over more recent periods for countries with similar levels of education and technological capacity exists. Comparing two years – 1960 and 1988 – Jones (1997) found converging tendencies. He compared, however, GDP per worker, assuming this would correct for the fact that non-market production is quite important in many SCs. As all evidence suggests that average income in the 'traditional' sector is lower than in the modern sector, his problematic assumption must produce biased results. Furthermore, GDP comprises imputed production for the traditional sector. It is not a measure of market sector production alone. The statement that 'both the numerator and the denominator then correspond to the market sector' (ibid., p.20) if GDP/worker is used is wrong. Countries must have a higher GDP/worker (which Jones apparently understands to be workers in the modern sector) than GDP/head, particularly if the traditional sector is comparatively large. Furthermore, industrialization drives of quite a few SCs, from Brazil to the Asian 'tigers', took place between 1960 and 1988. The relocation of industrial production was so strong that the 'de-industrialization' of the North was discussed. The period between these two years was exceptional. Whether Ceausescu's Romania was indeed a 'growth miracle' (ibid., p.22) might be discussed. But this qualification helps understand why Jones thinks growth miracles to occur more frequently than growth disasters.

Nevertheless, Jones finds a 'twin-peak' distribution in 1988, which is an indication of divergence between the groups of poor and rich countries. He also calls the term 'speed of convergence' unfortunate, 'because it seems to suggest that this equation has something to do with different countries getting closer together in the income distribution, which is not the case (at least not directly)' (ibid., p.29). While one might agree with him that 'rapid growth had been significantly more common' between 1960 and 1988 'than slow growth' (ibid., p.32), his optimism about the long run (beyond 2050), which is based on the assumption that all countries grow at the same average rate, seems unconvincing.

For large regions, such as India or China, international trade – and even more so the barter terms of trade – are (at least directly) less important for their total GNP performance than for smaller countries. But there has been an increasing income inequality in China and India, weakening their role as actors in a convergent scenario.

In the immediate post-war period, during the 1950s and 1960s, assuming convergence did not seem implausible: SCs were able to keep up even with the then high growth rates of the industrial countries in the 'Golden Age' of reconstruction and rehabilitation aided by the massive investment support of the Marshall Plan. It must not be forgotten that the rapid catching up of Korea and Taiwan was also supported by massive aid during the crucial early periods. The idea of stages of development, introduced by Walt Rostow (1960) into the post-war development debate, also lent itself to the idea that countries were more or less predestined to go through these various stages and end up in a state of general convergence.

The PST thus introduced a discordant element into the optimism of convergence. It argued that there are also elements of divergence operating in the world economy. Today this would no longer be such a heretical proposition as in 1950. It is not unusual now to say that, more recently, divergences or inequalities have increased between countries as well as within countries. The New Growth Theory emphasizes that investment has increasing rather than decreasing returns, that knowledge and technology feed upon themselves: those with access to and understanding of advanced knowledge and technology have the best chances of improving their knowledge and technology further. It seems to be widely agreed that the globalization process has its losers as well as winners, and that the losers tend to be the poorer and more vulnerable countries and groups within countries. Such terms as vicious circles of poverty, marginalization of Africa, poverty traps, social exclusion and endogenous growth permeate development literature.

A further new element has been added to support the PST, namely the debt pressure under which the poorer countries are compelled to export and earn foreign exchange at any price. The fallacy of composition ensures that the efforts of each country individually to improve its income terms of trade by increasing its own market shares must be at the expense of other countries under similar pressure which simultaneously try to increase their own individual market share. The practice of the BWIs to force countries to be outward-oriented and to improve their debt servicing capacity and balance of payments by increasing exports on a country-by-country basis, without much coordination between the different structural adjustment programmes, further strengthens the fallacy of composition. The vastly increased power of multinational corporations to shift production between SCs or out of SCs altogether introduces another element of racing for the bottom in production and export costs – in fact further supporting the PST. In all these respects the PST can be said now to have retained – if not increased – its relevance in the current development debate.

One indication of this is that the PST is now incorporated, both implicitly and explicitly, in the advice given by the Bretton Woods Institutions. SCs are now warned to be prudent even when export prices are temporarily favourable and to guard against currency overvaluation and Dutch disease. They are warned to remember that the outlook for commodity prices is not favourable, and that windfalls will tend to be temporary, with the subsequent relapse likely to be greater than the temporary windfall. This is exactly the warning which the PST would give. Emphasizing volatility is fully compatible with the PST. Its authors in fact drew attention to short-run fluctuations and their effects. Even if a long-term declining trend is established it will be in the order of perhaps 1 per cent per annum (calculations differ) whereas year-to-year fluctuations may average something in the nature of 15 per cent per annum. Volatility is a much greater and more immediate problem to macroeconomic policy in SCs facing a secularly declining trend of their terms of trade. In contrast to diversification into manufactures, which failed to provide a reliable escape from secularly declining terms of trade, there is a remedy in the case of volatility. The volatility of prices or unit costs of manufactured exports is distinctly lower than for primary commodities, although it is higher than the volatility of the exports of manufactures from the more fully developed countries.

The policy conclusion from this would be the same as the one reached by others starting from a different and wider perspective than the PST (cf., for example, Wood, 1994; Wood & Cano, 1996; Wood & Mayer, forthcoming). It appears that poorer countries with static comparative advantages in (non-oil) primary commodities, or in low-tech manufactures, would be well advised to try to create different and more dynamic comparative advantages in higher-tech manufactures or services. Otherwise, they may well be caught in the trap of deteriorating terms of trade and may be at the wrong end of the distribution of gains from trade and investment. Hence our conclusion emphasizes the importance of education, and development of skills and of technological capacity. In the light of recent mainstream thinking on growth and trade, there is nothing startling about this conclusion. But it is worth noting that the PST works in the same direction and strengthens this conclusion.

So far, we have discussed terms of trade as a factor in international divergence rather than convergence. But 'beyond terms of trade', there are forces at work which are linked with terms of trade but not included in their direct definition and measurement, although they are part of 'unequal exchange'. One factor is the unequal capacity of rich and poor countries to cope with and adjust themselves to changes in terms of trade by way of substitution of cheaper products and factors of production for those which have become relatively more expensive. Another is the tendency of technical progress and R&D to work more in the direction of substituting or replacing primary products rather than vice versa. Yet a third is the unequal capacity to produce and/or new superior products. The last point has been a main point of criticism of the PST of a long-term decline in primary commodity prices, since it is assumed that quality improvements apply more to manufactures than to commodities, and often escape measurement. This criticism has lost some force where terms of trade between countries are concerned since more countries now export both manufactures and primary commodities. Also a major part of world trade is intra-transnational company trade and TNCs can be assumed to apply the same degree of quality control in all their operations. To illustrate the importance of TNCs in the global economy one should recall that 'Sales of foreign affiliates of multinational companies are estimated to exceed world trade in goods and services' (WTO 1996d, p.7) in 1995. It is further argued in what follows that with increasing wealth and improved communications the superior quality of the new products is often more perceived than real: the concepts of 'conspicuous consumption' and 'status goods' are well established in the economic literature; increasing inequalities within and between countries may well tend to increase their importance. Insofar as innovations are new status goods or quality improvements are perceived rather than real, Schumpeter's 'creative destruction' would be more destructive and less creative. It is to such issues 'beyond terms of trade' that we now turn.

SCHUMPETER'S INFLUENCE ON THE PST

The PST was greatly influenced by Schumpeter in his emphasis on technical innovation as a stimulus to new investment. The original articles of 1949/50 both emphasized that one of the causes of deteriorating terms of trade for primary products was the capacity of the technically advanced consumer countries to produce synthetic substitutes for the natural primary commodities of SCs. The history of the impact of synthetic nitrates on the Chilean producers in the 19th century was well known to Prebisch and the development of synthetic dyestuffs and plastics was a current trend in 1949/50. In this sense the PST was also part of the neo-Schumpeterian approaches to the explanation of growth and development (for a distinction between neoclassical and neo-Schumpeterian approaches, see Freeman & Soete, 1997).

This also extends to Schumpeter's concept of 'creative destruction'. The creation of new technologies replacing primary commodities or economizing their use – or using them more efficiently for the production of higher quality goods – creates destruction for the producers of primary commodities. While this is not the concept of creative destruction that Schumpeter had in mind, it can be readily assimilated to his model. In the case of the PST the creation takes place in the industrial countries and in the industrial sectors while the destruction takes place in the primary producing countries and the primary producing sectors.

The case of the PST is not the only possible extension of Schumpeter's concept of creative destruction which lends itself to the introduction of an element of divergence in the convergence/divergence discussion connected with globalization. We could add another type of destruction, this time affecting the consumers and owners of the older or lower-quality goods preceding the innovation and technical improvements. It is to this neglected aspect of creative destruction that we now turn.

Everybody now agrees that the growth of real GDP per capita is not an accurate measure of people's welfare and quality of life. In that sense the concept of national income has been dethroned (to use the term used by Dudley Seers). The New Economics Foundation (1996), for example, calculates an Index of Sustainable Economic Welfare (ISEW). Without discussing the different adjustments made by the NEF in detail we would like to point out that, according to this index, real well-being has fallen by over 10 per cent while real GDP per capita has increased by over 40 per cent since 1973. This sharp divergence has mainly been a recent phenomenon. Between 1950 and 1973, the two indicators rose much more in line with each other. To keep things in perspective: even the lower ISEW in 1996 was still higher than in 1950, although much less so than GDP, which had more than doubled. The sharp divergence between GDP and ISEW arises mainly from correction for a widening cost of pollution of various kinds, depletion of non-renewable resources, ozone depletion and also growing inequality. This latter factor is difficult to measure quantitatively but it is clear that there is a positive aversion to inequality built into this index: an increase in income to a rich person would have less marginal utility or create less additional welfare than the same amount of increase in income accruing to a poor person. All this is common sense. The whole idea of aid is based on it.

There are two reasons why development may be unsustainable: one is a politically unsustainable polarization in incomes. The other reason is environmental degradation. Environmental factors are more clearly relevant to a distinction between sustainable and unsustainable growth. They reduce current welfare only to the extent that the present generation identifies itself with future generations. Ironically, the feel-good factor of the present generation is *too high*, rather than absent!

There is, however, another welfare loss. This concerns the destruction element in Schumpeter's creative destruction. This term recognizes that a new product or a new technology has destructive elements in its impact on the producers of old products or using the old technology. In the former case the new product will reduce the markets for the old products by competing with them for consumers' expenditures. In the case of new technologies it forces rival producers to scrap machinery prematurely or to adapt them at some cost to the new technology or engage in R&D activities. These additional costs which have to be set against the benefits of the innovation have been noted before and it has been pointed out that they reduce the gain from the innovation when measuring the gain in terms of social welfare. This cost is enhanced if the new technology is capital-intensive or labour-saving, in conditions of less than full employment (see Aghion & Howitt, 1994). But the impact on existing producers should, in principle, slow GDP growth and hence be captured by traditional GDP as well as by ISEW.

Schumpeter emphasized 'creative' rather than 'destruction'. Doing so, he assumed (a) that the new product satisfies a genuine social need and is genuinely additional or superior to the previous product; (b) that it spurs old producers to greater efforts to improve their productivity, to start production of the new product or, if possible, an even newer and even better product; and (c) that the displaced labour force among the old producers is rapidly reabsorbed into new employment, either by a macroeconomic full employment situation, or by the additional growth created by technical progress.

A different emphasis would obviously be appropriate if (a) the new product is not a genuine improvement on the old product but consists mainly of new gimmicks, packaging or clever advertising which gives consumers the impression that, because the product is new, it must also be superior; or (b) old producers close down rather than try successfully to fill the gap or leapfrog the new producer; and (c) there is no state of full employment. Displaced labour is not rapidly enough reabsorbed.

There is, however, also another element of destruction, which does not seem to have been sufficiently recognized. This is the effect of the new products on consumers rather than on other producers. Consumers of the old inferior product will become dissatisfied once they know that the superior product exists. This will be especially the case with items of prestige consumption – say computers or motor cars – where the use of the most modern product is taken as a mark of social standing. If, contrary to Schumpeter's assumption, the new product is essentially not superior to the old product, and the equation new equals superior does not apply, this premature scrapping of previous consumption goods serves no useful purpose. Even where consumers continue to use the old product their satisfaction derived from it will be reduced by the knowledge that a new and allegedly superior product is now on the market. Much advertising tries to hammer home the message that the new product is superior, and some is directly aimed at creating dissatisfaction with old products. Even if this is not the case, the dissatisfaction of consumers with their present goods will be increased and their welfare reduced, whether they continue to use the old product or are induced to use the new product with premature scrapping of the old product. Thus, if the impact of innovation on consumers as well as producers is considered, the chances that the creative factor is offset by the destructive factor is clearly increased. This would reduce the ratio of satisfaction to GDP.

Since virtually all consumers, at least in the North, possess a large stock of durable consumption goods, all simultaneously exposed to competition from superior or at any rate newer versions of the same goods, the loss of welfare arising from this factor must be quite considerable. It may well offset the welfare gain consumers derive from new products since the stock of old products may be large in relation to new products. Simultaneous replacement of all such goods conceived to be inferior to the newest versions or newest products, conceived as superior, would greatly exceed available resources. Perhaps this is one of the factors which helps to account for the absence of a feel-good factor in spite of rising incomes. In the long run, of course, the distinction between the stock of old products and the flow of new products disappears, but by that time there will be a flow of even newer products.

To keep things in perspective, this neglected impact of innovation on those possessing the old products does not in any way contradict the Schumpeterian assumption that innovation and technical progress are the key to growth and development. But it may help to explain why the increased growth and development is not fully felt as beneficial by the ultimate consumer. This follows from abandoning the assumption in traditional welfare economics that utility derives only from an individual's own income or consumption and is not affected by the income or consumption of other individuals. Yet in poverty analysis the concept of relative poverty is well known. It is implied in such measures of poverty as the percentage of people living at less than half the average per capita income of a country or region. In a study of long-term unemployment in the depressed areas of the UK during the inter-war period, it was found that the situation of the unemployed there – with almost everybody else also unemployed when the local coalmine or cotton mill closed down – was better than those unemployed in generally more prosperous areas, where unemployment was exceptional and had a stigma attached to it (Singer *et al.*, 1938). This finding is clearly related to the concept of relative poverty and corroborates our argument.

In his *Essays on the Frontiers of Economics*, Tibor Scitovsky (1989; see also his 1995 book) discusses such closely related subjects as happiness depending on relative incomes, the desire for novelty, the essentially self-frustrating insatiable nature of the demand for novelty and the importance of conspicuous consumption. In his version, the process appears as supply-driven by the innovating technician and entrepreneur. Keynes (1930) also argued in his essay on 'The Economic Possibilities of our Grandchildren' that above a certain income level welfare ought to depend on increased leisure and non-economic forms of enjoyment, rather than further accumulation of new goods. But this is more in the nature of normative prescription as to how civilized people ought to behave. As a projection of the future, of how our grandchildren will in fact behave, the idea of an insatiable striving for novelty, whether demand-driven or supply-driven, appears to be more realistic.

In this area, the demand for novelty creates its own supply, but it is also true that the supply of novelty creates its own demand. There is a cumulative interaction between supply and demand. On this Keynes, Schumpeter, Scitovsky and the New Economics Foundation all agree. But in spite of this apparently harmonious interplay between demand and supply, the market for novelties has an adverse externality in its impact on the welfare of those not able to participate in the market for novelties. Insofar as they hold earlier models or other close substitutes for the novelty, the market renders a disservice to them not taken into account in the market transactions. The exception are those users of earlier models or close substitutes by whom the services rendered by their possessions are entirely valued in absolute terms without any comparative element of conspicuous consumption. The relative extent of conspicuous and non-conspicuous consumption will be difficult to determine quantitatively and hence also the importance of the externalities in the market for novelty.

This is also closely related to the concept of conspicuous consumption introduced by Thorsten Veblen (1899) in his classic work on *The Theory of the Leisure Class*. However, Veblen's point was the value of the conspicuous consumption (which would include the novelties emphasized in this Chapter) to those able to afford it, whereas this argument concentrates on the impact on those *not* able to afford it. But the importance of conspicuous consumption emphasized by Veblen also gives added importance to this different emphasis.

As was pointed out by Gert Rosenthal (1997, p.6), the executive secretary of the UN Economic Commission for Latin America and the Caribbean (ECLAC) in Santiago, there has been a dramatic improvement in the access to communications in Latin America. This has tended to produce 'a common set of consumer aspirations'. The international demonstration effect was already identified in the 1950s (cf. Chapter 3), but it has become stronger and more widespread since then. However, because of the continuing and tenacious incidence of poverty and unemployment this means that 'whole sectors of society see their expectations frustrated, particularly urban youth. These young people are exposed to information and stimuli about a wide range of novel goods and services which are however inaccessible for the majority of them'. Rosenthal points to this as one of the reasons for threats to urban security and the rise of violence in the cities, 'which all seriously affect levels of social integration and governance'.

The argument is related to problems of measuring correctly price movements, rates of inflation and terms of trade. It is argued that data on price movements have an upward bias because sophisticated and novel manufactured goods which tend to fall rapidly in price after becoming more widespread are not sufficiently represented in the basket of goods or, if represented at all, only when they have become more widespread, which means after their prices have fallen. These earlier price reductions – which may be substantial – are thus not reflected in the index. To the extent that this is correct, it would lead to an overestimate of inflation and also to an overestimate of adverse movements in terms of trade of primary products against manufactured products. This point is additional to, and different from, the argument that prices tend to be over-stated because they do not take sufficient account of improved quality of manufactured goods. In the present context, however, there is another side to this coin: the argument implies that novel goods are initially introduced at a very high price. Hence the buyers of these goods pay a heavy price for the privilege of owning such novel goods and to that extent their real income is lower. The high price paid for novelty would be additional to the dissatisfaction of consumers not able to acquire the novel good and hence an additional element in reducing consumer welfare, reinforcing the argument.

3. The evolution of development thinking

Like the hems of skirts, mainstream development thinking is subject to ups and downs: dominant ideas are overthrown and restored after a while. Examples are the importance assigned to domestic and external factors as hindrances to development, the roles of the state and the market, monoeconomics versus development economics, cyclical phases of development optimism and development pessimism. One may identify further cycles in the history of development economics, such as between inward- and outward-looking policies, or trade and aid. These are just some illustrations of the influence of fashion and the political environment on scientific thinking. H.W. Singer (1989, p.2) concluded: 'our approach to development problems and lessons which we learn is simply the result of changing fashions and ideologies. It was the Keynesian consensus 40 years ago, it is now the neo-liberal tide of today, and goodness knows what tomorrow'.

It might be useful to keep these changes in mind when evaluating dominant currents in development studies or social sciences at large. But one must also not forget that problems remain while emphases change. Development is both hampered by external conditions blocking it, and by internal blocks. The problem is that a double barrier must be overcome. It is thus necessary to analyse both sets of blocks.

DOMESTIC AND EXTERNAL DEVELOPMENT BLOCKS

In the pioneer days of modern development thinking international market forces were perceived by most analysts as so benevolent and conducive to development that blockages could only originate within so-called 'backward countries'. Like runners simultaneously racing away from backwardness, some countries were faster than others. The task of development studies was to find out which individual shortcomings caused delays and to correct them. Leibenstein (1957, p.4; emphasis in original) provides a good illustration:

> The nature of the abstract problem can be outlined in the following terms: (1) We begin with a set of economies (or countries), each 'enjoying' an equally *low* standard of living at the outset. (2) Over a relatively long period of time (say, a

century or two) some of these countries increase their output per head considerably whereas others do not. (3) Furthermore ... the gap in per capita output between the advancing countries and the stagnant ones steadily increases .... Now our problem is ... why some countries should have developed while others remain more or less stagnant, or why some countries remain economically backward while others experience sustained secular advance.

This perception was – not always formulated so explicitly – the dominant base of development thinking. The heterodox exception drawing attention to the existence of negative effects of the world market was the Prebisch–Singer Thesis (PST). 'Non-economic' factors, such as 'traditionality', 'culture' or characteristics absent in advanced economies (such as high population growth) were singled out as impediments to development. 'Traditionally determined behaviour' became a social indicator for irrational backwardness, emulation of the West for progress and economic rationality. Rostow (1960, p.5) characterized these societies, after drawing attention to their long-run fatalism, as 'untouched or unmoved by man's new capability for regularly manipulating his environment to his economic advantage'.

Rational thinking in the South was not denied by all economists. Leibenstein (1957) pointed out that children were a potential source of security in old age. A rational motive was to 'a considerable extent' the driving force behind population growth. According to Meier (1964, p.45, emphasis added) the 'tradition-oriented' value system 'also tends to *minimize* the importance of economic incentives, material rewards, independence and rational calculation', which implies rational choice based on calculus.

A particularly telling misconception is Georgescu-Roegen's (1960) seminal paper on agriculture, where the author interprets 'traditional society' as big landowners trying to feed all other people for some romantic reason. A better explanation for so much generosity might be that Georgescu-Roegen's landowners do not own the land at all, but benefit from traditonal rights, such as entitlements to a share of production or to certain services in exchange for work on behalf of the community. Such rights of autochthonous legal systems might be quite sophisticated. When 'modernization' takes place the aristocratic 'landowner' may not start to fire people because he finally realizes how to maximize income, but simply chase the real owners from what now has suddenly become his property.

Baran (1968, p.76) observed with more realism that, instead of a complete substitution of capitalist market rationality for feudal or semi-feudal systems,

all that happened was that the age-old exploitation of the population of underdeveloped countries by their domestic overlords, was freed from the mitigating constraints inherited from the feudal tradition. This superimposition of business *mores* over ancient oppression by landed gentry resulted in compounded exploitation, more outrageous corruption and more glaring injustice.

Even within his philantropic food for work programme Georgescu-Roegen's feudal lord maximizes output, which yields the maximum income obtainable under the restriction of having to feed his flock. Thus people behave rationally in an irrational setting. Compared with ideas such as Rostow's fatalism and the inability to grasp the 'not all that difficult ... tricks of growth' (Rostow, 1960, p.166) such reasoning was progressive, because it conceded at least limited rationality to backward people.

Focused on internal development blocks, theoretical approaches such as dualism, trickle-down, balanced growth, backward and forward linkages, the inverted-U thesis of income distribution, the savings gap or the big push emerged. Even dissenting analyses were in a way dominated by the swing of the pendulum. Most notably in Latin America, the PST stimulated policies in SCs in the 1950s, directed at improving domestic economic structures by using import substitution, although with some neglect of export promotion and undue emphasis on substituting imports. In the 1970s, on the other hand, the PST was used to argue for buffer stocks to stabilize international commodity prices.

When efforts to overcome underdevelopment proved less successful than was initially thought, and especially when Latin America – the region thought to become developed relatively quickly – experienced an exhaustion (*estancamiento*) of growth, the tide turned. The debate started to focus on international markets and the insertion of the periphery into the global economy. The crisis of development euphoria and its easy tricks of growth give rise to dependency thinking. The 1970s especially were dominated by discussions on the global 'old economic order' as a hindrance to development, and demands for a New International Economic Order (NIEO) giving peripheral countries a fair(er) deal were voiced. Changes in the fields of raw materials, transfer of technology, information and foreign investment were attempted by the South, spurred by what was perceived as the successful example of OPEC.

Industrialized countries blocked these demands successfully. UNCTAD's Common Fund provides a good illustration. SCs demanded a Fund providing resources to bring new commodity agreements into operation, which would stabilize raw material prices via buffer stocks. Such stocks had already been advocated by Keynes (1974) in 1942 to smooth external shocks, facilitating the fine-tuning of economic management in the North as well (cf. Chapter 1).

The North continuously opposed this demand, advocating that the Fund should get resources from commodity agreements depositing part of their money with it. Such a Common Fund would, of course, be unable to create commodity agreements by providing the necessary resources. The resolution adopted in 1979 to head off North–South confrontation at UNCTAD V in Manila stipulated $400 million for commodity price stabilization, much too little for independent action by the Fund. After long delays in ratification the Common Fund came into existence in 1989, obsolete as an instrument of commodity policy because of insufficient resources and the breakdown of commodity agreements.

In the 1980s the pendulum started to swing back. Internal structures of SCs were again presented as the reason for development problems and global markets as the solution, although with less sophistication than in the 1950s. More elegantly expressed, 'we may be in the diminishing-returns range of the major advances of the early post war era. And each of us undoubtedly has his or her own idea of how the intellectual production function in development economics will once again be shifted' (Ranis & Fei, 1988, p.101).

While the swing of the pendulum sketched above serves well to illustrate shifts in development thinking, these shifts never excluded the opposite view totally. Explaining development problems by citing external factors, the PST is one example. The dual gap approach may be another less controversial example. It states that there was not only a domestic gap due to the insufficiency of savings to finance necessary investments, but also a scarcity of foreign exchange. The external gap was generated by the necessity to import most investment goods and posed a problem different from domestic savings owing to problems of convertibility. One could explain the foreign exchange gap by citing domestic shortcomings as well as failures of international markets. The foreign exchange gap had to be overcome by external finance and, inspired by the Marshall Plan, official aid was widely seen as the main instrument to do so. As marginal productivity of capital had to be higher in capital-scarce SCs according to theory, private capital was expected to flow eagerly across the North–South border.

Also it is 'a popular misconception' that *dependencia* 'explained under-development by the external factor only' (Blomström & Hettne, 1984, p.71). Palma (1989, p.91) sees dependency's 'most important contribution' in its analysis of peripheral capitalism 'from the point of view of the interplay between internal and external structures'. The role of domestic 'elites' collaborating with the centre to preserve their own material advantages is one important blockage to development. The concept of structural heterogeneity, like the concept of dualism, tackled the problem that most SCs disintegrate into two 'countries', the one modern and rich, the other decaying and impoverished. But while dualism will finally be overcome – as the whole country would eventually become developed – structural heterogeneity is bound to deepen and stay. Comparing dualism and structural heterogeneity shows how the same phenomenon is analysed by two schools: the main difference lies in their evaluations of development prospects. *Dependentistas* always put internal development blockages into their international context, which may justify classifying them as focusing more on external problems.

Regional and social disparities within SCs are direct results of their insertion
into the global economy or their colonial past.

DEVELOPMENT OPTIMISM AND DEVELOPMENT PESSIMISM

H.W. Singer (1964) pointed out that this cyclical movement started with
Adam Smith. Within this cycle the 1970s have to be called development
optimistic (U-optimistic). The reason was either the feeling that changes in
world economic structures would give impetus to Southern development, or
what was perceived as the 'successful' placement of exceptionally high
international liquidity in the South. The 1980s, finally, have been widely seen
as a decade lost for development or characterized by 'development in reverse'
(Singer, 1989, p.34), a view corroborated both by data on capital formation
and by increasing poverty in the South.

MARKET VERSUS PLANNING

Another swing occurred between market and state, or market forces and
planning. Immediately after World War II, planning was widely seen as *the*
necessary means to develop. There were several reasons for this view. First,
the old laissez-faire doctrine of letting the market work unhampered by state
intervention had been theoretically overcome by the ideas of Keynes and
discredited by the experience of the Great Depression. Second, the Marshall
Plan was as obviously successful as it was interventionist. Finally, there was a
widespread feeling that development could be speeded up by the state, or even
that the state had to intervene to break the vicious circle of stagnation and
underdevelopment.

The founding of the United Nations, Keynes's ideas of a supranational
currency plus equilibrating mechanisms forcing both surplus and deficit
countries to adjust, degenerating under US pressure into the Bretton Woods
system, and of an International Trade Organization were based on a strong role
of the state. The potential effectiveness of large-scale international income
transfers proved by the Marshall Plan made development activists think in
terms of multiannual, large-scale aid to developing countries. A target of 1 per
cent of GNP compared quite modestly with the amounts the USA had
channelled to Europe for several years: between 2 and 3 per cent.

Politically, though, the climate quickly changed. The only stabilization
scheme that did come into existence served to stabilize the US dollar – not
without success – well into the 1970s. Seen from the point of view of national

self-interest, the behaviour of the USA is easily explained. As any other nation could be expected to do, the USA used its political and economic power to establish an international system fostering its own interests rather than to press for arrangements limiting its power in the interest of the global community.

In the South, three-, four-, or five-year development plans were made to coordinate investment even after the strong emphasis on planning had been driven back on the international level. While some conservative economists noticed this with displeasure, if not disgust, development economists held that the particular situation of the South demanded approaches different from those useful in and for the North. The orthodox position that there are a number of simple but powerful economic 'laws' of universal validity, and that the market mechanism allows benefits to flow to all individuals or countries, was called the 'monoeconomics' claim. According to Hirschman (1981, p.3) the rejection of this claim means

> that underdeveloped countries as a group are set apart, through a number of specific economic characteristics common to them, from the advanced industrial countries and that traditional economic analysis, which has concentrated on the industrial countries, must therefore be recast in significant respects when dealing with underdeveloped countries.

By analogy with Keynes, who had called orthodox, traditional economics only applicable to the special case of full employment, but in contrast to his claim of a General Theory, the need for yet another approach appropriate for development was felt. Seers (1963) paraphrased Keynes and the established Keynesian view when pleading for a recasting of the teaching of economics to make it more useful for dealing with development problems. The special case that had wrongly claimed general validity was – as to Keynes the economy re-establishing full employment – to Seers the economy of industrialized countries that did not take Southern conditions properly into account.

Hirschman (1981, p.6) sees the Keynesian revolution as crucial for the establishment of development economics as a distinct area of research, because it had broken the ice of monoeconomics. He sees rural under-employment – in affinity with Keynes's thoughts on unemployment in the North – and late industrialization as the outstanding reasons for treating SCs as a group of economies *sui generis*. Long delayed industrialization, due to forced specialization in staples to be exported to the North, as Hirschman (ibid., p.10) points out, required a 'deliberate, intensive, guided effort'. While the historically correct remark about specialization was not the ruling view at that time, the need for a special effort, if only to speed up and smooth development, was almost universally accepted within the field.

The defenders of monoeconomics, on the other hand, claimed that there is just one economics, just as there is one physics (cf. Hirschman, 1981, p.4).

Unfortunately, this argument contains a fallacy. Claiming unconditional and universal applicability of theories irrespective of the peculiarities and constitutive characteristics of the case treated is tantamount to claiming in the name of 'monophysics' that the boiling point of water is the same anywhere in the world – on Britain's shores as well as on top of the Himalayas. Not surprisingly, science never knew a monophysics debate.

The 'Alliance for Progress', sometimes compared with the New Deal, might be seen as a new upsurge of – at least lip service – planning. Much of the money, though, was military aid to prevent another Cuba (Kay, 1989, p.232). The seeds of 'national security doctrines' of military dictators about to 'save the nation' are also seen in this programme. The idea of multilateral aid gained ground again, though in a different form. The World Bank dropped its reservations about soft aid when IDA was to be installed as its own soft window. Western donors were 'not ... willing to channel it [aid] through the UN where the developing countries had a major say, but through the World Bank which they controlled' (Singer, 1989, p.8).

The demand for a NIEO of the 1970s revived ideas such as Keynes's proposal for commodity stabilization, and interventions in the mechanisms of the world market were requested, not dissimilar to what happened in the era immediately after World War II. Very much like the outcome then, these wishes were aborted by the North. The 1980s saw a dismantling of planning, and a fanatically professed belief in markets and getting prices right (cf. Chapter 4). This fanaticism, though, has never been strong enough to make those recommending the 'market' enthusiastically to others apply the same prescriptions to themselves with equal enthusiasm. While the North and its institutions press SCs into opening their economies, ICs remain quite protectionist where it suits them (a telling example is provided in Chapter 13), showing themselves a healthy distrust of markets.

HARROD–DOMAR AND DEVELOPMENT THINKING

The Keynesian consensus manifested itself in the application of the new Harrod–Domar growth model on SCs. This theory had been developed to see under what conditions a Keynesian (static) full-employment equilibrium could be preserved over time in a growing Northern economy. The model rests on the assumptions of a fixed ratio between capital and labour employed, and the resulting value of output. Its famous growth equation relates the rate of growth (g) to the capital output ratio (k) and the rate of saving (s). Finally, g must be identical to the exogenously given rate of growth of the population (n):

$$s/k = g = n \tag{3.1}$$

From this formula the main theoretical approaches during the first phase after 1945 unfold. Given economies with an apparently abundant supply of labour, the problem was by definition capital scarcity, since the relation between capital and labour is constant. As there exists no technical progress in a Harrod–Domar world, capital intensity remains constant over time. Looking at the representative SC (distinctions did not suggest themselves at that time) two conclusions regarding capital become clear. First, the rate of savings, which is also the rate of investment, is too low. A savings gap exists. Second, the accumulation of physical capital is of paramount importance. This view could draw support from the historical experience of successful Soviet industrialization with its heavy bias towards capital accumulation, and the fact that readily investible funds were actually scarce in the South.

On account of the rigidities of the model, the process of development could be seen as a slot machine, where capital had to be inserted and development would emerge on pulling the handle. A virtually exclusive emphasis on physical capital accumulation is probably most clearly expressed by Maurice Dobb, lecturing at the Delhi School of Economics in 1951, who thought one would 'not go far wrong' in regarding growth in the stock of capital as 'simultaneously qualitative and quantitative' and the 'crux of the process of economic development' (quoted from Singer, 1989, p.10).

The problem of quality, though, was not neglected. There was ample research into the efficiency of investment, focusing on k, or more precisely the incremental capital–output ratio (ICOR), which is identical with k in a Harrod–Domar world. To gauge the amount of savings needed, ICOR was the strategic figure, therefore ICORs were estimated for sectors or whole economies. On the basis of empirical evidence for the USA and the UK, Bruton (1968, p.223) suggested that – cyclical swings apart – k remains constant. ICOR was expected to be very high in underdeveloped regions, which means that a lot of capital is needed to produce one additional unit of output, and low in developed, more efficient economies. Development had to go hand-in-hand with declining ICORs. This trend would be reversed if an increased supply of capital decreased its price, inducing more capital-intensive production – but not within a Harrod–Domar model. ICOR can be influenced by factors outside the model, such as learning by doing, education, but also if increased investment outruns administrative capacities to handle development projects efficiently. In this case the absorptive capacity of an economy becomes the bottleneck.

A model modifying growth theories to accommodate problems of development is Bruton's (1968), specifically introducing the effects of current accounts. A current account deficit (simplified: an import surplus) will allow a higher rate of growth, but has to be financed from without. Thus the availability of foreign exchange poses a definite ceiling. But foreign capital, a necessary yet not a sufficient condition for speeding up development, cannot solve internal problems (for instance, adapting foreign technology); it merely relieves their immediacy.

Especially for practical planning, the high degree of aggregation of the Harrod–Domar model posed problems. Therefore sectorally disaggregated models were introduced. Probably the most famous, and certainly the most influential in terms of economic policy, is Mahalanobis's (1953, 1955) model, initially developed for a closed economy (like Harrod–Domar), but later extended to include foreign trade by exogenously given export earnings. With a strong preference for the capital goods sector as the engine of growth, it influenced Indian planning enormously: 'The second Five Year Plan, whose analytical structure was largely the handiwork of Mahalanobis, stands out as a very distinguished document in the development of planning theory' (Chakravarty, 1989). Politically, Mahalanobis's inward-looking strategy – or autocentricity, as one might call it nowadays – gave support to J. Nehru's attempts at gaining economic independence after political decolonialization had been achieved.

Sectoral approaches raised the question of balanced or unbalanced growth: is there a need to coordinate (balance) sectoral growth, or will a speeding sector simply drag the rest of the economy along? Rosenstein-Rodan (1943) advocated a 'big push', the simultaneous establishment of several complementary industries, to use positive externalities, and to allow the creation of a domestic market big enough for creating its own, self-propelled effective demand. Nurkse (1952, 1953) coined the expression 'balanced growth'. Its advocates favoured planning, but it would be wrong to equate balanced growth with delinking from the world market. Rosenstein-Rodan, too, made his proposal explicitly to preserve the advantages of an international division of labour, assigning labour-intensive light industries to eastern and south-eastern Europe to avoid increasing global excess capacity in heavy industry. His big push was intended to achieve growth more quickly and with less sacrifice.

Hirschman (1958) opposed the balanced growth approach, arguing that governments should encourage strategic disequilibria, concentrating on key industries with strong linkages to other parts of the economy. Scarce (decision-making) capacities could be used to advantage and hidden, scattered or badly utilized abilities and resources would be mobilized. Hirschman (1989) understands his approach as a critique of the 'then dominant Harrod–Domar growth model' and its exclusive focus on capital. Similar ideas of growth poles (*pôles de croissance*), propellent industries (*industries motrices*), and impelled industries were advocated by Perroux (1950, 1955).

The theory of dualism can also be seen as a theory of unbalanced growth, where one leading (modern) sector grows until it encompasses the whole economy and the traditional (backward) sector has disappeared. Sir Arthur Lewis (1954), who introduced this concept into economics, built his growth model to criticize both Keynesianism and neoclassics as inappropriate for the situation of the South, essentially different from Northern economies. In SCs an oversupply of labour exists in the 'traditional' sector. People are not openly unemployed but contribute very little to total production, working on a family-owned plot or working only sporadically (hidden unemployment). As these people move towards modern (mostly supposed to be world market-oriented) production, wages remain fixed until this oversupply is absorbed and 'normal' labour markets come into existence, where wages are determined by demand and supply as in the North. Before this turning point is reached, SCs have to export at disadvantageous prices determined by costs, which means basically by low SC wages. Lewis is thus seen as a forerunner of unequal exchange theory by Emmanuel (1972).

The danger that growth concentrated in one part of the economy might increase disparities rather than give momentum to uniform development was seen by Myrdal (1944, 1957) and Hirschman (1958). In Myrdal's theory of cumulative causation, market forces bring about a vicious circle of impoverishment. These backwash effects (in Hirschmanite terminology: polarization effects) were expected to be stronger than positive spread effects ('trickle down' effects) although the latter were considered possible – a conclusion that went counter to orthodox economics. It called strongly for government intervention, while the trickle down theorem posited that benefits would trickle down from the rich to the poor, eventually spreading through the whole economy without government intervention.

The *s* in equation (3.1) gave rise to theories of income distribution. The most influential is Kuznets's (1955) inverted U, postulating that income distribution becomes more unequal in the process of development as 'traditional' society dissolves, and more equal again in 'mature' societies. It 'acquired the force of economic law' (Robinson, 1976, p.437), although it was based on the historical experience of ICs and Kuznets himself cautioned against applying his findings to contemporary SCs – with good reason, as quantitative research later showed.

The necessity of income concentration can be explained plausibly by economists: as *s* increases with income (the poor have no money to save), this inequality facilitates investments, for instance by big landowners transforming their surplus cash into investments in industry. Many other models combined perfectly with this perception, such as the famous Lewisian growth model: once the modern sector has grown large enough – beyond the turning point – surplus labour and disguised unemployment disappear, and the economy will emulate the structures of developed countries. Eventually, all benefits of development will trickle down. Inequality became a virtue – presumably not to the displeasure of the rich – and ideas of 'redistribution with growth' or satisfying 'basic needs' had to be defended by showing that greater equality did not hinder growth, or at least not too much (cf. Chapter 5).

To avoid an undue caricature it should be mentioned that economic growth was sometimes emphasized as the key to poverty eradication. Streeten (1993, p.16) recalls that sensible economists and development planners in the 1950s saw quite clearly

> that economic growth is not an end in itself, but a performance test of development. Arthur Lewis defined the purpose of development as widening our range of choice, exactly as the UNDP's Human Development Reports do today ... Even in the early days some sceptics said that growth is not necessarily so benign.

It was thought necessary first to build up capital, infrastructure and productive capacity in a 'backward' economy, as this would eventually improve the lot of the poor. If the rewards of the rich were incentives to innovate, to save and to accumulate, this would finally benefit the poor. The early hungry years would turn out to have been justified. Classical, neoclassical and palaeo-Marxist economists all agreed on this. Caveats on growth were eclipsed by a pervasive emphasis on the techniques of growth.

Greater inequality, however, does not automatically mean more investment. The rich might spend their money on luxuries and conspicuous consumption instead, as Nurkse (1952) and Adler (1952) argued convincingly. Presenting 'balanced growth', Nurkse worried that the international demonstration effect of the Northern lifestyle would make people spend their money on luxury imports rather than on investments promoting development. Prebisch (1976, p.70) denounced imports to 'ape certain forms of conspicuous consumption' as wasting foreign exchange needed for developmental investments.

Regarding the last term in equation (3.1), population growth n, 'economists lent their weight to the plausible conclusion that rapid population growth is an important deterrent to economic development' (Schultz, 1988, p.416). Basic mathematics illustrates this point: a GDP of 30 billion divided by 20 million people is only 1500 per head; dividing by 10 million, however, produces 3000. The amount of capital necessary to employ an apparently unlimited supply of labour increases as numbers swell. Reaching the Lewisian turning point marking the developed–underdeveloped border is postponed by population growth.

On the other hand, since the marginal contribution to GDP by people in the 'traditional' sector was assumed negligible – or, for the sake of mathematical elegance, zero – fewer people would leave GDP (practically) undiminished, but feeding fewer people would in turn increase funds disposable for investment. Population growth was seen as exacerbated by the success of modern medical science in decreasing mortality, so that birth control was urgently needed. Aid programmes to limit population growth were designed, usually by male donors and experts.

Leibenstein's (1957) critical minimum effort thesis classifies population growth as an income-depressing force. To get development going it is necessary to overcome the low-level equilibrium of a stagnant society where income-raising forces were kept at bay. If developmental stimulants are not strong enough, GDP/head would be raised shortly and fall back to the relatively stable stagnant equilibrium. Therefore a critical minimum effort, comparable to the big push, is mandatory. This minimum increases with population, more people demanding more effort. However, Leibenstein (ibid., pp.97f) sees the possibility of overcoming stagnation without drastic measures to limit population growth.

As population growth declines with income, one could also propose increasing development efforts to reach a lower population growth rate, but this alternative is more difficult and takes longer. In 1953, Clark (1968, p.53) pointed out:

> It may well be that many of those who advocate population limitation in the oriental countries do so precisely because they do not like the idea either of emigration or of leaving markets open to oriental goods, or of giving any capital assistance to weaker countries. If there are any such it is time that their uncharitable motives were exposed.

At the present time, population growth has again become an important argument to explain underdevelopment as internally caused.

Dominant technocratic and optimistic expectations based on the perception of development as a race away from backwardness were most pronouncedly expressed by Rostow (1960). The book's success seems to be explained by several factors: it corroborated existing prejudices, offered 'easy tricks' to attain the American Dream, and provided an acceptable though wrong historical figleaf for a basically anti-historical science by simply omitting the crippling effects of colonial policy on SCs. The book deserves mentioning because, through 'its influence on a whole generation of students of change, this publication is a major event in the prolonged obfuscation of the real issues contained in "development"' (Brookfield, 1979, p.37). Also catchy formulations such as take-off into self-sustained growth coined by the author have survived the discussion of his model.

Rostow was not the first to develop a theory of stages. List ([1841] 1920) had held similar views, although he limited development to the North, recommending a 'joint exploitation' of savage and barbarous tribes. In contrast, Rostow presented his theory to overcome theses of stagnation, declaring the American Way of Life to be within the eventual reach of anyone, offering quite precise dimensions of time lags, for instance about 35 years in industrial output between the Soviet Union and the USA (Rostow, 1960, p.93). Rostow called his book a non-communist, not an anti-Marxian, manifesto. One might ask whether he was aware that really existing communism was based on Lenin's anti-Marxian view that capitalism could be overcome before it had reached ultimate maturity. Marx himself and orthodox Marxists deny such a possibility. In their view the quickest way of overcoming capitalism would be to help it pass through its stages of development more rapidly. Similarities between these two schools induced Seers (1979) to speak of a congruence of Marxism and other neoclassical theories. Logically it could be argued that Marxian communism might follow Rostow's last stage of High Mass Consumption (only reached by the USA when the book was published). Although he stated the impossibility of predicting further development, Rostow would certainly not have espoused this view. Naturally, poverty in the USA (cf. Myrdal, 1944) or living conditions in 'reservations' for 'Indians' were unsuitable for his book.

Meanwhile, Latin American social scientists, stimulated by Raúl Prebisch, broke away from orthodox thinking. The structuralist school came into existence. As they were mainly centred at ECLA (Spanish: CEPAL) Kay (1989, p.25) refers to structuralism as the ECLA theory of development. As a result of the debate with monetarists, the structuralist view on inflation is best known in the North. Trade relations between centre and periphery, import-substituting industrialization and limits posed by small domestic markets to inward-directed development models were also analysed, following the lead of Prebisch. These ideas had a big impact on the subcontinent and a major influence on the creation of the Latin American Free Trade Association in the 1960s.

DEPENDENCIA: FOCUSING ON EXTERNAL FACTORS

Theories stressing the importance of external factors can be traced back to Mariategui's ([1928] 1955) ideas on imperialism in the 1920s. After World War II, the PST led, after an initial focus on diversification within SCs, to increased attention to external factors. The work of ECLA was an important contribution to the development of what later became dependency thinking. Sunkel (1979, p.23) warns against under-estimating ECLA's contributions by focusing on their weaknesses. Considering the ferocity of attacks by conservative groups, established (Northern) science, the US government and big firms against those doubting the dogma of the benefits of free trade, Sunkel finds ECLA's work already revolutionary.

The crisis of development at the end of the 1960s led to increasing scepticism of the Cepalistas at ECLA regarding the development possibilities within the present world system, and finally gave birth to *dependencia*. In contrast to neoclassics, dependency is not a school characterized by common, standardized concepts such as indifference curves or consumption functions, but a means of analysis based on globally unequal power relations, a theory explaining inhibited development in the periphery. 'Dependence' is, according to Dos Santos (1978, pp.76f) 'based upon an international division of labour which allows industrial development to take place in some countries while restricting it in others, whose growth is conditioned by and subjected to the power centres of the world'.

In marked contrast to the start from an 'equally low standard of living' and to neoclassicist anti-historical models, underdevelopment results from the history of North–South relations. Countries did not start from the same line, each having a fair chance, but the evolution of the global economy created and destroyed development in the North and the South, respectively. History documents, to use A.G. Frank's famous expression, a development of underdevelopment, a blocking of development by the North. 'The advent of an industrial nucleus in eighteenth century Europe disrupted the world economy of the time and eventually conditioned later economic development in almost every region in the world' (Furtado, 1978, p.33), which illustrates not only the shift of structuralist thinking towards dependency, but also its affinity with Wallerstein's (1974) World System approach. Underdevelopment was seen as the historical result of the genocide of the original populations of the Americas, slave trade across the Atlantic and colonial exploitation destroying economically active autochthonous classes and grafting the production of goods needed by 'motherlands' upon the conquered. In contrast to the ruling view of development starting from an equal base, underdevelopment was caused by present-day developed countries, a view that can be easily corroborated by historical facts.

Although underdeveloped countries are necessarily dependent, a dependent economy is not necessarily underdeveloped (cf., for instance, Furtado, 1976, p.104), as *dependentistas* often illustrate with the example of Canada. This is an important point routinely forgotten by critics of *dependencia*, accusing it of equating dependency and underdevelopment. Present economic and social structures are the result of a crippling history suffered by the periphery in the process of adapting it to the needs of the centre. Tobacco, sugar and coffee, as Marx cynically remarked in his 'Discourse on Free Trade' might have been the natural destiny of the West Indies, but 'Two centuries earlier, nature, which is unaware of commerce, had not placed either coffee trees nor sugar cane there' (quoted from Frank, 1978, p.76). This man-made division of labour created economic structures critically dependent on importing equipment, semi-manufactures and know-how from the centre. Braun (1977, p.106) defines dependence as 'the impossibility ... to effect enlarged reproduction, and also simple reproduction of capital'. Crippled peripheral economies cannot survive cut off from the centre. Commercial relations with the centre, though, are characterized by unequal exchange (for a survey, see Raffer, 1987a), external vulnerability and the power of transnational corporations. The ruling 'elites' experience a process of transnational integration – their ties to the centres of decision in the North become closer than to their own hinterland, the countries experience a process of national disintegration (Sunkel, 1973).

In contrast to Northern approaches, dependency is less economistic, following Myrdal's (1957, p.10) advice to differentiate between 'relevant' and 'irrelevant' factors, rather than clinging to the logically useless distinction between 'economic' and 'non-economic'. Economics forms the basis, but is by no means the only form of dependence. Political, military and cultural forms of dependence exist. Furtado (1976, pp.100ff) sees cultural dependence as the essence of dependence: the forming of consumption patterns from outside, which does not need foreign direct investments and cannot be abolished by economic policy alone. These changes in consumption habits were called the international demonstration effect by Nurkse.

Although some propositions are shared, many important differences remain between *dependentistas*. To equate *dependentistas* and Marxists, as is often done, is simply wrong. The group comprises both nationalist–populist and radical neomarxist authors. Kay (1989) calls them 'reformist' and 'Marxist', differentiating a third 'Caribbean' wing. Assuming a special kind of peripheral capitalism and sceptical views of possibilities of industrialization – also based on the secular decline of peripheral terms of trade – go 'counter to the spirit and letter of Marx's writings' as Palma (1989) points out. Orthodox Marxists have therefore criticized their leftist colleagues severely.

The diversity of views subsumed under the label *dependencia* is illustrated by the development prospects seen for SCs, which range from the assertion that genuine development is impossible within world capitalism to different forms of 'associated–dependent development' (Cardoso, 1972, p.94). While A.G. Frank (1972) argues that national bourgeoisies are unable to fulfil their capitalist duty of accumulating and developing their countries, Cardoso for instance argues that rapid economic growth and development of forces of production have taken place. Amin (1974) – to quote an African dependency thinker – sees the possibility of a new division of labour, where classical manufactures would be produced in SCs, while modern products and know-how would remain in the centre. The opinion that East Asian NICs contradicted *dependencia* simply because they existed – often voiced before the crash of 1997 – might thus result from infamiliarity with dependency thinking. No *dependentista* denied the possibility of development, although the more radical authors, such as A.G. Frank, thought it unrealistic, especially for Latin America.

To develop, however, these economies would have to protect themselves against the disadvantages of the world market. Two basic strategies were seen: (a) self-reliance for large countries such as China and collective self-reliance (through integration and cooperation) for smaller economies, (b) selective dissociation from the world market: allowing it to work where this is beneficial and intervening where market results would have a negative impact on development. Neoclassical critics of *dependencia* have often been accused of unfamiliarity with the approaches criticized and ignorance of literature. Kay attributes this lack of knowledge to the fact that most writings appeared in Spanish or Portuguese, translations took time, and therefore *dependencia* was identified with authors whose ideas happened to be readily available in English translations. Kay (1989, p.125) mentions Frank in particular, although he associates Frank with the world system approach as different from dependency, a debatable differentiation.

Blomström and Hettne (1984, p.79) stress a 'lack of communication and sympathy' between the two 'completely different paradigms'. Neoclassicists consider dependency unscientific, in these authors' opinion because of critical portrayals 'of neoclassical theory to which no selfrespecting neoclassical economist would put his name'. There is, however, a big gap between theoretical neoclassical economics of the advanced mathematical kind, whose disciples often stress that their necessary model assumptions are not met in reality, and the rather down-to-earth, simplistic prescriptions given to (or sometimes forced upon) SCs by 'practical' neoclassicists claiming that their advice would follow from those very models. Balogh (1963, p.201) detected a 'certain pride' among neoclassicists in the uselessness of their 'pure' theoretical models if they are subject to attack, 'though this pride is usually not manifested when, in the absence of attacks, they are used as a basis for policy recommendations'. *Dependentistas* concerned with reality and actual economic policies have apparently attacked practical neoclassics and its too often harmful effects in and on SCs.

Even more disturbing is an explanation by Raúl Prebisch (1988) for the neoclassical disrepute of approaches originating in the periphery. After presenting examples of misunderstandings and less than impeccable quoting, he concludes that the endeavour to free oneself from unconditional submission to theories formulated in the centres is frowned upon: 'Generally speaking, no serious effort is made to understand ideas before attacking them. No recognition has been accorded to our determination to free ourselves from a persistent intellectual dependence which has serious implications for the praxis of development.'

4. The neoliberal tide of the 'Washington Consensus'

The 1980s were not only a period of diminishing returns in development thinking, as identified by Ranis and Fei (1988, p.10), but also the decade of the victory of neoliberalism, a pronounced backswing of the pendulum towards anti-Keynesianism, anti-interventionism and monoeconomics. Lack of theoretical impetus was compensated by more enthusiastic belief in the benevolence of 'free' markets, deregulation and privatization. This conservative tide virtually wiped out critical thinking in the social sciences, completely muting critical approaches in development studies. The breakdown of the Soviet bloc, allegedly the final victory of capitalism, contributed to a practically unchallenged rule of neoliberal ideology, first shaken in 1997 by the Asian crisis.

Rodrik (1996, p.9) calls the extent of convergence about current fashions in economic development policy remarkable. What unites the 'vast majority of professional economists in the developed world who are concerned with issues of development' now is 'faith in the desirability and efficacy' of a strategy which 'emphasizes fiscal rectitude, competitive exchange rates, free trade, privatization, undistorted market prices, and limited intervention' (ibid.).

The prevailing attitude towards price distortions illustrates this fundamental change in a nutshell. Streeten (1994) draws attention to the curious transformation of the expression 'getting prices right'. In the 1960s, it meant the calculation of correct shadow or accounting prices instead of market or actual prices reflecting all sorts of distortions. Market power, externalities or highly imperfect markets in many SCs are reasons why actual prices are unlikely to reflect correct prices in the textbook sense. In an economy already 'distorted', additional distortions may be improvements. Government interventions can be beneficial correctives, rather than distorting an otherwise correct set of signals and incentives. Thus interventions had to allocate resources according to the 'right' shadow prices, to correct the distortions caused by the free play of market forces. The neoliberal consensus reversed this recommendation. SCs must now get rid of state interventions to permit market prices to reflect correct opportunity costs and benefits. Distortions are now regarded as caused mainly or only by governments.

The liberalization drive of the 1980s and 1990s cannot be justified by orthodox economic theory. One quick look at a good textbook will show that the results of the perfectly competitive market cannot be approximated by eliminating some but not all market imperfections (cf., for instance, Nicholson 1992, p.521). Reducing only the number of imperfections, liberalizing trade partially, might make things worse. Unless one assumes that a global, perfectly competitive market can be established, good introductory textbooks warn, liberalization may worsen a country's economic position.

Even the very founders of present trade theory themselves warned of its applicability to real life. Bertil Ohlin ([1933] 1967, pp.308f, emphasis in original) was quite outspoken:

> The obstinate conservatism with which the classical comparative cost thinking has been retained in theory as something more than a pedagogical introduction – or a model for the treatment of a few special problems – is evidence that, even today, there is in many quarters an insufficient understanding of this fundamental fact.
>
> It follows that not only the comparative cost model but also the factor proportions model can only be applied in special cases and used as a general introduction to illuminate the character of trade in some essential aspects ... It is characteristic of *the developing countries* that a good many factors do not exist at all and that the quality of others differs from factors in the industrialized countries. This means that a simple method of analysis – such as the factor proportions model – which does not take this into account is to some extent unrealistic.

Ohlin's attempts to approximate reality were lost in the process of formalization. Furthermore, while models work quite well under 2 countries/ 2 products/2 factors assumptions, they cannot be generalized in a meaningful way. Therefore it should be no surprise that empirical tests of the theorem contradict theoretical expectations. The best known test is the so-called Leontief paradox. Studying US trade data, Wassily Leontief (1953) found that US exports were more labour-intensive than imports, although the USA was doubtlessly the most capital-abundant country. Leontief's findings were corroborated by other studies later on. A long discussion followed. Its thrust, however, was not to find a theory more in line with reality but to find out why empirical results were wrong. All the same, the Heckscher–Ohlin theory of static comparative advantage has been successfully used to explain at least the broad composition of exports in some cases (cf. Wood & Mayer, forthcoming).

Eli Heckscher (1950, p.275; emphasis added) explicitly found his theory '*in full accordance with List's point of view, since his criticism of the "school" was directed only at the dynamic factors*' – a view fully shared by List ([1841] 1920, pp.234f). Nevertheless, the 'Heckscher–Ohlin theory' is used to advocate liberalization and to 'disprove' List's infant industry protection argument. The advice to SCs to diversify and to protect temporarily and selectively derived from the PST, would equally meet Heckscher's approval.

Academic theory and teaching have always centred on models displaying the advantages of 'free' trade according to what Thurow (1983) called the 'price-auction-view' of the world. Myrdal (1957, p.9) therefore pointed out that the 'theory of international trade, and, indeed, economic theory generally were never worked out to serve the purpose of explaining the reality of economic under-development and development'. In this context one should recall Balogh's (1963, p.201) dictum about a 'certain pride' among economists in the uselessness of pure theoretical models if they are subject to attack, which does not keep these economists from using the same models 'as a basis for policy recommendations'. Logic or mathematical facts are eagerly forgotten when it comes to recommending policies.

From this perspective, it is understandable that Rodrik (1996, p.17) saw the debt crisis as an opportunity seized by orthodox economists for a 'wholesale reform of prevailing policies' offering the chance 'to wipe the slate clean and mount a frontal attack on the entire range of policies in use'. A crisis brought about by overspending and overlending and the sudden change of economic policy in the North which sent interest rates rocketing – as the OECD (1996b, p.18) admits – was simply declared to stem from import substitution and 'inward-looking' policies. Distinctions between bad and proper import substitution were not made, even though the Asian tigers used these discredited policies to good effect. The World Bank in particular, as Rodrik points out, was strongly advocating that import substitution was better avoided, shaping economic policies in SCs accordingly. The IMF seconded helpfully.

The World Bank (1987, p.150) expressed most bluntly the ruling view that problems are caused by the inflexibility of SCs to adjust to the world market: 'The best response is flexibility – that is the ability to shift resources rapidly from an export where sales are proving difficult to an export or import substitute where profit opportunities are now superior'. As any importer can impose new trade barriers more quickly than any country could switch from one industry to another, this advice is clearly a recipe for disaster. The enormous costs of adjustment are not considered worth mentioning. It should also be recalled that trade restrictions in favour of industrial countries, such as the Multifibre Agreement, are justified on the grounds that these (developed) economies are not able to adjust so quickly. In this particular case the 'adjustment period' has been stretched over decades.

In his review article on policy reform, Rodrik (1996, p.33) concludes that reform is seen as needing 'a strong and autonomous executive, unhindered by the search for consensus and compromise'. Owing to lack of faith in people – who are assumed rational by orthodoxy – and democratic institutions, 'a lot of economists feel deep down but find [it] politically incorrect to articulate' (ibid.) that autocratic reforms are preferable to democracy, 'especially in new democracies'. Milton Friedman and his relation to Chile's junta is one example.

The best illustration is the history of the Compensatory Financing Facility summarized by Polak (1991, p.9, emphasis added), a leading theoretician of the Fund. Initially introduced to compensate shortfalls in export earnings beyond the control of SCs,

> conditionality was limited to an obligatory statement by the member to co-operate with the Fund ... to find, *where required*, appropriate solutions for its balance of payments difficulties ... Over the years, however, the Fund has increasingly come to the realization that *even though a country's export shortfall was both 'temporary' and largely beyond its control the country might still have balance-of-payments difficulties attributable to inappropriate policies and that large amounts of unconditional credit might cause the country to delay adopting needed policy adjustments.*

So even if the country's economic policy is not at all the reason for temporary problems, the country still has to change it if the Fund wishes so. This is illogical if one assumes that ways to overcome an economic problem are sought. It makes perfect sense if one shares Rodrik's (1996, p.17) perception that opportunities are seized 'to wipe the slate clean and mount a frontal attack on' policies disliked by the Fund and orthodoxy in general. Polak (1991, p.12) asserts: 'The purpose of the Fund's conditionality is to make as sure as possible that a country drawing on the Fund's resources pursues a set of policies that are, in the Fund's view, appropriate to its economic situation in general and its payments situation in particular'.

It should be recalled that conditionality did not exist in the original IMF Articles of Agreement. It was introduced later and has been strengthened over time. During the 1990s donors have generally increased conditionality while reducing official resources for development. Polak also advises how a country can be made to '*present itself as opting for adjustment on its own rather than under pressure from the Fund*' (ibid., p.13, emphasis added). His advice is increasingly heeded now: debtors often claim that the 'advised' policies are their own.

THE WASHINGTON CONSENSUS

The set of policies forced upon SCs is conventionally called the Washington Consensus. John Williamson (1996, p.15), its father, dates its origins to his Congress hearing in 1989 and to a visit to the Instititute of Development Studies, when he 'was challenged by Hans Singer to identify the policy changes that I regarded as so welcome.' Responding to this challenge,

Williamson made a list summarizing ten policy prescriptions – possibly recalling the ten commandments – as commanding consensus in Washington.

1. Fiscal discipline, 'typically' implying 'a primary budget surplus of several percent of ... GDP' (ibid., p.14). In the context of debtor SCs, that left room for debt service.
2. Public expenditure priorities, defined as redirections towards fields with high economic returns such as primary health and education. In practice, however, these sectors were most severely affected by fiscal discipline to allow higher debt service payments. Introducing user fees reduces the poor's access to these services. Research, in particular the famous UNICEF study on adjustment with a human face (Cornia *et al.*, 1987), proved that vulnerable groups were hurt.
3. Tax reform, including especially cutting marginal tax rates.
4. Financial liberalization: moderately positive real interest rates and the abolition of preferential interest rates (such as for developmentally useful projects).
5. Exchange rates: unified and competitive.
6. Trade liberalization: abolishing quotas (replacing them with tariffs) and reducing tariffs to a uniform low level within three to ten years. Williamson noted that there was some disagreement whether liberalization should be slowed down during crises.
7. Foreign direct investment: equal treatment with domestic firms. Reproducing Williamson's list, the World Bank (1999a, p.3) calls this the elimination of barriers.
8. Privatization.
9. Deregulation: abolishing regulations aimed at achieving developmental or social aims.
10. Property rights to be guaranteed.

This list was discussed at the Institute of International Economics and deemed to be an accurate report of the opinion prevalent in Washington, although Stanley Fischer 'suggested an alternative taxonomy that seemed to me to be less specific but largely to overlap in substance' (Williamson 1996, p.15). The one important exception was that Fischer, then chief economist of the World Bank, wanted to include social agenda far more explicitly than Williamson's point 2. The name was criticized too. It was argued that it should better have been called the 'universal convergence'. Agreeing to that, Williamson (ibid., p.16) regretted that it was too late to change the name.

Changes in applied orthodoxy occurred during the 1990s to which neither Williamson nor the World Bank (1999a) draw appropriate attention. In the early days of their structural adjustment, Bank and Fund used to insist on devaluations by the debtor. Later on, for instance in Asia or Brazil, they insisted on defending fixed exchange rates. This change occurred in line with a change of capital movements. In the 1980s, debts were in dollars or, less frequently, in other Northern currencies. Devaluing the debtor's currency increased the debt burden in domestic currency, without changing debt stocks in dollars or yen. The short-term placements dominating during the late 1990s were often in the debtor's currency. Speculators would have to take losses if this old recipe were still applied. Keeping the peg fixed allows them to leave the country without, or with reduced, losses.

The BWIs justified extremely high (instead of moderately positive) real interest rates – around 40 per cent in the case of Brazil – by claiming they would keep volatile capital in the country or attract new flows. In practice, though, this has not worked, quite understandably. These rates are interpreted as a clear signal of distress. They might provide an incentive for risk-loving speculators to stay a few days (longer), while more risk-averse ones leave immediately. But desperation interest rates are unlikely to attract long-term investment, while burdening domestic firms with huge costs.

During the period of the 'Asian miracle' (cf. Chapter 9) orthodoxy claimed that the tigers' success was the result of applying orthodox policies. The World Bank (1993a, p.9, original emphasis) stated that 'adherents of the *neoclassical view* stress ... an absence of price controls and other distortionary measures'. Even though there are short passages contending, for example, that 'East Asia does not wholly conform with the neoclassical model' (ibid.), the Bank stressed Asian openness to international trade, and an environment friendly to competition. In the text, the Bank concluded that the 'most difficult question' the study tried to answer was whether 'these interventions contributed to the rapid growth ... or detracted from it' (ibid., p.24; cf. also p.354). Demonstrating 'conclusively' that 'those interventions that were maintained over a long period accelerated growth' (ibid.) was considered difficult. The World Bank's president, Lewis T. Preston, summarized the authors' conclusions more briefly: 'rapid growth in each economy was primarily due to the application of a set of common, market friendly economic policies' (ibid., p.vi). This conclusion reinforced other research. Thus the 'market-oriented aspects of East Asia's policies can be recommended with few reservations'. Apparently, the Bank found it less difficult to demonstrate the beneficial effects of liberalization.

The fact that the tigers demonstrably did not follow the Washington consensus (cf. Rodrik, 1996; Raffer & Singer, 1996; World Bank, 1999a; Wade, 1990) was played down at best, but mostly disregarded. After the Asian crash, though, the World Bank stated that Mexico fulfilled most of the consensus conditions, but East Asia did not, reaching 'The conclusion: Washington consensus policies were neither the cause of high growth, nor the cause of the crisis' (World Bank, 1999a, p.2). This begs the question why they should be adopted, and why the Bretton Woods twins had propagated them so forcefully, unless one concurs fully with Rodrik that bringing about changes in economic policy was the real reason.

INCREASED DEPENDENCE OF SCs

Ironically, new and stronger forms of dependence developed at the very time when dependency analysis had practically vanished from academic debates. SCs have become perceptibly more dependent nowadays than during the heydays of the dependency school. The present situation of the South fully corroborates and confirms dependency analysis, but this triumph goes unclaimed. Dependency thinking was vanquished so completely that orthodoxy could wrongly claim until 1997 that Asian 'tigers' such as South Korea and Taiwan – two prime examples corroborating Raúl Prebisch's ideas and dependency thinking – would prove it wrong. This successful way to economic development is now largely closed.

The present global economy lends itself even better to dependency analysis than the world system of the 1970s (Raffer, 2000). The debt problem and its 'management', new and stricter forms of conditionality as well as changes in the global economic framework increased the dependence of SCs (or the periphery, as *dependentistas* would say) substantially, so much so that one may arguably speak of a de facto recolonization. The fact that dependency is nevertheless dead at present proves the completeness of the ideological victory of orthodox thinking, as well as a high level of intellectual dependence. Southern scientists no longer try to free themselves 'from a persistent intellectual dependence which has serious implications for the praxis of development' (Prebisch, 1988, p.37). Change is needed. Dependency analysis must be revived to play again an important role in scientific debate.

This new form of neocolonial dominance putting SCs under the control of multilateral institutions dominated by the North is an important new feature. The BWIs particularly exercise strong control over Southern economies and their policies. Increasingly, the present situation fits Friedrich List's recommendation of North–South relations. Better known for his opposition to the 'English philosophy' of free trade as harmful to Germany in its early development stages some 150 years ago, List ([1841] 1920, p.211) advocated joint exploitation of the South as 'promising much richer and more certain fruits than the mutual enmity of war and trade regulations'. This new form of dominance was thus called neo-Listian (Raffer, 1987b).

Present forms of dependence are based on foreign debts, new and tougher conditionalities – illustrated by the evolution of the Lomé treaties from a progressive model of contractual partnership to a means of control – and the discipline enforced on weaker partners by the new global framework of the World Trade Organization (WTO). As regards *financial dependence*, as early as the 1960s, *dependendistas* warned about this, seeing in it a most powerful means of controlling countries. The easy money of the 1970s may have made this warning look obsolete. The debt crisis of the 1980s, when 'sovereign' countries were de facto put into receivership, not only proves them right, but goes beyond what *dependendistas* would have thought possible then. As for *political conditionality*, the fact that conditionality has become more stringent and has been extended substantially during the recent past further corroborates the view of a neo-Listian world system. In perceptible contrast to the decades of the Cold War, donors have increasingly emphasized good governance, human rights, democratization, participatory development, transparency and accountability, but also environmental issues. These political demands are now manifestly present both in bilateral and in multilateral development cooperation. Most recently, poverty reduction strategies have been added to the list of conditions, rather than providing the base for a complete reorientation of development policy.

These principles have little impact on donor practice, as a comparison of ODA per capita received by democratic and authoritarian regimes showed (UNDP, 1994, p.76). In the case of the USA, the relationship between aid and human rights violations was even perverse. High military spenders received generous official finance. Multilateral institutions also seem to prefer martial law regimes, quietly assuming that such regimes will promote political stability and improve economic management – an empirical result corroborating Rodrik's thesis. The new political conditionality is a distinctive U-turn of donor theory not supported by corresponding aid volumes.

Their historical record as well as present policies make it difficult to believe that donor governments are honestly committed to these values. As colonial powers they ruled very undemocratically. After decolonization all Northern donors have supported dictatorial and undemocratic regimes, in some cases extending their 'assistance' as far as training special police forces to torture more efficiently. Baby Doc, Mobutu, Bokasa, Pinochet, Somoza, Suharto – the list of dictators dear to donors is quite long.

A telling illustration for the discrepancy between rhetoric and reality is the Dutch–Indonesian case. After a massacre in East Timor in 1991, the Netherlands decided to freeze aid, a move heavily criticized by other donors. In 1992, Indonesia severed its relations with the Dutch, requesting the World Bank to take over as the organizer of the Intergovernmental Group for Indonesia, which the Bank did with the consent of other donors. China is another example where human rights are considered not that important. When the Nigerian military put dissenters to death after a mock trial, only a token gesture, suspending aid, was imposed, but there was no trade embargo for oil, which would have been more effective but would also have been felt by a Northern transnational.

The double standard shows particularly clearly in the case of International Financial Institutions (IFIs) controlled by the North, such as the IMF or the World Bank (Raffer and Singer, 1996; Raffer, 1993). If principles such as participatory development, transparency, accountability, the rule of law or good governance were indeed as dear to OECD donors as their official declarations purport, they would equally apply them to their own aid administrations, multilaterals and all – not just some – recipients. Efficient management by public institutions, be they government departments or public finance institutions, is immensely desirable everywhere. Thus logic would demand that these principles be applied to bilateral aid, multilateral sources of finance controlled by OECD countries and all SCs with equal fervour. An example set by OECD donors would provide a most powerful argument against any scepticism about their honest intentions. It would also allow bilateral and multilateral institutions to reap the social and economic benefits to which the OECD draws attention, such as better use of scarce resources, or relieving delays and distortions of development. However, as the example of IFIs shows, this is not done.

The new world system of the WTO brought about fundamental changes, with the North mostly able to shape it according to their interests, as Chapter 12 will argue in greater detail. While able to retain high protection in the fields of textiles, clothing and agriculture, the North managed to restrict or outlaw protection where it could be in the interest of the South. Most notably, measures against infant industry protection were taken, arguing in some contrast to Eli Heckscher and Bertil Ohlin that these would contradict the Heckscher–Ohlin theory of trade. It should also be noted that the principles of the WTO are in many important respects the very opposite of the ideas behind the creation of UNCTAD. This is no surprise if one recalls that UNCTAD was largely the brainchild of Raúl Prebisch, whose ideas on appropriate trade-related development policies differ pronouncedly from the WTO's approach.

Potential advantages of SCs are, at best, quite limited. On the whole there is reason for concern that the new mechanisms will be used in the interest of the North, further compounding the South's disadvantages in the global economy. The textile sector (discussed in Chapter 13) illustrates international double standards particularly well. While SCs are forced by the North and IFIs controlled by Northern voting majorities to open their whole economies very quickly, the North protects sectors over decades where SCs have become competitive. In contrast to unacceptable infant industry protection this appears to be acceptable geriatric industry protection. Mechanisms considered necessary, useful and economically sound in the case of the North adjusting their structures are denied to SCs undergoing adjustment as unnecessary, harmful and economically unsound. Textiles and clothing are just one example. Agriculture, iron or steel could provide similar case studies. If the mechanisms used in the textile and clothing sector are useful, it appears logical to allow SCs to shape their adjustment according to this model of smooth transition, precisely because of the reasons brought forward by the North. Obligations under the WTO are currently used by the EU to remove those remnants of the 1970s from the Lomé framework that had been adopted in favour of and due to pressure by SC signatories. The history of Lomé mirrors the changes in North–South relations very closely.

The Final Act of the Uruguay Round also increased IFI influence. IFIs are to cooperate more closely with the WTO to achieve greater coherence in economic policy. One may assume that appropriate influence on national policies will be easier in the South.

NEOLIBERAL POLICIES IN THE NORTH

Quite in line with monoeconomics, neoliberalism rules in the North as well. While SCs were forced by the BWIs to adopt neoliberal policies, this was done voluntarily by Northern governments. In a way structural adjustment policies in the South may be seen as test runs helping to make these policies more easily acceptable. The failure of inefficient government interventions in Eastern Europe provided another argument in favour of what neoliberalism declares to be the 'market'.

The Rodrik thesis of a predilection for autocratic changes and the lack of faith in democracy is corroborated by the example of OECD countries, where government influence has been strongly reduced by cutting budgets for interventions, dismantling instruments to do so, and by international treaties, such as Maastricht, the Final Act of the Uruguay Round, or the North American Free Trade Agreement (NAFTA). We observe a weakening of democratic institutions by reducing their powers via international treaties. In contrast to the past, when newly elected governments were free to chose their policies, future governments are now bound by a new generation of treaties. Democratic changes and choices have been restricted. Long periods between withdrawal and termination of all contractual obligations make change extremely difficult. The MAI - now officially off the agenda after strong international public pressure – would have stipulated that its provisions should continue to apply for 15 years after the notification of withdrawal. Nations would have been bound for several election periods. Several future governments would be restricted in their possibilities to revise investment policies. They would have to continue to abide by the agreement even if there existed strong evidence of destructive impacts. If any of these future governments signed the treaty again, the process would start anew, making discontinuing these obligations virtually impossible.

This anti-democracy bias also shows in other, less important, examples. The Mexican government suppressed an open and fair discussion on the NAFTA treaty. In the USA, fast-track legislation was used, which reduces the influence of legislators considerably. This may have been the reason why the fast track option was denied for trade negotiations later on. The necessary new laws after her accession to the EU were whipped through Parliament so quickly in Austria that representatives publicly confessed that they did not even have the time to read first what they voted for. Democracy is rolled back and the state is reduced far beyond what liberals in the 1930s considered legitimate.

All international trade and investments treaties implement the Washington Consensus: national treatment for multinationals, restrictions on performance requirements, ensuring that host states will not restrict certain investment-related financial transactions, such as transfers of profits, and dispute resolution in the form of binding arbitration procedures to settle investment-related disputes between states and investors, putting investors even above democratically enacted laws. The potential effects of this kind of arbitration on the environment and social standards cast doubts on the concern for these issues expressed by OECD governments on other occasions.

Repeatedly presenting itself as a means to help and advance 'necessary' reforms, the WTO (1998a, p.4, emphasis added) stated most outspokenly in its *Annual Report 1998*:

> Finally – and perhaps most importantly – the WTO can help provide the response to the central government challenge of our new global age: *the fact that governments answer mainly to national constituencies, while increasingly the economic system must answer to global needs. The experience of the WTO, and the way it works via binding commitments reached by consensus, gives some guidance as to how these systemic gaps might be bridged.*

The WTO offers itself explicitly as an instrument to overrule national democratic processes, to roll back democracy. Measures against the will of constituencies are to be pressed through by entering international contracts. By accepting WTO obligations, administrations can undo the electorate's democratic control. Citing regulations they have themselves negotiated and signed before, politicians can argue that national laws and decisions have now to comply.

The desire to bypass and overrule democratically elected parliaments by binding international commitments is one important feature of neoliberalism. With its Maastricht criteria and the Dublin agreement to fine members not fulfilling them in the future, the EU locked in present neoliberal policies, practically excluding Keynesian policies for the foreseeable future. For the first time in history an 'institutional penalty on Keynesian policies' (Raffer, 1998b) was agreed on. Anti-Keynesianism was successfully institutionalized, making it next to impossible for future democratically elected governments to change economic policy in Europe, as they will be bound by EU common rules, which cannot be changed by any single country alone.

Under the cloak of the new European currency, those pre-Keynesian policies responsible for the economic crisis of the 1930s are relegitimated: budgetary cuts and the dismantling of social standards are now justified by the convergence criteria. If the Maastricht criteria were necessary conditions for a common currency, Belgium and Luxembourg could not have had one for decades, as one country usually fulfilled them while the other did not. Germany's failure to meet these criteria did not lead to perceptible devaluations of the mark, which casts doubts on whether these criteria are necessary for a hard currency. So does the decline of the euro's exchange rate during 1999–2000 while these criteria were fulfilled. The catchword 'Maastricht' has become a generally accepted reason to commit the errors of the 1930s all over again, plus a few new ones. In contrast to them the rich have received large tax cuts, which in turn have aggravated fiscal deficits and reduced effective demand, redistributing income to groups with a lower marginal propensity to consume. At the CDU party convention in October 1996, the then German Chancellor announced plans to cut taxes for the rich further, in spite of Maastricht and the heavy financial burden of reunification. This in turn increases pressures on other budget items, such as social expenditures and resources available for policy intervention.

Intervening more and more in member countries' decisions, the EU has a largely powerless 'Parliament'. Laws are made and relevant decisions reached behind closed doors by the executive branch and unelected bureaucrats, finally accountable to no one. Taxpayers are not even allowed to know their own government's arguments. This deprives them of any possibility to hold their governments responsible for what they did. Elected representatives of national parliaments have no choice but to accept decisions taken without democratic control. While busily rolling back democracy in Europe, the EU and its member governments insist at least as eagerly on more democracy and participation in SCs. However, the austerity policies implemented under the catchword 'Maastricht' might well be impossible if EU goverments themselves met the standards preached to others. A totally independent European central bank and a newly created police force, Europol, whose members are made totally unaccountable by enjoying lifelong immunity for whatever they might do, reduce democratic control further. Rodrik's reasoning is fully corroborated in Europe as well.

Introducing investor-to-state dispute resolution, NAFTA is another example of reducing democratic control. It confers the right to sue governments for damages before an international panel of arbitrators, not at national courts, challenging both parliamentary and judicial decisions. The first case was Ethyl Corporation suing the Canadian government for $251 million, arguing that it had suffered damages because Canadian legislators banned its gasoline additive as hazardous, and because its product was discussed in the Canadian Parliament, thus blemishing the firm's good reputation. Canada was forced to abolish this law, although this additive was banned in California as well. Parliamentary power to enact laws protecting the environment, but also social standards, was severely impaired. After Ethyl overturned the Canadian law other suits – all in the field of environmental protection – were immediately considered by multinationals. Swenarchuk (1999) presents a long list of law suits under NAFTA, among them a case against the USA, in which a corporation used investor–state legislation against a verdict of a Mississippi state court in a case between this corporation and a US competitor firm. According to Swenarchuk (ibid.) such cases demonstrate that a corporation can 'use ... the NAFTA investment chapter to essentially reverse the results of domestic court proceedings and to circumvent the course of normal commercial civil litigation. Having lost to a competitor in the courts, it claims compensation from the US federal government'.

The Multilateral Agreement on Investment, secretly negotiated under OECD auspices for quite some time, but now officially off the agenda after public protest, planned to confer this right to firms on a worldwide scale. If it had succeeded it would have reduced parliamentary powers substantially. Essentially, this instrument is but a further developed stage of WTO dispute settlement. There are attempts to revive MAI regulations within the WTO.

Globalization is always quoted as the factor forcing governments to adopt such policies. It is conveniently forgotten that it is itself the result of deliberate policies, decisions and international treaties by the same governments. Globalization serves as the basis for policies which result in redistribution in favour of the rich. Interestingly, this evolution was predicted by Kalecki (1971, pp.138f, emphasis in original) as early as 1943, analysing the political prospects and limits of Keynesian policies:

> The assumption that a Government will maintain full employment in a capitalist economy if it only knows how to do it is fallacious. In this connection the misgivings of big business about maintenance of full employment are of paramount importance. This attitude was shown clearly in the great depression in the thirties ... the *maintenance* of full employment would cause social and political changes which would give a new impetus to the opposition of the business leaders. Indeed, under a regime of permanent full employment, 'the sack' would cease to play a role as a disciplinary measure. The social position of the boss would be undermined and the self assurance and class consciousness of the working class would grow.

Powerful pressure by big business and rentiers – presumably disagreeing that their disappearance is a great advantage (Keynes [1936] 1967, p.376) – would prevent governments from pursuing full employment policies. Even higher profits under a regime of full employment would not change their view, Kalecki argued. This lobby, Kalecki (1971, p.144) wrote, 'would probably find more than one economist to declare that the situation is manifestly unsound. The pressure of all these forces, and in particular of big business, would most probably induce the Government to the orthodox policy of cutting down the budget deficit'.

As governments could not simply sit it out after Keynes, Kalecki predicted present policies such as lowering interest rates, income tax cuts or subsidizing private investment in one way or another rather than the government 'playing' with (public) investment. But government spending policy might again come into its own during a slump: the pattern of a political business cycle is therefore 'not entirely conjectural' (ibid., pp.144f).

In line with Kalecki's reasoning, a historically long period of full employment brought about by Keynesian politics was experienced in the North and finally stopped by an anti-Keynesian revolution justified by the necessity to fight inflation. Naturally, the arguments of the 1930s will not do after Keynes. Thus globalization is needed as a new argument. It has been widely used to justify neoliberal economic policies, to argue for real wage reductions, to push through anti-labour legislation in the North, and to justify policies favouring capital owners. Usually, the impression is conveyed that globalization just fell from heaven. If anyone is responsible for it at all, the culprits are SCs. Southern exports are often said to force the North to become 'leaner' and more competitive.

If neoliberalism is perceived as a policy of redistribution in favour of the rich, thinly disguised by 'arguments', one stops wondering why its advocates remain unperturbed by the fact that their policies cannot be deduced from neoclassical theory that is claimed to be their basis. Seen from the point of view of redistribution to the rich, these policies work. This might explain why a long history of crashes and fiascos does not seem to matter either. The first major débâcle occurred with Euromarket lending to SCs: the debt crisis. It started when the Euromarket established itself beyond regulatory interventions and began to lend to SCs. Before 1982, the 'recycling of petrodollars' was widely acclaimed as proof of the success of free and unregulated markets, but 1982 and the bail-out by taxpayers' money put an end to that claim. At the beginning of the 1980s, liberalization led to crisis in Latin America's Southern Cone.

The Chilean experience of 1982 is meanwhile called 'more relevant' as an explanation of the Asian crash than 'the lessons of the general debt crisis' (World Bank, 1999a, p.2). An audit report by the World Bank's Operations

Evaluation Department 'on Chile's structural adjustment loans highlighted the lack of prudential supervision of financial institutions in increasing the economy's vulnerability to the point of collapse' (ibid.). The OED's 'key lesson' did not make 'policy makers and international financial institutions give these weaknesses appropriate weight', who encouraged the same policies in Asia. In 1983, Chilean pension funds had to be bailed out by government money. An estimate by Roddy McKinnon puts costs at approximately 2·1 per cent of GDP. The armed forces, by the way, had not joined the new privatized pension system, compulsory for workers, but retained the pay-as-you-go variety (Ghilarducci & Liébana, 2000, p.756).

The breakdown of the deregulated Savings & Loans sector in the USA is another example. All in all, 1500 so-called thrifts had gone bust after deregulation had allowed them to start activities from which they had been barred before. FIRREA, the Financial Institutions Reform, Recovery and Enforcement Act of 1989, nicknamed the 'Thrift Bailout Act' by many Americans, cost taxpayers at least some $200 billion. Higher estimates exist, though. According to Litan (1992, p.391) 'many accounts in the media' put total costs 'at $500 billion or more' by including the costs of interest to the government to finance the resolution of the thrift crisis – a practice Litan criticizes.

In 1994–5, the Mexican crash occurred after some years of praising the good functioning of financial markets (cf. Raffer, 1996a). It should not be forgotten that this crash could not have happened without regulatory changes by OECD countries, such as the lowering of quality guidelines (ibid.), which allowed institutional investors to place money there. Bailing out investors who had made good profits before was again done with public money, socializing losses. In comparison with the S&L, the roughly $50 billion necessary was a small sum. The Asian crisis of 1997 moved well over $100 billion in bail-out funds. The Russian and Brazilian crises following suit cost public money too.

According to the *Washington Post*, the 'wide spread belief that the West would bail out Russia encouraged foreign investors to pour billions' into risky investments, 'setting the stage for a catastrophic reversal' (Dobbs and Blustein, 1999). The authors quote an IMF official working on Russia who received a 'deluge of phone calls from investment bankers and portfolio managers lobbying for a new IMF bailout'. After earning returns 'upwards of 50 percent' they 'wanted the fund to use taxpayer-backed resources' to ensure that they would not face losses. One person called 'three, four times a day' for that purpose.

Recalling the Mexican fiasco of 1994–5 and the problems of sustainability and stability of large global financial market-intermediated resource flows, the OECD (1996a, p.57) had identified systemic risks requiring 'the provision of a much larger officially provided safety net'. Less diplomatic and elegant language might simply speak of the prospect of officially subsidized speculation, whose losses are covered by governments, possibly even from donors' aid budgets. In contrast to aid, catastrophic private failures are interpreted as the manifest need for even more taxpayer's money, as recent events in Asia proved.

Some people might see the crash of the Long Term Capital Management hedge fund as particularly symbolic for neoliberalism, even though no public money, only public effort, was involved. Guided by two Nobel laureates honoured precisely for their theoretical contribution to liberalizing capital markets, LTCM was about to collapse. A rescue package of $3·5 billion was necessary. Although the fund's boss and his partners were removed from power, 'huge management fees that the partners had collected could still leave some ahead of the game by tens of millions of dollars' (*Time*, 5 October 1998, p.61) Thus this money was not used to internalize losses. According to any microeconomic textbook, rational decision making under such conditions would suggest producing more crashes as the optimal policy. In other words, present policies tend to destabilize rather than to stabilize financial markets. Just about a week before, the Chairman of the Fed, Alan Greenspan, had assured Congress that – though not technically regulated in the sense that banks are – hedge funds 'are strongly regulated by those who lend the money' and therefore 'under fairly significant degrees of surveillance' (ibid.). In other words: the market works – at least as well as official regulations.

The neoliberal record is by no means limited to financial markets. The huge losses of British agriculture due to 'Mad Cow Disease' occurred after the Thatcher government did away with 'unnecessary' restrictions on animal feed. The costs of this case of deregulation are again largely picked up by the taxpayer. This is another illustration of profits being appropriated by private actors while losses are socialized.

The Asian crash dented the Washington Consensus for the first time. It may have started the cyclical downswing of the currently ruling view, although this view has remained very strong so far.

5. Aid to development and the bipolar world

'Foreign aid originated', as Chenery (1989, p.137) rightly points out, 'from the disruption of the world economy that followed World War II.' Development aid is a phenomenon of the post-1945 period. Although quite a few independent countries existed before World War II which would have to be characterized as 'developing' according to present criteria, they did not receive transfers comparable to present Official Development Assistance (ODA). When the post-war order was discussed at Bretton Woods the intention was to provide international finance for Europe – albeit at terms too hard to qualify these flows as ODA according to the present OECD defintion. The Bretton Woods twins came into being. The IMF was to stabilize exchange rates vis-à-vis the dollar, considered equivalent to gold at that time, a far cry from its present activities. Originally, the Bank was intended to serve mainly as a financing institution for the reconstruction of Europe. The OECD (1985, p.140) describes the initial tasks of the Bretton Woods twins: 'The IBRD was there to guarantee European borrowing in international (North American) markets; the IMF was there to smooth the flow of repayments'. The words 'and Development' were added to the initial name, 'International Bank for Reconstruction' as a result of the presence of SCs, mainly from Latin America, at Bretton Woods, insisting on their share in resources.

The first aid programme after the war was the Marshall Plan, officially known as the European Reconstruction Programme (ERP). The initiative's original intention also included the Soviet Union, but it was soon strongly influenced by the new situation of East–West rivalry. It intended to reconstruct Western European economies as well as to contain communist influence. Like the aid programmes for Greece and Turkey – skipped by the OECD (1985) in its historical chronology of aid – the Marshall Plan is often seen as triggered by the aim of containing communism (Ruttan, 1996, pp.39ff). In a speech to a joint session of Congress, President Truman asked not only for funds for Greece and Turkey to takes sides in 'an ongoing struggle between democracy and dictatorship' (ibid., p.3), but also for 'support of a commitment to containing the expansionist tendencies of the Soviet Union'. European economic recovery was – rightly, one may assume – seen as necessary for a non-communist future of Western Europe.

In contrast to hard IBRD loans, the Marshall Plan operated almost entirely on a grant basis. It played a crucial role in setting a pattern for aid to SCs later on. Many guidelines and institutional arrangements for the subsequent aid programmes were developed under the Marshall Plan. One example would be the institution of counterpart funds, now a common feature associated with aid, including food aid. The Organization for European Economic Co-operation (OEEC), created as the self-monitoring agency for Marshall aid recipients and later transformed into the OECD, was also the cradle of the present donor club (Raffer & Singer, 1996, p.60). However, neither the high concessionality of Marshall aid nor its principle of self-monitoring by recipients was copied by ODA donors. Particularly during the 1950s and 1960s, soft financing, comparable to Marshall Plan terms for European countries, was out of the question for SCs.

The success of the Marshall Plan had strong effects on North–South relations, and it is not implausible to argue that ODA would not have become a characteristic feature of post-war North–South relations without this precedent. People perceived the Plan as a promising model for development policy on a global scale. US aid to Korea and Taiwan, which went on simultaneously and also turned out to be very successful, corroborated this view. The China Aid Programme was enacted as part of the ERP authorization in 1948 to support the nationalist government against the communists by fostering economic development (Ruttan, 1996, pp.42f).

George (1976, pp.195f) traces food aid under US Public Law 480 back to Marshall aid. By 1954, when European reconstruction was nearly complete, new outlets for surplus agricultural products had to be found. The Act had the officially stated purpose of increasing the consumption of US agrarian products in foreign countries.

The generous level of Marshall aid – the USA spent 2–3 per cent (excluding military aid) of its GNP under this initiative during the six years 1948–53 – raised high expectations. The 'wild men' at the UN advocated setting up a UN Fund for Economic Development (UNFED) to administer large-scale soft aid. Theoretically, this idea could be based on the Keynesian consensus, generally accepted at that time, that the availability of capital determined growth, which in turn was needed to improve the lot of the poor. It was also easy to argue that European countries had a moral obligation to help others as they had been helped by the USA.

But the idea of Marshall-type aid for development was foiled by the North opposing the idea of large funds administered by the UN. The World Bank was particularly strongly opposed to the principle of soft financing, demanding harder terms, nearer to the market. However, once it became clear that soft multilateral financing would be done by an institution administered by the World Bank, the Bank dropped all reservations (Raffer & Singer, 1996, pp.54ff). Van der Laar (1980, p.57) sees US interests as a major cause for the establishment of the International Development Association (IDA): US surplus agricultural commodities sold under Public Law 480 for domestic currencies of recipients (a practice called 'quasi-grants' by the OECD) had resulted in embarrassingly high and practically useless holdings of inconvertible currencies. In 1958, Senator Monroney therefore proposed the establishment of IDA as an affiliate of the World Bank, where the USA would pay in these surpluses. Helped by the Cuban revolution, which sparked a wave of 'generosity' of the USA, IDA came into being in 1960.

IDA is run by World Bank staff and reimburses the Bank for administrative expenses with a management fee. In spite of proposals to establish a more democratic voting structure, also supported by some industrialized countries (essentially the Netherlands and the Nordic countries) voting rights in IDA followed the World Bank model: the dollar-a-vote model instead of the country-a-vote model of the UN. The OECD (1985, p.141) is quite outspoken, stating that 'developed countries' preferred this solution to the UN Fund 'because the structure of the World Bank ensured weighted voting in their favour'. The participatory and recipient-friendly approach of the Marshall Plan in Europe was not to be repeated.

The International Finance Corporation (IFC), established as an affiliate of the Bank in 1956, is further evidence that managing larger financial resources was reserved for the World Bank. Five years before, the UN's 'Lewis Report' had proposed it for precisely the purposes it still serves nowadays. The OECD (ibid., p.146) observed a certain differentiation regarding multilateral aid: 'by and large the largest donors have favoured the World Bank, while the smaller donors have favoured the United Nations'. In other words, countries where global power politics matter have preferred tighter control.

AID AND THE COLD WAR

Donors give aid for a mixture of motives, ranging from humanitarian reasons to self-interest. As was argued in Raffer and Singer (1996), aid may but need not be help. Advocates of aid have frequently argued that it is in the interest – certainly the long-term interest – of the rich countries themselves. Unsurprisingly, the element of self-interest is reflected in what donors claim to be aid.

The Cold War was one, if not *the* major cause of aid. The sharp drop of ODA in the 1990s would support this view. Particularly in the case of European colonial powers, historic and political links played an important role too. In 1946, France established the 'Fonds d'Investissements économique et social des territoires d'outre-mer'. The UK passed the Overseas Resources

Development Act setting up the Colonial Development Corporation in 1948 (now the Commonwealth Development Corporation). European colonial powers established the predecessor of the present Development Assistance Committee (DAC), the Overseas Territories Committee, within the OEEC in 1949 (OECD, 1985, p.66). The OECD (ibid., p.92) identified three major periods of DAC aid. During the 1950s and early 1960s, aid built up rapidly owing to 'accumulation of new and broadened development assistance efforts and strategically motivated economic aid'. By watching the regional distribution and concentration of aid the major political interests and their shifts can be clearly discerned. According to the 1963 Clay Report, '72 per cent of total (military and economic) assistance appropriations' were concentrated on 'allies and other countries at the Sino-Soviet border'. After criticizing dispersion of aid to an excessive number of countries, the report claimed that economic assistance to some non-allied countries was beyond that 'necessary for our interests' (Ohlin, 1966, p.21). In the 1950s and 1960s, South Korea and Taiwan, as well as India, were major recipients of US aid, which the US used to try to get countries away from Soviet influence. Aid was given relatively generously, but not always without discussion. In the end, however, the feeling that it was a necessary or at least useful measure against Soviet expansionism prevailed.

Between 1952 and 1961, the 'Mutual Security Act' was the legal basis of US aid. US food aid was seen in close connection with military and political considerations (George, 1976). Shifts in aid flows have remained closely connected to policy interests. First, Taiwan and Korea received extremely generous aid (Raffer & Singer, 1996, p.63), then Vietnam became one of the major recipients of US aid, after the Vietnam war, Israel and Egypt topped this list. With nearly a quarter of US aid in 1995-6, they left Haiti, ranked third with 2·3 per cent, far behind (OECD, 1998a). In 1991-2, Egypt received 29 per cent of total US ODA, Israel another 9·9 per cent.

Communist aid was equally dominated by politics. Soviet aid was immediately available to nations facing problems with the West, for instance in the case of the Aswan Dam in Egypt, or in Guinea where Soviet aid arrived promptly after the French had announced their withdrawal. Communist initiatives, such as the visit to Asia by Soviet Premier Bulganin and party head Khrushchev in 1955, had profound effects on the USA. 'The economic aid contest began to dominate U.S. foreign policy' (Ruttan, 1996, p.73). The essential point – later advocated by Robert McNamara as president of the World Bank – was that aid would obtain more defence than military expenditures. India managed to profit substantially from this East-West competition for some time. Annual US promises of aid rocketed from $4·5 million in 1951 to $87 million in 1954 (Goldman, 1967, p.197).

Like the West, communist countries concentrated their flows on political allies and 'friendly' countries. As there were by far fewer SCs orienting themselves towards the East, communist aid was more concentrated than ODA from the West. Cuba under Castro became the main beneficiary of Soviet funds. North Korea, Mongolia and, later on, Vietnam and Afghanistan were other important aid recipients. Mongolia, Cuba and Vietnam also became members of the Council of Mutual Economic Assistance (CMEA, also called COMECON in the West), the integration movement of communist countries. The financial burden of these developing members on Eastern economies became apparently so great that the East turned down Mozambique's application for full membership in 1980. This was a strong indication of the economic constraints of communist economies. It led to a reorientation of Mozambique and Angola to the West, and ultimately to their becoming signatories of the Lomé treaties.

Not surprisingly, aid statistics became one weapon in the Cold War's arsenal. As communist countries never provided information worth mentioning, this was easy. The strategy of 'annihilation by numbers' is described by Kaiser (1986) and Raffer and Singer (1996) in detail. Kaiser identified three phases of the DAC's reporting of Soviet ODA: (a) 1961 to 1974, when the DAC tried to estimate it as correctly as possible, which was no easy task given the lack of transparency of communist countries; (b) 1974 to 1980, when Soviet aid was deliberately under-reported to provide propaganda ammunition; (c) upward revisions after 1980, when the DAC was apparently afraid of losing credibility.

Two main areas of statistical manipulation can be singled out: the conversion of Soviet statistics to the Western accounting system using GNP, and sudden exclusions of flows recognized before. Manipulations started when the GNP percentages of US aid fell perceptibly and the Soviet Union came uncomfortably close according to the DAC's own figures. The exclusion of price subsidies to Cuba reduced Soviet aid in 1970 to 0·27 per cent of GNP, well below the US figure of 0·31, while Soviet aid including these subsidies would have resulted in 0·34, well above it. US embarrassment was thus avoided.

Owing to substantial massaging of data, widely differing figures for Soviet aid granted in the same year coexist in OECD publications. Thus for 1970 or 1971 several figures between 0·25 per cent and 0·12 per cent exist (Kaiser, 1986, p.40). Their distribution is a distinct U: high percentages before 1974 (0·25 per cent), minima in the *Report* on 1977 (0·12 per cent and 0·10 per cent, respectively) and perceptibly higher percentages in the 1980s (up to 0·17 per cent for 1970, and 0·2 per cent for 1971). The OECD must have assumed that no one would compare their figures for the same year in different reports. Why the Soviet Union did not defend its record properly is also likely to remain a riddle.

THE QUANTITATIVE EVOLUTION OF ODA

Foreign aid was quite high during the first years compared with present levels, but relatively low and at hard terms compared with Marshall aid. This might be interpreted as an indication that solidarity within the North was stronger than solidarity across the North–South divide.

The evolution of ODA after World War II is shown in Figure 5.1. For 1950–55, the earliest period for which the OEEC collected data on a reasonably comparable basis (OECD, 1985, p.92), the average had to be used. Annual data are not published for this period. From 1956 onwards annual figures are used.

Data show that the optimistic view of the 'wild men' at the UN was not unfounded. Even in percentages of the aggregated GSP of all DAC donors, ODA increased quite significantly until 1961, peaking at 0·54 per cent. By present standards that may seem wonderfully close to the famous 0·7 per cent target, officially accepted by most DAC donors. War-torn countries on the European continent had recovered and started to grant aid themselves. With 0·55 per cent of her GNP, Britain surpassed 0·5 per cent in 1959, a steep increase from 0·43 in 1958 or 0·35 in 1956. In 1961, British ODA peaked at 0·59 per cent (ibid., p.335). Australia had just started to give aid in 1960, Austria, New Zealand and Finland in 1961. Due to this steep upward trend it was not irrational to expect substantial and even increasing transfers until the mid-1960s – though realistically not anywhere near the level of Marshall aid.

US aid, still about 60 per cent of total aid at this time, reached a peak during Kennedy's presidency (1961–3), not least because of the Cuban revolution, but

> the year 1961 itself contained certain special elements, notably an exceptionally heavy volume of I.B.R.D.-bond purchases by the central banks of Germany and other countries, which tended to exaggerate the increase in that year and made the subsequent levelling-off in the total seem more abrupt than was the case for the distributions directly financed by governments. (OECD, 1967, p.29)

Another factor was a major change in France's policy, which 'accompanied the evolution of France's political and economic relationships with countries in North Africa, and in particular Algeria' (ibid., p.35). French aid started to decline in the 1960s after many French colonies had become independent. Apparently 'aid' by some 'donors' was to some extent just financing their colonial policy, a conclusion not contradicted by the time series for Britain, which underlines the importance of colonial expenditures presented as aid.

ODA, measured in GSP percentages started to decline after 1961, the very year when the UN designated the 1960s as the first Development Decade,

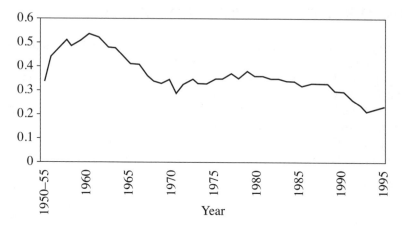

Source: Figure based on OECD data.

Figure 5.1   DAC–ODA as a percentage of GSP, 1950–99

setting a target for aid and capital inflows to SCs of approximately 1 per cent of GSP. This decline turned into a dramatic fall in the mid-1960s, down to 0·29 in 1973 (OECD, 1985). It would not be implausible to see one reason for this pronounced fall in the South's attempts to gain 'economic independence' and to establish a New International Economic Order. The rise of oil prices in 1973–4 and the 'anxiety' and 'fear' it caused at least in Europe (European Commission, 1996, p.9) might have pushed ODA percentages up again. Between 1969 and 1982, ODA stabilized at a level around 0·35, slowly declining afterwards. Also the communist bloc was still there and very vocal about quantitative shortcomings of Western aid. The recent evolution, discussed in more detail in the next chapter, is a steep drop after three years of 0·33 per cent during 1990–92 to 0·23 per cent in 1998.

Expressing aid in real dollar terms produces a different picture: there is no pronounced fall during the 1960s, which means that aid was delinked from GNP growth. The OECD (1985, p.92) speaks of a relative stability of aggregate levels of DAC aid between 'the mid-1960s and the early 1970s in which the downward drift of US aid' was compensated by new donors. The rapid expansion of ODA by the Nordic countries and the Netherlands (ibid., p.100) is classified as the most striking development of this period. The OECD's chart of DAC aid in 1983 dollars shows a steep increase until 1960, then a levelling off, but still a positive slope until the peak in 1965. Then real aid falls, recovering again in 1972 (clearly visible in Figure 5.1 as well) to the level of 1965. The dent of 1973 and the increase afterwards resemble the line in Figure 5.1.

The OECD (ibid., p.92) sees the following reasons for the increase after 1973: 'new pressing developing country needs resulting from the oil price shocks, a variety of external factors including serious harvest failures, the effects of world economic recession and the African development crisis'. It fails to mention the steep increase in wheat prices brought about by US agricultural policies. US farmers were paid subsidies to withhold 'fully 15 per cent of all US cropland' in the summer of 1972, when the US government already knew about massive grain purchases by the Soviet Union (George, 1976, p.142). A price increase comparable to that of oil resulted, financially squeezing net food importers very hard too. Also the strong political pressures by SCs, including demands for more aid, are not mentioned by the OECD. As OPEC aid surged as well after 1973, total ODA received increased considerably.

THE QUALITY OF AID

To understand quantitative evolutions, one must be aware of the substantial qualitative changes of what has passed as ODA. Since the donor club DAC has the unchecked prerogative of the Red Queen in Wonderland, that ODA means what they say it means, donors have always exercised the privilege of self-control. ODA figures produced by each member state itself are reviewed by other DAC members, a process called 'peer review'. Participation by recipients or independent experts has never been considered by the DAC. A double monopoly on data production and performance evaluation has allowed 'donors' substantial leeway.

Initially 'donors' simply regarded any flow to SCs as 'aid', based on the philosophy that whatever emanates from them must be good for the South. This idea seems to enjoy a revival within the donor community nowadays, as many OECD publications show, again blurring the distinction between the developmental effects of commercial flows and aid. Although a purely commercial investment, offered to private investors as well, purchases of World Bank bonds by the Bundesbank boosted aid in 1961. Normal profit seeking was sanctified aid, in line with the very accommodating DAC definition. At that time purchases of multilateral bonds and loans to multilaterals by official institutions were automatically aid. So was government lending over one year (OECD, 1967, p.21). Further qualification, such as better terms than normal market transactions, was not required. Technically, loans at above market interest rates stuffed down an unwilling but dependent country's throat qualified as aid. Some countries such as Germany and Britain even 'raised objections of principle against soft loans, especially with respect to interest rates' (OECD, 1985, p.109) at this time.

Germany was a beneficiary of soft Marshall aid. Britain had received money from the USA at 2 per cent over 50 years with the right to waive or cancel interest payments unilaterally if necessary. Not being any longer at the receiving end, both countries had dramatically changed their views on loans. Defending the Bundesbank's investment, Germany argued that soft loans would distort allocative efficiency and 'impair the role of private capital' (ibid.). The UK 'generally' made 'loans at the rate at which it can borrow plus a small management charge' (ibid.), routinely making profit on underdevelopment. Briefly summarized, high GNP percentages of aid (Britain was above the DAC average at the beginning of the 1960s) often veiled self-interest. One could make money on what officially passed as help.

Gunnar Myrdal (1970, pp.315ff) disturbed this cosy understanding of altruism. Criticizing the OECD's concept of aid, he pointed at regularly and systematically blurred distinctions between ODA and 'flows' in official DAC statistics. Economists, experts, officials, journalists – everyone equated 'flows' with 'development aid', a malpractice tolerated and occasionally supported by the DAC 'by some of the titles of tables and comments on the tables' (ibid., p.316). Thus Portugal, one of the poorest European countries and itself an 'aid' receiver at that time, had the place of honour in DAC statistics. It fought a protracted and costly colonial war in Africa, recording substantial flows of resources to Angola and Mozambique. Myrdal's critique contributed greatly to a change of perception and to a clearer definition of ODA, formulated in 1969, which is still *de jure* valid, but was eroded considerably in the 1990s. Furthermore, the DAC has never totally dropped the notion that flows across the North–South divide are always conducive to development, and is reviving it at present.

The DAC's present ODA definition demands the promotion of the economic development and welfare of developing countries to be the main objective and a minimum grant element of 25 per cent. The definition is so vague that critical minds might call it well chosen. The first criterion allows practically anything to pass. People do disagree on what 'welfare' or 'economic development' means, and there is even more disagreement on what measures promote them. Actual increases in welfare or an actual promotion of development are not necessary – the intention is sufficient. Unless the donor's main intention to the contrary (such as doing harm or having another main objective) can be conclusively proved, which is next to impossible, it applies automatically, even if substantial damage is inflicted upon recipient countries and the people affected by a project. At present no mechanism of assuring damage compensation exists. If one looks at the standards considered normal and demanded by the rule of law within any OECD country, such a mechanism should be introduced.

Obviously, the donor club is not very keen on enforcing its own rules strictly, allowing cosmetic tinkering with aid statistics to make them look better. Some members have continuously reported export credits as ODA, a practice routinely condoned by the DAC. Austria is probably the best example to illustrate this point. Although by no means the only DAC member using aid to promote exports, the share of export credits in total ODA has traditionally been perceptibly above other DAC members'. This fact has been criticized by researchers, NGOs, the Austrian aid administration itself and the DAC for quite some time (cf. Raffer, 1995). In 1983, for instance, the official *Dreijahresprogramm 1984–86* (Three Years Programme) published by the Federal Chancellery of Austria (1983, pp.24f; our translation) stated that the OECD found fault with these credits 'evading primarily development-oriented planning, structuring (intention), assessment as well as international ODA comparison and used with an orientation towards competitiveness' of exports. A few lines further down, the Chancellery stated that 'the benefit of the developing country [is] a secondary effect after all'. A few pages above it declared: 'Currently no application of developmental criteria. Review urgently needed' (ibid., p.19).

In its peer review, the OECD (1996c, p.26) calculated that a 'stricter interpretation' of ODA would have reduced Austrian aid by 0·06 GNP percentages in 1993 and by 0·11 GNP percentages in 1994, or by two-fifths and one-third, respectively. The Federal Chancellery of Austria (1994, p.10) stated in its main official publication on ODA that if reporting 'according to the reporting practices applied by the majority of DAC members the volume would be about 0·25 per cent of GNP' in 1992. Officially, it was 0·30 per cent. The table that follows this statement contains a row specifying the ODA subtotal considered 'in accordance with DAC [criteria]' ('davon "DAC-gemäß"'; ibid., p.11). Thus both the competent Austrian authority and the DAC declared publicly, officially and repeatedly that these flows were not ODA because they violated the first DAC criterion of being 'administered with the promotion of the economic development and welfare of developing countries as its main objective'. Nevertheless, with few exceptions these credits have been recorded as ODA by the DAC (Raffer, 1995; 1998a). Austria claimed that she could not separate concessional and non-concessional components, thus recording the whole credit package as ODA – in breach of DAC rules (OECD, 2000c, p.19).

As Austria also felt unable to separate aid to refugees within Austria during the first year (ODA according to the DAC) from assistance provided later, she recorded all expenditures irrespective of how long refugees had actually been in the country, also in breach of DAC rules (ibid., p.11). The peer review (in 1999) criticized such practices once again, noting that the share of three components (export credits, imputed student costs and assistance to refugees in Austria) which 'do not have development as their primary objective' had been reduced significantly but still amounted to 'a considerable share' (18 per cent) of total ODA (OECD, 2000a, p.77). Large backflows from past loans combined with reduced growth of new exports to the South in 1998. The share of export credits fell to 4 per cent of total ODA, which also reflects strong export ties with Indonesia and Asia in general. Fewer refugees from the Balkans, and the effects of tighter immigration laws on foreign students combined. One should also mention that the Department of Development Cooperation tried to introduce stricter application of OECD criteria to export credits against strong vested interests in favour of the status quo. While courageous and laudable, these efforts had limited results. The peer review points out that the Department 'usually' gets the relevant documents on export credits 'only a few days before' the decision is taken. Examinations of the developmental nature of a credit can thus only be done cursorily 'in most cases', as also shown by the examples reviewed (OECD, 2000c, p.19).

By contrast, the minimum grant element is a more objective measure. However, as it simply measures the difference between the present value of loans at what the DAC calls the 'market interest rate' (taken as 10 per cent, perceptibly above the actual market rate at present) and its present value at the interest rate actually charged, a sufficiently high grant element does not necessarily mean any economic gain. Actual export prices can be much higher than competitive world market prices, particularly in cases where price comparisons are difficult. The more excessive the overcharge, the higher the loan reported as ODA, and in final consequence, the more 'generous' the donor, as Raffer and Singer (1996, p.10) observe. It is possible that over-charging may (over)-compensate financial 'concessions' of an ODA loan. Furthermore, a 'donor' able to get money at sufficiently less than 10 per cent can lend it on to the 'recipient' with a mark-up, thus again combining profit with charity. The DAC Terms of Recommendation specify a minimum grant element of 86 per cent on average to discourage such practice. Thus over-pricing cannot (over-)compensate the grant equivalent of any donor's total ODA with present average concessionalities. Nevertheless, a profitable loan with a low grant element still qualifies as ODA.

As the OECD imputes the market interest rate as 10 per cent, even normal commercial transactions have grant elements at present: the real market is concessional compared with itself, according to the DAC. Quite logically, the World Bank (1998) shows grant elements for private creditors. In the case of the Severely Indebted Low-Income Countries new private commitments in 1996 had an average grant element of 20·9 per cent (ibid., vol.I, p.175), nearly reaching the DAC's minimum grant element. As during the 1960s, any flow from North to South seems again to be interpreted as helping the latter.

It might be helpful to recall that aid is not help, unless one includes the notion of 'donors' helping themselves, but merely a technical term (Raffer & Singer, 1996). In practice, ODA can be anything from really selfless altruistic help to hypocritical profiteering. Even items whose qualification as aid is openly doubted or denied by the OECD itself have been included (Raffer, 1998a), a point further elaborated in Chapter 6.

Both political and commercial donor self-interest have always played an important role. The argument that aid should make up for the shortage of capital in the South combined well with donors' export interests. As shown in Chapter 3, the dual gap theory was the main justification of aid, understood as transfers from IC governments to SC governments. As SCs were unable to produce needed capital goods during the first period after World War II, this should not simply be misunderstood as a criticism of donor behaviour. Under these conditions it did make sense to provide capital goods needed for development, which SCs could not buy owing to insufficient foreign exchange income, even though practice did not always live up to theoretical, academic perceptions. What must be criticized, though, is that ODA also comprised goods not needed for development, supplied to cater to donors' export interests.

SHIFTING FROM GROWTH TO OTHER GOALS

Around 1970, doubts began to emerge about the adequacy of accelerating growth as the main thrust of development policy. In 1969, the ILO's World Employment Programme (WEP) was created to tackle the problem of unemployment and underemployment more directly. Employment missions were sent to countries to focus on the issue of poverty and to analyse possibilities of creating employment. For the first time the issue of inequality was officially emphasized. According to Jolly (1998, p.173) this programme was 'one of the formative influences on development thinking and policy in the 1970s'. The report of the mission to Kenya was the first international report recognizing the positive side of the informal sector, recommending how its contribution could be made more effective. It was the 'forerunner' (ibid., p.174) of the Basic Needs Approach.

Jolly (1998) recounts how the mission's head sketched the idea that the incomes of the poorest must increase more rapidly than they would by growth and 'trickle down' alone. Redistribution from the increment of growth would mean adding to the incomes and assets of the poor without having to take away from anyone else, an idea that run counter to the ruling perception of the Kuznets curve. This challenge to achieve greater equality by redistribution from growth as formulated in the Kenya Report gave rise to the strategy of

Redistribution with Growth, as Jolly (ibid., p.174) describes, based on the joint World Bank/IDS study of the same name (Chenery *et al.*, 1974), which even spoke of trickle-up effects from greater incomes of the poor. Arguing in favour of investing in the poor became acceptable.

Streeten (1993) describes the reorientation from GNP growth via redistribution with growth to basic needs. Once it was discovered that the results of redistribution remained modest in practice, at least for low-income countries, basic human needs emerged as the next logical step in development thinking. Streeten argues that better nutrition, health, education and training can be very productive forms of developing human resources, investments in the future, which, with the exception of some forms of education, were considered as consumption and therefore neglected.

Basic needs finally became an accepted approach when the World Bank under McNamara propagated it. Following the Bank, many aid administrations adopted poverty orientation. McNamara forcefully advocated helping the poor, which he – quite in line with early US policies – saw as a means to fight communism. To do so more efficiently, he increased the volume of Bank lending considerably and established country and regional targets that had (and still have) to be met. Thus he established the 'approval culture' of quick disbursement criticized by the Wapenhans Report (World Bank, 1992; see also Mosley *et al.*, 1991; Raffer & Singer, 1996).

The World Bank's projects have had debatable results on the ground, as quick disbursement and reports written in beautiful English have commanded a premium over economic returns. Regarding poverty the results were underwhelming. At that time the Bank often published impressive-looking figures alleging positive effects of its projects, but remaining sufficiently vague to resist verification. Illustrative examples are 'benefits of 210 of these projects are expected to accrue predominantly to the rural poor' (Christoffersen, 1978, p.20), or 'They aim at affecting directly between 15 and 20 million rural families or some 90 to 120 million individuals' (ibid.). The meaning of 'affected' is not revealed. Does it include people driving on, walking on, seeing a new road, those able to see it if they walked 50 kilometres first, or even those just knowing about a new road? Reviewing World Bank publications, Tetzlaff (1980, pp.438ff) called such figures a bluff, because the exact meaning of benefiting or affecting is nowhere explained. Owing to the bank's structures the poor were hardly reached, although Bank money did sometimes trickle a bit further down than before. Even according to its own sources the Bank did not reach the poorest 20 per cent (Lipton & Shakow, 1982).

As late as 1982, the conclusions of a working group on poverty calling for measures to alleviate the effects of structural adjustment on the poor were officially approved, but a little later the tide had turned. Bank and Fund insisted that carrying on structural adjustment had positive impacts and was in the very interest of the poor. Special measures to protect them would thus be superfluous, if not harmful. Emphasizing human needs might obstruct needed reforms (cf. Raffer, 1994a). The World Bank (1980, p.62) described the 'major drawback' of efficient food subsidies as costly, often using up 'scarce foreign exchange or aid'.

After the demise of the communist bloc, 'an important paradigm shift, with some quite radical implications for the practice of development co-operation' (OECD, 1998a, p.17) occurred, 'a dramatic widening of the scope and ambition of the development co-operation agenda' (ibid., p.18), which is discussed in the next chapter.

CRITICISMS OF AID

From early on aid, particularly ODA, has been criticized. Examples for evaluations of its usefulness are Cassen *et al.* (1986), Lipton & Toye (1990), Toye (1995) or White (1993). Contending that there is no good evidence that aid is beneficial for growth, White argues that there exists no good evidence to the contrary either. Thus he thinks that results are not sufficiently sound to justify radical policy conclusions such as the reduction or abolition of aid. As he finds evidence that aid does indeed increase investment, a rather unflattering conclusion of average effectiveness follows logically: it may boost investments that do not result in growth. This does not of course imply that each single aid project failed.

Criticism came from such divergent poles as Milton Friedman (1970), P.T. Bauer (1976) and Gunnar Myrdal (1985) for quite different reasons. Arguing that the market would promote economic development better, Friedman (1970, p.65) objected to ODA, but not to military aid and defence support to military juntas defending 'freedom'. Myrdal (1985) saw ODA as mainly self-serving as well as supporting 'corrupt, exploiting cliques' in SCs. Therefore he advocated discontinuing any aid except (a) emergency aid, (b) support for the very few countries where governments actually cared for the population (he specifically mentions the 'liberated' Nicaragua of the Sandinistas and Tanzania under Nyerere), and (c) help to dissidents within SCs.

'Aid fatigue' has become a popular slogan and a phenomenon that has even been growing in the South (UNDP, 1994, p.72). To critics arguing that aid has failed altogether and calling for a total stop, the UNDP (ibid., p.69) replies that 'legitimate criticism should lead to improvement, not despair'. In line with this view, Raffer and Singer (1996) made proposals for change of aid practices. The UNDP (1994, p.69) points out that, in spite of disenchantment on both sides, donors and recipients, 'the development process – along with foreign assistance – has had more successes than its critics usually concede'.

Prolonged and sometimes very harsh criticism of aid, many examples of projects not yielding expected benefits, negligent implementation causing grave damages, or absurd projects and 'aid' expenditures have certainly contributed to aid fatigue (for examples, see Raffer & Singer, 1996, pp.20f). Recording the transport of thousands of rolls of toilet paper to and from Africa to cater for the needs of a US AID employee during his assignment is just one embarrassing case.

Heavy criticism of official aid increased NGO involvement, seen by bureaucracies as a way to avoid criticism (Raffer & Singer, 1996). But NGOs are also considered better able to perform aid reaching the poor, particularly as a means to overcome institutional restrictions on official aid favouring large projects. The political swing away from government involvement towards the private sector in all DAC countries since around 1980 has led to a stronger emphasis on NGOs as well. Delegating the execution of projects to NGOs allows implementing more projects with fewer civil servants. Finally, as structural adjustment was imposed on SCs, NGOs were increasingly seen as a channel for funds aimed at mitigating the effects of the policies of the Bretton Woods twins. Using NGOs, official donors heal some of the wounds their own policy within the World Bank and the IMF has inflicted.

6. ODA after the Cold War: Less money on tougher conditions

Two events characterized 1989 as a watershed year for ODA. Overtaking the USA, Japan became the world's biggest ODA source in dollar terms, an event that marked the end of an era. Much more important, however, was that communism collapsed in Europe, an event often symbolized by the crumbling of the Berlin Wall. The demise of the Eastern bloc gave rise to great hopes. Large parts of expenditures on armaments had suddenly become unnecessary, so at least some of these resources would be available for development. An enormous 'peace dividend' was expected to increase aid to both East and South. The élan of these expectations suggests a comparison to the period immediately after World War II, when North–South cooperation was propagated on a scale strongly influenced by the Marshall Plan.

Quantitative expectations were accompanied by suggestions for qualitative changes. The UNDP (1994, p.69), for instance, saw the end of the Cold War as a 'rare opportunity to make a fresh start', calling for a restructuring of aid: it should be made more participatory and people-centred to genuinely benefit the poor – something it had hardly done so far. The peace dividend failed to materialize. Quite to the contrary, ODA even dropped substantially, as depicted in Figure 5.1. The 'precipitate fall in ODA since 1992 is almost entirely due to cuts in aid from G7 countries, particularly the "big four"' (OECD 2000a, p.54), the USA, France, Germany and Japan. From 1992 to 1997, DAC aid experienced the largest declines both in GSP and in real terms 'since the inception of the' DAC 'in 1961' (ibid., p.67). Asking why the peace dividend failed to free resources for development, the OECD (1998a, p.55) sees pressures on donors' budgets and attempts to cut fiscal deficits as the reasons. Presumably, resources for armaments would nevertheless have been available had the Cold War continued. Unilateral Western disarmament because of budget pressures and fiscal deficits seems unlikely.

Great expectations were aroused when centrally planned economies were about to shake off communism, apparently influencing political evolutions. But generous promises soon gave way to less generous reality. The end of the Cold War had negative effects on SCs, but the gains promised to former communist countries, now called Countries and Territories in Transition (CTTs) or Central and Eastern European Countries/Newly Independent States

(CEECs/NIS) remained quite modest too. The importance of East–West rivalry for ODA is acknowledged by the OECD (1992, p.5) warning that the end of the Cold War was an impediment to increased concessionary flows because of 'growing uncertainty as to the context and rationale for development assistance in the post Cold War world. The search for this new rationale is most notable in countries like the United States, but to a considerable degree a re-examination is under way in most DAC Member countries'.

HAS AID SHIFTED TO THE EAST?

The end of 'bipolarity' also gave rise to concern. SCs feared that aid transfers would now be channelled away from them to the East. When the EU signed Lomé IV, the Commission's vice-president, Manuel Marin (1989), felt compelled to assuage fears about the future of the cooperation between the EU and countries from Africa, the Caribbean and the Pacific (cf. Chapter 7). As it soon turned out, EU interest shifted perceptibly away from these countries.

Fears were fuelled by the idea to subsume flows to CTTs under ODA. After some discussion, DAC donors opposing this proposal more or less prevailed. The compromise differentiated between so-called 'Part I' and 'Part II' recipients. Part I comprises SCs as well as some NIS, such as Armenia and Kazakhstan, or Albania. One might argue that countries such as Kazakhstan would have been listed as recipients long ago had they not been part of the Soviet Union. Most CTTs, including Russia, Hungary or the Czech Republic, are Part II recipients. Furthermore, the DAC graduated a few SCs to Part II status as from 1996: the Bahamas, Singapore, Brunei, Kuwait, Qatar and the United Arab Emirates. None of these was an important aid recipient anyway. In 1997, seven further countries were transferred to Part II, among them Israel, an important aid recipient of the USA, whose inclusion in the list of 'developing countries' dated from the early period, when this list was stretched to include as many countries as possible to be able to subsume more flows under ODA. Spain, Portugal and Greece were ODA recipients as well. To illustrate this point: Israel accounted for 14·3 per cent of US aid, which was 0·11 of GNP on average in 1995–6 (OECD, 1998a, p.A8). With Israel off the list, US aid would have been (rounded) 0·09. Had Israel been graduated a year earlier, DAC-ODA would have been 0·24 (instead of 0·25) per cent of GSP in 1996, as aid to Israel was particularly generous in its last ODA year. In 1997, US ODA actually dropped to 0·09 per cent (OECD, 2000a) In 2000, further countries, including Korea, were 'graduated', none of them a substantial ODA recipient. Malta and Slovenia are scheduled to join Part II in 2003 (ibid., p.267).

This graduation is quoted by the OECD (ibid., p.67) as one of two technical factors adding to the fall in ODA/GSP ratios. The combined aid receipts of 13 countries removed from Part I would have added $1·2 billion to ODA recorded for 1997. This argument is correct as far as it goes. One must, however, be aware that this addition was 2·48 per cent of total DAC aid, or 0·00546 per cent of DAC GSP. Adding it would push up the GSP ratio from 0·22 to 0·23, not changing the picture drastically. As one country accounted for 95·76 per cent of this sum, the other 12 for $53 million, we may call this the Israel effect. The OECD does not mention the also small but compensating effect of newly included formerly communist countries.

The second point is the introduction of the new national accounts system, expanding donor GNPs 'by between 2% and 8%, reducing reported ODA/ GNP ratios accordingly' (ibid.). No figures are quoted, nor is the average effect for all DAC members provided. Illustratively, one may say that correcting a DAC GSP expansion of 2 per cent yields 0·23 instead of 0·22 but only because of rounding, correcting 8 per cent for all DAC members results in 0·24. Correcting for both effects – adding the 13 countries' ODA and correcting for GSP expansion – would have produced between 0·23 and 0·25 (precisely 0·246), depending on the GSP percentages used. This looks better than 0·22, but the fall since 1992 is still 'precipitate'.

'Official aid' and 'flows of financial resources' to Part II countries are recorded separately, but like ODA. Officially they are not 'development assistance' but 'Official Aid' (OA) defined in exactly the same wording as 'ODA', except that 'developing' is replaced by 'recipient' countries. But language has already been blurred. The OECD (1994, p.5) called 'concessional development assistance' to the East explicitly a 'new demand on development co-operation'. This *Report* was the first to include OA data. The *Report* on 1998 (OECD, 1999a, p.47) already subsumed ODA and OA under Official *Development* Finance (ODF). The currently given definition of ODF (OECD, 2000a, p.262), however, does not do so.

Statistical separation is of course irrelevant to the real question whether funds are actually being rerouted. Donors claim that aid to CTTs is additional. DAC statistics show the following evolution of the two types of aid expressed in percentages of DAC GSP:

	1989	1990	1991	1992	1993	1994	1995	1996	1997	1998	1999
OA	—	0·01	0·04	0·04	0·04	0·04	0·04	0·03	0·02	0·03	n.a.
ODA	0·32	0·33	0·33	0·33	0·30	0·30	0·27	0·25	0·22	0·23	0·24

In GSP percentages ODA has fallen since 1961. Using the above figures, one might argue that this trend was briefly stopped after 1989, even though 0·33 remained well below the level of 1978–88. The period 1990–2 suggests both a slight recovery of ODA and additionality of OA. A relatively steep fall in ODA expressed in dollars between 1992 and 1993 was a strong argument for a shift of aid to the East, particularly so as OA remained fairly constant, nominally even increasing by 2 per cent. But as has been argued before (Raffer & Singer, 1996, pp.211f) the short time series until 1993 available then did not support the thesis of a clear general shift of DAC resources from South to East, although Germany and the EU budget were apparently exceptions proving the rule.

Regarding the EU, the shift thesis does not only remain plausible but seems further corroborated by the recent past. Its ODA fell in both 1997 and 1998 in nominal dollar terms, while its OA soared by 67·5 per cent between 1997 and 1998, in line with official declarations (see Chapter 7). Germany's OA (in current dollars), on the other hand, fell monotonously and substantially between 1995 and 1998, by 85·5 per cent, while its ODA fell by 25·8 per cent (OECD, 2000a). These recent data would rather support the thesis of less to both East and South as the present trend. They corroborate our opinion. It would be difficult to argue the case of a general OA increase at the expense of ODA. According to official OECD data, OA appears to be additional. For all DAC members both fell in 1996 and 1997, which would suggest a decrease in their interest in any type of aid. One of the reasons is certainly economic austerity policies aimed at substantially reducing budget deficits. Both types of aid recovered slightly in 1998. In 1999, ODA increased very slightly according to the most recent information, while OA from DAC members and multilateral institutions fell by $0·5 billion (OECD, 2000b). Officially, no GSP percentages were provided, but for our argument it suffices to see that OA has fallen while ODA has not.

Moving Israel to Part II had pronounced effects on OA. In 1997, Israel received 21·4 per cent of all DAC OA. Aid to the former eastern bloc was thus only some 0·015 per cent (0·016 if rounded), roughly half the percentage of 1996. US OA jumped by 50 per cent from 1996 to 1997. In 1998, OA was roughly $1·5 billion higher than in 1997. Israel's share sank to 15.17 per cent.

Statements by the EU, and contrasting the sobering experience of the second financial protocol of Lomé IV with significant increases of aid to the former eastern bloc, at that time might have supported the thesis of shifting. Also, when negotiations on the new treaty after Lomé IV/2 were about to start, the EU argued that its 'geopolitical' interests had shifted to Eastern Europe. After a small decline in 1995, the Commission increased its OA by 15·6 per cent, or $193 million, between 1995 and 1996. However, aggregate OA by EU member countries fell by more than half, or $3675 million, at the same time, after a strong increase from 1994 to 1995. In GSP percentages EU members' OA fell from 0·09 in 1995 to 0·04 in 1996 (OECD, 1998a). These figures hardly suggest a great deal of interest in backing declarations with money. The OECD (1994, p.128) described OA quite pithily: 'disbursements of concessional assistance continue to lag far behind the large commitments announced at international conferences'.

Official data do not show any shift to the East but suggest additionality of OA. However, Raffer (1998a) showed that donors boosted ODA figures considerably after 1989 by increasingly including items which the OECD itself does not consider ODA according to its own definition. This practice could hide a rerouting of resources, visible if one corrects ODA data. To check whether a shift occurred, one must therefore look the DAC's gift horse in the mouth to correct discontinuities.

BROADENING THE CONCEPT OF ODA

Particularly after 1989, donors busily undermined checks of what passes as ODA, moving downwards to pre-Myrdalian recording practices. Claiming that the definition of ODA has not changed, the OECD (1998a, p.114; 2000a, p.265) concedes that 'changes in interpretation have tended to broaden the scope of the concept'. Present DAC performance would be noticeably worse without this broadening.

Broadening is illustrated by three 'main' (OECD, 1998a, p.114) examples: administrative costs (ODA since 1979), imputed costs of students from the South (since 1984) and assistance provided to refugees from recipient countries during the first year after arrival in the donor country ('eligible to be reported for some time but widely used only since 1991'). The wording makes it clear that these are not the only cases, but no other examples are given.

Further examples of 'broadening' not specifically mentioned in this passage are the 'inclusion from 1970 of ... official contributions to these [private voluntary] agencies' activities (which are recorded as ODA)' (OECD, 1985, p.173) the second 'major break' in continuity according to the OECD; emergency and disaster relief, debt forgiveness, and changes regarding capital subscriptions of multilateral institutions. For the sake of precision, Raffer (1998a) added ODA received by former communist countries. Lengthening the list of recipients is a factor potentially increasing ODA. However, flows to these countries were negligibly low, never more than 0·003 per cent until 1994. Thus they were only included to capture all changes broadening ODA. In 1995, they remained below and in 1996 very slightly above that level (OECD, 1998b), fluctuating perceptibly. However, in 1995, ODA would have had to be rounded down to 0·26 per cent without the longer list. The inclusion of Moldova in Part I from 1997 onwards will make staying above psychological thresholds such as 0·25 or probably 0·20 per cent in the future marginally easier.

It is important to stress that, with the exception of geographical broadening, all items enumerated above have been severely criticized by the OECD itself as not being ODA pursuant to its own definition. With this one and relatively minor exception, the list above therefore simply compiles what should not be recorded according to the OECD's own judgements. Quotes from official OECD publications proving this statement are provided by Raffer (1998a). It is not any outsider's choice.

In the jubilee edition of the so-called *Chairman's Report* (women have never been allowed to chair so far, although the word 'chairman' was removed) the OECD (1985, p.173) defines 'in particular export credits extended by an official sector trade promotion body ... , debt relief funded by the National Treasury or other government departments' as Other Official Flows (OOF), explicitly denying them qualification as ODA. As shown in Chapter 5, practice was softer on DAC members than official statements. In the case of communist donors the OECD (ibid., p.118) stated consistently that debt cancellations and debt reschedulings softening outstanding loans to more concessional terms were 'not taken into account'. A few years later the situation had changed. The Cold War and its exigencies being matters of the past, debt forgiveness including non-ODA export credits is now readily recorded, increasing total aid, without any change in definition – as the OECD insists.

Capital subscriptions made in the form of notes encashable on demand were reported either on encashment or on issuing (on deposit) before 1980, depending on the donor's choice. All donors now report on a deposit base irrespective of whether notes are ever encashed, which in practice boosts ODA. Unifying on the deposit basis clearly contradicts the cherished general principle of recording disbursements, not commitments, and the OECD (ibid., p.173) once considered it worth debating and changing. Not any longer, although – or maybe because – this practice boosts figures perceptibly. Commenting on the World Bank's board's decision to raise the costs of World Bank loans, Wade and Kapur (1998) criticized the fact that – owing to the practice of capital increases by depositing notes – ICs determine World Bank policy without having to pay in proportion to their voting rights. 'In practice the amount of money paid into the World Bank from the budgets of member countries is nearly zero.' Large reserves and the World Bank's preferred creditor status mean that liabilities are 'also, in practice, zero', and all costs are simply shifted onto borrowers. The privilege of a voting majority is enjoyed by the North without bearing a fair share of the costs.

Emergency and disaster relief, always subsumed under ODA, thus boosting figures, has rightly never been considered ODA by the OECD. Traditionally, its share was small, but it grew substantially in the 1990s. The OECD (1995, p.84) even calls aid to refugees and disaster relief 'extreme examples of the way circumstances can thwart intentions', explaining: 'The definition of ODA requires that, to be eligible for inclusion, resources should be "for the economic development and welfare of developing countries"'. They are laudable and necessary expenditures helping to alleviate human suffering, thus real help. But these flows, strictly speaking, do not contribute to development and are - as the OECD rightly observed - not really development aid.

Raffer and Singer (1996, p.196) noted 'the rapid increase in emergency aid [which] has been at the expense of normal development aid' coming 'under threat'. Therefore they proposed combining actual relief work as much as possible with development work, for instance by offering refugees an income for building infrastructure useful for future development of their own or another country.

Data on member countries exist, and can be found by looking at official national sources. But the OECD refuses to specify the quantitative impact of broadening, quoting difficulties with data collection and coverage, although the 'amounts involved can ... be substantial' (OECD, 1998a, p.114). If whole items involving 'substantial' amounts of money cannot be traced and quantified by the DAC because of the statistics provided by its own members, severe doubts about the quality of both its published figures and the system of peer reviewing are justified. It is difficult to see how flows can be audited in detail to check whether they meet the criteria demanded for ODA if statistical returns are so bad that whole important items are difficult to quantify. It also prompts the question why members are not encouraged to provide better data.

Proving that OECD sources are occasionally able to report astonishingly exact figures on quantitative dimensions of broadening factors, Raffer (1998a) sees two possible conclusions. Either no corrections could be made to produce consistent time series, because the DAC could not quantify these factors – which would be surprising, considering that it was once able to do so - or it is unwilling to disclose these sums because they are too 'substantial'. In both cases ODA time series are flawed - the OECD (1985, p.173) speaks of 'major breaks in the continuity of the long-term series' - and the falling trend resulting from sticking consistently to the original method would be more pronounced.

Finally, one has to ask what precisely the OECD means, stating that revising historical records for 'substantial' changes 'is not always feasible' (ibid.). From a purely statistical point of view, consistent time series are usually not considered unfeasible. Including items previously not subsumed under ODA is one method of pushing up the downward sloping trend of aid in GSP percentages. This has been done for some time. These new items are not necessarily by themselves unjustified additions, as the examples of administrative costs or contributions to NGOs illustrate. 'One can justify administrative costs incurred by providing ODA as part and parcel of total costs' (Raffer, 1998a, p.10), although the OECD excludes administrative costs of NGOs when calculating private (that is, non-ODA) aid – another example of unjustified self-preference by DAC members, tilting the relation between ODA and private generosity a bit in their favour. It is difficult to see why a minister's salary is considered development aid, but the (much lower) salary of an NGO employee is not. While there is no reason why funds given by governments to NGOs for aid work should not be recorded as ODA, adding such items without correcting the amounts of previous years produces a statistical discontinuity. The decline of ODA looks less steep than it is. Whether considered morally laudable activities or the opposite, logically justifiable as ODA or not, all broadening factors inflate the total and have to be deducted to show the real trend of aid hidden by broadening.

The second type of broadening concerns outlays that are not oriented towards promoting development, but which have been traditionally counted as ODA. They have not, strictly speaking, been considered ODA by the OECD, although they have always been subsumed under ODA. The fact that these items used to account for relatively low shares of the total until the recent past might explain why this inconsistent practice was tolerated. They are emergency and disaster relief as well as what one would nowadays call support for structural adjustment: 'economic support assistance' (OECD, 1985, p.171) was 'also reportable as ODA' even though not really aid. Owing to the data situation, Raffer (1998a, written in 1996) could not correct for structural adjustment. Deflated ODA in Table 6.1 therefore still includes it.

Removing the broadening factors mentioned above, Raffer (ibid.) calculated these GSP percentages of DAC ODA for the period 1989–94. The

Table 6.1   ODA by DAC members, broadened and deflated totals (% of GSP)

	1989	1990	1991	1992	1993	1994
Official DAC value	0·32	0·33	0·33	0·33	0·31	0·30
Deflated ODA	0·260	0·245	0·239	0·235	0·221	0·211
ODA inflator	1·231	1·347	1·381	1·404	1·403	1·424

Source: Raffer (1998a).

second line of Table 6.1 shows ODA corrected for broadening factors, and may be called deflated ODA. The relation between officially broadened figures and deflated ODA is called ODA inflator. This shows by what percentage official figures are higher than they would be if the original concept had still been applied without 'major breaks in the continuity of the long-term series' (OECD, 1985, p.173).

Most of the figures necessary for the calculation of Table 6.1 were readily accessible, particularly in the most recent *Reports* laudably itemizing ODA disbursements in more detail. The OECD's (1996a, p.126) statement that quantification is difficult (later changed to 'precise quantification' (OECD, 1998a, p.114; 2000a, p.265) is therefore incomprehensible.

Broadening has demonstrably and increasingly inflated ODA, by more than 40 per cent during the last three years in Table 6.1. This result is obtained with very conservative calculations, restricted to correcting for items on whose eligibility as ODA the OECD itself has officially expressed doubts, and which are readily accessible from OECD publications. It does not and cannot include ODA granted only to bail out official creditors including IFIs, such as the Bretton Woods Institutions, that is subsumed under other titles than debt forgiveness. It was also not possible to correct for export credits accepted as ODA by the DAC with some grumbling. Official data are not provided and all one could do would be to go through national statistics trying to find out which ODA export credits might be mainly motivated by self-interest. Nor does the fact that the OECD stopped making data on associated financing available in 1985 (Morrissey & White, 1996, p.214) inspire confidence. Even without agreeing with those harsh critics arguing that the justification of tied aid as ODA must generally be challenged, one has to assume that correct application of the present definition would yield noticeably lower ODA figures. This point is corroborated by the OECD's unwillingness to enforce ODA's being recorded according to its own rules.

Regarding tied aid, which is an indication of donor self-interest, it should be recalled that consensus on a recommendation to untie aid to LLDCs, an enterprise welcomed by the OECD ministers and the G8 at Birmingham, could not be reached. Concerns that 'untying aid might result in declining aid flows' expressed by some OECD countries (OECD, 2000a, p.154) were one reason. This makes one wonder whether ODA would already have fallen below 0·2 if tying had been abolished.

This may suffice to show that the figures of Table 6.1 are not unduly biased against the DAC and that ODA inflation may well have been higher than shown. The perception that deflated ODA was in reality even less than 0·2 per cent of DAC GSP in 1994, which would mean a broadening of aid of roughly 50 per cent, cannot be discounted as unfounded.

As deflation was done according to the DAC's accounting and publishing practice, quality checks on a case-by-case basis were by necessity disregarded. Since war, repression, human rights violations and the destruction of the environment have also been funded by ODA (cf. Raffer & Singer, 1996) aid in the sense of real help has certainly always been lower than donors' figures.

But such qualitative aspects can only be discussed by detailed case-by-case studies beyond the scope of this chapter.

According to Table 6.1, officially recorded ODA was 42 per cent higher in 1994 than it would have been according to the initial scope of the concept. Furthermore, broadening almost doubled over the six years shown. In other words, what the OECD itself initially considered and still considers proper development aid decreased quite visibly, particularly if one assumes that sums that could not be included because of lacking information, such as debt determined 'aid' bailing out other creditors, are likely to have become substantial. This statistical growth of volume due to boosting factors reveals a disturbing trend. The OECD (2000a, p.50) defends itself against this criticism, stating: 'On the whole DAC members have only added to ODA reporting items which, in principle, lead clearly to development outputs, *e.g.* associated financing and the administrative costs of delivering ODA programmes'.

It should be noted that the OECD does not claim that these activities had the promotion of economic development and welfare as their main objective, as required by its own ODA definition. Recognizing administrative costs as part and parcel of ODA, Raffer (1998a) granted them more developmental focus than the OECD. That these items may, in principle, have developmental effects was never denied. What Raffer primarily criticized was not a dilution of the developmental focus (OECD, 2000a, p.50) - which happened as well, for instance when including expenditures for refugees in donor countries - but higher figures produced by inconsistencies in recording. Combined with the claim not to have changed ODA's definition since at least 1970, these produced a wrong and misleading picture. Keeping ODA constant at 0·33 by increased 'broadening' during 1992-4 is a prime example. It was proved by showing that the OECD itself did not consider these items as proper ODA, but recorded them all the same. This is not logically equivalent to whether they are developmental or not, but simply a proof that the OECD did not obey its own rules. Finally, referring in a footnote to Raffer's conference paper (not the published version, which is more easily available), the OECD (ibid.) asserts: 'There is no statistical evidence to support these claims.' As Raffer's conclusions were obtained exclusively on the basis of officially published - and appropriately quoted - OECD statistics, this assertion is incomprehensible.

Extending these calculations would have been interesting, but is not possible owing to the data situation. Imputed student costs are not regularly published. The 1996 review of Austria (OECD, 1996c) contained these data for all DAC members until 1994, which seems a unique exception. Also further data on emergency food aid from the source used by Raffer (1998a) were not available to the authors. These are important caveats, but it can nevertheless be said that the trend towards higher and higher ODA inflators stopped after 1994. Assuming that the missing two items remained constant at their 1994 nominal values in 1995-6, ODA inflators of 1·374 and 1·345 obtain in 1995 and 1996, respectively. Considering the dimensions involved, general information on aid, and the difference to 1·424 in Table 6.1, one may therefore safely maintain that the increasing trend was at least halted, if not clearly reversed.

A change in recording deserves mentioning: until 1997, the OECD (1997, p.A41) provided the DAC totals of encashments by multilateral institutions. One year later, the OECD (1998a, p.A41) declared these sums 'not available', even for the years 1993-5 for which these data had already been published by the OECD (1997, p.A41). For 1995, for instance, the only difference between the two *Reports* is the missing total in OECD (1998a). Adding all figures for members would result in the same total as published in OECD (1997). However, referring to the OECD's authority when using DAC totals as done by Raffer (1998a) is no longer possible. This change occurred after Raffer (1998a) had started to circulate as an unpublished paper in 1996.

Interesting facts emerge from these figures. The highest boost both nominally and in percentages occurred between 1989 and 1990. Boosting took off precisely during the three years when official data held ODA percentages constant at 0·33, which must have strengthened the argument against the shift thesis. Critical minds might point out that ODA inflators declined once it became clear that the further decline of ODA could not be made up any longer this way.

Returning to our initial question whether resources were shifted to the East, the answer is somewhat less apparent after correcting for broadening (see Table 6.2). Percentages in the table were rounded to two digits, as is

Table 6.2   Corrected ODA and OA by DAC members (% of GSP)

	1990	1991	1992	1993	1994
Deflated ODA	0·25	0·24	0·24	0·22	0·21
OA	0·01	0·04	0·04	0·04	0·04
Total	0·26	0·28	0·28	0·26	0·25

customary in OECD publications. During 1990-2 at least some OA must have been additional, as the totals (corrected ODA plus OA) increased, even though ODA itself declined slightly (hidden by rounding for 1992). In 1994, however, the sum of both types of aid is precisely the same as corrected ODA alone in 1990. This could be interpreted as giving some support to the thesis of a slow shift happening over several years, but this conclusion would be based on a single year. With the same caveat, the decline of both types of aid in 1996 and 1997 does not contradict the view that, once the Cold War was over and any danger of CTTs returning to communism gone, donors saw little reason for 'generosity'. Less money for all recipients rather than shifts of available resources between groups still appears to be the most plausible conclusion from available data, even though slight increases for both types of aid were recorded in 1998.

The ODA increase in 1998 itself grew between June 1999, when the OECD (1999b) had put the figure at 0·23 per cent, an increase of $3·3 billion instead of $3·56 billion over 1997, and the publication of the last *Report* (OECD, 2000a). A total of $1·9 billion (OECD, 2000a, p.68) – still $1·3 billion the year before (OECD, 1999b) – in US aid reflects 'increased deposits of promissory notes with multilateral development banks and rises in food and emergency aid' (OECD, 2000a, p.68), bringing the USA up to a less embarrassing 0·1 per cent, partly without any real expenditures. Another $1·3 billion reflects a 'surge' of Japanese 'loans to countries affected by the Asian crisis'. This information would not contradict the suspicion that ODA inflating might become popular again. Most recent figures available in September 2000 decrease the percentage of 1998 again to 0·23 (OECD, 2000b) owing to upward revisions of GNP. With the preliminary figure of 0·24 for 1999, this happens to yield a monotonous increase since 1997, a short but encouragingly upward-moving line.

Over the period 1992–8, the cumulative drop in DAC ODA 'amounted to $88·7 billion' (OECD, 2000a, pp.13ff) compared with a situation where the average GSP ratio of the previous 20 years had been maintained. Ireland, New Zealand and Luxembourg are shown to have no cumulative drop, but an increase over the period 1992–8. Denmark, a generous donor, also showed an increase in 1998 over 1992 as measured by the OECD, but a small cumulative drop over the period. In the more recent past there are further positive examples. Italy and the UK increased their aid, the UK by 8·6 per cent in real terms. In the British case this reflected the 'commitment to increase aid by 25% by 2001' (OECD, 2000a, p.68).

The overall picture is bleak, though. The OECD (ibid., p.24) warns that 'the political impulse required' to reach again some 0·3 per cent of DAC GSP 'should not be underestimated', even though the amount would be 'relatively small'. It will ultimately rest on whether there is a strong political conviction that partnership with SCs works and on whether there is a convincing case for investing in global and regional public goods. Compared with times when aid was widely seen as an obligation and nearly all DAC countries officially and voluntarily bound themselves to reach 0.7 per cent – legally still a binding obligation for these countries - this is a marked difference. This illustration of what international obligations in favour of the poorest mean in practice should induce us to share the OECD's pessimism about whether reaching 0.3 again is likely in the near future.

AN UNSUCCESSFUL ATTEMPT TO BOOST ODA

Not all attempts to 'broaden the concept' were successful. The prime example is the attempt to have one type of military assistance recognized as ODA. For a short period it was successful, and it has left its traces in ODA statistics (for instance, in Annex Table 6b in OECD, 1998a). In 1990, the USA started to include substantial amounts of military debt cancellations ($1·2 billion; 1991: $1·86 billion) in its ODA statistics. Washington forgave Egypt military debts because the country sided with the West in the Gulf war against Iraq. Following US advice, the DAC agreed to review the appropriate recording of debt forgiveness – whose qualification as ODA was fervently denied not so long ago – particularly of military debt. These debt reductions were first accepted as ODA, although with 'appropriate footnote indications and further explanations where required' (OECD, 1992, p.86). The DAC recorded them for members reporting military debt reductions but did not include them in the DAC total. For those years the sum of ODA by all members was bigger than the DAC total – an example of having one's cake and eating it.

During the review it was argued that military debt forgiveness was not military aid. If undertaken in the context of supporting effective policy programmes its economic effect was said to be similar to programme aid. Finally, the US attempt to have military debt reductions recognized as ODA within the DAC was unsuccessful, although it was declared to be ODA. The DAC confirmed that forgiveness of military debt was

> a new and separate transaction dissociated from the purpose of the original transaction, that the inclusion as ODA is based on the development motivation of the act of forgiveness, that this logic is also the basis for including as ODA forgiveness of debt arising from export credits and that therefore both types of debt forgiveness should be treated statistically in the same way. (OECD, 1992, p.86)

But it was agreed not to record this type of ODA in the future 'in deference to concerns expressed over public opinion impacts' (ibid.). The fact that donors encourage recipient countries to reduce military expenditures and arms imports was also seen as a reason why military debt reductions should not be recorded as ODA. Another logically convincing point was not raised by the DAC. Once debt forgiveness for military aid is accepted as ODA, any military transaction can easily be transformed into ODA. All that would be required would be to 'sell' arms first 'on credit' and to 'forgive' these debts afterwards. Logically, it would also be difficult to argue that an outright grant for military purposes cannot be counted as ODA, if a transaction which is economically a grant with a time lag can be recorded without problems. This would also have been at odds with the OECD's repeated claims and assertions that no kind of military activity can be subsumed under ODA, a fact that apparently did not disturb the DAC.

In practice, this highly laudable and ethical rule was not always obeyed anyway, as the financing of activities during the Vietnam war by ODA or the use of aid funds to pay Somoza for his permission to use Nicaragua as the base for the Bay of Pigs invasion document (Raffer & Singer, 1996, p.20). But in theory the DAC had remained adamant for more than two decades until the beginning of the 1990s, stating for instance that 'any kind of military assistance is excluded' (OECD, 1985, p.171) from ODA. By accepting forgiven military debts at least some kind of military transaction has become eligible in theory, but not in practice, if debt relief is based on development motivation. One may assume that, in the case of Egypt, the West's comrade-in-arms against Iraq, development was clearly seen as the main reason for substantial cancellations. The DAC must be applauded for withstanding successfully US pressure to include military debt cancellations. It was thus able to reaffirm: 'Grants, loans and credits for military purposes are excluded' (OECD, 1996a, p.123). However, financial support given to friendly countries in the region because of the war – in some countries even explicitly referred to as 'Gulf aid' – was recorded as ODA. Deducting this as well from deflated ODA would strengthen the shift thesis further. But military debt cancellations, although theoretically eligible, will be forced to remain unrecorded ODA.

Technically, the OECD was right. Its 'unchanged' official ODA definition provides no logical reason against including military activities as long as soldiers shoot mainly to promote welfare and economic development and the grant element is at least 25 per cent. Nevertheless, the DAC claimed after Myrdal's critique that transfers financing military purposes were excluded, an assertion honoured in practice both in the breach and in the observance. The World Bank (1990, p.253) cautions that 'the borderline is sometimes blurred; the definition of the country of origin usually prevails'. It concludes: 'Many "aid" programs in donor countries cover an assortment of activities (including commercial and strategic initiatives) which often have, at best, a tenuous connection with development' (ibid., pp.127f).

THE NEW AID PARADIGM

A policy of 'granting less and demanding more' and ODA decreases have been accompanied by justifications for these reductions. The 'role of aid in filling "financial gaps" will become less relevant, as domestic resource mobilisation and capital inflows strengthen over time' (OECD, 1998a, p.36). The fear of the 1960s that aid may impair the role of private capital has returned. Private capital is to be substituted for ODA.

This highly uncritical enthusiasm about private flows, somewhat toned down after the Asian crash of 1997, resembles the enthusiasm about Euromarket lending in the 1970s and the enthusiasm of the early 1990s when the end of the debt crisis was announced. There were indications that the pattern of private profits and socialized losses might become institutionalized. The OECD's (1996a, p.57) view of systemic risks requiring 'a much larger officially provided safety net' is a prime example. Of course, such a safety net would only be needed for more volatile flows. In contrast to aid, catastrophic private failures are interpreted as the manifest need for even more taxpayers' money. The US Savings & Loans deregulation, which cost US taxpayers several hundred billion dollars, shows that public money is available to clean up the results of neoliberal policies within ICs.

The OECD (ibid., p.58) announced the end of state-led development: 'With the shift to market-based economic strategies, these issues matter much more than they did when there was a common assumption that development would be state-led.' The role of official finance is formulated quite succinctly: it 'helps to seed and reinforce' (ibid., p.55) expanding private flows from abroad. Aid is seen as a handmaiden of private profit interests (cf. OECD, 1998a, p.57), more precisely of Northern profits, as most capital originates in the North. In many SCs, privatization means selling to foreigners because locals lack the necessary money. State-led development seems to be replaced by state-subsidized private business. In contrast to the lack of coherence too often found with aid politics, where viable projects have frequently been destroyed by decisions of the same donors in other areas such as trade (Raffer & Singer, 1996), the thrust of privatization and liberalization is quite coherent.

Reducing official aid combines naturally with privatization and liberalization, as well as with present austerity policies practically everywhere in the North. Combining budget cuts, for instance to comply with the Maastricht criteria, with substantial tax cuts in favour of the rich and people with high incomes (often including top politicians) makes it necessary to look for savings wherever possible. Criticizing aid and the rather opaque nature of political conditionality, which allows donors unrestricted arbitrariness as to whether recipients comply with conditions or not, may be useful tools to justify aid cuts.

Apart from cutting ODA further, it is also being redirected to expenditures in the interest of donors. The OECD (1998a, p.17) speaks of an 'important paradigm shift, with some quite radical implications for the practice of development co-operation', and of 'a dramatic widening of the scope and ambition of the development co-operation agenda' (ibid., p.18), which now include quite a few purely political demands. Documents refer repeatedly to this new ODA focus, concisely presented by the OECD's (1996b) document *Shaping the 21st Century*. It argues that the future of SCs will be ever more tightly linked to that of OECD countries. Once perceived as a means to help SCs to overcome internal problems, development cooperation is now seen as a way to address, as this document put it, common global problems and to pursue common aspirations.

The new thrust is helping the international community to manage global issues. Sustainable development expands the community of interests and values necessary to 'manage a host of global issues that respect no borders' (OECD, 1996b, p.6) such as global environmental policies, limiting population growth, nuclear non-proliferation, control of illicit drugs, controlling AIDs or combating epidemic diseases. Building new legal and economic systems compatible with new globalized structures is another new task. The choice of a more liberalized international system is clearly an issue overwhelmingly in the interest of OECD countries. These issues are doubtlessly important. Addressing them can be easily justified. But they are not ODA in the traditional sense nor – strictly speaking – according to the still valid DAC definition. They finance at best tasks of common global interest or remedial actions against international externalities. Some expenditures have the character of global public goods, of actions safeguarding global commons, or of managing global issues. Such activities are a necessary and laudable reaction to global changes, of common interest, and thus also – though not necessarily 'mainly' as the donors' own ODA definition requires – in the interest of SCs. Nevertheless, they have increasingly been recorded as ODA, reducing the shares of traditional ODA. Societal organization according to values and concepts propagated by donors after the Cold War, such as democracy, human rights, participation or good governance, is supported by flows subsumed under aid. Quite often goals mainly in the donors' interest are financed. Controlling illicit drugs appears to be more of concern to donors than to recipients. Unconditionally opening SC economies to Northern capital and transnational firms, which often has detrimental effects on SCs, is another example.

The OECD argues that vital interests at stake have caused this perceptible shift of ODA. More of what little money might be left should go to issues donors are interested in: 'Although a sustained aid effort by DAC countries would still be essential, by the year 2020 it would represent a significantly lower level of DAC countries' GNP, allowing room for the expansion of aid directed at global issues of sustainability and other international public goods' (OECD, 1998a, p.40).

The ODA target of 0·7 per cent of donor GNP, officially pledged by most DAC members, is thus dead. Suggesting that all ODA should serve the purpose of some form of globalized internal policy, the OECD declared ODA to be one means to support their own foreign policies: 'Our crucial interest in the broad goals of peace, economic growth, social justice, environmental sustainability and democracy obviously goes far wider than aid programmes' (ibid., p.14). OECD statements inferring all ODA to be a GPG can be found. However, a blanket classification covering all ODA is not useful. Traditional ODA functions are best characterized by the dual gap theory: aid has to close both the savings and the foreign exchange gaps in developing countries, thus accelerating the catching-up process. Chenery (1989, p.140) described ODA's traditional role quite succinctly: 'In macroeconomic terms it adds to the resources available for investment and it augments the supply of foreign exchange to finance imports.' By contrast, the new paradigm focuses on helping the international community to manage global challenges and problems.

General issues of equity are still addressed, such as poverty and, notably, the question of gender-based discrimination, a problem by no means unique to SCs. Poverty is embedded in this new perception by redefining the notion of security: 'Everyone is made less secure by the poverty and misery that exists in the world' (OECD, 1996b, p.6). The OECD's (ibid., p.9) first goal is halving the proportion of people living in extreme poverty by 2015, as a step towards eradicating poverty demanded by the Copenhagen Declaration and Programme of 1995. Additionally, universal primary education, eliminating gender disparity in primary and secondary education, reducing infant and child mortality and access to the health system are to be achieved by 2015. These goals are traditional ODA activities, still influenced by ideas reaching back to redistribution with growth and basic needs.

But, in perceptible contrast to the decades of the Cold War, donors have increasingly emphasized good governance, human rights, democratization, participatory development, transparency and accountability, and also environmental issues recently. While reducing ODA, donors started at the same time to demand more and far-reaching concessions from recipients. Conditionality became increasingly elaborate, interfering more and more with recipients' political decisions. Given the dependence of most recipients on OECD countries as the only source of aid or other financial flows, the North has an opportunity to dictate conditions, which is used to the full.

Already during the 1980s the World Bank connected its lending openly with measures diminishing state activities, favouring private enterprise and implementing its 'free market' ideology. However, these conditionalities were said to be economic rather than political. Meanwhile, all donors have become more openly political. Aid has become increasingly conditional on what donors consider appropriate behaviour. They do not always go as far as to observe themselves what they preach to others. Raffer & Singer (1996, pp.168ff) give examples of double standards, most notably the lack of appropriate reactions to the World Bank's so-called 'Wapenhans Report' by ODA donors controlling the majority of votes. What the OECD (1998a, pp.67ff) calls 'reform process' is certainly not adequate. Thus, not meeting their own standards, not all donors would qualify as their own aid recipients. The example of the EU demanding separation of state powers from SCs while busily undoing this very separation in Europe where 'laws' are passed by councils of ministers behind closed doors is a case in point.

As illustrated by the examples of the US *African Growth and Opportunity Act* and the European Union's basis for negotiating a new treaty after Lomé IV (see Chapter 7), this new OECD ideology comes down in practice to obtaining substantial concessions from SCs. Both make ODA contingent on demands such as decentralization, democratization, good governance, human rights or environmental policies. At the same time, donors increasingly insist on the need for flexibility of decision making, meaning decisions on short notice whether to continue aid or trade preferences or not, and without any objective criterion or legal obligation of donors. This increases insecurity and dependence of recipients, reducing ODA increasingly to a means to ensure compliance with donors' perceptions of how global or domestic issues should be managed by SCs.

The catchword 'partnership' has become increasingly popular with donors at the very time when their practice dictates conditions in a way unimaginable before. The OECD's (1996b, p.14) crucial document on aid in the 21st century demands 'A Stronger Compact for Effective Partnership', speaks of 'a process of dialogue and agreement in a true spirit of partnership' (ibid., p.9) or simply 'true partnership' (ibid., p.13), to quote a few passages.

The OECD sees a catalytic role of country-level frameworks (2000a, pp.107f) for partnership. In particular, it refers to the World Bank's Comprehensive Development Framework, proposed by James Wolfensohn. The Framework's record is underwhelming so far. The complicated nature of the matrix proposed to coordinate efforts, the lack of will to be coordinated of quite a few donors, as well as the 'lack of sustained commitment' (ibid., p.117) by donors identified by a forum organized by the OECD, the World Bank and the UN as one main obstacle to development partnership do not suggest that this scheme can be implemented well. Assertions such as 'Countries must be in the driver's seat and set the course' (ibid., p.122), may soon provide a 'good' reason to reduce aid, namely that the country is unable to use inflows properly.

Donors have busily relaxed standards of what passes as ODA recently, moving downwards to pre-Myrdalian recording levels, the cosy situation of the 1960s before the present debatable definition of ODA existed, which logically excludes some flows. Looking at 'Development Finance' illustrates this time warp too. The expression 'official development finance', including ODA as well as Other Official Flows, was initially coined to provide a nice sounding name for multilateral lending too hard to qualify as ODA, such as typical World Bank loans. The aim was 'to recognize the developmental value of lending by multilateral development institutions' (OECD, 1985, pp.172f). There are no objective criteria to measure this alleged developmental value.

When it comes to daily business, official development finance is described in more down-to-earth terms. In May 1995, for instance, the World Bank advertised in US newspapers, informing the business community that its loans 'give you more bang for your buck' (*Time*, 29 May 1995). The fact that even official sources, such as the Wapenhans Report, prove that a lot of harm is done by IFIs (cf. Raffer & Singer, 1996, who quote this and various other sources) did not influence donors perceptibly. 'Development finance' is a positive-sounding expression without content created by DAC members holding the majority of shares in IFIs such as the World Bank. Bilateral loans, by contrast, require a minimum grant element to qualify as development aid.

Meanwhile, 'development financing' was expanded to cover 'market-driven' private flows (OECD, 1996a, pp.58ff). 'Market-Driven Development Financing' (ibid.) or simply 'private development finance' (OECD 2000a, pp.9f) again implies that everything emanating from the North – including highly speculative capital – is good for development. The Asian crisis of 1997 is logically a result of development financing. Occasionally, the OECD (1998a, p.57) is quite frank, though: the 'flow of reward seeking private capital' to SCs 'is at its highest real level since the wave of decolonisation of the early 1960s'. Decolonization reduced development finance.

After the Cold War, flows labelled 'ODA' are increasingly used in the donors' own narrow interest, to obtain concessions from 'recipients' or to help shape the world according to the perceptions of OECD countries. There is also a shift towards projects whose successes or failures cannot be checked, thus reducing criticism. In contrast to dams or factories, where failures can be easily proved, this is virtually impossible in fields such as voters' education, constitutional development, electoral assistance or training of journalists. Understandably, donors might be keen to reduce potential targets of critics. This is not at all to say that such projects are bad or unnecessary, but simply to point out that checks and criticism have become more difficult, if not impossible.

The present official focus on poverty reduction is greatly to be welcomed. Poverty reduction is indeed the true meaning of development. Aid that is also help does increase the standard of living of poor people. But focusing on poverty can also be used as an argument to leave substantial parts of what used to be financed by aid to 'reward seeking private capital'. Finally, the OECD's statements on poverty – like the rhetoric on democracy and human rights – may be used to make aid practice more acceptable to the public, even to parts of the critical public.

7. Lomé: reflecting North–South relations since colonial times

The history of Lomé mirrors North–South relations very well, including their origin in the colonial past. When the Treaty of Rome creating the European Economic Community (EEC) was signed in 1957 several signatories were colonial powers. Since they had no intention to sever economic links with their colonies the treaty had to contain clauses (Article 131 et seq.) linking these colonies with the Community. The first European Development Fund (EDF 1) was established. Naturally, the colonized were not asked for their approval.

After decolonization, international agreements became necessary to continue these relations with what now were independent countries. Yaoundé I and II were signed, the first Agreement of Yaoundé between the Six (original EEC members) and 18 newly independent African states. It abolished tariffs and trade barriers for nine agrarian commodities, reducing them for other products except for those considered sensitive by the Europeans (whose production was of interest to EEC agricultural policy). Provisions for capital movements and locations of firms were included, aid by EDF 2 and the European Investment Bank was agreed on. In return, European exports had to be granted preferential treatment – or 'reverse preferences' – by the Yaoundé countries. Other SCs complained about massive trade diversions. This led to the Arusha Agreement with Kenya, Tanzania and Uganda, less generous than Yaoundé I, but the first breakaway from the strong concentration on francophone Africa. Yaoundé II invited all African states with 'structurally similar' economies to join. Mauritius did.

Reverse preferences were heavily criticized by the USA and the UK, worrying about their export markets. Britain stopped her attacks when she decided to become a member of the Community herself. Britain's accession, more precisely her relation to the Commonwealth, made new arrangements necessary. Under the UK Treaty of Accession, Asian Commonwealth countries were not offered association. There was only a declaration of intent to seek 'appropriate solutions' for problems that might arise in the field of trade. On 28 February 1975, a totally new treaty was signed in Lomé, the capital of Togo – Lomé I – thus preserving the dominating influence of francophone states.

Lomé I was very progressive. Blocking the demand for a New International

Economic Order, the EEC made far-reaching concessions, granting ACP (African, Caribbean, Pacific) states an unprecedentedly strong position, including a contractual right to aid. Lomé I was the best arrangement SCs ever got from any group of donors. Its great innovation was Stabex, the STABilization of EXport revenues (cf. Raffer & Singer, 1996), deliberately offered as an alternative to Southern demands for commodity price stabilization. Like an insurance scheme it conferred contractual rights of compensation for export earnings shortfalls of selected commodities. Special regulations for bananas, rum and, most notably, sugar were laid down. The Sugar Protocol guaranteed a minimum sugar price linked to the price of beet sugar within the EEC for a quota of roughly 1·22 million metric tons per year. Thus ACP exporters participated automatically in intra-EEC policies preserving European farmers' incomes, another unique feature. The European Commission (1996, p.9) frankly acknowledged that such generosity was based on the

> concern to defend ... economic and geopolitical interests in the age of the Cold War ... the international situation ... European anxiety at the first oil crisis, i.e. a fear of raw material shortages and a desire to hold on to valued overseas markets, united with geostrategic interests.

Negotiations for Lomé I started in 1973, the year of the 'first oil crisis', after which SCs tried to follow OPEC's example by establishing more commodity cartels. They were perceived to be on the brink of wielding commodity power. Frisch (1996, p.61) stresses the bargaining power sub-Saharan Africa had, remarking that the establishment of the ACP Group in Georgetown foiled the European approach of parallel negotiations with three regional groups. This unexpected solidarity might well have increased European anxiety.

Lomé I also did away with reverse preferences. This, however, was the result of US pressure rather than of ACP power. The UK, now a member, had dropped her reservations. Seeing reverse preferences as a means to secure advantages in ACP markets, the USA demanded their abolition. The informal 'Casey–Soames understanding' committing the EEC not to insist on reverse trade preferences paved the way for Lomé I (cf. Raffer, 1999a, pp.132f).

Evolutions after Lomé I are a prime example of successful policies of flexible response. Lomé II already saw a slight shift towards greater influence by the European donor side, a tendency strongly accentuated during the 1980s, as documented by Lomé III and IV. Geopolitical conditions have changed perceptibly since 1973–5, and the EU's anxiety with them. Slowly but tenaciously concessions granted in a period of anxiety have been rolled back by taking advantage of the worsening position of SCs. Later Conventions including the new 'post-Lomé' arrangement slowly changed the balance of power, moving from contractuality to conditionality. The history of Lomé highlights the loss of political weight by SCs due to the debt crisis and the end of the Cold War.

ACP countries were well aware of this. When Lomé IV was signed, the Commission's vice-president, Manuel Marin (1989) had to assuage ACP anxiety that Lomé cooperation might become as much a thing of the past as the bipolar world. He insisted that signing 'only a few weeks after the Berlin Wall came down, underlines a permanency in ACP–EEC cooperation which goes beyond the historic events we are living through'. Seven years later, European interests had shifted and political and security interests were redefined to fit a 'post-Lomé world' (Commission, 1996, p.i).

Commissioner Patten stated at a hearing of the International Development Committe of the House of Commons that the goal of projecting stability around the EU has made 'the proportion of our external assistance which is traditional ODA' decline (IDC, 2000, p.23). Much money is going to accession candidates. The East, the Balkans and the Mediterranean are generously funded. Poland received twice as much as Asia and Latin America together (ibid., p.27). Both in 1997 and in 1998, no ACP country was among the top ten recipients of OA or ODA (OECD, 1999a; 2000a), with Poland topping the list in both years. According to Oxfam, more than half of the budget of the European Commission's Humanitarian Office went to ex-Yugoslavia in 1999, 'four times the amount of aid going to 70 ACP countries' (IDC, 2000, p.77). Both in volume terms and on a per capita basis, the ACP group has been marginalized.

FROM LOMÉ TO MAURITIUS

Lomé II was negotiated at a time of lessened European anxiety. Donors turned more self-assertive (for more details, see Raffer & Singer, 1996; Raffer, 1999a). ACP countries demanded the extension of Stabex, which covered some agricultural products and iron, to include other important commodities. Considering minerals much too important for Stabex, the Europeans offered a new system for mineral exports, Sysmin, proposing to move iron ore into the latter. In contrast to Stabex's automaticity – payments depended only on losses in export revenues – Sysmin was tightly controlled by the Commission having the exclusive right to approve financing. Klaus Meyer, then director-general for development, declared that automaticity was out of the question because of European interests in these commodities (Raffer & Singer, 1996, p.93). Regarding iron ore, a compromise was reached: pits already in operation continued under Stabex. Officially labelled 'Aid for Projects and Programmes', Sysmin covered copper and cobalt, phosphates, bauxite and alumina, manganese, tin, as well as iron ore and pyrites from new sites.

Sysmin proved quite unattractive to ACP countries. It only committed 35 per cent of the funds available for 1986–95 (Lister, 1999a, p.151).

Stabex experienced minor changes under Lomé II. Some ten more items were included. Thresholds – minimum percentages of products in countries' export revenues and minimum export revenue losses triggering payments – were reduced. Repayment conditions were made more favourable. Plummeting commodity prices at the beginning of the 1980s proved too much for the system with its fixed maximum resources per year calculated on the basis of much less pronounced income reductions experienced before. In 1980, only 53 per cent of legitimate ACP claims could be covered. In 1981, financial manœuvring finally allowed paying around two-thirds of established claims. To deal with such steep declines either the amount of money would have had to be increased substantially or claims would have had to be reduced. These 'difficult years' for Stabex resulted in a new Article 155 in Lomé III containing more detailed rules than Lomé II on how to reduce transfers if allocations were insufficient. The huge backlog of undisbursed EU funds would suggest increased allocations for an underfunded Stabex. This would have reduced the Commission's administrative problems and backlogs, and provided enough money for stabilization. But this would have strengthened Stabex, the concession granted out of fear.

Lomé III introduced strict control of the use of all Lomé funds, including Stabex. The whole Convention was now subjected to strong conditionality, which had been restricted to Sysmin before. Cumbersome administrative procedures were introduced that later proved useful as an argument against Lomé. ACP countries were sceptical about the European idea of elaborate coordination (for a simplified and schematic description, see Raffer & Singer, 1996). The term 'policy dialogue', also used initially, strongly recalled the 'dialogue' with the IMF. But again Europeans prevailed. Edgard Pisani, the commissioner for development whose ideas largely formed Lomé III, declared that these mechanisms were designed to make the Convention clearer, more solid and stricter in its execution. Official sources saw them as a means to render cooperation more effective in development terms. Considering that disbursements for the less bureaucratic Lomé I (signed in 1975) were not completed until 1990 (when Lomé IV was signed; see Greenidge, 1999, p.111) there would have been scope for simplification. At the end of 1992, two years after the end of the period covered by Lomé III, only 64 per cent of funds had been disbursed (ibid.). The manner in which procedures were implemented was seen as one reason. Although no longer considered efficient, these cumbersome procedures were preserved by the new Convention of Cotonou – unlike other, more progressive features.

Nevertheless, the ideas of participation, discussion and equality were still present in Lomé III. The Directorate General VIII tried to work out an alternative to BWI-type 'structural adjustment'. These attempts and the goodwill acquired in the past were doubtlessly useful in making the changes of Lomé III more palatable to ACP countries. However, the search for alternative adjustment was soon discontinued. Meanwhile, the EU fully supports the BWIs, although they could not deliver lasting positive results.

Formal support for structural adjustment was an important innovation of Lomé IV. Interestingly, this was accompanied by strong criticism of the Bretton Woods approach by practically all EU organs, from the Commission to the European Parliament. Even the relevant part of the Convention reads like a compendium of criticisms of the BWIs. The subtle final touch was pointing out that Community support was in the form of grants, not loans. Legally, an ACP country need not have a reform programme approved by multilateral institutions in order to qualify. But the BWI seal of approval automatically means eligibility for Lomé resources. Since the EU stopped attempts to create an alternative, this means practically submission to BWI-type adjustment.

Lomé IV consolidated and continued the process of 'Sysminization' with minor changes. To give examples: the Commission finalizes the financing proposal and forwards it to the Community's decision-making body. ACP countries shall be given an opportunity to comment on any amendment of substance which the Commission intends to make. The chief authorizing officer (an EEC organ) approves the tender dossier before invitations to tender are issued, subject to the powers exercised by the EU delegate. The list of tasks of the delegate has grown slightly.

The so-called 'Mid-Term Review' of Lomé IV in particular increased conditionality and European leverage (cf. Raffer & Singer, 1996). The Convention was concluded for ten years (1990–2000), but its financial protocol was to be renegotiated after five years. Lomé IV/2 was the first Convention not signed in Lomé but in Mauritius. The sobering results of the protracted and sharp wrangling on the second financial protocol 1995–2000 (EDF 8) also documented that Lomé had outlived its usefulness to the EU. Although the Union had grown with the accession of new members, only a small nominal increase could be agreed on at the Cannes summit. EDF 8 was 12 967 million ECU (the euro's predecessor currency). The European Investment Bank (EIB) added 1·66 billion. To put this into proper perspective, the ACP Council president calculated Lomé IV/2 to provide 5·5 ECU per head over five years to his group, or 'two pints of beer and a packet of chips in an average London pub' (*The Courier*, no. 155, 1996, p.4).

On this occasion changes could be demanded, a clause used by the EU to revamp the system substantially. Flexibly responding to political changes and eroding ACP bargaining power, the EU has finally turned a once participatory system into a means of domination. The money earmarked for ACP countries under national indicative programmes is paid in two separate tranches. The second tranche is conditional upon the country's performance as well as 'the situation in each ACP State' (*The Courier*, no. 144, 1994, p.6). The *Courier* concedes that 'There is some uncertainty over what this exactly means' (ibid.), but it goes in the direction of donor 'flexibility' – meaning that the donor may decide without contractual restrictions – and IMF conditionality. The Commission gained more competences (cf. Raffer, 1999a). Examples are the sole responsibility for carrying out studies, or dealing directly with tenderers. This was believed to permit easier comparison of proposals and to enable the Commission to use its knowledge of markets to negotiate directly and untroubled by outside interference. This is likely to affect trade in a way conducive to EU export interests. The chief authorizing officer was given powers, reducing those of the national authorizing officer (of the ACP country).

An *essential elements clause* was introduced, allowing the suspension of the Convention in the event of serious violation of the principles of democracy, human rights or the rule of law, without clearly defining serious violation, thus creating space for arbitrariness. Regarding democracy, one should note that the EU, where 'laws' are passed secretly by ministers, lacks the democratic structures it demands from ACP countries. Apparently, it is now largely forgotten that the inclusion of human rights in Lomé III was an ACP demand directed against the EEC states that were in

> a close economic (and political in some cases) embrace with the Apartheid regime of South Africa. For this reason the EU insisted that it be relegated to an annexe rather than being incorporated in the body of the text. Today the tables have turned somewhat. (Greenidge, 1999, p.116)

With Lomé IV, political and ideological orientation has become part of the system. Before, Lomé was based on the recognition of the right of ACP states to determine their development models in all sovereignty. Lomé's political and ideological neutrality was an asset during the Cold War, allowing Europeans to maintain links with countries that had reduced or severed diplomatic ties to Western governments, even to integrate countries oriented to the East into the Western sphere of influence (Frisch, 1996). Thus Angola signed the treaty as its first step of reorientation to the West. When Cuba wanted to join the ACP group in 2000, its formal application immediately received ACP support, but two EU members opposed it because of Cuba's failure to meet the criteria envisaged by the new convention. Cuba finally withdrew its application. The development commissioner also believed that supporting the country's health sector was 'not in line with the EU's common position on the country' (*The Courier*, August/September 2000, p.28). He wants to shift the money to financing human rights organizations, democracy building, economic reform and a free press. Political neutrality, once a 'pragmatic approach' and 'plain common sense' (Commission, 1992, pp.16f) has outlived its usefulness to Brussels. The EU embraced neoliberalism fully: privatization, liberalization, supporting the Washington Consensus and express political conditionality became part and parcel of Lomé.

A process of differentiation was started. Joining Lomé IV, the Dominican Republic, a country heavily dependent on sugar exports, was denied access to the Sugar Protocol. When post-apartheid South Africa wanted to join, Brussels got what it had often demanded, as Lister (1999a, p.150) points out: a greater African response. But as the country wanted to become a full fledged member, rather than joining a free trade area, the EU was 'dismayed by this response'. Lister sees this case as a reason to ask whether the EU actually wants 'more dialogue ... or simply more effusive agreement with its policies'. Politically, formal membership could not be denied. But Brussels largely avoided financial commitments, de facto denying membership to the country. The general trade arrangements, the protocols on bananas, rum, beef, sugar, coal and steel products, Stabex, Sysmin, structural adjustment support and EDF resources (except for refugee assistance) are not applicable. South Africa has the right to participate in the Joint Assembly. It is eligible for tenders for EDF 8, but not under preferential ACP conditions. A new two-class Lomé – to avoid the word 'apartheid' – was created, although the country would have needed resources to overcome the legacy of a racist regime that was also supported by EU members. These two cases mark the change towards differentiating ACP countries continued by the present treaty.

THE DISCUSSION ON THE 'POST-LOMÉ' WORLD

Issuing a Green Paper on the future of Lomé, the Commission (1996) encouraged discussion in an unprecedented way. Its thrust was to dismantle the remnants of the Lomé system, finally establishing the situation the EEC had wanted in the mid-1970s. The Commission seemed determined to reshape relations, getting rid of the last compromises of the past. The continuous dilution and undermining of Lomé was used against it. In the foreword of the Green Paper, the commissioner for development summarized: 'The post-colonial era is coming to an end.' Taken literally that means that colonialism is supposed to start again. Breaking up ACP countries into groups was the preferred option. Continuing one overall agreement was only possible 'with different arrangements and priorities' (ibid., p.viii). Referring to obligations of the WTO regime shaped by the EU and the USA, the end of reverse preferences and 'the move away from trade protection (bananas, sugar, rice etc.) to open competitive trade' (ibid., p.32a) was demanded. The official

Courier (no. 164, 1997, p.29), also prepared the ground by speaking of the necessity to discontinue preferences on sugar and rum, 'the most important benefit of the Lomé Convention' to Caribbean countries. Contending that these privileges postpone adjustment, Barbados's prime minister already accepted change.

The Commission (1996, p.39) thought the principle of partnership had 'come up against a number of difficulties'. It 'has proved hard to put initial intentions, based on the principle of equal partners, into practice'. Among the reasons that 'seriously undermined' partnership are 'growing conditionality' or the Community's tendency to decide for recipients 'like other donors'. By arguing so the Commission uses its own undermining of partnership to justify its abolition. Europeans seem to forget that they themselves forced rather cumbersome and absurdly complicated planning and execution procedures into Lomé III, so cumbersome that even the EU is not always adequately aware of procedural issues. Thus errors, shortcomings and inefficiencies have to be expected. They were documented by the post-Fiji study (Price Waterhouse, 1992), both within ACP countries and within the EU. Greenidge (1999, p.111) points out that commitment rates of 'funds under the discretionary control of EU institutions' lagged far behind those driven by unforeseen events or dialogue during the first two years of Lomé IV. Decisions taken by the EU alone were slower than others. According to Greenidge (ibid., p.112) 'unhelpful interpretation of the articles', and a Commission saddled with minutiae contributed to frustrating effective implementation. While partnership creates problems absent in a command-obey relationship, this cannot be blamed on SCs.

Lomé's implementation problems and their causes cannot be properly understood without discussing the Commission's own efficiency as a donor. The peer review of the EU 'again identified aid management as the weakest point of the Community's programmes' (OECD, 1999a, p.108). The Commission's preoccupation with procedures, controls and administration rather than results is quoted as a reason. At the enquiry into the effectiveness of EU aid in the House of Commons, the British secretary of state for international development stated that 'the Commission is the worst development agency in the world. The poor quality and reputation of its aid brings Europe into disrepute' (IDC, 2000, p.xxiii). Delays and inefficiencies in disbursement forced a local NGO director in Pakistan to take out a personal loan, using her residence as a collateral, to be able to pay staff salaries. The secretary of state testified that there were 'lots of trouble' in Britain. The government had to intervene to avoid NGOs and people committed by the Commission to do things going bankrupt. She qualified such slowness as 'unforgivable' and spoke of a 'disgracefully bad administration' (ibid., p.16). One committee member suggested 'some form of compensation' for consultants and NGOs if something goes wrong in some way through no fault of theirs. A lot of organizations ceased to apply for EU funds, he stated, because they could not afford the risk involved. Commissioner Nielson called the case of 'the fabulously well organised and successful agricultural research network' CGIAR 'very embarrassing'. The Commission was 'unable to pay because the dossier was moved from one Directorate-General to another and the patient did not survive that transfer' (ibid., p.41).

During the last five years the average delay in disbursement of committed funds has increased from 3 to 4·5 years. By the end of 1999, the backlog of outstanding commitments had reached over € 20 billion. For some programmes the backlog was equivalent to 8·5 years of 'payments' (ibid., xvi). According to Commissioner Nielson, the ACP countries fared better than the Mediterranean programme regarding the general overall time lag (ibid., p.37) even though some states have practically collapsed in Africa. None of the money for Nicaragua in the wake of hurricane Mitch was spent by 6 July 2000. Questioned in detail by an MP familiar with the situation on the Atlantic coast, the Commissioner had finally to admit that this delay was not caused by corruption or problems in Nicaragua: 'It is a Brussels problem' (ibid., p.43).

This should suffice to show that simply putting the blame on the ACP Group or on the concept of partnership allegedly making implementation difficult is unjustified. One also wonders why the Commission wants to expand its activities, given its present problems. Its greater efficiency seems hardly to be a credible reason.

Complaining that 'automatic triggering ... is making them less relevant', the Commission (1996, p.72) attacks export revenue compensation declared in 'need to be abolished or at least amended'. As compensation is always relevant if and when shortfalls occur, this is illogical, unless increasing leverage is the relevant goal. Arbitrarily granted compensating aid would, of course, increase leverage enormously. The Commission declared, 'support is appropriate only when certain conditions – primarily political – are met' (ibid., p.40). Economic goals, such as development, seem to have less importance now. One may also expect this support to arrive with considerable delay.

[P]ost Lomé, the Commission (ibid., p.72) wanted to concentrate grants on the poorest countries and those 'least favourably placed to attract foreign ... investment'. Because of the 'increased supply of investable resources seeking profitable placement in developing countries', the Commission favoured 'a new instrument to make it easier for ACP countries to gain access to capital markets' (ibid.). Since EDF resources were largely grants under Lomé IV, this meant the end of Lomé aid to quite a few countries. This is in line with budgetization (integrating Lomé resources into the EU budget) which was also proposed. Budgetization as such does not necessarily mean less money, but the overall impression, in particular statements on aid effectiveness, suggests that the ground was prepared for less aid (cf. Raffer, 1999a).

Although the main intentions of the Green Paper form its backbone, the Commission's (1998b) basis for negotiations was more accommodating, though still somewhat vague on details. It proposed to preserve parts of the original Lomé arrangements until 2005. Renewed US interest in sub-Saharan Africa (SSA) – the Commission (1998a, p.18) referred explicitly to the US African Growth and Opportunity Act (HR 1432 EH, 105th Congress, 2nd Session) – might explain this. So would the common bargaining manœuvre of demanding more than intended to allow for 'compromise'. Clearly, a system such as Lomé cannot be totally abolished at one stroke. It should be noted, though, that the EU and the US documents contain very similar ideas, increasing donor leverage (Raffer, 1999a).

The WTO is immensely useful for cleansing trade relations of disliked historical obligations. Lomé needs a WTO waiver, which the Commission (1996, p.34) qualified, while emphasizing the need to honour WTO obligations, as unlikely to be achieved for any new Convention. Reciprocal trade preferences will have to be part of any new treaty. The pre-1975 situation of reverse preferences will finally be restored.

To guarantee WTO compatibility of Free Trade Areas (FTAs) by including substantially all trade, ACP countries would have to liberalize substantially. Quite frankly, the Commission (1998a, p.18) declared its strong economic interest and its hope that European firms 'themselves under the pressure of globalization' would benefit greatly. SADC countries would have to liberalize to an extent, which even in the Commission's (ibid., p.13, English in the original) opinion is 'politically ... certainly not defendable and would even run counter to the principle of asymmetric liberalisation, as conceived by the Commission'. The Commission (ibid., p.28) does not consider liberalizing its system of agrarian protection. Very sensitive products, such as rice, will remain as protected as before, regardless of ACP export potential. Rightly, the Commission does not foresee noteworthy impacts of FTAs on its Common Agricultural Policy. While there logically is a larger potential for liberalization in ACP economies, the Europeans are apparently unwilling to establish a level playing field, reserving the right to protection where it suits them.

Trade preferences were attacked by pointing at the loss in market shares of ACP countries. While these may have happened because of, as well as in spite of, preferences, they are more limited than is often thought. Even the Commission (ibid., p.51) documents the fact that EU–ACP trade has fared better than total ACP trade: while their share in global trade was more than halved between 1976 and 1996 (from slightly more than 3 per cent to less than 1·5 per cent), the ACP share in European imports shrank by roughly 43 per cent. As ACP countries are strongly concentrated on raw materials whose prices deteriorated considerably after 1975, a substantial part of this loss is due to price effects. Zambia, for instance, saw a decline of GDP by 'a factor of 2·63' (Greenidge, 1999, p.107). Frisch (1996, p.69) clarifies the fact that only 7 per cent of all ACP exports enjoyed a 'significant preference margin – defined as "above 5%"' in 1989. Products of particular interest to the EU remain highly protected. The complex rules of origin appear 'more of a penalty than an advantage for trading with the EC' (Bossuyt *et al.*, 1993, p.40). Nevertheless, some countries, such as Mauritius, Kenya, Zimbabwe and Jamaica, were able to increase exports thanks to Lomé (Frisch, 1996, p.69). In the case of Mauritius, the Sugar Protocol was also extremely helpful.

Like all components of Lomé, trade has suffered from policy incoherence. An example would be subsidized EU exports undermining EU aid. The Maastricht Treaty as well as Article 15a inserted into Lomé IV demand coherence. The Green Paper repeatedly invokes its importance. Nevertheless, the Commission (1996, p.46) refuses expressly and steadfastly any commitment to coherent and consistent policies, even quoting the articles it intends to breach. In 2000, the Commission (2000a, p.13) reasserted this position. Under the heading 'Avoiding unintended incoherence' it stated:

> It is still possible that the EU makes the political choice to go ahead with a policy despite its potentially negative, indirect and unintended impact on developing countries. In these cases it is important that this decision is made in full knowledge of its indirect consequences.

Offsetting measures 'may' – but need not – be devised. Incoherence will be 'highlighted', which is hardly much help to SCs having suffered damages. While it is argued that the Maastricht Treaty must be respected to the digit behind the decimal point in the case of austerity policies politically justified by the euro, and WTO discipline is keenly cited to justify changes, the Commission has no intention of obeying the Maastricht Treaty when it comes to aid (cf. also Commission, 1996, p.ix). European taxpayers' money is going to be wasted for projects whose success will be destroyed by taxpayers' money, as in the past. This bodes ill for the efficiency of ODA and is a somewhat sobering illustration of European bureaucrats' perception of the Rule of Law.

Coherence would also demand dealing with the debt overhang. The Commission (ibid., p.35) stressed the importance of progress in debt management, speaking of the 'bankruptcy of many African states' (ibid., p.5), declaring: 'In the light of the enormity of the foreign debt problem facing many ACP countries, it is hard to turn a blind eye to international initiatives in this area' (ibid., p.57). But the Commission manages. The only trace of the debt problem in the Commission's proposals (1998b, p.30) is that EU money may be used to repay the EU itself in the case of internationally agreed debt relief measures accepted by all creditors. These sums would not be additional but part of Lomé's Programmable Resources Facility, thus reducing resources available for real aid to development. It must be recalled that total debt forgiveness under all schemes and programmes 'never exceeded 2 per cent of total debt stock in any year since ... 1982' (Greenidge, 1999, p.115). Except for 1·93 per cent in 1989 and 0·79 per cent in 1990, it was usually well under 0·5 during 1985–92. Thus debt pressure goes on choking development in ACP countries. The enlarged policy dialogue supposed to cover all common and regional interests, as well as 'the great problems of society, especially drugs and organized crime', does not include debts. Obviously the Commission (1998b, p.10) does not see the debt burden in this category. Migration, by contrast, was expressly cited as part of an extended policy dialogue.

The EU wanted to include budget resources 'wherever possible, i.e. where they are programmable on a year-by-year basis' (ibid., p.32). Aid tranches should depend on a 'global evaluation' instead of specific conditions, whose compliance could be checked more easily (ibid., p.33). The political dialogue should become 'as flexible as possible ... It must be possible to conduct dialogue at the level and the moment most relevant' (ibid., p.10). The 'merit' of the recipient is to become the main touchstone of further resources. It remains undefined and one may expect the EU to define it in concrete cases. More non-project aid and the power to define who 'deserves' money allow the Commission largely unrestricted power unhampered by quantitative factors. Dependence on short-term evaluations and vague criteria makes long-term planning problematic, making recipients totally dependent. The Commission (ibid., p.34) strictly refused to bind its own internal procedures by treaty, which does not alleviate such fears.

Things like environmental and social standards, which were largely kept out of the WTO's Final Act, were proposed as part of a new treaty (ibid., p.21). Further reciprocal liberalization in services is demanded (ibid., p.27), because of differences in the competitiveness of service industries, with foreseeable results. The EU even prepared the field for making ACP countries accept unspecified future multilateral treaties: the now shelved Multilateral Agreement on Investment, not negotiated by ACP countries, would have fitted that description.

STABEX: THE END OF LOMÉ'S BEST KNOWN INNOVATION

Stabex was the unique feature of Lomé. A remnant of the period of stronger political clout of the ACP side and in a way of the demands for a NIEO, it was a privileged target for attacks. Its slow dismantling is characteristic of the evolution of the treaties. Therefore we continue to give it more space than other instruments which differ gradually (if at all) from usual aid practice, even though that may expose us again to criticism of concentrating on it, although it only accounted for some 12 per cent of total resources (McQueen, 1997, p.1639), a fact to which we had drawn attention (Raffer & Singer, 1996, p.98). The heavy attacks that such a comparatively small amount triggered are all the more remarkable.

Stabex was criticized from left and right (Raffer & Singer, 1996). To champions of 'free markets' it was the first sign of dawning global interventionism, its high concessionality a dangerous deviation from market mechanisms. Criticism from the left attacked its very market conformity. Calculating losses by comparison with gliding averages of export incomes during the years before losses occurred reduces transfers progressively when the trend of export revenues is falling. Stabex was introduced to stabilize revenues but not to guarantee certain income levels forever. Existing trends should be smoothed, but – unlike the EEC's agricultural policy – not eliminated. It also moved ACP countries away from price stabilization schemes. While Stabex was still sufficiently funded under Lomé I, insufficient resources and the necessity to reduce compensation claims as much as possible have weakened Stabex further. Consultations on reductions are often thought to have been merely of a token nature. While money was piling up which the Commission was unable to spend, Stabex remained under-funded. Redirecting money towards Stabex would have been possible. Recently EDF money was reallocated for HIPC-II, because, as Commissioner Nielson explained, the G7 did not provide sufficient finance for their own brainchild (IDC, 2000, p.38). Any new convention, of course, could have increased allocations or introduced more flexibility in the case of large shortfalls, as the availability of money was not the problem. One may assume that Stabex, unpopular with the Commission, was to be undone rather than improved.

Stabex was also criticized for its disincentive to industrialization as only (some) agrarian commodities plus iron ore were covered by this kind of income insurance. This, it was argued, would encourage undue specialization on unprocessed or semi-processed raw materials. This criticism is to some extent valid, even though export stabilization has to focus on actually exported commodities. But, as funds could be used without restriction, the statement that Stabex hinders diversification had to be qualified initially. Later on, raw material production was given preference contractually, a change which may be seen as in the interests of the commodity-importing EU. Article 186.2 of Lomé IV restricts diversification to 'appropriate productive sectors in principle agricultural, or for the processing of agricultural products'. In the case of tropical timber ('sawn wood' pursuant to Article 187) devoting transfers to the sector concerned reinforces environmentally harmful effects, which are already quite perceptible in the case of West African wood exporters. The EU may be accused of subsidizing the destruction of tropical forests. Reducing options of industrialization, these restrictions were a late vindication of those critics claiming that Stabex hindered diversification.

Stabex as well as Lomé were criticized for their small impact. The funds allotted to Lomé have been quite small in comparison with total ODA by EEC members. Stabex was also criticized as worse than the IMF's Compensatory Financing Facility. Even when the CFF was largely unconditional – before it fell in line with other IMF drawings – this was simply wrong. The CFF never did offer interest-free loans or grants, in sharp contrast to Stabex, which formed a valuable alternative to the IMF. Arguably, the loss of automaticity was less important than the introduction of strict control and restrictions of the use of funds. Having to justify the use of Stabex money outside the sectors for which compensation was paid discouraged diversification measures essential for economic development. After successfully insisting that Stabex had to be used for purposes related to 'structural adjustment', as enforced by the BWIs, this new orientation forced on ACP countries provided Brussels with an argument against a separate Stabex. Lomé IV/2 (Article 209.4) integrates it fully into structural adjustment and reform programmes. After forcing their 'partners' to accept divesting Stabex of its special function, the Europeans argued that it should be abolished because it has no special function.

Annex II of the new Convention contains provisions to finance short-term fluctuations in export earnings. Additional financial support may be mobilized from the programmable resources for the country's long-term development. Special allocations for Stabex and Sysmin are gone. The degree of dependence of an ACP state's economy on exports of goods, and in particular from agricultural and mining products, shall now be 'a criterion for determining allocation of long-term development' (Annex II, Art. 8). Resources are no longer restricted to lists of eligible products. But eligibility criteria are a 10 per cent loss of export earnings compared with the arithmetical average in the first three years of the first four years preceding the application year (2 per cent for LLDCs) and a 10 per cent worsening 'in the programmed public deficit programmed for the year in question or forecast for the following year' (ibid., Art. 9.1(b)). Lomé IV contained no such restriction, but a reduction of 4·5 per cent of reference averages. Entitlement is limited to four successive years, a restriction likely to remain largely theoretical given the huge reductions in export earnings necessary for transfers. The minimum loss of 10 per cent is not unlikely to reduce transfer cases, which would in turn provide an argument for abolishing these provisions altogether. Article 11 of Annex II subjects them 'to review at the latest after two years of operation and subsequently at the request of either party'. Article 68.5 obliges the EU to 'provide support for market-based insurance schemes designed for ACP States seeking to protect themselves against the risk of fluctuations in export earnings'. One will have to see whether an insurance market for this risk will come into being. In any case this clause is a strong indication that such schemes are scheduled to be abolished.

COTONOU

The new treaty – initially scheduled to be signed in Suva – was concluded for 20 years, with Financial Protocols for five-year periods pursuant to Article 95. Pursuant to para. 4 of Annex I (the Financial Protocol), 'The overall amount of the present Financial Protocol, supplemented by transferred balances from previous EDFs, will cover the period of 2000–2007', which does not look like a five-year period at first sight, but seems connected with Article 93.3. Pursuant to this article, Cotonou shall enter into force on the first day of the second month following the date of deposit of instruments of ratification of the member states, at least two-thirds of the ACP states, and of the instrument of approval by the Community. One may thus expect Cotonou to start not before 2002, if the Commission can deposit its approval by then. As some delay was also caused by the political situation in Fiji, one should recall that the ethnic frictions in this country are a colonial legacy. Indians were brought into Fiji as indentured labourers (a euphemism for temporary slaves) to work in sugar production. The present problems of Fiji show very clearly what strong and long-lasting effects colonialism has in the countries that suffered under it.

Remaining funds from previous EDFs are to be transferred to EDF 9 and used in accordance with the new conditions. The Financial Protocol demands an assessment of the realization of commitments and disbursements. This will serve as the basis to re-evaluate resources needed in the future. If the past record is any guidance, that should result in a nominal reduction of funds. Furthermore, the Commission can influence the outcome by dragging their feet – a case of moral hazard. It should also be noted that the slowness of the EU's aid administration has been criticized repeatedly, and led to a reform plan launched in May 2000 (Commission, 2000a, see also 2000b).

The new Financial Protocol amounts to euro15·2 billion (Lomé IV/2: euro14·625 billion). Assistance under EDF 9 is, according to Annex I, 'up to' euro13·5 billion over five or possibly seven years, an increase of 4·1 per cent in nominal terms, if the whole maximum amount should be available. Even with modest inflation this means a remarkable reduction in real terms. At the present weak exchange rate of the euro, this means noticeably less than the two pints of beer and the packet of chips per head in an average London pub used to illustrate the impact of Lomé IV/2. The meaning of 'up to' – an innovation in EU–ACP conventions – must be interpreted with the disbursement backlogs and the Commission's 'efficiency' in mind, which cannot be reassuring to ACP countries. This formulation would also allow shifts. Inter-Press Service reported on 17 May 2000 a proposed shift in EU resource flows. The EU commissioner for external relations told reporters that stabilizing the western Balkans, in particular Kosovo, was a priority, and that the Commission was proposing cuts in commitments in most other external actions to finance this. For reconstruction of the Balkans, euro5·5 billion were immediately promised, even before concrete projects were assessed. According to the commissioner, 'we had to raid other parts of the budget' (IDC, 2000, p.25). The British secretary of state for international development saw it as 'raiding money that would otherwise be used for development of the poorest' (ibid., p.5). Such reallocations will be easier under Cotonou.

Euro2·2 billion are allocated to the Investment Facility, which the Commission had proposed (Raffer, 1999a). Loans under this facility – a term strongly recalling the IMF – will be administered by the EIB, like euro1·7 billion of loans from its own resources. This brings the share of grants down from 92·29 per cent (EDF 8) to 83·7, more than doubling the share of loans. Euro10 billion, the envelope for long-term development, are grants. A special allocation for regional cooperation and integration (euro1·3 billion) underlines the shift away from raw material policy, for which no special allocations exist any longer. Regional integration shall be 'encouraged and supported' to 'foster the integration of the ACP countries into the world economy in terms of trade and private investment' pursuant to Article 1.

As in the DAC, the catchword 'partnership' is used frequently by the Convention, and ranked before gender issues and sustainability. The EU was apparently able to overcome its reservations against partnership mentioned above and to overcome the number of difficulties it poses. It is a biased partnership, as real decision power rests with Brussels, which it always has done under Lomé. As before, the Commission 'shall be responsible for taking financing decisions on projects and programmes' (Art.57.5). Since the treaty fixes the total amount of money available, it could have been used in a pioneering way to test self-monitoring, which was successfully done by European recipients under the Marshall Plan, in the case of SCs. Pointing at the economic success of Marshall aid, Raffer & Singer (1996, pp.197f) proposed this as a model for aid in general, which, however, would reduce donor power. Raffer (1998c, 1999a) specifically recommended simplifying Lomé procedures by self-monitoring.

Dealing with post-emergency action, Article 73 demands that the transition from the emergency phase to the development phase must be eased, that the affected population should be reintegrated, and that the causes of crises should be removed as far as possible. Having advocated a relief–development continuum (Raffer & Singer, 1996, pp.195ff) we are happy to see that the EU is stipulating the connection of emergency action with long-term development and crisis prevention.

Trade provisions are strongly shaped by WTO agenda. Economic and trade cooperation shall be implemented in full conformity with WTO provisions (Art.34.4). Liberalization, privatization and support for the private sector have become as dominant as within the WTO. Chapters on trade in services and trade-related areas corroborate this impression.

TRIPS (trade related intellectual property rights) are fully integrated (Art. 46) including the protection of patents on plants. As in the respective WTO treaty, no appropriate protection of traditional knowledge or clauses against so-called 'bio-piracy' are stipulated. The clause from the TRIPS agreement that countries may decide not to allow patenting of plants and animals is not referred to. The tendency to go beyond the WTO, visible in the first proposals by the Commission (cf. Raffer, 1999a) is occasionally reflected in the Convention. Article 50 contains the agreement to enhance cooperation regarding trade and labour standards, an issue that SCs had struggled to keep out of the WTO agreements. The reason was an understandable fear that such clauses might be used as 'justification' for protectionist actions. Liberalization in the field of information and communication technology will benefit the EU more than the ACP side. Article 43.3 obliges ACP countries to participate fully and actively in any future international negotiation in this field, which restricts their options. A 'need' is also stipulated for ACP states to participate in multilateral trade negotiations. Compared with earlier formulations, that seemed to prepare the field for making ACP countries accept unspecified future multilateral treaties, such as the now shelved MAI, not negotiated by ACP countries, this is less binding.

Particular emphasis on private financing of infrastructure investments (Art.75(*f*)) is demanded. One might ask whether poor people, even small ACP firms, are really able to pay for these facilities if market fees are charged, as suggested by 'revenue-generating infrastructure'. This will certainly be less of a problem to European investors who are to be encouraged. The text uses the word 'diversification' only twice. But Article 21 speaks of the diversification of enterprises. Only Article 28 uses it in relation to ACP economies heavily concentrated on raw material exports. Diversification strategies are apparently not seen as important enough to merit more attention, although the Commission (1998a, p.53) found 'lack of supply capacity and competitiveness of most ACP countries which renders them unable to cope with external demand and competition'. Liberalization is easily granted under such conditions, and a one-way street. Free Trade Areas (FTAs) must therefore be expected to reflect mainly if not solely European interests: to soften the pressures of globalization on Europe, as the Commission formulated, giving European exporters an advantage over other industrialized countries. This does not suggest development considerations as the main reason. Frisch (1996, p.68) points out that FTAs would serve European export interests better.

To guarantee WTO compatibility of FTAs by including substantially all trade, ACP countries would have to liberalize substantially. As mentioned above, the Commission did not foresee noteworthy impacts of FTAs on its Common Agricultural Policy. A preparatory period until the end of 2007 is foreseen to negotiate trade agreements (called 'partnership agreements') on this new basis. As intended before Lomé I, the ACP Group will thus finally be split into regional groups. Several FTAs will allow Brussels to target restrictions more specifically on items the EU does not wish to liberalize, thus remaining more protectionist. Beef, for instance, can remain subject to restrictions only for country groups that actually do or could export it, but liberalized vis-à-vis countries unlikely to export any. Liberalization can thus be minimized by splitting. If all ACP countries formed one FTA with Brussels, that would not be possible.

The new WTO regime shaped by the EU and the USA will apparently serve to cleanse trade relations of disliked historical obligations. The EU did not try to protect the Lomé model during WTO negotiations. The present result may be welcome. With the WTO many specificities of Lomé, such as non-reciprocity, can be undone without unpleasant new negotiations. Emphasizing the need 'to achieve respect for the relevant WTO rules' while 'securing to the extent possible the benefits provided through the commodity protocols' the Commission (1996, p.34) noted that a waiver for Lomé would be unlikely. What 'securing to the extent possible' precisely means can be guessed from a passage on the challenges of Caribbean countries, which includes 'the move away from trade protection (bananas, sugar, rice etc.) to open, competitive trade' (ibid., p.32a). Meanwhile, a waiver is obviously seen as more likely, but commodity protocols are the other characteristic element of Lomé where it remains to be seen to what extent they can survive WTO conformity tests. Falling product prices – because of agrarian reforms within Europe, as the Commission (1998a) envisages, or for other reasons – would reduce export values, increasing the share of liberalized trade to WTO-compatible levels. 'A decrease of 30% in guaranteed prices for sugar or beef and veal alone' would increase 'total liberalized imports to 89%' in the case of the SADC countries (ibid., p.13). As 'such elements' would make an FTA 'perfectly feasible', one should not be surprised if the economic value of the protocols should become obsolete.

The best known case of WTO scrutiny is bananas. A panel ruled that Lomé's banana system 'violated the world trade rules in several ways' (*The Courier*, no. 164, 1997, p.9). Duty-free preferences covered by a WTO waiver were not condemned. The licensing system provided an incentive to companies to import higher-cost ACP fruit. Producers fear that maintaining their market shares on trade preferences alone would at least be very difficult. However, waivers are only granted for limited periods of time. It remains to be seen how long the main scope of the banana protocol, to secure present treatment, will be able to survive. Producers are now encouraged to diversify, although, as Greenidge (1999, p.113) points out, bananas have been produced by ACP states in pursuit of diversification.

The banana case is pathbreaking in another way as well. It was the first time that the USA had ever used Section 301 in connection with a product not exported by it. Chiquita exports bananas from Latin America. In a ten-page report on that case *Time* (7 February 2000, pp.36ff) described how donations and campaign contributions from people connected with the firm flowed generously. The magazine also connected these flows to actions of the US government, claiming that they had influenced them in this unprecedented case. It argued that the US trade representative's decision regarding bananas was 'sharply at odds with its handling of similar agricultural issues'. It compared negotiations with Japan to allow US companies an import share of 3 per cent for US rice with Chiquita's 20 per cent market share in Europe for non-US bananas that caused a trade war. Finally, it pointed out that US importers big enough to finance lobbying were not hurt by US sanctions – in contrast to smaller US firms.

Preferential access to the European market for sugar and rum at prices much higher than world levels is unlikely to survive WTO scrutiny. The really unique but costly arrangement of guaranteed prices connected to intra-EU prices and of guaranteed purchases of sugar (Article 5) can be abolished because goalposts were moved during the bargaining of WTO rules from outside the playing field of new EU–ACP negotiations, avoiding the political embarrassment of denouncing the protocol pursuant to Article 10. Reaffirming the importance of commodity protocols, Article 36.4 of the new treaty speaks of the necessity to review them 'in particular as regards their compatibility with WTO rules, with a view to safeguarding the benefits derived therefrom'. They are subsumed under the heading 'new trading arrangements'. This might indicate that they are to become part of trade treaties, losing their status as special protocols. As in the case of reciprocity a preparatory period can be expected, but it must be doubted whether the essence and thus the benefits will survive.

Migration is strongly emphasized by the Convention, another example of the shift towards accommodating European interests more explicitly. Article 13 makes this issue 'the subject of in-depth dialogue in the framework of the EU-ACP partnership'. ACP countries are obliged to readmit nationals deported from Europe without further formalities. The same obligation is stipulated for the EU as well, but one may assume that fewer Europeans will be expelled from ACP countries to EU members reluctant to allow them to return than vice versa. The EU, on the other hand, has great problems with immigrants from ACP countries, and not only from there. Dearden (1999) concludes that concerns about migration pressures have been an important reason for Europe's reorientation towards economies in transition. The EU's increased attention to the southern Mediterranean is also influenced by migration concerns. Although overindebtedness is a pressing problem for ACP countries, no initiatives are stipulated, but 'business as usual' is to continue in spite of its dismal record. Money may be used in support of structural adjustment; the level of indebtedness is one criterion for assessing resource allocation. The latter would be compatible with the present practice of bailing out IFIs with bilateral resources. So would the reallocation of EDF money for HIPC-II, which means using money that was already promised and committed to be used in another way. ACP countries had to agree – as it was legally their money – which they did in the middle of tough negotiations on the new arrangement. Some ACP countries spoke against it, pointing out that not all HIPCs are ACP members. For the EU it does not involve any additional expense and is a simple and agreeable way of getting rid of parts of the backlog. Under the heading 'Support for debt relief', Article 66.4 finally states that the EU intends to do nothing to remove the debt overhang:

> Given the seriousness of the international debt problem and its impact on economic growth, the parties declare their readiness to continue to exchange views, within the context of international discussions, on the general problem of debt, and without prejudice to specific discussions taking place in the relevant fora.

This inactivity regarding the debt overhang means that, as in the past, indebted countries will not have the resources to 'improve the coverage, quality of and access to basic social infrastructure and services and take account of local needs and specific demands of the most vulnerable and disadvantaged' (Art.25), let alone for 'improving health systems and nutrition, eliminating hunger and malnutrition'. The special attention demanded by this article to ensure adequate levels of public spending in the social sectors is likely to remain lip service if one considers the amounts of aid.

Defining essential elements, Article 9.2 includes 'an executive that is fully subject to the law'. Within the EU the executive branch makes 'laws' behind closed doors. The Commission has failed to present the annual reports pursuant to the 1991 Council Resolution under the heading of human rights over a number of years (IDC, 2000, p.41), a fact which one MP contrasted with the EU's promoting good governance and democratization in other countries. Irregularities led to the forced resignation of the Santer Commission, an event Africans in particular liked to discuss in connection with political conditionality. But its own performance does not keep the EU from demanding standards that are not met in Europe from ACP countries, and from reserving the contractual right to appropriate measures, including the suspension of the Convention if these standards are violated according to its understanding.

While a good mirror of changing North–South relations, EU–ACP relations may be said to have changed even more dramatically. While Lomé I was the closest SCs ever came to their demands for a NIEO, the present treaty continues to roll back what was once agreed in a period of anxiety, catching up with the neoliberal *zeitgeist*. The EU has now turned into a normal donor, although a donor with more than normal leverage vis-à-vis the ACP Group and joint institutions to keep up the appearance of partnership. Post-colonialism is indeed over. Considering the shift in EU interest towards stabilizing the Balkans, ACP countries might, on the other hand, be lucky that the Convention is already agreed, even though it remains to be seen how much money will actually be forthcoming. It seems that our conclusion in 1995 that there appeared to be little interest to 'preserve and reform the Lomé system' (Raffer & Singer, 1996, p.102) is vindicated by later evolutions, even if giving appropriate consideration to the EU's Green Paper (cf. McQueen, 1997, p.1639) published after our book.

8. Oil: temporarily a special case

Crude oil, frequently seen as a special commodity, deserves closer analysis. OPEC and the 'oil crises' of the 1970s are still often quoted as an example of Southern pricing power. As mentioned in Chapter 3, these price increases of oil spurred Southern demands for a NIEO as well as attempts to follow the OPEC example by coordinating action of commodity-exporting SCs. OPEC's price hikes scared the EU into granting unprecedented and unique concessions. Conservative colleagues used to quote OPEC as an example against *dependentistas*, claiming that the North, too, is dependent, and one would thus have to talk of interdependence rather than dependence. Emmanuel (1980) presented OPEC as an example how unequal exchange was overcome. The drastic fall in oil prices after 1980 changed perceptions, but 'petrodollars' are still occasionally singled out as the culprit for the debt crisis of SCs, for the Northern recession in the 1970s and for the end of the Keynesian Consensus. Crude theories about crude oil abound.

OIL PRICES UNTIL 1973–4

As mentioned in Chapter 1, the 1973–4 hike did little more than restore the real price of oil in terms of manufactures to what it would have been if it had not deteriorated since the 1950s. This would have been achieved smoothly and without any shock if Keynes's ideas had been implemented. Although OPEC had been established in 1960, its role was restricted to protesting and demanding higher prices for roughly a decade. It was founded after two unilateral oil price reductions by oil companies, amounting to nearly 14 per cent, of which producers had not even been informed beforehand. In spite of OPEC's existence, real oil prices were at their absolute minimum since the 1930s before the price hike of 1973. Between mid-1971 and mid-1973, the dollar lost roughly 25 per cent of its value relative to the four other SDR currencies (German mark, yen, French franc, British pound). This depreciation induced a significant increase in dollar prices of manufactures: by 30·4 per cent between 1971 and 1973 (Schulmeister, 1998, p.5). The income situation of oil exporters whose export product is priced in dollars deteriorated drastically. Schulmeister thus sees the reason for the shock as endogenous to a system of unstable exchange rates based on the double role of the dollar as both a domestic and an international currency. Adopting Keynes's ideas of a really international currency would have avoided this.

Falling real prices between the 1940s and the 1970s (see Figure 8.1) rendered other sources of energy unprofitable, increasing the market share of oil. In 1994 dollars, crude (Arabian Light) cost $12·61 in 1947, and $6·87 in 1970 (Williams, 1999, p.9). Not all oil products had the same evolution of prices. Heating oil, directly competing with coal, was particularly low-priced over the years (Raffer, 1987a, p.161). Coal mines were bought cheaply, often by oil companies diversifying into other energy sources, in spite of relative prices. After oil companies had brought substantial shares of coal mines under their control, the price of heating oil in relation to coal started to rise again. In 1974, the Federal Trade Commission published findings that the top four oil companies controlled 23·4 per cent of the US production of oil, gas, coal and uranium, the top eight 37·8 per cent, and the top 20 companies 57·2 per cent (Oppenheim, 1975, p.55).

The fall in real oil prices was possible because production concentrated on the Middle East, a region with low production costs, thus increasing the shares of OPEC in global production and exports. Technically, prices paid by oil companies were taxes. In 1950, when aid for Saudi Arabia could not pass Congress, tax provisions had been worked out to qualify oil prices paid as income taxes to provide money to potential buyers of US armaments. Actually paid prices were thus calculated from imputed, so-called 'posted prices'. In 1973, OPEC accounted for 58·4 per cent of world and 64·7 of Western production, or 86·6 per cent of crude exports (Raffer, 1987a, p.168). In 1973, OPEC supply was more important than ever before or after that year. Ten years later, OPEC's share in world production had fallen to some 30 per cent. It recovered to over 40 per cent in 1998, although OPEC had lost two members, Ecuador and Gabon.

In 1971, OPEC countries controlled only some 8 per cent of Western refinery capacity. This control of downstream activities is important, as crude cannot be sold to consumers without refining. This share has increased little over time, in spite of OPEC's 'fat years'. In 1982, it was 8·9 per cent. OPEC's share in tanker capacity was 5·7 per cent. At the end of 1998, OPEC's share in world refinery capacity was 10·5 per cent, a share that has to be seen in relation to a slight decrease of refining capacity in Eastern Europe. OPEC members controlled 4·2 per cent of the world's tanker fleet capacity in 1998 (OPEC, 1999). Distribution has always remained firmly in the hands of oil companies.

Oil is the one industry strongly characterized by repeatedly cooperating oligopolies. The 1928 agreement of Achnacarry was the first agreement ever to split up the global market. In 1927, oil companies created the 'Red Line Area', considered to be the region of the former Ottoman Empire, within

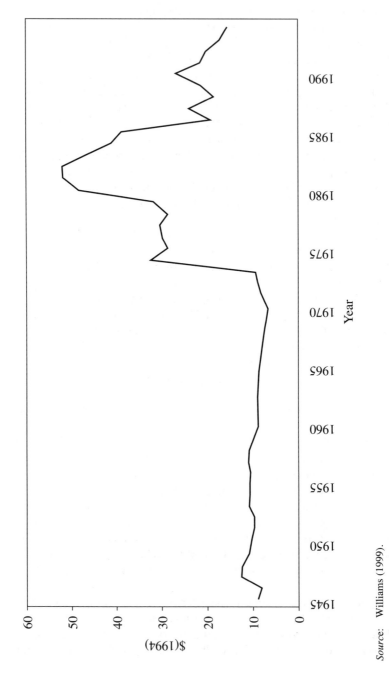

Source: Williams (1999).

Figure 8.1 Real oil prices, 1945–94 (1994 US$)

which they would not compete. The so-called 'Gulf-plus' pricing system cost the Marshall Plan and European governments an enormous amount of money. Under it any oil – even next to its production well – was sold at a price as though it had been produced at and transported from the Gulf of Mexico. Pressure by European countries and the Marshall Plan administration forced companies not to charge phantom transport costs, but crude was still priced as though it had been produced at the Gulf of Mexico, where production costs were perceptibly higher than in the Middle East. The Teheran–Tripoli agreements, which brought about the first relatively modest price increases in 1971, were negotiated between OPEC and the oil companies, which bargained collectively, backed by a waiver of US antitrust laws (Raffer, 1987a). With the Teheran agreement (signed on 14 February) the companies accepted a 55 per cent tax rate, an immediate increase in posted prices and further successive increases (EIA, 2000a). Companies claimed they had come to sign, not to fight. Tripoli was similar. In January 1972, some OPEC members reached an agreement with oil companies in Geneva to raise posted prices by 8·49 per cent to offset the loss in value of oil concessions due to the weak dollar (ibid.). Both sellers and buyers in the international oil market were thus highly oligopolized in 1973. The stage for price increases was set well before 1973, even though such a dramatic hike was unexpected.

THE OIL CRISES OF THE 1970s

The two substantial price hikes in 1973–4 and 1979–80, commonly referred to as 'the two oil crises' were brought about by a coincidence of interests. The interest of oil-producing countries in higher prices was obvious. The political climate was favourable around 1973, as SCs demanded a NIEO with 'remunerative' prices for their commodity exports. The Arab–Israeli war provided a political trigger.

The interest of oil companies, now owning large investments in other energy sources that suffered from low oil prices, is easy to see. Owing to relatively low price elasticities of final demand, oil companies could expect substantial profits if prices went up, not least because higher prices increase the values of stocks of oil (bought at cheaper prices in the past) quickly and substantially. Profits increased strongly in 1973 and 1974. Net profits of the so-called 'majors' nearly doubled in 1973, rising to some $11·6 billion in 1974. Considering the tax privileges enjoyed by oil transnationals, this figure cannot be compared with other companies (cf. Raffer, 1987a, p.162). Exxon and Royal Dutch/Shell became the world's biggest transnationals. Higher oil prices led to a boom in the nuclear industry, as well as to increases in uranium prices of 300 to 400 per cent, which also increased the amount of economically recoverable uranium. New sources of energy, such as the North Sea, became economically viable. Domestic producers in the USA, hard squeezed by low oil prices, benefited from higher crude prices.

Many authors (for examples, see Raffer, 1987a) point out that the US government, too, was interested in higher oil prices in 1973. Higher prices would help domestic production and make non-traditional reserves economically viable. Such reserves had already been assessed in 1964 and parts of them had been reserved, for example for the Navy (Galbraith, 1979, p.6). Price increases could be expected to help 'Project Independence'. This was a plan of the Nixon administration to make the US energy-independent, officially unveiled on 11 February 1974 (EIA, 2000a). Higher prices would also curb the growth of US oil imports.

According to Oppenheim (1975) the US government wanted to use OPEC as a tool for pushing up prices to change the price relation between oil produced within the USA and cheaper oil available from main exporters. Higher oil prices would give the USA competitive advantages vis-à-vis Europe and Japan, regions heavily dependent on oil imports. One might call price increases a possible remedy to the situation where the rest of the world had access to cheaper energy, while the USA protected domestic energy sources at high cost. In 1959, President Eisenhower had limited imports of crude and oil products east of the Rocky Mountains under the 'Mandatory Oil Program' as a protectionist measure. This programme was ended in 1973. The idea of increasing prices of oil from foreign wells was the core of an internal document of the US administration already published in the USA by the *National Journal* on 7 July 1973, and reprinted by *Le Monde Diplomatique* in November 1974.

Odell (1983, p.219) speaks of a 'deliberately initiated diplomatic effort' and of the USA having 'its representatives talk incessantly to the oil-producing countries about their low oil prices and ... showing them the favourable impact of much higher prices'. At the Eighth Petroleum Congress of the League of Arab States a State Department official even suggested a concrete higher price (Oppenheim, 1975, pp.31f). Also, the USA made it clear that no force would be used, even in the case of an oil embargo (Raffer, 1987a, p.161). By contrast, President Ford threatened to stop exports of wheat in a speech at the UN General Assembly in 1974 should SCs further try to copy OPEC's example (NACLA, 1976, pp.47f).

The North reacted to higher oil prices with inflation. Import prices of OPEC countries increased disproportionately. Inflation had particularly adverse effects on non-oil-exporting SCs for which higher import prices were not attenuated by higher oil revenues. Suffering from the depreciation of the dollar, OPEC exporters saw a steady decline in real oil prices and balance of payments surpluses. In June 1978, some OPEC countries therefore attempted to fix OPEC prices in a stabler currency, a move blocked by Iran and Saudi Arabia defending the dollar (EIA, 2000a). Oil companies benefited considerably from the weak dollar, increasing their profits hugely. The first quarter of 1979 saw increases of 81 per cent for Mobil and Texaco, 61 per cent for Gulf, and 37 per cent for Exxon. The champion was probably the relatively small Ashland Oil, with 517 per cent. This development must have influenced OPEC's decision to increase prices substantially again.

In September 1979, real oil prices were not higher than in 1974. Although real prices differ according to the deflator used, it is agreed that this second shock could only preserve the real price of 1974 (World Bank, 1979, p.11; Raffer, 1987a, p.165). The nominal increase of 1979 was thus just correcting for inflation. As in 1973-4, there were no shortages of oil. During the last quarter of 1979 up to 2 million barrels per day above daily consumption were produced. Experts considered price reductions by the spring of 1980 as very likely. In 1973, too, production had been increased over the last months of the year (Schulmeister, 1998; Raffer, 1987a). As in 1973, political turmoil, this time the coming to power of the ayatollahs in Iran and the Iraq-Iran war, provided the trigger.

The second 'crisis' again produced high profits for oil companies. Shell netted nearly $6·5 billion in 1979 and, like Exxon, more than $5 billion in 1980. Coal exports increased so drastically that port capacities limited further growth. The Carter administration, though, was not interested in another price increase. President Carter openly attacked the oil companies. Petrol happened to become unavailable to consumers in the USA at the very moment that Carter's attacks started, even though stocks were full and it was sometimes difficult to find storage space. Finally, OPEC and the oil companies prevailed. Oil prices rose substantially again.

To understand the events of 1979, it is useful to look at global consumption figures. World consumption of oil fell in 1974 and 1975, but recovered quickly. In 1976, it again surpassed the quantity of 1973, continuing to climb until 1979. The first crisis had not led to a long-lasting reduction of demand, which had picked up again after a short hiatus. One might thus have expected no drastic and prolonged fall of demand in the 1980s. This fall, however, happened. It may partly have been the result of lagged reactions to 1973-4. Between the peak of 1979 and 1983, global consumption fell by roughly 10 per cent. The reduction in market economies was significantly more pronounced as communist countries increased consumption slightly. In contrast to 1973-4 consumer reactions, higher than expected conservation effects, and global recession, had reduced demand. The 1979 peak of world consumption of refined products was not surpassed again until 1992, and then only by a very slight margin (OPEC, 1999, p.23). Seen from a long-term interest in preserving a market for oil, the second oil crisis seems to have gone too far.

THE REVERSE OIL CRISIS AND RECENT DEVELOPMENTS

From 1981 onwards, nominal and real oil prices dropped (OPEC, 1999, p.122). From 1985 to 1986, both roughly halved. In the 1990s, they fell until 1998, when the real price of oil (adjusted for inflation in Geneva I countries – the countries whose currencies were the basis of the agreement of January 1972 – and the USA) was \$3·13, slightly more than the \$3·05 in 1973 before the famous price increase. UNCTAD (1999, p.34) compares the 1974 price (\$10·4) with the average of the OPEC basket in 1998, 'an estimated \$4·0 a barrel' in 1974 prices, or one-fifth of the price of 1980. The lesson of the events of the 1970s is that 'commodity power without control of financial institutions, and not backed up by technological power, is empty and temporary' (Singer, 1989).

In the 1980s, the same instruments were used as in the case of other commodity exporters. OPEC's shares in global production and exports decreased substantially. OPEC exports fell from 28.6 million barrels per day in 1979 (67 per cent of world exports) to 12·9 million in 1985 (42·4 per cent). Its share in world production fell below 29 per cent in 1985 (OPEC, 1999, p.15). OPEC oil was substituted by oil from other sources. Britain, Norway and also Mexico became large producers of oil. The high concentration on the Middle East of the early 1970s vanished. During 1982 and 1983, stock operations undermined OPEC's attempts to stabilize crude prices through quotas. Technical progress spurred by efforts to save energy had further depressing effects on demand. The oil intensity of output in the North has been reduced markedly since 1973–4, by about 40 per cent according to the WTO (2000c, p.9). As in the cases of the Southern commodity exporters trying to overcome unequal exchange by substantial and persistent price increases, the mechanisms of substitution described by Raffer (1987a) brought oil prices down as well during the 1980s.

When OPEC could not stop the gradual erosion of its market share it abandoned its policy of restricting supply, which led to the price collapse of 1986. This policy was mainly based on Saudi Arabia's willingness to be a 'swing producer', the country reducing its production substantially. Between 1980 and 1985, Saudi production declined by more than two-thirds. It fell so low that associated gas production could no longer meet the kingdom's internal needs (IPE, 1999, p.214). Maintaining their idle capacities in a state of readiness caused considerable costs. In August 1985, Saudi Arabia linked prices to the spot market, and raised output to 5 million barrels per day in early 1986. The emerging new pricing system linked transaction prices closely to prices established in organized trading markets. This change highlighted OPEC's new situation. In the 1970s, Saudi Arabian Light served as the so-called 'marker crude', the basis on which all oil prices were calculated. At the beginning of the 1980s, spot prices started to dominate official OPEC prices. Nowadays non-OPEC crudes, such as Brent (UK) or West Texas Intermediate (as traded at the New York Mercantile Exchange), are usually quoted as *the* oil price.

UNCTAD (1999, p.35) describes the present situation:

> a new pricing system dominated by future markets has emerged. Under this system, traders set up key futures prices based mainly on expectations of market conditions. Transaction prices have become closely linked to prices established in the organized trading markets. The large influence and the functioning of futures trading have resulted in more transparency in the petroleum market, enabling not only consumers but also speculators to react to shifts in supply or demand more rapidly.

The former direct link between changes in supply and prices does not exist any longer. Heavily dependent on oil exports, OPEC members experienced a shock in 1986 when their revenues plummeted, which is sometimes referred to as the 'third oil shock' or the 'reverse oil crisis'. As both volumes and unit prices declined, the effects were particularly pronounced. As in the case of all countries heavily dependent on one or two commodities, the effects of changes in income terms of trade were much higher than the effect of the first oil crisis on OECD economies, which was on average some 2·5 per cent of national income. Nevertheless, the first oil crisis – small in comparison to shocks commodity exporting SCs are often exposed to – is still referred to as the cause of years of economic problems in the North. UNCTAD (ibid., p.39) estimated that the 1998 drop in oil prices caused an export revenue shortfall of 6·4 per cent for all OPEC countries (excluding Iraq). The heavily indebted member countries Nigeria (12·2 per cent) and Venezuela (8 per cent) were significantly worse off.

Declining revenues in the 1980s had negative effects on output, budgets and the balance of payments in OPEC economies. Because of the deteriorating economic situation, the quantity of non-performing loans increased. The whole banking sector in the Gulf states looked at times on the verge of collapse during the period 1982–8 (Stevens, 1993). Countries with small populations and large exports felt the squeeze less. Gulf states, which had accumulated foreign assets, could use these to fill gaps at first. Kuwait in particular received substantial income from foreign investments. Countries with less favourable population/oil ratios which had borrowed heavily to finance diversifying industrialization were worse off. OPEC members such as Venezuela, Nigeria, Algeria or Ecuador were heavily indebted. Mexico, though not an OPEC member, was also heavily dependent on oil. Like some OPEC competitors in severe need of money, it was said to undercut OPEC prices to gain urgently needed foreign exchange. Some OPEC countries, too, were said to sell more than agreed. North Sea oil production expanded.

After the price collapse of 1986, the situation changed. World oil demand picked up again, particularly in the South. 'During 1986–92 there was a steady decline in non-OPEC oil production. A remarkable expansion by North Sea producers and in a number of non-OPEC developing countries was more than offset by a progressive decline elsewhere, particularly in the United States and CIS' (UNCTAD, 1999, p.37). World demand again became increasingly dependent on OPEC and the Middle East, also owing to the latter's favourable production costs, even though rapid technical advances reduced exploration and production costs substantially. In a way, the situation started to resemble that before 1973: increased concentration on OPEC, low prices, an interest of domestic US producers in higher prices, and increasing demand. Last but not least, oil companies became stronger, by consolidating, forming alliances and merging, the 'mega-mergers' of Exxon–Mobil and British Petrol–Amoco being just the two best known examples. After the wave of nationalizations, OPEC countries are again opening their doors to them, creating new investment channels 'that should result in lower growth in non-OPEC production in the longer run' (IPE, 1999, p.218). UNCTAD (1999, p.36) sees reduced revenues as a reason, because necessary investment 'to expand or even maintain oil production, let alone to explore and develop new oil fields' became difficult to finance. Saudi Arabia and Kuwait, two capital-strong economies, held out longest against this new trend.

Low demand in crisis-ridden Asia – South Korea's refineries had difficulties buying crude and cut operations in January 1998 (EIA, 2000a) – an unusually warm winter in the northern hemisphere and excess supply led to a large build-up of stocks and depressed prices in 1998. UNCTAD (1999, p.38) estimates that the one-third drop in 1998 resulted in 'a transfer of real income of over $80 billion from oil exporters to oil importers'. OPEC's revenues plummeted by $54 billion to just over $100 billion in 1998, 'the lowest level in real terms since 1973'. Industrial countries gained about $60 billion through lower oil prices, a gain which exceeded their ODA, as UNCTAD points out. Export growth in the Middle East of more than 20 per cent in 1999 'did not fully offset a corresponding decline in 1998' (WTO, 2000c, p.9). This recent collapse apparently triggered cooperation between OPEC and other oil exporters.

On 30 March 1998, agreement was reached between OPEC and key non-OPEC exporters (EIA, 2000a; UNCTAD, 1999, p.34) to cut production. As Norway also pledged to reduce production by 3 per cent, one may speak of a coalition across the North–South divide. But prices continued to fall. Another round of production cuts was agreed in Vienna on 24 June 1998. Mexico and Oman promised to go along. Russia joined to cut world production by some 3·1 million barrels per day.

As prices stayed low, another output reduction was agreed on in March 1999. Prices recovered. On 15 April, the US Department of Energy started to take oil deliveries to add 28 million barrels to the government's strategic petroleum reserves (SPR). On 22 September 1999, OPEC decided to maintain current production cuts until March 2000, although crude prices had doubled since early 1999 (EIA, 2000a). In January 2000, heating oil prices in the USA had risen so high that Senator Schumer demanded oil sales from the SPR, a demand supported some four weeks later by the American Trucking Association (EIA, 2000b). The US Secretary of Energy started to visit oil exporters. In real terms, oil prices in mid-2000 were slightly less than half the 'historical highs seen in 1981', as the director of the EIA testified before the US Senate on 13 July 2000 (Cook, 2000). But 'for many, the pace of these increases may be as disruptive as the higher absolute levels'. This deserves quoting as not many in the North believe in disruptive effects of commodity price volatility in the case of Southern exporters.

On 28 March, OPEC ministers agreed to increase production. Several major non-OPEC producers, including Mexico and Norway, followed suit. Prices fell, and the EIA expected a gradual decline due to low world demand, non-OPEC production growth, growing leakage by OPEC members and growth in Iraqi production. On 21 June 2000, OPEC ministers agreed to a further increase in production quotas. Eight days later, Norway announced it would rescind its production cut. As Norway's cuts were subtracted from planned, not actual, production, the effects of this move were considered unclear by the EIA (2000b).

In spite of further increases of production, prices have not fallen. As prices are now determined on exchanges speculators may well be able to raise prices further while output expands, thus reducing the pricing power of producers, as OPEC (2000a) pointed out. After the summer OPEC (2000b) became more outspoken. After three agreements by OPEC members to raise output in 2000 and a total increase of 'no less than 3·3 mb/d [million barrels per day], bringing supply to the market well in excess of anticipated oil demands', crude prices had 'fallen noticeably over recent days'. According to OPEC, the real reasons for market volatility were therefore refining bottlenecks, 'speculation in the futures markets, manipulation of the Brent market due to the dwindling volumes of this crude', and widening differentials between certain types of crudes. These are all elements 'about which OPEC can do little or nothing at all' (ibid.). Naturally, the approaching winter is one reason fuelling speculation. Should it be very cold, this would strongly affect demand for heating oil.

As in 1973–4, recent price hikes had a fall-out for US domestic producers. On 16 May 2000, Senate majority leader Trent Lott and other Republicans introduced legislation to boost domestic crude production. Among other measures, the bill foresees tax credits of up to $3 per barrel for production from marginal wells during periods of low oil prices and the opening of the coastal portion of the Arctic National Wildlife Refuge to oil exploration (EIA, 2000b). An EIA study released a week later put the quantity of recoverable oil at 5·7 to 16 billion barrels (ibid.)

On 12 July, China ended its ban on foreign ownership of natural gas infrastructure, allowing foreign investors a majority stake in the planned Xinjiang–Shanghai natural gas pipeline project (ibid.).

PRODUCER RECEIPTS AND CONSUMER PRICES

As in the case of all commodities, prices received by producing countries are only a fraction of the prices of final products bought by consumers. Oil products in particular are heavily taxed by OECD governments, especially in Europe. In 1998, EU member governments collected over $250 billion in oil taxes (UNCTAD, 1999, p.38). This compares with world exports of oil of $192 billion. In three EU countries alone (France, Germany and Italy), 'the tax revenue exceeded the value of oil exports from OPEC' (ibid.). When oil prices rise, taxes levied as percentages (such as VAT) rise automatically with them. In contrast to the price of crude, this automaticity has not received much attention in the past. The idea of reducing petrol consumption by special energy taxation within OECD countries did not raise concerns similar to those about oil price hikes, although the two would serve the same purpose. But in 2000, reactions from the public differed dramatically from this attitude. On 22 February 2000, Senator Ben Nighthorse Campell proposed to remove the federal excise tax on diesel for one year. Germany's opposition suggested that a new and relatively low additional tax on petrol for ecological reasons should be scrapped. Protests and blockades by lorry drivers and farmers have attacked high tax revenues of Northern governments for the first time, for instance in France and the UK. Several governments have reduced their takes, often by refunding money to groups such as transport industry or farmers, or by granting special assistance for heating to poor people.

Table 8.1 shows the split between producers, companies, and governments. As this Table illustrates, the whole debate on oil prices has, until very recently, focused on a relatively small layer of the total price cake. Except in the USA, a country exercising particular restraint in taxing petrol, crude prices are less than 18 per cent. Even in the USA they were the smallest share in 1998. But this was the result of the fall in oil prices during 1998. Due to the small differences between the three components crude oil commanded the largest shares during 1994–7. As prices are cif, the real producer share (fob producing

Table 8.1   The composite barrel and its components (US$ and percentages in 1998)

	USA		EU		Japan		OECD*		UK	
	$	%	$	%	$	%	$	%	$	%
Comp. b.	39·9	100	94·5	100	80·8	100	72·7	100	131·7	100
Crude cif	12·0	30·08	12·4	13·12	13·7	16·96	12·5	17·19	12·6	9·57
Tax	13·5	33·83	64·2	67·94	32·6	40·35	35·4	48·69	89·6	68·03
Ind. margin	14·4	36·09	18·0	19·05	34·5	42·70	24·8	34·11	29·4	22·32

Note: * OECD countries excluding Australia, New Zealand, Turkey and Iceland.

Source: OPEC (1999, p.125).

country) is even smaller. Except for Canada and Japan, a country far away from any wells, cif prices differ very little. Industry margins were quite high in Japan and the UK, more than twice the $14·4 of US industry. But price differences are mainly explained by taxation.

To put the effects of OPEC price hikes into perspective, one should note that doubling the OECD's average cif price in 1998 would result in a price increase of the composite barrel of less than 17·19 per cent, as one may assume that insurance and freight costs will not double as well. If cif prices trebled, the final price would increase by less than 34·39 per cent. The impact of such price increases could be absorbed by the average EU country by reducing its taxes, compensating any inflationary effect. It could be reduced if consumer governments would keep those taxes constant in absolute terms that are levied as percentages of the consumer price, growing automatically with price increases. But, while commodity exporters are blamed for getting higher revenues, Northern finance ministers point out that this is not a viable alternative as they need this additional money. In the 1980s, consumer governments absorbed some of the lower price by increasing their fiscal take in sales taxes or in setting utility prices (Stevens, 1993, p.88).

In 2000, OPEC started a perceptible information campaign on the split of the composite barrel for the first time. Rejecting blame for high consumer prices, OPEC (2000b) drew attention to 'exorbitant levels of taxation on petroleum products' in the North. It contrasted the average share of taxation in the EU of 68 per cent with the shares of oil exporters and refiners and marketers of about 16 per cent each in 2000. Having taken action to bring down crude prices, OPEC expected 'a reciprocal response from the governments of consuming nations to help alleviate the burden of high pump prices to their citizens'.

On its homepage, OPEC (2000c) explained 'Why you pay so much for gasoline and other oil products'. It drew attention to the fact that some ICs 'take the opportunity to increase taxes on gasoline' when crude prices fall, 'thus maintaining prices on the same level or even higher'. The UK is picked out to illustrate this point: 'UK prices for crude, which were $17·3/b rose to $21·1/b in 1996, slumped to just $12·6/b in 1998, before rising again in 1999 to $17·6/b.' The price for the composite barrel, though, rose constantly over the period from $109·1/b in 1995 to $127·1 in 1997, and further to $141·5/b in 1999. The explanation is simple: every year the UK government increased its taxation take on the refined barrel, from $64·6/b in 1995 to $80·1/b in 1997, and then even higher, to $96·1/b in 1999.

Expressed in euros, taxes per litre increased by 0·09 euro in Britain between 1999 and 2000, while the shares of OPEC and TNCs together increased by 0·08 euros (*Time*, 25 September 2000, p.35). The former Tory government had introduced a provision 'that raised fuel taxes 6% above inflation' (ibid.). At the moment it looks as if this so-called 'accelerator' is likely to be dropped by the government as a result of recent protests.

In the case of continental Europe, one may add that the steep fall of the artificial new euro currency vis-à-vis the dollar increased import prices perceptibly, a cause for which OPEC can hardly be blamed. Also some of these governments have used the period of low crude prices to reach the self-set Maastricht target by creaming off reductions in crude prices. By reducing the price elasticity of demand in consumer markets, this low share of crude is a disadvantage when prices fall. In spite of plummeting crude prices world oil demand remained stable in 1998, roughly the same as in 1997. Consumption was not stimulated, as UNCTAD (1999, pp.36f) noted, because

> with the exception of the United States, taxes on oil account for so much of the price to end-users that the latter scarcely benefit from any fall in international crude oil prices. In Western Europe for example, over 70 per cent of the end-user price is constituted by taxes ... Consequently, even a prolonged period of low oil prices is not likely to increase demand in the developed countries by more than 1–2 per cent a year.

While the expression 'prolonged period' is indeterminate, and one may expect increases in demand eventually, the short-run price elasticity is certainly very low. This is the case with all commodities. Prolonged troughs of coffee or copper prices do not increase final demand strongly, because producer shares, and thus their effects on consumer markets, are small. Price reductions are usually not passed on immediately, as this would mean selling stocks below the price at which they were bought. Intermediaries holding stocks have an interest in selling these before lowering their prices. Income terms of trade must be expected to decline like prices in the short run. A long and pronounced price decline, though, is likely to increase demand, not least from poorer countries.

Reactions by companies holding stocks will thus be asymmetric. While increasing prices quickly after commodity price increases means hefty additional profits from more cheaply bought stocks, 'windfall losses' due to a price decline are usually avoided. Oil companies are known to have argued that they have to sell their stocks before they can pass on new lower prices, a restraint not shown in the opposite case.

EFFECTS OF OIL PRICES ON SCs

While it is undeniable that increased oil bills were one important factor influencing the balance of payments of SCs, the usual practice of singling out oil prices as *the* explanation for imbalances and increasing debts needs to be put into perspective. The GATT (1980, pp.8f, emphasis added) compares the effects of the two 'oil crises' on all SCs with other factors:

> The overall trade deficit of the non-oil developing countries grew steadily from $15 billion in 1973 to $40 billion in 1975. *The largest part of this increase resulted from an increased deficit in manufactures, essentially in trade with industrial countries; the rise of the deficit in fuels, while substantial, was relatively less important.* Between 1974 and 1978, the overall deficit of non-oil developing countries levelled off, the further rise in the manufactures deficit being offset by a higher surplus on trade in non-fuel primary-products. In 1979, however, the overall trade deficit increased once again reflecting *a sharp rise in the deficit on trade in both manufactures (to $71 billion) and fuels (to $21 billion).*

Even excluding net exporting non-OPEC SCs (which GATT subsumes under 'non-oil developing countries') the combined deficit is estimated at 'nearly $35 billion' (ibid.), or less than half the deficit in manufactures alone. The impact of interest rate hikes in the 1980s is shown by the findings of the IMF's Padma Gotur (1983). Of the total increase of current account deficits of non-oil SCs ($66 billion for 1978–81), $18 billion were caused by oil trade, $24 billion by net interest payments and $21 billion were traced to terms of trade changes. In spite of the 'second oil crisis', the impact of interest rates was 1·33 times the impact of oil.

OPEC's net effect (increases in oil import bills minus inflows from OPEC) on net importing SCs has usually been exaggerated, as an estimate by Raffer (1992) for 1973–87 corroborates (see Table 8.2). Net importers (NIs) comprise all Southern net importers of oil except so-called 'refining centres', countries importing huge amounts of crude oil to export after refining. Three NICs (Brazil, Taiwan and South Korea) usually accounted for well over 40 per

Table 8.2 The effects of oil price changes on groups of SCs, ODA and total receipts from OPEC, 1973–87 (US$mn)

Group	1973	1974	1975	1976	1977	1978	1979	1980	1981	1982	1983	1984	1985	1986	1987
Direct Effects of Oil Prices															
NISs	748·8	8 596·7	9 211·2	11 397·9	13 350·6	14 994·2	23 508·8	41 716·3	45 082·6	37 345·7	37 711·0	32 516·2	30 250·0	19 171·7	16 618·2
NI—NICs[a]	452·2	4 912·6	5 225·1	6 247·6	7 482·6	8 410·0	13 025·2	22 989·1	24 947·5	19 614·4	22 190·4	19 166·3	18 846·9	12 896·2	8 384·2
LLDCs	63·8	350·7	333·8	590·1	753·5	792·2	982·6	1 804·5	2 093·3	2 438·0	2 071·0	1 914·6	2 170·4	1 302·6	738·6
Total Receipts (net) from OPEC[b]															
NIs	1 352·1	4 072·8	6 659·2	6 760·5	6 333·5	5 379·3	5 409·0	6 797·3	9 403·5	6 071·6	4 899·3	4 191·2	2 963·3	3 872·6	3 211·4
LLDCs	78·3	632·4	797·1	831·7	941·7	769·0	793·2	1 038·8	1 199·2	1 121·2	1 142·2	675·0	714·6	641·3	565·1
OPEC-ODA[b]															
NIs	1 208·2	3 131·9	5 106·3	4 955·3	5 173·5	4 212·8	5 190·5	6 382·7	7 916·5	4 922·6	4 603·1	3 800·0	3 104·2	4 018·9	3 031·8
LLDCs	78·3	632·4	797·1	831·7	881·8	607·7	691·4	951·5	968·7	1 171·0	1 106·7	669·6	684·2	667·7	565·1
Net Effect: Direct Price Effects minus Total Receipts															
NIs	-603·3	4 523·9	2 552·0	4 637·4	7 017·1	9 614·9	18 099·8	34 919·0	35 679·1	31 274·1	32 812·5	28 325·0	27 286·7	15 299·1	13 406·8
NI—NICs[a]	-899·9	839·8	-1 434·1	-512·9	1 149·1	3 030·7	7 616·2	16 191·8	15 544·0	13 542·8	17 291·9	14 975·1	15 883·6	9 023·6	5 172·8
LLDCs	-14·5	-281·7	-463·3	-241·6	-188·2	23·2	189·4	765·7	894·1	1 316·8	928·8	1 239·6	1 455·8	661·3	173·5
Net Effect: Direct Price Effect minus ODA															
NIs	-459·4	5 464·8	4 104·9	6 442·6	8 177·1	10 781·4	18 318·3	35 333·6	37 166·1	32 423·1	33 108·7	28 716·2	27 145·8	15 528·8	13 586·4
NC—NIC[a]	-756·0	1 780·7	118·8	1 292·3	2 309·1	4 197·2	7 834·7	16 006·4	17 031·0	14 700·8	17 588·1	15 366·3	15 742·7	8 877·3	5 352·4
LLDCs	-14·5	-281·7	-463·3	-241·6	-128·3	184·5	291·2	853·0	1 124·6	1 267·0	964·3	1 245·0	1 486·2	634·9	173·5

Notes:

[a] Net importing SCs minus Brazil, South Korea and Taiwan.

[b] As defined by the OECD; the sums in the table were obtained by adding the figures for 'OPEC' (after 1983, 'Arab Countries') and 'Arab Agencies' (initially 'OPEC Financed Agencies').

Source: Raffer (1992).

cent of the total impact of higher oil prices on NIs. The group NIs without these NICs (NI−NICs) shows the impact on other net importers. LLDCs is the group of Least Developed Countries, as defined by the UN. Economies of space prohibit detailed explanations of data problems, including problematic recording practices by the DAC. They are presented in Raffer (1992) and Raffer & Singer (1996, pp.127ff). But it should be noted that lower rather than higher OECD values for OPEC aid and other flows were consistently used, even when substantially increased figures for the same year exist in other OECD publications. Avoiding under-estimating the impact of crude prices, these figures have thus an 'anti-OPEC' bias. There is reason to suggest that flows from OPEC have been somewhat higher and net effects correspondingly lower than shown in Table 8.2. Net inflows of oil importers are shown by a minus sign and are made more visible by bold figures.

The absolute gross effect on LLDCs was surprisingly small, which does not exclude relatively heavy additional burdens on some LLDCs' balance of payments. OPEC aid was by no means distributed according to oil price effects, but determined by other criteria, such as ethnical proximity, political calculus and whether Islam was a country's official religion. The small group of half a dozen 'least developed Arab countries' received particularly large inflows. Available evidence suggests that balance of payments effects of Arab ODA, other flows, and remittances by migrant workers − which were substantial − were higher than the direct effects of increased oil prices for this group (Raffer, 1992). Effects varied strongly between countries. The conservative Arab Republic of Yemen was by far the largest recipient, also receiving generous ODA inflows. But as a group these countries experienced a net inflow of foreign exchange, thus actually gaining from oil price increases. On the other hand, Tanzania, a non-Arab, non-Muslim country with a socialist president, received very little, and was consequently hard hit by increased oil prices.

The two Yemens were traditional sources of foreign labour to oil-rich neighbours, in particular to Saudi Arabia. Estimates put the number of people working in neighbouring oil-producing countries during the boom years at up to 1·2 million for North Yemen, and half the domestic labour force for South Yemen. Yemenis worked mostly in Saudi Arabia. They were expelled when their country chose to support Iraq diplomatically during the Gulf war. Estimates put the number of Somalis employed abroad (mostly in other Arab countries) at 100 000. Furthermore, the movement of private unrequited transfers to the two Yemens, Somalia and the Sudan suggests a strong correlation with oil prices and the income of rich oil exporters (ibid.). Immigrant labour was attracted from far off SCs such as Pakistan, India and the Philippines. Once at the Gulf, these people were too often not treated in a humane way, but their remittances were important for their countries. These, as well as the procurement of construction and other contracts in oil-rich countries, 'helped to maintain growth' on 'a more solid basis than lending from commercial banks' (Singer, 1989, p.31). But they also turned out to be a temporary and precarious source to finance development.

Like OPEC-aid, this income was dependent on the continuance of large OPEC surpluses. Instead of laying new foundations for sustainable growth in the 1980s, the OPEC engine merely served to replace the failing engine of Northern economies and postpone the impact of this failure. When oil prices fell drastically, OPEC countries themselves faced a severe crisis, sometimes referred to as the third oil crisis. After 1973/4, aid from OPEC countries – Arab aid in particular – accounted for the bulk of South–South aid. During the second half of the 1970s, OPEC accounted for some 22 to 30 per cent of ODA from all donors according to the OECD (1983a, p.14). It is little known, though, that OPEC aid was already 1·18 per cent of OPEC's GSP in 1970, well before the first oil price hike (ibid.), when the corresponding DAC average was 0·34. In 1973 and 1974, OPEC aid rocketed to 2·25 and 2·53 per cent of GSP, respectively. For the Gulf states (Kuwait, Qatar, Saudi Arabia and UAE) 12·76 and 7·78 per cent were recorded by the OECD (1983a, p.21) for these years. Qatar (15·62 per cent of GSP in 1973, 15·59 in 1975), Saudi Arabia (14·80 in 1973) and the UAE (1973: 12·67; 1975: 11·69) even surpassed 10 per cent of GNP (ibid.), while the averages of OECD countries were 0·29 and 0·35 per cent, respectively. During the 1980s, the sharp fall in oil prices, the 'third oil shock', resulted in sharp cuts of financial flows from all OPEC members. Some, such as Nigeria, ceased to be donors. It is worth mentioning that aid from Nigeria and Venezuela consisted exclusively of grants in most years. The Gulf war and the destruction of Kuwait's economy reduced Arab aid flows further.

Like OECD aid, OPEC aid was concentrated according to political criteria. In the early 1970s, 90 per cent of net disbursements went to Egypt, Syria, Jordan, Gaza and the West Bank (ibid., p.31), a clear sign of the financial support for the fight against Israel. As a result of Egypt's peace talks with Israel, President Sadat's visit to Jerusalem in 1977, and after the signing of the Camp David Agreement in 1979, aid from Arab countries to Egypt plummeted drastically. Over many years, Bangladesh, a country joined with Arab OPEC members in a common faith, Islam, was the largest non-Arab recipient.

Finally, a few lines on the indirect effect of OPEC money via the Euromarket are necessary, as the Southern debt problem has so often been presented simply as the result of OPEC surpluses. Commercial banks drowning in liquidity, a popular Northern line of argument runs, simply could not help 'recycling' this surplus cash to SCs. According to data published by the Bank of England, $130 billion of the petrodollar surpluses accumulated between 1974 and the end of 1983 were channelled to private banks, and thus available for credits internationally (Reichmann, 1988, p.230). As SCs were not the only borrowers, one cannot argue that this money was exclusively lent to them, while others, for example Northern governments, did not borrow petrofunds. Direct loans from OPEC countries to other SCs amounted to US $55 billion during this period. Singer & Roy (1993) point out that the responsibility for Southern debts was widely shared. In addition to OPEC and commercial banks, some responsibility also attaches to the BWIs, two institutions which strongly encouraged and advised SCs to borrow, Northern and Southern governments.

Quantitative evidence apart, the recycling argument is theoretically wrong. If doubtful loans had not been urged upon SCs, excess supply of international money would have driven interest rates down towards an equilibrium allowing investments unprofitable under actual interest rates. The assumption that sovereign debtors can at most become illiquid, but not insolvent, and the knowledge that their claims would be protected against the market by Northern governments, on which commercial banks operated during the 1970s, disobeying the most elementary rules of banking, led to massive misallocations of resources, both directly in borrowing countries and indirectly by preventing otherwise possible investments elsewhere. The imperfections and interventions that kept the market mechanism from functioning properly cannot be blamed on OPEC.

9. The Asian tigers: what do they prove?

East Asia, in particular South Korea and Taiwan, has a curious history. In the 1950s, its economies were considered hopeless basket cases, particularly the two largest 'tiger' or 'dragon' countries of the 'first generation'. During the 1980s, the region became the 'Asian miracle', hailed as a model of successful development, and wrongly used as a vindication of neoliberal ideology. The crash of 1997 brought about a very abrupt change of mainstream opinion. Suddenly, the World Bank (1999a) asserted – in contrast to its 'Asian Miracle' study – that East Asia had not followed the Washington Consensus. The economic systems and the very same policies that had led to the 'economic miracle' were now described as deplorably inefficient and flawed, mostly by the same people who had marvelled at the Asian success story shortly before, claiming it to be the result of applying their policy advice. This new interpretation makes one wonder how and why success could be achieved in the past. One may wonder even more about the quick change of opinion happening virtually overnight. Ignoring one's own recent views actually appears to be bliss.

Our analysis of economic policies before the crash focuses on the first generation of tigers, in particular on the two main 'old tigers', Korea and Taiwan, because interventionist policies were most pronounced there. They were the most advanced in 1997. Also the discussion on the Asian success has mostly centred on them.

NON-ECONOMIC FACTORS: THE HELPFUL PANACEA

During the 1950s and 1960s, Latin America, not least because of its Westernized elites, was seen as the growth pole in the Third World, while virtually all economists considered East Asia hopeless. Scarcity of resources, high population growth and – quite important at that time – non-economic factors were cited to corroborate this view. This pessimism was forgotten later on, as Balassa (1988, p.S275) recalled:

> In offering an ex post rationalization for the success of (South) Korea, people also tend to forget the dire predictions made about this country less than a generation ago. Cut off from industry in the North, saddled with abject poverty, it was

considered a hopeless basket case in the writings of the time, including the World Bank reports.

Non-economic factors were widely used to explain the predicted development catastrophe. The 'Chinese factor', Buddhism, or Confucian tradition were routinely quoted as reasons for Japan's and South Korea's economic stagnation and a hindrance upon China's economic development.

In 1959, Taiwan was chosen as the country to which President Eisenhower would pledge particular support to increase its exports in his State of the Union address of 1960. The resident representative of the Agency for International Development (AID) opposed this vehemently, arguing it would be nonsense to assume '[T]hese Chinese' could ever 'go into manufacturing for export' (ibid.). The fact that Taiwan had already exported manufactures to Japan during colonial times did not affect this expert's opinion.

One has to concur fully with Balassa's (ibid., p.S274) vehement rejection of such social or ethnic factors: 'Those who have failed to understand, nay foresee, actual developments because of faulty or inadequate economic reasoning fall back on noneconomic explanations, just as our ancestors thought to find the causes of lightning and thunder in the supernatural.' On the other hand, these non-economic factors proved quite useful. Once the miracle had started, they were used to explain it too. Confucianism, seen as a development blockade earlier because of its fatalism and lack of proper interest in material advance, was now seen as the very reason for success. Confucian ethics – like Max Weber's protestant ethics – were now understood as the engine of growth thanks to virtues such as hard work, modest consumption and obedience to superiors. Since 1997, 'Asian values' again enjoy great popularity for explaining the crash brought about by cronyism, corruption and economically inadvisable policies. If present signs of quick recovery lead to sustained new development and growth, one may again hear a lot about Asian values explaining it.

A MIRACLE OF FREE MARKET POLICIES?

As long as they were success stories, orthodoxy quickly and resolutely presented these Asian countries as a vindication of its free market ideology, disproving dependency analysis or similar conclusions by Raúl Prebisch. Few economists went as far as Linder (1985, p.281) to speak of 'market economy superstars', or Lal (1984), who presented Korea – of 'all countries' as Palma (1998, p.793) comments – 'as an example of "virtual free trade"' to show the 'Poverty of "Development Economics"'. But most orthodox economists claimed or implied that economic success was due to the adoption of their textbook wisdom (cf. Krueger, 1997). The distinction between 'export orientation' and 'free trade' was usually blurred, deliberately or otherwise, thus implying that actual growth of exports equals free trade. The mercantilists had already proved this wrong.

Looking at the facts shows that all 'tigers' were successful precisely because they did not apply orthodox advice. Selectively, they picked those policies they considered most appropriate. Therefore the range of policies is very wide, from extremely protectionist South Korea to non-interventionist Hong Kong. Naturally, optimal policies of harbours and city states such as Hong Kong and Singapore must differ from the options of larger, 'normal' countries. This eclectic choice of policies is precisely what was recommended as 'selective dissociation' by *dependentistas* in lieu of blind faith in the world market.

Suffice it to recall that Hong Kong's 'positive nonintervention' (Krause, 1988) and state minimalism was a pragmatic, not an ideological, choice. The crown colony earnestly considered more intervention in the 1970s, but finally decided against that option and for continuing free trade policies (ibid., pp.S61f). Obviously, the harbour Singapore is quite open to foreign trade. Nevertheless, a World Bank study found selective protectionism there (Rhee *et al.*, 1984, p.6). Government influence has always been pervasive in this small economy. A relatively large share of state-owned firms proves that there appear to be no ideological barriers to the government entering any economic activity. In spite of its openness, Singapore 'was not about to rely on the invisible hand of the market' (Krause, 1988, p.S52).

Quite often the mere fact that impressive economic development took place in North East Asia was presented as a proof that the dependency school was wrong, although it has always differentiated between underdevelopment and dependency, and no author excluded the theoretical possibility of dependent development (see Chapter 3). The argument that the economic success of the 'tigers' as such proves dependency theory wrong is untenable. Taiwan and, especially, South Korea applied the ideas of Raúl Prebisch and of the dependency school (Raffer, 1996b). Governments intervened strongly, opportunities to export were used to the full, but they opened their own economies slowly and selectively to the world market. Both imports and foreign direct investment remained heavily restricted; domestic industries enjoyed heavy protection. Simultaneously, exports were massively subsidized and supported. The array of government incentives and interventions was particularly impressive in South Korea, as Rhee *et. al.* (1984) documented. This detailed World Bank study is not even mentioned in the 'miracle' study. As one of the former's authors, Bruce Ross-Larson, was also a member of the latter's research team, unawareness can hardly account for that omission. Apparently, strong evidence (cf. Fishlow *et al.*, 1994; Wade 1990; Raffer &

Singer, 1996, pp.114ff; Raffer, 1996b) is simply 'forgotten' whenever inconvenient.

Even though 'many of the discredited policies had long been in use in South Korea, Taiwan, and Singapore, and apparently to good effect' (Rodrik, 1996, p.17), the view developed soon among 'professional economists' that Asian success 'could be attributed to market-oriented policies and the reduced role of government intervention' (ibid., p.13). Ironically, neoliberal reforms in the 1980s were 'inspired at least in part by the East Asian experience' (ibid., p.11). Facts had to be ignored to be able to use the 'tigers' to justify neoliberal policies.

Export subsidies, as given to Korean firms, were strongly recommended by Raúl Prebisch (1984, 1959), who is also an important intellectual root of dependency thinking. Prebisch (1959) thought that selective protectionist barriers should equalize the disadvantages of infant industries in promising branches, allowing them to compete with established Northern producers. He warned (ibid., p.259) that 'protection itself does not increase productivity. On the contrary, if excessive, it tends to weaken the incentive to produce'. Noting that in 'some cases indiscriminate protection' had 'gone far beyond the optimum point, to the serious detriment of exports and world trade' (ibid., p.265) Prebisch advocated a 'cautious and selective policy of protection' not conflicting with 'the advisability of reducing and eventually eliminating protection' (ibid., p.260). Prebisch (1984, p.181, see also 1988, p.35) demanded selective export subsidies combined with continued protection of the domestic market. Advocating selective protection, he also warned of the 'obstacles that have to be overcome in practice' (Prebisch, 1959, p.257). Korea in particular followed his advice faithfully. There is reason to assume that specific political facts let Korea and Taiwan 'get away' with it. By demanding export targets, granting substantial benefits uniquely to firms fulfilling them, and even by introducing penalties for underperformers, the Korean government forced domestic firms to increase productivity in spite of a comfortably protected domestic market. The government even inspected the quality of export products (Rhee *et al.*, 1984, p.66). This strategy, as well as the government's strong intervention in picking industries, looks as if it were carbon-copied from Prebisch's recommendations.

Singer (1986, p.6) emphasizes the strong influence of Prebisch's ideas in Korea, pointing out that many Korean economists were very conscious of that heritage. In contrast to Latin America, which is usually associated with dependency and Prebisch, economic policies recommended by these approaches were rigorously followed through in Asia, while 'exaggerated' protection 'to shelter inefficiency' (Prebisch, 1959, p.257) was quite frequent in Latin America. Robert Wade's (1990) phrase 'governing the market' characterizes East Asian economic policy in a nutshell. Prebisch's advice (later repeated by *dependencia*) not to rely on the market but to intervene and to use existing possibilities selectively instead of opening one's economy was successfully heeded.

Even the waves of privatization differed strongly between Asia and Latin America before 1997. Between 1988 and 1992, privatization proceeds amounted to slightly more than $40 billion in Latin America and to $7·5 billion in East Asia (World Bank, 1994, p.105). The share of foreigners was 56 per cent and 2 per cent respectively: in East Asia, 98 per cent of assets remained under domestic control. The lack of strong domestic firms and the resulting strong dependence on Northern transnationals has always been standard criticism of Latin American policies by *dependentistas*.

Economic success bred self-reliant proposals, such as the idea of an Asian Monetary Fund to deal with crises in the region. Interestingly, Japan proposed a fund for refinancing short-term debt in the summer of 1997 (Wade, 1998a, p.1548), which met stiff US and IMF opposition. Although this was precisely what would have been needed to defuse the crisis, any form of regional funds would have reduced the IMF's clout and US influence with it. The Asian crisis put an end to such attempts. From the point of view of institutional self-interest, this must have been welcome to the IMF.

FACTORS CAUSING THE MIRACLE

Analysing the Asian miracle shows some distinct differences from other SCs. Focusing on the two 'first generation' tigers that are not city states, Taiwan and South Korea, shows these specific factors more clearly. These factors are:

Generous Aid Flows

As countries threatened by communists, both South Korea and Taiwan received massive aid inflows from the USA, just as North Korea did from the Soviet Union (cf. Chapter 5). From the end of the Korean War until the early 1960s, South Korea received aid amounting on average to 8 per cent of GDP, which financed around three-quarters of its imports of goods, more than half of all investment, plus, in some years, part of consumptive state expenditures (Serfas, 1987, p.204). This does not include military aid, data on which have not been disclosed until this day. During 1951-61, US aid amounted to roughly 6 per cent of Taiwan's GNP per year, covering some 34 per cent of imports, 40 per cent of capital formation, 37 per cent of infrastructure and 26 per cent of human capital development (Bräutigam, 1994). These percentages are comparable to aid receipts of SSA countries today; some countries even get more. Aid to Asia was, however, more generous. The grant ratio was 84 per cent, 13 percentage points above the African average in 1980, 18 above the average in 1987 (ibid., p.116). Taiwan's debt service ratio in 1974 (almost entirely from aid loans) was 2·7 per cent, a fraction of the ratios of SSA countries. It deserves special mentioning that aid comprised raw materials ready for industrial processing in Asia – over 73 per cent in Taiwan – which is very exceptional indeed.

These flows must not be forgotten when analysing the 'miracle'. Generous aid is certainly not a sufficient condition for success. Funds have to be used judiciously, which is only possible if they are available. Rodrik (1996, p.31) calls it 'conventional wisdom' that Korea and Taiwan became successful in the 1960s 'in large measure because U.S. aid, which had been plentiful during the 1950s, was coming to an end'. This is logically compatible with the argument that aid was important to rebuild these economies after the War. It could be understood in the sense that the decline itself was the reason for success, but this is hardly convincing. If it were, quite a few other economic miracles should be discernible in the 1990s.

Interestingly, the important part of aid in the Asian success story is played down nowadays. The World Bank's (1993a) miracle study does not do it justice. The European Commission (1996, p.5) asserts that 'aid had played a marginal role in the economic success of certain Asian ... countries'. Although at severe odds with the truth, this might come in handy to 'corroborate' claims of a 'loss of legitimacy' of aid (ibid., p.36), unless one uses it on someone familiar with historical facts.

Land Reform

Both South Korea and Taiwan had land reforms, a distinct difference from other SCs, most notably in Latin America, where the power of big landowners usually precludes land reform. Naturally, Singapore and Hong Kong had no large landowners. In Korea and Taiwan, formerly Japanese land, acquired by the Japanese in one way or the other during the colonial period, could be distributed without expropriating national elites. In Taiwan, Japanese plots amounted to one-quarter of arable land, and formerly Japanese industrial assets provided money to pay landowners affected by reform (Bräutigam, 1994, p.117). Land reform also served Chiang Kai-shek's interests: by destroying the power base of autochthonous Taiwanese elites, he could consolidate his grip on the island. He did not rely on land reform alone. The massacres of 1947 killed off many influential Taiwanese. Bräutigam (ibid., p.136) speaks of the elimination of 'an entire generation'. In South Korea, World War II and the invasion by North Korea are likely to have reduced the land-owning class.

Chen and Stocker (1993) see one potential cause of Taiwan's extraordinary growth in the fact that land reform rendered highly esteemed investment in real estate unfeasible for most people. Land reform and the hyperinflation of the 1940s certainly contributed to a reduction in differences in wealth. It is interesting to note that both South Korea and Taiwan had a relatively egalitarian income distribution, which – although contradicting Kuznets's inverted-U curve – was repeatedly cited as one reason for economic success.

Production Structures Inherited from Colonial Times

Ingham (1995, p.8) cites Korea and Taiwan as exceptions accelerating growth during the period between the two world wars due to Japanese colonial policy relying heavily on food production in the two colonies: 'Taiwan and Korea constituted the Japanese "rice basket". In Taiwan and Korea infrastructral investments increased, agricultural productivity rose, and the foundations of today's manufacturing base were laid.'

Although guided by self-interest rather than altruism, Japanese colonial policy differed markedly from the Western model. While the West reshaped their colonies, forcing them to export raw materials and to import manufactures from 'motherlands' – physically destroying competing capacities and occasionally even competitors – the Japanese started to industrialize their colonies and to modernize agriculture there. They invested in the health system (Louven, 1983, p.154), made school attendance compulsory, even established research institutions (Bräutigam, 1994, p.113) – a glaring contrast to colonial policies by Europe and the USA. A relatively well educated labour force was the result.

During the second half of the 1930s, manufactures already accounted for more than half of Korea's exports (Serfas, 1987, p.20). At the end of the 1930s, heavy industry produced roughly half the industrial output, chemical industry about one-third (ibid., pp.16ff). Industrial production grew by 6 per cent annually during the 1930s (Bräutigam, 1994, p.113). Japanese firms relocated labour- and wage-intensive industries to Korea's Pusan region and to Taiwan (Luther, 1983, p.120). According to Chen and Stocker (1993), Korea was the preferred location for industrial investments.

Naturally, Japanese colonial policy was primarily driven by Japan's self-interest. To increase rice exports to Japan, for instance, Korean rice consumption was reduced. High positions in the colonial administration were mostly reserved for Japanese. Wages of Korean workers were roughly half those of Japanese workers in comparable positions. But, irrespective of what discrimination, injustice and exploitation might have been done by the colonizers, an economic base was formed, which was much more favourable than what most colonies had at independence. The World Bank's (1993a, p.32) 'Asian miracle' rightly mentions the good infrastructure of former

Japanese colonies as a positive factor. Finally, Serfas (1987, p.211) mentions compensation paid by Japan for the colonial past.

Economic Policy

Hong Kong apart, the state played a crucial role in the first generation 'tigers'. Massive export promotion along mercantilist lines was one important factor of the success of the three other original 'tigers'. A World Bank research publication subtitled 'Managing the Entry into World Markets' (Rhee *et al.*, 1984) describes Korean intervention in great detail. Preferential interest rates exclusively available to export firms, which could be more than ten percentage points cheaper than domestic credits – the World Bank (1993a, p.282) speaks of up to 20 percentage points until 1982 – are just one example. Lower taxes, subsidies and licences to import highly restricted 'luxuries' are others. The fate of firms diverging from agreed targets is described quite ornately by Rhee *et al.* (1984, p.36): 'all ministries and firms have been part of the team, and if one member wandered astray, others would rein the wanderer back in'. Less flowery language could be used by pointing out that about half the firms asked felt pressure to reach export targets; more than one-third even felt strong pressure. Government involvement and directed credits were major causes of complaints by the West.

Imports to Taiwan were subject to government approval, banking was reserved to public banks, as in Korea; selective credit policies, interest differentials and foreign exchange control, including decisions on what foreign exchange could be used for, were all important elements of Taiwanese economic policy. The fact that both Korea and Taiwan allotted foreign exchange for developmentally important investments, while restricting expenditures for conveniencies and consumption of goods considered 'luxuries', also deserves to be mentioned. Even in Singapore, Rhee *et al.* (ibid., p.6) found selective protectionism.

Like Japan, Korea and Taiwan restricted technology transfer, allowing imports of techniques considered essential for the country's development policy, unbundling expensive technology bundles. Rhee *et al.* (ibid., p.28) report that permission to import techniques, but also to import foreign consultants or to send staff abroad, was linked to export success. Taiwan's policy of improving technological standards demanded the use of domestic inputs, a practice now outlawed by the WTO. Wade (1994) reports a case illustrating the subtlety of intervention. One day, the Industrial Development Bureau thought that domestic firms could produce inputs for a transnational firm that had to be imported. A little help was needed from the foreign firm, but denied. Inexplicably, permits to import needed inputs, granted immediately before, took longer and longer, which started to be felt by the foreign firm. This bureaucratic inefficiency stopped once the firm had agreed to help Taiwanese firms to produce the quality of inputs needed. Soon, these inputs were produced in Taiwan.

It has been pointed out that the East Asian 'tigers'' performance with respect to productivity was not outstanding, as output growth was largely if not virtually totally accounted for by capital increases and growth of the labour force (Rodrik, 1996, p.13), a point also made by Krugman (1996), who compared Asia to the Soviet Union. According to Krugman, both achieved rapid growth in large part by mobilizing resources, by rapidly growing inputs of labour and capital. One may discuss, though, whether this 'extraordinary mobilization of resources is no more than what the most boringly conventional economic theory would lead us to expect' (ibid., p.184). Quite a few countries have not been able to mobilize resources in the same way, and the whole discussion on dualism or structural heterogeneity would not have taken place if boring convention would have sufficed. Lack of technology is certainly a problem and might have impaired future growth. Nevertheless, first generation tigers achieved historically high growth rates, the mobilization of production factors and the transformation of their economic structures, which remains to be achieved by quite a few developing countries. Apparently, these Asian economies achieved something uncommon in SCs, if only the better use of resources.

Transnational Firms

Regarding FDI, Taiwan and Korea were quite restrictive. Modest liberalization occurred during the 1980s, but it remained far from what OECD countries pressed for. Korea in particular fostered the growth of large domestic oligopolies, creating its own transnational corporations which became international players.

Role of the State

At first sight, the shares of public and nationalized enterprises seem to be relatively small. But as Kuznets (1988, S24) showed, incompleteness of data and inconsistent definitions of 'government' explained low official shares of government activity. Korea's state enterprises and parastatals, such as the tobacco monopoly or KEPCO (Korea Electric Power Company) were, in contrast to going practice of other countries, listed as private business. In Singapore, the government's share in economic activity could not be estimated precisely, nor could the share of the Kuomintang party in Taiwan. Until 1990, banking was reserved for state banks in Taiwan, with less strong restrictions regarding international transactions. An informal capital market and private savings clubs (known as 'Hueas') played an important role for private entrepreneurs unable to gain access to the official market (Chen and Stocker, 1993).

According to census data of 1980, Singapore's government employed 19·5 per cent of the workforce, but as 'the total size of government enterprise is not public knowledge (by any useful measure)' (Krause, 1988, pp.S62f) the real share may have been higher. According to official sources the public sector accounted for 33·4 per cent of gross domestic fixed capital formation in 1984. Krause (ibid., p.S63) concluded: 'Indeed, there appear to be no ideological barriers to the government entering any economic activity.'

Both Korea and Taiwan increased their reliance on public enterprises during the crucial decade of the 1960s (Rodrik, 1996, p.18), but public ownership offers one means of influencing a country's economic policy, not necessarily the most important one. Literature describes a wide array of formal and informal methods of influencing economic policies, ranging from encouraging telephone calls by the president to outright banning of specific investments. Industries considered to have little economic future were told to reduce production capacities or to close eventually. Even lists of business branches that were fostered and those where entry was 'banned' were published, as Serfas (1987, p.159) quotes from the *Korea Newsreview* of 12 July 1986. Tax privileges and subsidies were stopped and rerouted to other branches which the government considered more promising. Singapore's government was qualified as 'very intrusive' (Krause, 1988, p.S62). One may assume that economic development was not uninfluenced by the government in a country where the president even regulated the length of boys' hair and girls' skirts.

'Tiger' governments governed the market efficiently and pragmatically. Conservative fiscal policies and competitive exchange rates can be singled out as the areas 'where Korea and Taiwan followed the orthodox path most closely' (Rodrik, 1996, p.18). Not everyone doubting the applicability of the orthodox model is by necessity pursuing policies of unsustainable spending and reckless overvaluation. Pragmatic choices are typical of eclectic approaches likely to adopt those policies considered useful; whether recommended by orthodoxy or not. The Korean payments crisis of 1979/80 and its quick fix show that the country experimented with the amount of debt which would be sustainable. None of the Asian success economies could be egged on by the BWIs' applause to borrow as heavily as other SCs before 1982. Consequently, none became a problem debtor in the 1980s.

With the exception of Hong Kong – which intervened perceptibly in the housing market, though – the original 'tigers' did not apply the policies which IMF and World Bank have forced on other SCs. The so-called 'next-generation tigers' had interventionist governments, too. The 'miracle study' (World Bank, 1993a, p.43) describes an important difference between these high performers and other SCs. During the 1970s, levels of public investment did not differ markedly, but during the 1980s East Asian economies diverged: 'In other economies, the fiscal contraction of macroeconomic adjustment was reflected in lower public investment rates.' In Asian 'high performers' they were substantially above the levels of the 1970s. 'In short, in striking contrast to elsewhere, public investment in 1980–87 in these East Asian economies was countercyclical to the reduction of private investment' (ibid.). The events of 1997 changed the situation fundamentally, depriving Asian economies of such possibilities to follow their own – apparently not unsuccessful – policies.

THE CRASH OF 1997

Two rivalling strands of explanations thrived immediately after the crash. The first, championed by the World Bank and especially by the heavily criticized IMF, ascribes the fault basically to domestic problems: bad economic policies, 'crony capitalism' and 'notably government involvement in the private sector' (IMF, 1999). This diverges remarkably from these institutions' analyses even shortly before the crash. In its Asian miracle study, the World Bank (1993a, p.359) for instance stated that high performance could only be achieved as a result of 'high government institutional capability ... because their civil services and public institutions were largely stuffed by competent and honest civil servants'. Export was the single yardstick for performance. Directed credit programmes 'were designed to achieve policy objectives', but, as the World Bank (ibid., p.20) assured at that time, 'nevertheless included strict performance criteria ... These performance-based directed-credit mechanisms appear to have improved credit allocation, especially during the early stages of rapid growth (see Chapter 6 [of the World Bank's publication])'.

Without a 'clear link to economic performance' (ibid., p.367) similar interventions 'have failed' elsewhere. A 1992 World Bank report 'cited Indonesia as "one of the Bank's greatest success stories overall in the 1980s", and [claimed] that "[t]he impressive growth of Indonesian industry was a testimony, among other things, to the Bank's sound analysis, advice and influence"' (quoted from Pincus & Ramli, 1998, p.724). As late as June 1997, Indonesia was praised by the IMF for prudent macroeconomic policies, high investment and savings rates, and reforms to liberalize markets (ibid., p.725). After 1997, all these objective, competent and honest institutions that had served as an argument for the impossibility of the East Asian experience being duplicated had suddenly and surreptitiously turned into corrupt crony-capitalists that could only be expected to go bust. Reading post-1997 publications, one wonders why the BWIs obviously did not expect it, let alone why they ever claimed East Asia as their success, praising Korea's and

Thailand's economic performances on the very eve of the crash (Sachs, 1997).

The second strand explains the crash as basically triggered by unduly quick liberalization, or – more politely – problems of transition. The Thailand Department of Export Promotion and the Industrial Authority of Thailand acknowledged this in costly three-page advertisements (for instance, in *Time*, 24 November 1997) placed to reassure investors:

> Simply put, the winds of change blew in too quickly, catching Thailand offguard. A lack of mature systems and safeguards for control meant trouble for an economy that had neither time nor macroeconomic managerial experience to adjust. Such are the pitfalls of the development cycle in today's rush to modernization and prosperity ... we have realized that transition from poverty to prosperity must be made in a deliberate manner, with controls and vigilance to prevent over-ambition and over-zealous borrowing.

Liberalizing private lending – in the wording of the Thai authorities: 'a runaway financial sector' – while banks and investors were still subject to obligations of the old and, that far, successful system was likely to create problems of compatibility, particularly as most new debts incurred had rather short maturities. The pronounced concentration on short-term debts against all textbook wisdom remains puzzling.

This is not to deny problems, such as investments in real estate, large corporate debts or the effects of exchange rates pegged to the appreciating US dollar. But government intervention and regulation would have been necessary to allow smooth transition and to avoid the crash. This, meanwhile, is recognized by the World Bank (1999a) speaking of the need of 'institution building', and the IMF (1999) demanding 'better prudential regulation and supervision'. There was also, however, a governance issue. Following the neoliberal creed, these countries had liberalized too quickly. The IMF (1998) recognized that the crisis was 'not primarily the result of macroeconomic imbalances' and that 'private sector expenditure and financing decisions led to the crisis'. Ex post, the IMF (ibid.) saw a need for prudent liberalization of capital markets, as well as for fostering 'orderly and properly sequenced capital account liberalization'.

The World Bank (1999a, p.3) rightly concluded that a system that 'seemed adequate as long as the boom lasted' proved fatally flawed once external conditions deteriorated. The 'unprecedented volume and reversibility of short-term capital flows, weak banking institutions and ineffective regulation systems proved a lethal combination'. If Asian countries had not liberalized their economies so strongly, the crisis could not have happened. Money that cannot enter a country hardly leave it. Sticking to the old Asian model would have prevented the crisis, as it prevented the debt crisis of the 1980s – or controlled debt problems, as in the Korean case. High debt–equity ratios –

Wade (1998a, p.1544) quotes for instance 5:1 for Daewoo – which posed no problem under government protection in the Asian system make an enterprise extremely vulnerable in a Western-type financial system, even without the additional risk of volatile short-term inflows. These ratios alone were enough reason not to liberalize so speedily, exposing actors to an environment for which they were extremely ill-equipped.

Nevertheless, more liberalization of capital flows was demanded and enforced as the solution. If one agrees with the World Bank (1999a, p.3) that building institutional capacity is expensive, slow and complex, even more liberalization before one has the needed regulatory structures in place does not seem good advice. One wonders why it was given. By naming *chaebols* that went bankrupt before the crash, Chang (2000) and Chang *et al.* (1998) have proved that the perception that *chaebols* would always be protected by the government was unfounded. As rescue operations 'almost always' implied ceding corporate control in Korea, management clearly had incentives to avoid them (Chang, 2000, p.782). Chang contrasts the Korean situation, where financial help was always accompanied by tough terms, with the rescue of the LTCM hedge fund in the USA, 'which did not involve the removal of the incumbent management'. Chang (2000) and Chang *et al.* (1998) convincingly show how the demise of industrial policy and the dismantling of the mechanisms of government intervention in the 1990s contributed critically to the crisis. Chang (2000, p.779) argues that the removal of rational criteria that had been part and parcel of planning possibly created more room for cronyism in Korea.

What may be most surprising is that there was no need to liberalize so quickly. In contrast to debtor countries in the South, the Bretton Woods twins could not force the tigers to do so. In the case of Korea, OECD membership was certainly a factor. The Republic of Korea had traditionally maintained strict capital controls, which enabled authorities 'to prevent excessive speculative foreign exchange trading' (Park, 1996, p.216). These were liberalized in preparation for OECD membership: McKinnon (1999, p.97) speaks of 'premature removal of the controls as a condition for Korea's joining the OECD three years before'. Although Korea had fared quite well under the old system, Park (1996, p.193) justified liberalization of the capital account with 'the inefficiency of these regulations and ... the worldwide trend towards economic liberalization' – in 1997, Korea repeated the experience of efficient liberalization Mexico had undergone in 1994.

As early as 1990, Wade (1990, p.367; see also 1998a, p.1552) had warned that control of international financial flows must be maintained to avoid exchange rate movements 'with damaging consequences for the real economy'. Wade warned of 'speculative inflows', '[U]ncontrolled outflows' and vulnerability to an 'investment collapse'. Both this warning and the World

Bank's (1999a, p.2) acknowledgment of knowing 'the relevant institutional lessons' since the early 1990s prove that the crisis was foreseen.

Stating that '[M]any fundamentals were sound' in Asia, the World Bank (ibid.) draws parallels with Mexico. Identifying 'premature financial liberalization and weak financial discipline in domestic banking systems' as creating vulnerability to speculation, it draws attention to the Southern Cone crisis in 1982 and to Mexico's in 1994–5. In 1990, an audit report by the OED on Chile's structural adjustment loans 'highlighted the lack of prudential supervision of financial institutions in increasing the economy's vulnerability to the point of collapse'. The neglect of proper sequencing and institution building 'featured prominently in the Chile and Mexico crises' (ibid.). In short, the problem was known years before the crash. The Argentine crisis of 1995 goes unmentioned in this source, although it was of a 'similar variety' (Radelet & Sachs, 1998, p.9) to Asia, triggered by private sector debts. Indeed, one has to ask: 'Why did not policymakers and international financial institutions give these weaknesses appropriate weight?' (World Bank, 1999a, p.2). Why did the BWIs (neither normally known for their restraint in giving advice) not warn those countries to proceed more slowly with cautious sequencing – as they do today – pointing at already available evidence, instead of applauding too quick liberalization and those inflows of volatile capital? Before 1994–5, the BWIs had applauded and encouraged inflows to Mexico, presenting them as a proof that the debt crisis was over (Raffer, 1996a). As in the case of Asia, official euphoria must certainly have fuelled inflows further.

We do not, of course, assume that attempts to establish an Asian Monetary Fund had anything to do with the fact that the BWIs did not warn Asian countries. Nor do we comment on conspiracy theories that emerged as a result of the crisis, also fuelled by cheap sales of Asian assets to Euro-American foreigners. But it should be recalled that as distinguished an economist as Jagdish Bhagwati (1997) spoke of a 'Wall-Street–Treasury complex' dictating the agenda. He also drew a parallel to the S&L crisis in the USA. The fact that the IMF even identified two foreign buyers for Korean banks (Krause, 2000, p.6) has certainly not counteracted such perceptions. Expanding that expression to the 'Wall Street–Treasury–IMF complex', Wade (1998a, p.1545) asked why the IMF insisted on further capital account opening in countries 'awash with domestic savings', and why it did 'so little to organize debt *rescheduling* negotiations'. Short-term debts were finally renegotiated after two rescue packages 'and the foreign exchange crisis ended' (Krause, 2000, p.4).

As is often the case, IMF interventions were also occasionally used to serve agenda of domestic interest groups, most notably in Korea (Mathews, 1998, esp. p.752). Changes in labour regulations regarding redundancies to make firing easier are a prime example.

After 1997, the World Bank (1999a, p.2) states that 'decisionmakers overlooked the failure of the Asian countries to comply with the basic tenets of the much abused Washington consensus'. The World Bank's (1993a) own study on the Asian miracle would be one perfect corroborating example. To support the thesis that the Washington Consensus is not to blame, the World Bank (1999a) now uses and expands Rodrik's (1996) Table 3, produced to show that Taiwan and Korea – in contrast to what the BWIs postulated at that time – did not follow the Washington Consensus.

Indonesia, Korea, Taiwan and Thailand complied with only six or seven of the Washington Consensus's ten tenets (see Chapter 4). Privatization and deregulation in particular were insufficient, and barriers to foreign direct investment were found (World Bank 1999a, p.3). Except in Taiwan, property rights were seen as not secure enough. In the case of Korea the World Bank's Table 1.2 quotes Rodrik's information that leading businessmen were imprisoned and threatened with confiscation in 1961. There is a subtle change in emphasis, though: while Rodrik (1996) mentioned this before the crash, writing the same in 1999 might convey the impression that this was one reason for the crash. The Bank's method might be refined to explain a future crash in China by recalling some of Djingis Chan's atrocities.

The point that the crisis countries did not comply with the tenet of deregulation is particularly interesting, since too rapid deregulation was singled out as one of the main reasons for the crash. The World Bank (1999a, p.2) sees the capital account as the main vulnerability. Lack of transparency was identified ex post as another main reason for the crash. This is equivalent to stating that foreign investors pushed their money on and into these countries without bothering about fundamental information on their debtors – hardly best business practice. As Wade (1998a, p.1542) rightly observed, Western prudential guidelines should have prohibited such lending. But Western traditional prudential criteria were only applied ex post. Wade (1998b) quotes a complaint by the US comptroller of the currency that 'only four of the largest 64 North American banks practice state-of-the-art portfolio risk management, and that loan standards are therefore laxer than they ought to be'. This finding supports the theory of creditor moral hazard. Under the assumption of no exchange rate risk, so-called 'carry trade' (Wade 1998a, p.1539) profiting from interest rate differentials flourished. Investment in short-term Asian notes yielded relatively higher interest rates; under the assumption of a fixed exchange rate, profits seemed riskless.

The moral hazard argument stands out prominently in the discussion. We believe it to be a valid argument, in particular with regard to foreign investors. Of course, money was not invested in Asia because investors hoped to go bust to be then bailed out, but because of the euphoric view on these Asian economies' trajectories. The OECD's (1996a, p.57) call for 'a much larger officially provided safety net' must have had effects on investors, as well as experiences from past crises going back to the bail-out in the Indonesian Pertamina crisis of the early 1970s. Such effects can only be the reduction of perceived risks, providing an incentive not to practise all those advanced risk credit assessment techniques that are now preached so eagerly to Asian institutions.

Asian economies absorbed high liquidity, or what the OECD (1998a, p.57) called 'reward seeking private capital'. The crisis was thus a crisis of overlending and overborrowing (Palma, 1998) like Latin American crises before. Palma puts it down to endogenous market failures of over-liquid underregulated markets along the lines described by Kindleberger's (1978) *Manias, Panics, and Crashes*. The perception that the IMF–Treasury cavalry would arrive if – rather than when – needed would hardly be a disincentive to overlending.

Wade (1998b) gives examples of warning signs being ignored by investors. Also BWI staff trying to ring the alarm bell were overruled by superiors. Thus, during a visit to Indonesia in the autumn of 1997, the World Bank's president, Wolfensohn himself removed a passage by the resident mission that warned of serious problems, 'substituting it by even more fulsome endorsement of Indonesia as an Asian miracle'. According to Wade, one typically did not want to hear news that went against one's ideological preferences, in this case for free private capital markets that had to be proved right by the Asian example. Private rating agencies did not do better either. As late as the first quarter of 1997, spreads of loans to Asian economies fell, even for the two most vulnerable economies, Thailand and Indonesia.

As in the case of Mexico, the bail-out of international investors followed immediately. Although debts were incurred by private Asian companies, the governments of the borrowing countries were taken to task: someone had to pay for the bail-out and, as private business can go bankrupt, governments had to guarantee that investors would get paid. Stiglitz (2000, p.1) puts it in a nutshell. While 'reckless lending by international banks and other financial institutions combined with reckless borrowing' and 'fickle investor expectations' led to the crash,

> the costs – in terms of soaring unemployment and plummeting wages – were borne by workers. Workers were asked to listen to sermons about 'bearing pain' just shortly after hearing, from the same preachers, sermons about how globalization and opening up capital markets would bring them unprecedented growth.

Living standards deteriorated drastically. Nevertheless, the issue of the right of workers to participate in the decisions which did affect their lives so thoroughly was never raised, as Stiglitz notes.

Although the budgetary situation was excellent by international standards, the IMF insisted on its usual austerity measures. During 1990–94, average budget deficits of Korea, Malyasia and the Philippines were 0·4, 0·7 and 1·4 per cent of GDP, respectively, which compared favourably with the deficits of most Euro-countries. Indonesia and Thailand had surpluses. During 1995–6, all five countries had budget surpluses. Nevertheless, and although the problem lay with private debts, the IMF immediately called for budget restraint. The room for manœuvre the governments had could thus not be used to soften the crisis by increasing public expenditure. Naturally, as private debts had to be socialized, public money was needed for bail-outs rather than for cushioning the impact of the crash on the populations. Foreign exchange borrowed from the IMF was used to allow speculators to leave the countries with smaller losses than they would have had to suffer without cover.

The IMF's crisis management came under severe attack. Best known is probably Sachs's (1998) dictum about the IMF screaming fire in the theatre. It refers to the fact that the Fund demanded the freezing of many finance companies in Thailand, which sent investors into panic. 'Later the IMF imposed the closure of some domestic banks in Indonesia with the same result' (Wade, 1998c, p.699). The fact that the criteria applied to decide which banks to close were not published, and an unclear legal basis, have apparently been major factors in creating a bank run (Pincus & Ramli, 1998, p.727). Radelet & Sachs (1998, p.34) show that the IMF was aware of the risks, as Indonesia's request for the stand-by arrangement mentioned that a run on healthy institutions could be triggered by bank closures. They point out (ibid., p.17) that the 'original Fund programs in Thailand, Indonesia, and Korea were discarded within months. Korea's first program lasted but three weeks'. In Indonesia, the IMF believed a 32 per cent increase in spending in nominal rupiah terms to be inconsistent with its programme, although the 'increased spending was entirely due to pass through effects of the depreciation, and in real terms the budget represented a reduction in spending' (ibid., p.31.). Apparently realizing the difference between nominal rupiahs and real values, the IMF soon approved a budget with an even larger increase in spending (46 per cent), but 'the damage from the original statements' by the Fund and the US Treasury 'had been done'. These examples show grave shortcomings in the IMF's response.

Neoliberal agenda, though, could be pushed forward. The WTO (1998a, p.29) commented favourably on APEC's agreement on 'a "fast track" trade liberalization programme', and on the 'landmark agreement on financial services' (WTO, 1997f) also signed by Asian countries hit by the crisis, even though it has to acknowledge 'China (which, with a non-convertible currency largely isolated from speculative attack)' (WTO, 1998a, p.26) was doing comparatively very well. Many SCs, including prominently some Asian countries, had opposed this agreement committing them to opening banking, insurance and securities markets to foreign firms. While heavy criticism of the bail-out of speculators was widespread and heard from conservatives as well, the WTO remained absolutely silent. In spite of the crash, the process of market opening could be 'kept on track': 'most countries in Asia have accepted, either unilaterally, as part of IMF-sponsored adjustment programmes, or as a result of recent sectoral negotiations in the WTO and in APEC, substantial liberalization – and commitments to further liberalization – of their trade and investment policies' (WTO, 1998a, p.27).

Not without pride, the WTO adds that Indonesia, the country most severely affected by the crisis, liberalized most. With the whole WTO–IMF package implemented as planned, Indonesia 'will have one of the most liberal trade policy regimes of all developing countries' (ibid.). If the WTO was right about the 'virtual elimination of non-tariff barriers to trade', though, it would also be more liberal than virtually any OECD member.

Indonesia could have increased its average applied tariff by 25 per cent without breaching its WTO obligations but, convinced by whatever means, did not do so. The steep fall of the rupiah, which increased import costs drastically, may be one reason why higher tariffs might have been considered unnecessary. Though 'not extensively used' in South East Asia, selective tariff increases by some Asian countries remaining within the gap between bound and applied tariffs, thus 'within the flexibility allowed by bindings under the WTO agreements', nevertheless 'give cause for concern to the extent they may distort the pattern of production and trade' (ibid., p.28). In contrast to IC policies regarding textiles and clothing, using one's contractual rights raises the WTO's concern if done by SCs (cf. also ibid., p.23). Similar concern over potential distortion by the Agreement on Textile and Clothing was not expressed by the WTO, nor was it with regard to the rather long phasing-out period of GATT-inconsistent restrictions. But 'the absence of recourse to new "legal" measures of protection' in crisis countries was a 'striking feature' (WTO, 2000c, p.20). There was not even an unusual level of activities such as transitional safeguards, as the WTO reports. The fully legal use of measures ICs have continuously applied without a comparable crisis and comparable concern by the WTO seems to be seen as highly problematic in the case of crisis-stricken SC members.

Although it highlights the fact that crisis countries did not use its rules within legally correct limits, the WTO (ibid., p.2) claims that 'WTO rules and disciplines' were 'crucial in making the Asian recovery possible'. The WTO no longer draws attention to the fact that 'Trade contraction in Asia has been the biggest factor in the global trade slowdown' in 1998 (WTO, 1999b, pp.1f). Crisis countries reported the strongest import decline. The fact that exports were choked by lack of foreign exchange and credit lines in spite of substantial devaluations as necessary imports could not be financed – the Korean refineries mentioned in Chapter 8 are one example – goes unmentioned. South Korea did export more, but not enough to avoid a decrease in revenues. Only the Philippines were able to increase their export value with an increased volume in spite of a drop in unit values in 1998 (UNCTAD, 1999, p.26). One wonders about the qualities of an 'effective rule-based multilateral system' (WTO, 2000c, p.2) if it seems only to work if weaker members refrain from using their contractual rights.

THE ASIAN CRISIS IN PERSPECTIVE

The lending spree has tamed the 'tigers'. These economies had to open up for foreign investment and to reduce public spending, although the latter did not create the problem. Their assets were sold at highly reduced prices; the successful 'tiger' model is likely to be dead, at least in its traditional form. Wade (1998c) points out that the old growth model of high debt–equity ratios will be difficult to sustain in the future. It allowed higher investments propelling fast growth, but without adequate protection high debt ratios create vulnerability to shocks. In the changed environment this protection will no longer be so easy.

The Asian case is a good illustration of Rodrik's thesis that chances 'to wipe the slate clean' are immediately seized (cf. Chapter 4). One can fault Asian governments – as Akyüz (1998, p.5) put it – for 'failing to prevent market failure – an approach that underpinned successful policy intervention in post-war East Asia'. The failure of the private sector was used to increase its role even more, to change policies that had nothing to do with the crisis, and to dismantle public control further. IMF conditionality went much further than usual, triggering fundamental systemic changes.

First signs of recovery in Asia were quickly noted. In July 1998, governments in the region started to follow expansionary policies representing a considerable change of direction (Wade, 1998c, p.701). Krause (2000, p.1) noted that the 'resolution of the crisis is being done in a very Korean way' with the government centrally involved. As he sees more talk and planning about reforms in Korea than reforms actually accomplished, he concludes: 'Fortunately, the continuation of economic recovery does not depend on the completion of reforms' (ibid., p.19). Malaysia, the one country that introduced capital controls against all neoliberal warnings, did not fare that badly. A paper based on material initially prepared for discussion in the IMF's executive board in September 1999 (Ariyoshi *et al.*, 1999, Part II, p.60, emphasis in original) concluded that '*preliminary evidence suggest* [sic!] *that the controls have been effective*'. But it is also seen as important to resist temptation to draw firm conclusions from Malaysia's experience with the use of controls on capital outflows, not least because of the difficulty in separating the impact of the controls from that of the accompanying macroeconomic and financial sector reforms, as well as from the broader international and regional developments.

This language recalls the World Bank's Asian miracle study's reluctance to admit that state intervention was successful. However, ten pages earlier, the paper found that '*The effectiveness of the controls was also evident*', and that '*Available evidence suggest* [sic!] *that the controls have so far been effective in achieving the objective of eliminating the offshore ringgit market*' (ibid., p.50, emphasis in original). According to this study, the overall balance of payments continued to strengthen, net portfolio outflows were contained, foreign exchange reserves continued to increase and the reduction of interest rates that accompanied controls helped contain increases in non-performing loans (NPLs). 'In its most recent upgrading of Malaysia's credit outlook, Standard & Poor indicated that if interest rates had not been cut sharply ... NPLs would have risen to above 30 percent of total loans, computed on a three-month basis' (ibid., p.51). One should recall that the IMF demanded higher interest rates to gain investor confidence. In economies with high debt–equity ratios, such increases are likely to push quite a few firms into bankruptcy. There were no signs of speculative pressures on the ringgit 'despite the marked relaxation of fiscal and monetary policies to support weak economic activity' (ibid., p.12). The introduction of the exit levy system in February 1999, which replaced the outright prohibition of repatriation of portfolio investment for a 12-month holding period, improved investor confidence, although it amounted to 30 per cent on early repatriations. Controls impacted on short-term speculative flows as dividends, interest earned or rental income were excluded. Measures taken obviously differed from Prime Minister Mahatir's somewhat emotional verbal reactions to the crisis. What appears most important, though, is that 'The Fund conducted an immediate on-site review to determine whether the measures were in *conformity with Malaysia's obligations under Article VIII*, Sections 2, 3, and 4 of the Articles of Agreement; the measures were found to be in conformity with the Articles' (ibid., p.55, emphasis in original).

Thus other tigers – or any SC in trouble – could have introduced such controls as well without violating their obligations as IMF members, but IMF conditionality forbade it. The recovery in Asia, and in particular the Malaysian experience, could be a sign of waning neoliberal influence. Wade (1998c, p.1535) might be right: 'Paradoxically, the crisis may be looked upon not as the triumph of benign globalization and neoliberal economic doctrine but as the beginning of its end.'

10. The debt crisis: historical roots and 'debt management' during the 1980s

August 1982, when Mexico declared itself unable to honour debt obligations as contractually due, is conventionally seen as the beginning of the debt crisis, although Poland's default in 1981 was already a major shock. However, dating the beginning of the debt crisis in the 1980s veils the fact that the underlying structural causes of the debt problem had existed long before. The date also disguises the long and dismal record of debt management and the ineffectiveness of the policies enforced by the BWIs in restoring the sustainable economic viability of debtor countries.

The debt problem results from structural inequalities and disequilibria in the global economy, putting SCs at a disadvantage: the structural resource gaps to which the PST had drawn attention when showing evidence for secularly falling terms of trade. This problem was covered up by the 'easy money' of the 1970s – more precisely, the increasing exposure of commercial banks in the South, starting as early as the end of the 1960s. The end of high international liquidity in the 1980s brought it again to everyone's attention.

The Pearson Report (Pearson *et al.*, 1969, pp.153ff), prepared on request of the president of the World Bank, already identified structural origins of the debt problem. Debt relief was strongly recommended. The report warned of 'many serious difficulties' that could result from 'very large scale lending', emphasizing that 'The accumulation of excessive debts is usually the combined result of errors of borrower governments and their foreign creditors. Failures on the part of the debtors will be obvious. The responsibility of foreign creditors is rarely mentioned' (ibid., p.156). This sounds as modern as its finding that debt management had emphasized spending cuts and credit restrictions while neglecting the need to sustain sound development outlays.

The Pearson Report considered the debt problem already so urgent that it suggested the application of a unique feature of the $3·75 billion US–UK loan in 1945 (at 2 per cent interest), the so-called 'Bisque clause', to provide 'a timely policy alternative to moratoria or debt rescheduling when a country is in temporary balance of payments difficulty' (ibid., p.159). This clause allowed the debtor (the UK) to waive or cancel interest payments unilaterally, on certain conditions. It was agreed to change it in 1957: the UK was then entitled to postpone up to seven instalments of principal and interest. Four of these seven deferrals had been used when the Pearson Report was written. Deferred payments were to be paid after 2001, carrying an interest of 2 per cent.

In its last *Report*, the OECD (2000a, p.43) started a 30-year retrospective on aid with the 'pathbreaking' Pearson Report, recalling some of its findings as 'still relevant today'. However, the latter's recommendations regarding over-indebtedness are not mentioned, even though they are highly topical at present.

THE DEBT BUILD-UP UNTIL 1982

In spite of these warnings, Southern debts exploded during the 1970s. It is important to recall that these debts started to take off at the end of the 1960s (Reichmann, 1988), when international liquidity increased because of an oversupply of US dollars, possibly connected with financing the Vietnam war. The former Austrian chancellor Bruno Kreisky used this 'dollar overhang' to argue that his proposed New Marshall Plan for the South – often called the Kreisky Plan after its advocate – could be easily financed. The OECD (1983b, p.57) summarized:

> At the beginning of the 1970s ... a major jump in private bank lending occurred ... It is evident from the tables that it was in this period, essentially before the first oil shock, that the decisive increase in the role of bank lending occurred, both in absolute terms and proportionally ... In the wake of the first oil shock, capital market financing of developing countries fell away in 1974 ... the period 1975–1978 can be regarded in retrospect as almost a repetition of the early 1970s ... [but] the rise in bank lending was not as dramatic as in 1971–1973.

During the second half of the 1970s, the share of SCs in publicized Eurocredits was always well above 50 per cent of the total, peaking at roughly 63 per cent. This growth of Southern debts occurred at a time of slack demand in the North and high liquidity of commercial banks; also of strong inflation in the OECD countries and negative real interest rates.

Commercial bank loans, however, were strongly concentrated on richer SCs. Balance of payments surpluses of some OPEC countries, classified as 'capital surplus oil exporters' by the World Bank, increased international liquidity further after the first oil price hike of 1973–4. While undeniably one important factor influencing the Euromarket, its quantitative impact has often been exaggerated (see Chapter 8). Some OPEC members were themselves among the big borrowers. Indonesia, for instance, borrowed roughly as much in the Euromarket in 1979 as all other Low Income Countries. The net amount of OPEC money available for the Euromarket was thus much less than the trade surpluses of capital surplus oil exporters.

When the Fed adopted a restrictive monetary policy to fight inflation at the end of the 1970s, and US budget deficits increased under the Reagan administration to finance military expenditures, interest rates increased swiftly and dramatically. Previously negative real interest rates turned into historically high positive levels. LIBOR went above 16 per cent and real interest rates, still around −7 per cent in 1980, peaked at around 22 per cent in 1982 (cf. World Bank, 1987, p.19). With a large share of debts at variable interest rates this increase was quickly transmitted to borrowers, pushing up debt service considerably.

At about the same time, raw material prices started to fall dramatically, and terms of trade with them. Between 1980 and 1982, they reached historic lows, comparable only to the 1930s. Increased Northern protectionism was one reason for falling export receipts (World Bank, 1985, p.6). Debtors suddenly faced a situation where interest rates – or the cost of borrowing – rocketed while their income plunged. Until August 1982, the unsustainable situation was covered by new loans made to allow debtors to service their debts. After the Mexican crash, syndicated lending fell sharply. In two years, between the end of 1982 and 1984, the stock of syndicated loans outstanding was reduced by nearly 25 per cent (ibid., p.118, Box 8.6). With the exception of East Asia, 'spontaneous' lending ceased. 'Concerted' or 'involuntary' lending occurred in conjunction with debt restructuring. It was necessary as no bank was willing to increase its share in total exposure. Concerted action ensured that the burden of additional exposure would be shared by all. In this respect it can be seen as an alternative to insolvency.

The borrowing and lending spree was fuelled by several factors, as well as by a nearly universal convergence of interests of borrowers, lenders and OECD governments. A period of negative real interest rates and relatively high commodity prices encouraged SCs to borrow cheap money. Spreads, the surcharge over LIBOR demanded from borrowers, fell dramatically, reaching 0·5 per cent for ICs at the end of the 1970s. Differences in spreads between ICs and SCs, supposedly reflecting differences in risk, were also perceptibly reduced. In June 1978, the *Institutional Investor* wrote of a move towards a 'unispread' market.

Furthermore, SC governments saw commercial banks as an opportunity to diversify their sources of finance. Declining ODA, the practice of tying aid, the fact that ODA was not infrequently used by 'donors' for political purposes or to obtain economic advantages, must have made commercial loans attractive. Apart from a few exceptions confirming the rule, commercial banks have not tried to influence their clients' policies. This new option improved the position of SCs vis-à-vis their official lenders, reducing the power to impose conditions. In 1981, India even used the IMF as a lender of 'first' resort, preferring Fund access to private borrowing (Williamson, 1983a, p.614). Last but not least, the liberal attitude of commercial banks may have made it easier for corrupt government ministers and officials to channel money into their own private bank accounts. A large proportion of official borrowing returned as flight capital to creditor countries, sometimes to the very banks that had given the official loan. In the Philippines, for instance, firms connected with the Marcos clan borrowed with government guarantee to go bankrupt after disbursement, leaving the public sector with more debts. According to the *New York Times* (30 March 1986) such loans amounted to nearly $10 billion. Capital flight was rampant: during 1979–82 it was estimated to be 47·8 per cent of gross capital inflows in Mexico, 65·1 per cent in Argentina and 136·6 per cent in Venezuela (World Bank, 1985, p.64). Liberal lending by commercial banks opened a bonanza for corrupt 'élites'. After amassing huge debts and filling their pockets, military juntas, especially in Latin America, simply handed power and the debt problem over to civilians. The military were not troubled with accounting for disappeared money or persons.

Official creditors, too, made similarly dubious loans. Over decades, bilateral creditors have given money to corrupt governments they supported. Nor have multilateral institutions always had scruples. The IMF, for example, granted Zaire the largest drawing ever by an African country in the year just after the so-called 'Blumenthal Report' of 1982, which warned that there was no chance of Zaire's creditors getting their money back because of the corruption of the team in power. The German banker Erwin Blumenthal had been seconded by the World Bank to monitor and manage the Bank of Zaire. Between the publication of his report and 1989, the IMF trebled the volume of its lending to Zaire. Predictably, the money disappeared. This is not the only example. Shortly before the Sandinista victory in Nicaragua, the IMF made a sizeable loan to Somoza, who fled with the money. The country was supposed to pay back. According to *Time* (2 July 1984), $20 million disbursed by the Fund to alleviate Haiti's balance of payments problems vanished without a trace, although the movement of a similar amount into the Duvaliers' palace account could be noticed. The IMF went on disbursing, insisting, however, that more money must not disappear in the same way. Thus one should not single out commercial banks alone as making dubious loans.

For commercial banks, lending to SCs was a bonanza just at a time when demand in Northern credit markets was slack. Following Walter Wriston's view that countries could not become insolvent, would always exist, and thus repay, banks urged loans on SCs without obeying the most elementary rules of banking. It was considered profitable business. In 1982, for instance, Brazil produced over a fifth of Citicorp's profits although it accounted for only 5 per cent of the bank's assets (*The Economist*, 19 March 1983, p.73).

The handling of small crises in the 1970s, such as in Zaire or in Indonesia, convinced commercial banks that sovereign lending was riskless. The latter case illustrates this very clearly. The Indonesian national oil company Pertamina had amassed uncontrollable debts: according to a report by the US Senate Committee on Foreign Relations (1977) no one, including commercial banks themselves, seemed to know how much precisely. A one-year stand-by agreement was concluded with the IMF, which – like subsequent agreements – put a ceiling on Indonesia's external borrowing and a specific sub-ceiling on Pertamina's. Foreign banks rushed in to go on lending, using technical tricks (such as rolling over short-term loans) to escape these ceilings. Even 'direct representation' (ibid., p.22) and warnings by the US embassy went unheeded. Convinced that they would be bailed out, banks went on lending. When the crisis broke, the US government immediately helped. The Committee concluded that 'the Indonesian situation' could be repeated any time and Senator Sarbane expressed his fears that the Senate would soon be forced to vote for payments to debtor governments to bail out US banks. The Committee concluded: 'Conceptually, the independence of private bank lending activities overseas would be fine if the banks were actually made to bear the ultimate risk.' But intervention of creditor governments 'calls into question the justification – the high degree of risk involved ... – for the high rate of interest banks charge to developing countries. Thus it is the creditor governments, not the banks, which are really bearing the risk' (ibid.).

Economically, bank behaviour was perfectly rational, a clear case of moral hazard, produced by IC governments. Banks apparently charged what they could get and lent as much as they could, being 'very annoyed' when Colombia, a prudent borrower, 'refused to borrow money that it did not need' (Williamson, 1985, p.31), restricting consumption and investment instead to a reasonable estimate of its permanent income. Nevertheless, Colombia did not get new loans any more easily than other Latin American countries after 1982.

Some facts corroborate the impression that commercial banks must have been convinced that no real risk to the banking system existed. First, spreads increased drastically after the Mexican crash. One would expect that creditors eager to avoid default would help their problem debtor to get out of trouble by not charging higher interest rates, rather than increasing debt service obligations. Also commercial banks were reluctant to agree to multi-year rescheduling until 1984, which would not allow them to charge front-end fees every year. Finally, pressure had to be used to make commercial banks participate in the Mexican rescue package of 1982. If they had thought that Mexico could trigger a major banking crisis, they would have been eager to help avoid it. However, reliance on the official sector to avoid a crash would explain why commercial banks were not prepared to use more of their own money to avoid Mexico's default.

Profits from early rescheduling were enormous. It was believed in 1983 that some US lawmakers might try to require banks to refund excessive fees already collected from Latin American sovereign obligors (Bransilver and Patrikis 1984). Hayter and Watson (1985, p.27) quote Antony Harris in the *Financial Times* of 10 February 1983: 'there would be something deeply offensive about the current spectacle of bankers boasting about the profits they make out of rescheduling if one seriously believed that the debts would ever be repaid in full'.

If banks had actually considered their debtors on the brink of collapse they would not have charged these high fees, worsening the debtor's position further. The US International Lending Supervision Act indeed limited fees in order to avoid excessive debt burdens. As banks had recognized fees in current income, thus boosting their profits, accounting concerns seem to have been a reason for these changes too.

IC governments finally benefited as SC borrowing increased demand for their products, securing jobs in the North. Calculation of jobs lost due to the crisis were published repeatedly. In 1981, 'North America sold more manufactured goods to the developing areas than to Western Europe and Japan *combined*' (GATT, 1987, p.24; emphasis in original). This preponderance could also be observed for Western Europe, while Japan exported as much to SCs as to the other two regions. During the 1970s, SCs stimulated IC exports 'in high productivity sectors such as machinery, transport equipment or chemicals, which made up 70 per cent of the manufactured goods' imported by SC from the North (World Bank, 1979, p.23). The World Bank warned that IC protectionism reduced the South's import capacity. Until 1982, growing SC debts had temporarily but conveniently solved the contradiction between exporting and protecting for IC governments, with positive effects on Northern job markets. Until August 1982, OECD governments and IFIs congratulated everyone, including themselves, for the successful 'recycling' of OPEC surpluses. On the other hand, warning voices were raised throughout the 1970s. Abbott (1972) saw the roots of the debt crisis in sub-Saharan Africa in the 1960s, when foreign debts first began to accumulate faster than economies or foreign exchange earnings were growing. Defining insolvency rather than illiquidity as the problem, he (like the Pearson Report) proposed debt cancellation ten years before the official start of the debt crisis.

Accepting the need for debt alleviation, the major creditors adopted the so-called 'Retroactive Terms Adjustment' (RTA) in 1978 to provide debt relief and improve the net flow of bilateral official aid to Low Income Countries. These debts were mostly caused by official flows, including aid, clearly documenting the co-responsibility of official creditors deciding and monitoring where and how their money is spent. The programme's long-winded, clumsy name evidences the creditors' desire to avoid the words 'debt relief' or 'debt cancellation', not to mention 'insolvency'. This steadfast refusal to recognize realities officially has remained the most important hindrance to proper debt management and to a viable solution of the crisis until the present day. The word 'insolvency' remained ostracized until the first shock after the Mexican disaster in 1994–5. To this day, creditor governments are still unwilling to accept insolvency procedures as a solution to the debt problem.

Warnings against overindebtedness had been heard in Latin America during the 1970s. Citing dramatic proportions of foreign public debts, Wionczek (1978, p.118) thought a debt crisis comparable to the 1930s possible in 1968. A conference in Mexico City in October 1977 discussed solutions to the debt problem. Helleiner (1979) demanded rules for debt relief, including the reduction of present values of repayments. The World Bank's C.S. Hardy (1979, p.196) warned of debt problems, classifying refinancing as 'not really a credible alternative'. The coordinator of this conference, M.S. Wionczek (1979, p.93), explained the post-1977 wave of optimism in the face of a deteriorating situation: 'in terms of institutional interests and social psychology rather than economic and financial analysis'.

Without ignoring the co-responsibility of SC governments that borrowed eagerly, it must be recalled that Third World leaders warned repeatedly of the dangers inherent in debt accumulation and proposed relief measures, for instance at UNCTAD IV and V, or during the negotiations of the Conference on International Economic Cooperation in Paris.

The BWIs themselves started structural adjustment lending well before 1982: according to *Finance and Development*, their official quarterly, the IMF started in Africa after 1973 (Kanesa-Thasan, 1981). Officially the Bank started programme lending in 1980, but it had exerted influence in connection with projects before. The Bank always used its leverage to support the IMF and its policy against resistance from SCs.

During the early phase, when the Fund was apparently glad to find clients, conditionality was considered lenient 'in relation to the required adjustment effort' (ibid., p.20). At that time, adjustment programmes were usually planned for one year, as 12 months fitted in best with administrative time horizons. In 1979, conditionality became stricter; 88 arrangements were approved by the IMF between January 1979 and December 1981, to support adjustment policies, particularly measures to reach a sustainable balance of payments position (Crockett, 1982). All countries asking for rescheduling in 1981 'had adopted an adjustment program' with the Fund when negotiating with their creditors (Nowzad, 1982, p.13).

In spite of RTA, the Pearson Report, explicit warnings, the fact that new loans were mostly used to service old ones on time well before August 1982, or their own experience with macroeconomic interventions and adjustment programmes, the BWIs strongly encouraged SCs to borrow. The BWIs, particularly the IMF, did not arrive on the scene after August 1982 to solve a problem created by others, but had been part of the process leading to it (cf. Raffer, 1994a, 1997b). Their type of adjustment did not prevent the debt crisis. The first unsuccessful adjustment programmes existed before its official start. The IMF might counter by pointing out that it did not have sufficient leverage before 1982 to force countries into necessary reforms. Then one would have to ask why programmes were financed if and when the IMF was aware that necessary reforms were not undertaken and the money could thus not be put to good use. The argument of lack of leverage would be at odds with the claim that debtors themselves 'own' programmes only 'supported' by BWIs. The claim of country 'ownership' is more often heard recently. But both official sources and publications by leading BWI staff show that countries do not 'own' programmes (cf. Raffer, 1993). The issue of 'ownership' is another peculiar feature of the BWIs. Depending on occasions and audiences, they claim either to be only supporting a country's own programme or to make a country adopt 'sensible' policies – a clear logical inconsistency.

They completely failed to realize in time how serious the situation was. That it took them an embarrassingly long time to acknowledge the nature and the dimension of the debt problem can be proved by a host of evidence from their own publications. As late as 1982, a paper in their official quarterly allayed fears that private banks might not cover SC deficits. These widespread concerns of 'two years ago' had become unfounded 'nowadays' (Nowzad, 1982, p.14), although it could not be excluded that some groups of non-oil-exporting SCs might not be able to borrow all the funds they might need in the future. Nowzad echoes the findings of an IMF working group on international capital markets published in *Finance and Development* in March 1981 in an unsigned article and as an *Occasional Paper*.

Even after August 1982, the BWIs thought the money market functioned well, seeing no signs of liquidity bottlenecks, or of restrictions regarding the capital base of private banks limiting lending to SCs, which was supposed to continue on a large scale (Versluysen, 1982). The Task Force on Non-Concessional Flows established by the BWIs in 1979 presented their findings in May 1982 (ibid., p.33). Pointing out that the conclusions had been presented before the crisis and that there was currently even less reason for optimism, Versluysen insisted that they did still hold (ibid., p.34).

DEALING WITH THE CRISIS AFTER 1982

The year 1982 is an important one with respect to BWI influence on debtor economies, which increased dramatically from that time. Any financial support to debtors has been made contingent on the 'seal of approval' by the

BWIs. Debt management by Bank and Fund has received unconditional support by their major shareholders, in spite of apparent and protracted lack of success. Even grave failures officially documented, for instance by the internal Operations Evaluation Department or the Wapenhans Report (World Bank, 1992), have not made creditor countries, dominating the BWIs with their voting majority, question the effectiveness of the BWIs seriously, let alone demand appropriate reforms.

The literature on structural adjustment and debt management after 1982 is voluminous. A huge array of proposals on ways to deal with the crisis were made, ranging from interest caps to public institutions buying debts from banks at a discount – which might or might not be passed on to debtor SCs – thus transferring commercial bank claims into official claims. Clearly, a survey cannot be provided here owing to limitations of space. Nor is it attempted. The rest of this chapter will show how debt management moved too slowly towards more and more, yet still insufficient, debt relief, drawing attention to what we believe to be important historical milestones.

Debt management after 1982 was based on the so-called 'illiquidity theory', the assumption that there was no fundamental crisis but only a temporary inability to pay. William R. Cline and the US Treasury Secretary James Baker, as well as the BWIs, were firm defenders of this thesis. On the basis of optimistic assumptions, for instance with regard to debtors' export volumes and prices, or relatively high growth in OECD countries, Cline (1985) claimed just before the 1985 IMF/World Bank meeting that, by the late 1980s, debt-export ratios would be back to levels previously associated with creditworthiness. Optimistically, he concluded: 'The emerging evidence in 1983–84 has tended to confirm the analysis that the debt problem is one of illiquidity and subject to improvement as international recovery takes place' (ibid., p.187).

During this meeting in Seoul, James Baker expressly called on IFIs to support comprehensive macroeconomic and structural policies in SCs, demanding a continued central role of the IMF together with multilateral development banks, and more intensive IMF and World Bank collaboration. As countries would grow out of debts, Baker insisted that not a single cent of debts be forgiven. Financial help was proposed in the form of additional net lending of $29 billion over three years. Commercial banks were supposed to lend $20 billion, IFIs $9 billion. To put this amount into proper perspective: Mexico alone paid $9·4 billion in interest in 1985; its total debt service was $14·5 billion, Brazil's 10·3 billion (WDT, 1988, vol. II).

Supported by all creditors, Baker firmly rejected any general solution, insisting on solving SC problems case by case. Eventually, a group of debtors was singled out, called 'highly indebted countries' (HICs) but sometimes dubbed 'Baker countries', on which debt initiatives were to focus.

Membership of this group clearly reflected US economic and political interests.

To overcome the debt problem during the perceived period until recovery, 'involuntary lending' by commercial banks was seen as the solution, which appeared a good policy on the assumption that debtors would grow out of the problem. Officially favoured was the so-called 'menu approach': as with a menu, banks were supposed to chose their options. Small banks with relatively little money in SCs lent during the heydays of sovereign lending could chose a way out: exit bonds allowing them not to participate in further concerted lending. Larger banks might sell their claims on the secondary market to reshuffle their portfolios. Cataquet (1989) provides a good survey of the many options, including the establishment of a subsidiary on the Cayman Islands by Japanese banks. The so-called 'secondary market', where claims were traded below nominal values, was not a market in the textbook sense, since participation was restricted. Great pain was taken to ensure that debtors themselves could not buy their own debts. Understandably, creditors feared that SCs might otherwise have a strong incentive to drive secondary market 'prices' down. On rare occasions it was believed that a debtor had been allowed unofficially to buy back on these conditions. In the case of Bolivia, a buy-back occurred for an SC by other countries, not by the debtor itself (Sachs, 1988a). Occasionally, a debtor may have managed to conceal who was actually buying.

Although secondary market rates implied a reassessment of the values of Third World debts, the belief that more could eventually be recovered remained strong. The chairman of Lloyds, Sir Jeremy Morse, explained in 1987: 'Lenders that have stayed in Latin America generally have not lost except those that lent to private companies which went bust', and 'Those that wanted to get out quickly have lost the discount on the assets they sold or swapped' (*The Economist*, 21-7 March 1987, Survey, p.18). J.P. Morgan and Co reacted to the establishment of secondary markets by setting up a unit selling other banks' SC loans at a discount and for a fee, but not their own. Sir Jeremy's remark on private companies deserves further elaboration. Some commercial banks forced SC governments to assume retroactively losses from private lending initially done without any government involvement. The reason is simple: private debtors can go bankrupt, official debtors are denied this relief by the North. This shows that the lack of international insolvency is a market imperfection. Although based on rather unorthodox legal foundations, these debt increases have never met audible protest from the BWIs. They chose to ignore it. This ex post socialization made debt management more difficult, but the BWIs insisted on punctual service of these debts as well.

The instrument 'on the menu' receiving most attention was debt–equity swaps. They allowed investors to buy from banks at secondary market discounts and to finance direct investments worth the face value of acquired claims. Somewhat later, a fee was charged by SC authorities, which eventually could become quite substantial. However, with austerity programmes restricting domestic demand and IC protectionism restricting export possibilities, debt–equity swaps have usually not exceeded a relatively modest level. Exceptions were most notably Mexico and Chile. If effected on a larger scale - political resentment against selling out to foreigners apart - they only postpone balance of payments problems. Once the repatriation of profits starts, foreign exchange pressures make themselves felt again. The effect is thus the same as a grace period.

Further problems were mentioned in the literature: inflationary effects and subsidizing investments that would take place anyway. It is interesting to note that Mexico, which introduced debt–equity swaps in 1986 on a significant scale, suspended its scheme for exactly these reasons in November 1987 (Blackwell & Nocera, 1988). Irrespective of one's opinion on direct investment in general, these swaps were not a viable tool to solve a debt crisis, as shown by the relation of the stock of debts to available swap opportunities.

These subsidies of investments were available not only to foreigners, but also to nationals of the debtor. If nationals or residents are allowed to participate, another problem emerges: capital flight gets a premium. It pays to get one's money out of the country first to benefit from the inherent subsidy. With an amount of $2·6 billion, Chile was the biggest converter during 1983–7, ranking nearly half a billion before Brazil (ibid.). It was the first country allowing its own residents to engage in this activity, regulating it with a special provision, Chapter 18 of the rules set by the central bank. Assuming that the military junta and its supporters were more likely to have the necessary foreign exchange, one may call it a clever move by the junta to use governmental powers for reaping private profits. The Chilean repatriation of flight capital via debt–equity swaps is most surprising. During the 1980s, when capital flight was - quite correctly - seen as a sign of wrong economic policies, statistics on Chile showed no capital flight and the country was therefore generally presented as a model of sound economic policy, not least by the BWIs. It was argued that one could not sweepingly qualify Latin America as a capital flight region because of Chile. It was even regretted that Chile would not be able to benefit from repatriation since it had not had any capital flight (Arellano & Ramos, 1987). Chile was nevertheless able to benefit massively from returning flight capital as soon as repatriation became the touchstone of soundness, and Chile could again be presented as a model (Raffer 1996a).

Throughout the 1980s, fears of a debtors' cartel were voiced, but the only working debtors' cartel occurred in 1984, when big debtors such as Mexico,

Brazil and Venezuela joined to help Argentina to pay in time to save US banks from having to classify loans as non-performing because of inflexible and inappropriate banking laws. A whole literature on 'legal risk' came into existence, analysing the problems that a crash might be brought about by national banking laws in OECD countries (cf. Grueson & Reissner, 1984; Raffer, 1989) rather than by debtor action. Crises were frequently reported at quarters' ends during the 1980s owing to US quarterly accounting, triggered by awkward and economically debatable regulatory constraints, such as the 90 days clause, the impossibility of capitalizing interest arrears, or unpredictable and allegedly discriminatory decisions of regulators. On one occasion the hands of the clock were reportedly held back to book payments 'in time'. By contrast, legal rules governing loan loss provisioning on the European continent proved to be stabilizing (Raffer, 1991).

When commercial banks withdrew from the South after 1982, multilateral funds poured in, allowing commercial banks to receive higher (re)payments than otherwise possible. A remarkable shift in the structure of debts occurred. In 1988, the World Bank complained that concerted lending by banks since 1982 had just been sufficient to refinance around a quarter of interest payments by HICs, making the World Bank 'the principal net lender to HICs' (WDT, 1988, p.xxix). The substantial bail-out of private banks by multilaterals was aptly called an 'implicit taxpayers' subsidy' by Sachs (1988b). In a major process of risk shifting, risk was reallocated to public multilaterals, increasing their share of debts substantially. This hardened conditions for debtors since multilaterals, in marked contrast to private banks, refused to reschedule or reduce their claims until quite recently. A financial merry-go-round started in order to keep up the pretence that multilaterals do not reschedule. Funds from, say, the Bank were used to repay the IMF, allowing it in turn to lend again to the debtor, so that the World Bank's loan could be serviced 'in time'. Not infrequently, OECD governments participated as intermediary financiers. The whole bill had to be picked up by debtors.

Apart from shifting risk to official IFIs, this also shifted risk from the USA to other countries. US banks were much more heavily exposed in HICs than others, accounting for a higher percentage of total bank debts than the US share in IFIs. Seen as a country, the USA could thus reduce its risks, being bailed out by other countries. The idea that other countries should use their money to allow the USA to reduce their exposure was advocated for some time. In particular, the idea was propagated that balance of payments surplus countries, such as Japan or Germany, should use their surpluses to become larger creditors. The USA accused Japan of not properly sharing the burden of necessary international expenditures, which were mainly military, although Japan's low military outlays were due to the restrictions imposed by the USA itself after World War II. Japan's Capital Recycling Programme of 1986 resulted from this pressure, as the name indicates (Raffer & Singer, 1996, pp.111ff). Apparently (and understandably), Japan was not prepared to pick up other people's debt problems. Rather than lending directly to problem debtors, it preferred channelling funds via IFIs.

In May 1987, US money centre banks finally acknowledged that some money was irretrievably lost. In a spectacular move, Citicorp set aside $3 billion in additional reserves to cover loan losses. Without doing so Citicorp would have expected profits of $2 billion. This move, and the favourable reaction of the stock exchange, set the stage for other banks to follow. The argument that default by Latin America – it was routinely assumed that the whole region would behave like one country, forming some kind of cartel – would wipe out the primary capital of major banks and lead to a crash of the banking community was no longer valid. The fact that US banks, unlike banks on the European continent, had not used their high incomes from SC loans to build up reserves for quite some time is not what one would expect if higher spreads had actually been charged because of higher (perceived) risk. Backed by their new strength, US banks started to favour tougher bargaining – another proof of the lack of debtor power.

ACCEPTING DEBT REDUCTION IN PRINCIPLE

The 'Baker Plan' was put aside when its author left the Treasury to become secretary of state, a position where, in the opinion of *Time* (20 February 1989), his holdings in Chemical New York Corp., a bank significantly exposed in the South without sufficient provisions against losses, posed a potential conflict of interest to debt initiatives.

At the 1988 IMF/World Bank conference in Berlin, the new US Treasury secretary, N. Brady, referred to the necessity of debt reduction. The 'Brady Plan' presented on 10 March 1989, after violent riots in Venezuela, called explicitly for debt reduction, although only commercial banks were supposed to recognize losses. Brady's proposal was very similar to the ideas of Japanese Minister of Finance Miyazawa Kiichi, made a few months earlier without receiving much attention.

Brady's official statement was not the first deviation from the 'Baker Plan'. The US Treasury had actively backed a deal between Mexico and its creditors in 1987–8, involving a reduction of the principal owed. The idea was to use US Treasury zero coupon bonds as collateral for securitized Mexican debt amounting to $20 billion. Even though the outcome was very modest, falling far short of the quantitative target, and interest rate increases already eroded the result during the same year (Navarrete, 1988), this Mexican deal was a recognition by the USA that the 'Baker Plan' did not work.

The *Venice Terms* of the Paris Club still insisted on full repayment in 1987, but stretched maturities for poor debtors (WDT, 1991, p.28). Opposition to initiatives to reduce the debt burden of poor countries was eventually overcome at the Toronto summit. The UK proposal was accepted. These *Toronto Terms* involved debt reduction of some official debts owed by poor (so-called 'IDA only') SCs to members of the Paris Club (IC governments). Official creditors were to forgive either one-third of the stock of eligible debts or grant an equivalent reduction of the rate of interest. On US insistence, a third option was agreed upon, which was considered equal: stretched maturities and grace periods of 14 years. Officially, the 'Baker Plan' was upheld as the general principle.

By recognizing the necessity of debt reduction not only for the poorest countries, Brady's initiative was an important first step towards a viable solution. Suffering from severe shortcomings it provided, on the other hand, no solution to the debt problem. Its two main elements were voluntary debt reduction by commercial banks and public guarantees via IFIs. But Brady also wanted banks to lend new money, an option not enthusiastically received. Banks were reluctant to grant voluntary reduction of debt and debt service, all the more so as they were the only ones supposed to do so. Creditor governments and IFIs, such as the BWI, would insist on full repayment. Understandably, this unequal treatment of creditors was strongly resented by banks that wanted symmetrical treatment of all creditors.

The bail-out was the carrot. The stick was a change in IFI disbursement practices. Disbursement by the BWIs would no longer depend on prior completion of full commercial bank financing packages, thus weakening the position of commercial banks. The executive board of the IMF stated that a loan package to a heavily indebted country could be approved before the completion of a debt reduction agreement with its commercial creditors, provided the Fund felt such prompt support to be essential, and negotiations were already started with commercial banks with an agreement expected within a reasonable time. The Fund also softened its position on arrears to commercial banks, recognizing that a debtor's financing situation might not allow them to be avoided. The policy of non-toleration of arrears to IFIs remained unchanged.

The first tangible product of the Brady Initiative, reached under prolonged pressure by the US government, was the Mexican agreement of July 1989, hailed as the first Brady Plan deal. Warnings that Mexico's overall debt might rise because of new lending by IFIs and Japan, as well as the capitalization of interest on Paris Club debts, did not materialize. But the reduction of bank debts by $7 billion was balanced by increases in debts vis-à-vis IFIs and Japan. An effective cash flow relief of less than $1 billion was calculated by banks (*Neue Zürcher Zeitung*, 6 February 1990). According to the World Bank

(WDT, 1990, p.33) the net debt service effect of Mexico's Brady package during 1990–94 was $1·8 billion a year on average. Fewer banks than expected opted for new money instead of relief.

After Mexico, further Brady restructurings occurred. Free-riding of banks unwilling to participate was prevented by 'political pressure' (WDT, 1993, p.39). Argentina, Costa Rica, Brazil, Venezuela, Nigeria, the Philippines and Ecuador benefited from Brady schemes, called 'debt and debt service reduction schemes' after Brady's term at the US Treasury. The results were not encouraging. Except in the case of Costa Rica, time series of the debt overhang did not reflect positive impacts on debt servicing in the early 'Brady countries', not even in the Philippines, which had a second helping. Costa Rica and the Philippines still could not service their debts as due afterwards (Raffer, 1996a).

The BWIs embraced the 'Brady Plan' as fully as the 'Baker Plan', possibly because it, too, increased their importance. After defending the illiquidity theory for some years they seemed to have forgotten their own arguments and analyses, as well as the fact that the policies advised to (or forced on) debtor countries by them were based on this error. Their 'advice' or – paraphrasing a sterner source – their 'firmer understanding' (Stern, 1983) of monitoring had created economic and social damage in SCs. The countries, not the BWIs, had to pay for such damage, thus increasing debt burdens, not least by new multilateral loans to finance rehabilitation measures necessitated by IFI projects.

Debt management based on the wrong illiquidity assumption hurt creditors as well. Between 1982 and 1989, the year when the US decided that debt reduction was necessary, long-term debt of all SCs roughly doubled, from $546·9 billion (WDT, 1985) to $1114·9 billion (World Bank, 1997), growing at a compound rate of 10 per cent per annum. This was due to reschedulings relieving the immediate liquidity problem, but increasing present values of debts. Delaying a proper solution by clinging to the illiquidity theory and giving more loans ultimately increased unpayable debts. Delaying debt relief makes it look costlier and costlier. A quick and sensible insolvency solution would have been less costly in 1982 than in 1989 owing to phantom debts, claims capitalized and added that exist on paper but can never be recouped.

While of limited financial importance, the Brady Initiative definitely opened the door for debt reduction. In 1989, IDA introduced a Debt Reduction Facility. In 1990, President Bush declared debt reduction an option under the *Enterprise for the Americas* initiative. In 1991, UK Chancellor of the Exchequer John Major urged that Paris Club debts be reduced by two-thirds. These *Trinidad Terms* were considered so radical that OECD governments refused to apply them. A compromise of 50 per cent reduction was agreed on, the *Intermediate Trinidad Terms* or *Enhanced Toronto Terms*. The *Naples*

Terms adopted three years later by the G7 were still less generous than the UK Trinidad proposal: 50 to 67 per cent debt reduction. Eventually, the discussion on the multilateral debt overhang (see next chapter) brought about reductions surpassing the original proposal by Britain.

VICTIMS AND DAMAGES OF DEBT MANAGEMENT

While quite successful in extracting payments for creditors, debt management during the 1980s had considerable negative effects on both the poor in the South and debtor economies. Huge net transfers to creditors were achieved by drastic import compression, with crippling effects on debtors. The burden of real transfers, measured in relation to GNP, was historically unprecedented. In 1982–5, it was higher than Germany's burden after 1918, France's after the lost Franco-Prussian war of 1870, and higher than Marshall Plan payments.

The GATT (1986, p.25) concluded that 'virtually the entire burden' of adjustment had been put on debtors. Pointing out that adjustment had 'involved mostly import contraction rather than export expansion', the GATT worried that this 'will prolong rather than resolve the debt crisis' and about a 'vicious circle of reduced imports and reduced export potential' (ibid., p.26). In 1986, the dollar value of merchandise imports of 15 HICs was more than 40 per cent below their 1981 level. Gross capital formation fell drastically. In 1985, the relation of gross capital formation to GDP had fallen to just over two-thirds of the value in 1980. The fall of investment ratios was so steep that the BWIs themselves started to worry that 'even minimal replacements may no longer occur in important sectors' (World Bank, 1988, p.3) and that the 'severity of this prolonged economic slump already surpasses that of the Great Depression in industrial countries' (ibid.). It had 'already taken a heavy toll on growth' and 'will continue to hold back future growth' (WDT, 1988, p.xix). But the Bank did not see this – or the 'Lost Decade' in general – as a result of structural adjustment.

Debt management also caused great hardship to the poor. At first this was denied, but the BWIs had to admit that the poor actually suffered. Poverty is another issue where the BWIs made a distinct U-turn (Raffer, 1994a). After 1982, the BWIs insisted that carrying on structural adjustment had positive impacts and was in the very interest of the poor, while special measures to protect them would be superfluous, if not harmful. Emphasizing human needs might obstruct needed reforms. Strong public pressure, in particular after the famous UNICEF study on adjustment with a human face (Cornia *et al.*, 1987), has changed the picture. Special programmes to help those affected by structural adjustment are now officially accepted. It is argued that this will make structural adjustment more acceptable and thus more efficient – a point strongly denied before. In practice, though, little was changed and measures for the poor largely remained lip service, not only during the 1980s. Social Dimensions of Adjustment (SDA) were recognized in publications rather than acted on in practice.

If the BWIs are right now, that means that their previous adjustment efforts were flawed and inefficient, causing damage to their clients. If they were right, then they are causing damage now. But the effects of IFI errors have to be borne by their clients. The exemption of IFI from financial accountability and from paying any damage compensation is patently unjustified. The World Bank particularly has been keen to stress that it has learned for some time – it was quite recently joined by the IMF – but at whose cost?

To support the claim that their policies work, the BWIs have repeatedly singled out countries as examples of successful policies, dropping them after a short while when they became untenable. Statistically debatable groupings of adjusters and non-adjusters have often been compared without producing convincing statistical differences. Occasionally, claims were made that the debt crisis was over for one region or the other. In the case of Africa, the famous statement, 'Recovery has begun' (World Bank and UNDP, 1989, p.iii) had to be withdrawn quickly because of massive criticism even from within the UN family. The UN Economic Commission for Africa (ECA, 1989) presented an *official* critique of the measures forced upon the region's debtor nations, and an African alternative. The optimistic conclusions of the World Bank/UNDP publication which arranged data to support the BWTs' claim of economic success were soon no longer upheld by the Bank itself. Quite rightly so, as experience showed.

11. Too little, too slowly: dragging the debt problem into the third millennium

While the 1980s became known as the 'lost decade', the 1990s began with officially heralded hope and recovery, if not for all debtors, at least for those having adopted 'prudent' economic policies. Latin America was used, with an occasional, cautious caveat regarding sustainability, as a practical vindication of adjustment policies based on the Washington Consensus.

In 1991, the Inter-American Development Bank's report, *Social and Economic Progress* in Latin America titled its first part, 'The Nineties: A Decade of Hope'. In spite of a GDP per head at the level of 1977 and a drastic fall in standards of living not experienced in the region for half a century, it thought greater optimism for this decade justified (IDB, 1991, p.5). The following report of 1992 starts with the ominous formulation, 'The Recovery Begins' (IDB, 1992, p.1) strongly recalling the famous 'Recovery has begun' (World Bank and UNDP, 1989, p.iii), used to herald economic recovery in sub-Saharan Africa (SSA).

In its *World Debt Tables 1992/93*, the World Bank (WDT, 1992, p.3) concludes with regard to 'a number of' Latin American countries: 'With debt indicators now back to pre-1982 levels, most of these countries are emerging from the debt crisis, helped in some cases by the catalytic effects of reductions in their commercial bank debt.' It was fast becoming generally accepted wisdom according to the Bank (ibid., p.41) that the resumption of large capital flows into some Latin American countries heralded the end of the debt crisis. For 'commercial banks and some of their middle-income developing country borrowers, the debt crisis ... is largely over', as proved by 'renewed portfolio flows [which] are part of a wider (albeit still fragile) return to market access' (ibid., p.7). In short, Latin America had dealt with its debt overhang (WDT, 1993, p.5). In this enthusiastic climate no one seemed to recall the enthusiasm about private flows to SCs during the 1970s, when OECD governments, the BWIs and private banks were all equally enthusiastic about increasing private lending, or the results of these loans, the still not overcome debt crisis.

Pointing at over two dozen Low and Lower-Middle-Income Countries still under debt pressure, the World Bank saw a growing dichotomy between

175

middle-income and poor debtors. It was generally agreed that the debt crisis was still felt in some countries, notably in SSA, or by Severely Indebted Low Income Countries (SILICs), a group largely identical to it. These countries, the argument went, had not embraced 'sound' policies as eagerly, even though SSA had been subject to structural adjustment for nearly two decades.

The World Bank took care to place caveats more visibly than in 1989 – possibly a good example of learning by doing. It warned, for instance, that complacency might be premature: 'The newer portfolio flows are generally more volatile and their marked redirection to a few developing countries is to some extent an outcome of low interest rates in their home markets, as well as one-off adjustment in the composition of individual and institutional investor portfolios' (WDT, 1992, p.3). Strong concerns about the sustainability of some of the new capital flows were also noted (WDT, 1993, pp.4f).

A closer look at the World Bank's own data did not show that the debt overhang had been overcome in Latin America, nor did it justify the vindication of successful adjustment policies (Raffer, 1996a). Conventional indicators such as the debt service ratio (DSR) did indeed fall because Latin America's arrears increased steeply. As the World Bank measures payments on a cash basis (payments made), not on the basis of payments due, low ratios of debt service or interest payments to exports or GNP can result from two very different situations. A country without any debts would obviously have ratios of zero. So would a country with huge debts not paying a single penny. If used to describe a country's debt overhang, these indicators might be misleading. Calling debt service obligations 'the real measure of debt burden', the World Bank (1989, p.21) recognized this fact.

The World Bank's comparison with pre-1982 debt indicators, supporting the notion that debt management had – at last – been successful in Latin America, only held if one disregarded arrears. This, however, is definitely wrong if one follows literature unanimously defining debt overhang as a situation where the debt burden is so disproportionately large that conceivable efforts to pay according to contract could not improve the debtor's situation. The fruits of such efforts would thus accrue exclusively to creditors. Krugman (1988) defines debt overhang as the expected present value of potential future resource transfers being less than a country's debt, or – less formally – existing debts 'sufficiently large that creditors do not expect with confidence to be fully repaid'. Similarly, the WDT (1992, p.11) define the 'reduction of debt obligations in line with ability to pay' as removing the debt overhang. According to both definitions growing arrears (that is, incapability to service debts in line with obligations) are a clear and undeniable proof of a debt overhang. Furthermore, arrears should make creditors cautious.

Raffer (1996a) suggested an index to reflect the debt overhang, using arrears, which are the clearest proof for it:

$$0 \leqslant DSR/DSR_d* \leqslant 1 \qquad\qquad (11.1)$$

the relation between debt service payments effected and due. *DSR* is the debt service ratio as defined by the World Bank (cash base). The subscript *d* denotes payments contractually due. The denominator of (11.1) contains debt service plus arrears. Theoretically, the real debt service ratio must include all payments due but not effected, including interest arrears and amortization of short-term debt and capitalized interest. Furthermore, it should include rescheduled principal arrears for every year. Owing to constraints of data availability, Raffer (ibid.) had to define DSR_d* as the contractual debt service ratio (DSR_d) plus interest capitalized. While this is an improvement on traditional debt indicators, it still understates the burden of debt service.

The index is 1 if payments are made on time, 0 if the debtor does not pay. It does not suffer from the ambiguity of the World Bank's interest service ratio or debt service ratio, which are equally low if a debtor has small debts or simply does not pay as stipulated.

The *World Debt Tables* show dramatically increased arrears. Apparently, the ability to pay deteriorated substantially. Even if it had not been the ability but the willingness to pay, this, too, should have dampened optimism. Latin America's interests arrears were perceptibly higher than actual interest payments for the first time in 1990, then again in 1991, and nearly as big in 1992. Principal arrears were higher than repayments in 1990 and 1991, and 82 per cent in 1992 (WDT, 1993). Naturally, the global decline in interest rates since their peak in the 1980s had beneficial effects as well, lowering interest service ratios perceptibly. Not surprisingly, considering the privileged position of some official lenders, private creditors accounted for most of these arrears, between 83 and 87·8 per cent in the case of interest, and from 69·7 to 73 per cent in the case of principal.

Until 1991, Latin America's contractual debt service ratio was markedly worse than SSA's (cf. WDT, 1993). Excluding countries with no arrears according to the World Bank, such as Mexico, Uruguay and Chile, the situation for the rest of Latin America was even more drastic. The index proposed by Raffer was between 0·46 and 0·49 between 1990 and 1992 for Latin America, and between 0·3950 and 0·3736 for Latin America without Mexico (Raffer, 1996a): what was paid was less than half of what should have been paid.

If calculated as the relation between contractually due debt service and exports, Latin America's debt service ratio had deteriorated massively, while indicators using actual payments indeed fell to pre-1982 levels because of tolerated non-payment. Since the World Bank itself published the data on arrears allowing Raffer to recalculate their indicators, it must have been aware of this precarious situation when voicing optimism.

In a nutshell: the heralded end of the debt crisis in Latin America was basically due to the toleration of extremely large non-payments, or breaches of contract. If creditors had accepted much lower, let alone similar, arrears in 1982, whether in percentages of long-term debts or in current dollars, there would have been no debt crisis. Rather than a recovery, the situation recalled Maddison's (1985, p.28) description of Latin America in the 1930s when 'debt default eased payments constraints' and creditors acquiesced in the situation.

Steeply growing current account deficits for Latin America did not suggest a recovery either. Between 1990 and 1992, the latest year available for individual countries in the summer of 1994, Mexico's deficit more than trebled, growing at 179 per cent per annum. Argentina, Venezuela and Uruguay changed considerably from surpluses to deficits. Brazil, however, not a model debtor, changed from –$3·8 billion to a surplus of $4·1 billion. Argentina, Brazil, Mexico and Venezuela were the main countries in the region able to place bonds. Honouring only one-third of its contractual obligations Brazil got large reschedulings in 1992 and was second in attracting new bonds in 1992 and 1993, right after Mexico and before Argentina, whose DSR/DSR_d* was 0·26 in 1992. Apparently, new bonds worth billions of dollars can be placed by debtors with huge arrears if the 'climate' is right.

The World Bank acknowledged insolvency as the root of the problem when the end of the debt crisis was proclaimed and it could be argued that insolvency relief was no longer necessary. In spite of their embarrassing record, the BWIs lectured on prudent borrowing. *The World Debt Tables 1992/93* (WDT, 1992, pp.10ff), for instance, explained that 'the principal policy lesson of the debt crisis is that domestic resources and policy, not external finance per se are the key to economic development'. The World Bank went on:

> heavy reliance on external finance is a risky strategy because it increases vulnerability to adverse external development and their attendant long-term development impact ... *Prudent lending and borrowing policies should take into account the vulnerability to adverse external shocks.* Current interest rates are a poor guide for external finance decisions. Seemingly cheap variable-rate loans may turn out to be expensive if interest rates increase. Negative terms of trade shocks may be permanent rather than transitory and merit adjustment rather than external finance. *In a solvency crisis, early recognition of solvency as the root cause and the need for a final settlement are important for minimizing the damage.* ...protracted renegotiations and uncertainty damaged economic activity in debtor countries for several years ... It took too long to recognize that liquidity was the visible tip of the problem, but not its root. (Ibid., emphasis in original)

Ahmed and Summers (1992, p.4) quantify the costs of delaying the recognition of the 'now' generally acknowledged solvency crisis as 'one decade' lost in development. This delay was caused by defenders of the illiquidity theory in the 1980s, notably the BWIs. Among its most explicit advocates, they supported this theory with overly optimistic forecasts 'showing' that debtors would 'grow out of debts'. In line with US policy, they defended the view that debt reductions were unnecessary until the 'Brady Plan' abandoned this view.

DIRECTING AND ENTICING NEW CAPITAL INFLOWS

The improvement in SC access to international capital markets did not just happen in the 1990s. New flows from new sources, namely bonds (as in the 1930s) and foreign direct as well as portfolio investment poured into some SCs, allowing voluntary repayments to commercial banks and easy servicing of multilateral debts. Commercial banks themselves knew better than to put substantial sums of their own money into these countries again. Similar to the shift from commercial banks to IFIs described in the previous chapter, another shift took place in the 1990s.

This shift 'has been supported by regulatory changes, particularly in the Japanese bond market. Quality guidelines for Samurai bond issues ... were relaxed further in 1992 and the minimum credit rating ... was lowered from A to BBB' (WDT, 1993, pp.21f). Changes in regulation regarding equities making private placement in general more attractive occurred in the USA too.

These regulatory changes, and a trend toward explicitly rating developing country borrowers at least partially triggered by them, allowed institutional investors to place money in SCs. Without these changes the Mexican crisis could not have happened. Official optimism, relaxed quality guidelines and lowered minimum credit ratings induced institutional investors to place money there. Interest rate differences helped to attract new money until the Mexican crash. Risk was shifted again, this time away from IFIs onto institutional investors and the public at large. Lured by regulatory changes and official optimism, they had replaced banks and IFIs to such an extent that these 'tens of millions of little-guy investors' (*Time*, 13 February 1995) were one, if not the main, argument for a new $50 billion bail-out in Mexico.

The Mexican fiasco of 1994–5 vindicated strong scepticism. Official optimism about renewed market access and claims that the debt crisis was overcome – often backed by the example of Mexico – were dashed by the new Mexican crisis and the rescue package required to defuse it. As in many other cases, the BWIs had not foreseen the crash of their model debtor, a country which had implemented BWI 'recommendations' faithfully. The only 'success' of orthodox debt strategies seems to have been shifting some risk onto mutual funds, pension funds and retirement accounts – or the public at large. The fact that the crisis broke in the very country always enjoying privileged treatment as a debtor, and showing excellent debt indicators, should be taken into account when evaluating this period of official optimism. This crisis also strengthened the case for an international insolvency procedure for sovereign borrowers modelled on the US Chapter 9 (the insolvency of municipalities) as an efficient and durable solution with a human face (Raffer, 1990a; Raffer & Singer, 1996).

The need to find a permanent and viable solution to the debt problem was felt again in a forceful way. Shortly after the Mexican crash, the chairman of the Federal Reserve System, Alan Greenspan, suggested thinking about international insolvency. US Treasury Secretary Robert Rubin said that some procedures were needed to work out the obligations of debtors. The chairman of the House Banking and Financial Services Committee, Rep. Jim Leach of Iowa, recommended international insolvency proceedings, even briefly mentioning the little-known Chapter 9 proceedings for debtors with governmental powers, which is particularly well suited for sovereign debtors. But the shock was quickly overcome. Instead of some form of international insolvency, the G7 Halifax meeting of 1995 chose to strengthen the IMF.

After this brief hiatus, enthusiasm about private flows to the South continued. But, as mentioned above, at least one institution learned the lesson: expecting frequent crashes in the future. The OECD (1996a, p.57) called for officially subsidized private speculation, implying that private failures require taxpayers' bail-out money. This expectation was proved right in 1997 by the Asian crisis.

THE DEBT PROBLEM OF SUB-SAHARAN AFRICA

In contrast to the case of Latin America, IFIs showed less optimism regarding Africa, no doubt also because of the World Bank's experience with announcing that recovery had begun. Nevertheless, some 'good news' on SSA was cautiously put about during the optimism of the 1990s. It was again posited that structural adjustment was the first and decisive step towards recovery in Africa, although there was still a long way to go (cf. Jones & Kiguel, 1994). Optimism was expressed that growth prospects would 'doubtlessly' increase if adjustment policies were not impeded, although they would not be able to overcome poverty in African countries (Husain, 1994). To achieve this, Husain declared increased investments in human capital and infrastructure to be necessary, precisely those investments that had to be cut under SA programmes.

Interestingly, SSA's conventional debt indicators were dramatically lower than Latin America's at the beginning of the 1990s, as Table 11.1. shows. However, IFIs did not interpret them as optimistically as in the case of Latin America, a fact which must be taken into account when evaluating their optimism on Latin America's recovery. Table 11.1 also illustrates the dubious character of official data on debts, particularly on SSA. It compares debt indicators for the same years taken from two consecutive years of the Bank's *World Debt Tables*.

Table 11.1   Sub-Saharan Africa's arrears and debt service, 1980-93 (%)

	1980	1986	1987	1988	1989	1990	1991	1992	1993^p
			DSR and ISR on Cash Base*						
WDT 1993									
ISR	6.2	11.4	9.4	10.3	9.7	9.0	9.2	8.6	7.3
DSR	9.7	24.9	19.6	21.0	18.0	18.0	17.1	16.9	13.5
*WDT 1992**									
ISR	5.7	11.6	9.2	11.5	10.2	8.9	10.0	8.8	—
DSR	10.9	28.2	22.1	24.7	21.8	20.0	19.8	18.5	—
			Contractual DSR and ISR						
WDT 1993									
ISR$_d$	6.4	15.8	16.3	19.7	20.5	20.9	23.4	25.7	26.8
DSR$_d$	11.2	39.4	39.1	50.5	48.0	50.2	56.7	64.9	68.0
*WDT 1992**									
ISR$_d$	6.1	18.7	20.3	26.9	27.7	27.2	32.6	34.5	—
DSR$_d$	11.2	49.4	49.4	67.9	64.6	64.0	76.6	—	—

Notes:
* DSR = debt service ratio: (actual) total debt service/exports of goods and services (TDS/XGS);
ISR = interest service ratio: (actual) interest payments (INT/XGS).
** Data for 1992 provisional estimates.
$_d$ indicates that actual payments plus arrears are used in the numerator.
^{p} indicates projected.

Source: WDT (1992, 1993).

From one year to the next, debt indicators for SSA 'improved' dramatically, but without any explanation. The country grouping of SSA had not been altered. *DSR$_d$* for 1993 was finally 77·6, notably higher than the optimistic estimate. After two decades of IMF adjustment, SSA's arrears were roughly five times the amount of debt service actually paid in 1995 and 1996 (World Bank, 1997).

Although statistics provided by the BWIs are used by practically everyone working on debts, and the BWIs have used them to support their own conclusions, these data have not received the scrutiny they deserve. Such scrutiny both questions the reliability of statistics and casts doubt on the professional standards of those producing them. Raffer (1996a) has shown unexplained changes for Latin America as well. The total debts: GDP ratio published in various *World Debt Tables* display great and unexplained differences of up to 10.1 percentage points for the same year in the case of years long before the issue was published. The ratios of external debt to GDP in various issues of the IMF's *World Economic Outlook* show a maximum difference of over 13 percentage points. Raffer (1996a) noted that the time series published in 1989 displayed a constant (and monotonously falling) reduction of the debt burden since 1984, thus supporting the illiquidity theory. The time series of the *World Economic Outlook 1993* increased, peaking in 1987, supporting Brady's call for debt reduction. Chile, the no-capital-flight-high-repatriator country, may serve as one more illustration of the data problem. Its DSR improved dramatically from WDT (1992) to WDT (1993). For the year 1991, it 'fell' from 33·9 to 23·1, although the country had no arrears.

Irrespective of data quality, however, the situation of SSA and the poorest debtors is dramatic. Relief is urgently needed. Like debts of the poorest countries in general, SSA's debts have another distinctive feature, characterized very trenchantly by Svendsen (1987, p.27) as being 'creditor-determined', in contrast to Latin America's 'debtor-determined' debts. The difference is simple: commercial banks did lend aggressively but have usually not interfered with their clients' economic policy, while official creditors, most notably IFIs, have strongly influenced and monitored the use of their loans, exerting massive influence on their debtors' economies. The World Bank has been particularly proud of the detailed monitoring of its projects for decades. Recently, emphasis has shifted from monitoring to 'ownership'. Considering that commercial banks have reduced their claims substantially, the position of official creditors in debt negotiations must be called exceedingly hard. To a considerable extent official creditors make the poorest and most vulnerable pay for their own errors and shortcomings. In this respect official debts are perceptibly harder than commercial loans. Multilateral reluctance to grant debt relief is indefensible.

Much of what little progress has been made so far is owed to NGOs and their advocacy work, continuously pressing for debt relief and measures in favour of the poor. They have formed continental networks and coordinated advocacy globally. Jubilee 2000, a campaign for debt reduction to a level that allows the poor a dignified life, initially started in the UK, provides an example.

THE HIPC INITIATIVE : RECOGNIZING THE
MULTILATERAL DEBT OVERHANG

Many SCs, particularly the poorest, remain burdened by a high share of multilateral debts they have to service with priority. Other creditors must wait as IFIs receive the lion's share of debt service payments actually made. At the end of 1993, IFIs received more than half the payments made by poor SCs; 62 per cent of all multilateral debts were owed to the BWIs.

According to the World Bank (WDT, 1996, p.170), 'Seventy percent of outstanding debt [in SSA] at the end of 1995 was owed to official creditors – 90 percent if Nigeria and South Africa are excluded.' The share of the World Bank group, the IMF and the African Development Bank and its fund were 30 per cent of long-term debt outstanding. Until September 1995, the BWIs denied officially that multilateral debts were a problem. Then a leaked discussion document of the World Bank acknowledged for the first time that something had to be done about multilateral debt, since it is a heavy burden on many poor countries. Tackling the problem of the multilateral debt overhang, which is of particular relevance to the poorest countries, is a great merit of the present World Bank president, James Wolfensohn. He proposed and backed a Multilateral Debt Facility, against strong internal opposition.

The idea is simple: a fund financed by bilateral contributions and by IFIs themselves would pay off multilateral debts of eligible SCs, thus maintaining the fiction that IFIs neither reschedule nor reduce debts. As creditor countries had to bail out multilaterals repeatedly in the past to keep this fiction 'intact', this is not entirely new. The suggestion that IFIs should finance reductions of their own debts by outright grants financed by IFIs themselves is new. The precise contribution by IFIs to the new Facility remained unclear, although the World Bank expected a $850 million windfall surplus in 1995 according to *The Economist* (16 September 1995), which was seen as one source to finance the fund. *The Economist* reported that many people within the BWIs still clung to the old idea that new money and growing out of debts were the best solutions, although this had been practised unsuccessfully for decades.

Despite high net transfers, HIPCs often had to reschedule from 1980, as the World Bank (1997, p.42) acknowledges, recognizing the effects of delaying relief: 'The surge in borrowing, coupled with increasing reliance on rescheduling and refinancing, increased the nominal stock of debts of HIPCs from $55 billion in 1980 to $183 billion in 1990 ... by the end of 1995 it had reached $215 billion.'

The slowdown from an annual growth rate of 12·77 per cent to 3·28 per cent in the 1990s was achieved by a shift towards more grants, higher concessionality and forgiving ODA debts. This clearly shows that wrong debt management by creditors unwilling to accept economic facts and powerful enough to keep debtors from making reality felt has exacerbated the problem. Trying to avoid smaller write-offs to go easy on their budgets, official creditors allowed debts to grow further, thus forcing themselves to accept much bigger write-offs. One can protect the illusion that bankrupt borrowers will eventually repay by going on lending or by capitalizing interest arrears on paper for quite a while. This does not make the money actually repaid. On paper one increases one's claims, though. But these new claims are unrecoupable, 'phantom debts' just making the 'costs' of debt relief look higher on paper.

In early 1996, the BWIs assessed the outlook for debt sustainability in 38 heavily indebted IDA-only countries, projecting the likely availability of external finance and estimating the effects of *Naples Terms* debt relief from the Paris Club and similar treatment from other bilateral and commercial creditors. Former BWI success stories such as Ghana and the Côte d'Ivoire were among the countries assessed. The debt burden was classified as sustainable if the net present value (NPV) of debt to exports was expected to fall below 200 per cent, and the debt service ratio below 20 per cent within five years. Eight countries were found to have unsustainable debts defined as ratios above 250 and 25 per cent after ten years, while 12 countries falling between these categories were classified as 'possibly stressed'. Liberia, Nigeria and Somalia were finally not assessed, the remaining 18 considered 'sustainable'.

After the G7 had agreed on up to 80 per cent debt relief by the Paris Club – thus finally going further than Britain's Trinidad proposal – the Highly Indebted Poor Countries (HIPC) Initiative was adopted by the Bank's Development Committee and the Fund's Interim Committee in the autumn of 1996. Its declared aim is to bring debts of eligible countries to sustainable levels, to enable a country 'to meet its current and future external debt-service obligations in full without recourse to debt relief, rescheduling of debts, or the accumulation of arrears, and without unduly compromising growth' (Boote & Thugge, 1997, p.10). It was supposed to provide a durable exit strategy from debt problems. The need to reduce multilateral debts was officially recognized. Wolfensohn's proposed fund became the HIPC Trust Fund established by the World Bank, allocating $500 million as its initial contribution. IDA was assigned the task of administering it on the basis of decisions made by donors and multilateral creditors. Decision making on the use of its resources is related to each creditor's relative contribution. IDA does not charge any fees, which the World Bank presents as one further contribution to the HIPC Initiative. The HIPC Trust Fund may pre-pay debts, cover debt service when it falls due, or purchase and subsequently cancel debts. The World Bank is also prepared to provide enhanced support in the form of IDA grants during the interim period.

The HIPC Initiative relies heavily on non-IFI creditors. Higher reductions by other creditors allow IFIs to reduce their own claims less than others. This still preserves a preferred status – or a bail-out – of IFIs. The World Bank (1997, p.44) formulates: 'Any debt relief provided by multilateral creditors will preserve their financial integrity and preferred creditor status.' In the meantime, some donor countries have transferred aid money to the HIPC Trust Fund. But bilateral contributions to the HIPC Trust Fund remain a problem. Creditor countries willing to contribute have remained reluctant to make large contributions as long as some major creditors are unwilling to pay up as well.

Initially, the IMF refused to contribute cash, wanting its 'contribution' to be financed by bilateral donors, a proposal attacked as unacceptable by many NGOs. Then the Fund proposed to contribute by replacing current ESAF (Enhanced Structural Adjustment Facility) loans (5·5 years grace, 10 years maturity) with softer ESAF loans (10 years grace, 20 years maturity). Eventually, the IMF established the HIPC ESAF Trust Fund for the concessional part of HIPC, hoping other creditors would contribute, and agreed to grants. These are to be used to repay the IMF itself to pretend that the IMF is not reducing debts. The proposal to sell some of the IMF's gold to finance its contribution to the HIPC Initiative was particularly strongly supported by NGOs.

Resistance by major shareholders, such as Germany and Japan, but also smaller members, such as Austria or Sweden, prevented this at first. Historically, some IMF gold was sold in the 1970s, after the decision to demonetize gold. The IMF Trust Fund was established with those proceeds in 1976. But in the case of debt relief sales were declared impossible by hard-line IC governments. Paying for one's errors in the way private consultants have to was still anathema at the IMF.

By contrast, the IMF wanted to expand its monitoring and controlling of cash-strapped debtors in the future. ESAF funds with longer maturities or a permanent ESAF, which it expected to become operational by 2005 (IMF, 1997, p.14) would achieve this. Considering the IMF's past record, this may seem questionable (cf. Raffer & Singer, 1996). Suffice it here to recall that the US Congress withheld $70 million of its $100 million contribution to ESAF in 1994 after US NGOs had complained that ESAF loans, conditional upon structural adjustment policies, caused more harm than good, and that the IMF was extremely secretive. Funding this permanent ESAF by selling gold was also proposed. Once internal opposition to gold sales was overcome, gold producers, notably South Africa, strongly opposed this move, fearing that massive sales would depress gold prices in an already difficult market and reduce employment in gold mines. One may discuss what the effect of sales by the IMF alone would have been. But several countries, most notably Britain, decided to sell large portions of their gold reserves at precisely the same time. It remains to be asked why these sales had to occur precisely when the IMF wanted to sell. In any case, this had the effect of hindering market sales. Warnings against this price effect were already being voiced within the IMF in 1995.

Finally, it was agreed to 'sell' gold in 'off-market' operations, which basically meant that this gold with a low book value would be revalued. Technically, the IMF sold gold at market value to members who were about to repay the Fund, generating profits in the IMF's books. Then the settlement of the country's obligation in gold valued at the same price instead of cash was accepted. Profits are then invested to finance debt operations. Mexico and Brazil were the first countries participating in such innovative transactions.

The HIPC Initiative's objective was to reach overall debt sustainability by coordinated action, allowing the country to exit from continuous reschedulings (World Bank, 1997, p.44). To qualify, the country has to have a good track record with the BWIs. The Initiative is composed of two stages. During stage 1, BWIs continue to lend, thus increasing debts and making more relief necessary at the completion point. It seems totally incomprehensible that countries already classified as 'unsustainable' should have to wait six more years for debt relief. The World Bank (ibid., p.45) points out that preliminary assessment and country classification do 'not constitute an assessment of debt sustainability under the HIPC Debt Initiative'. The relevant analysis will be done by Bank, Fund and the HIPC according to the same criteria, 200–250 per cent debt exports (in present value terms) and 20–25 per cent debt service ratios. Specific vulnerability indicators, such as export concentration and variability, are to be taken into account. Fiscal indicators, such as debt (NPV) to fiscal revenue, were added following French pressure in favour of the Côte d'Ivoire, and NGO lobbying. Officially, this modification was for 'highly open economies'.

If the preliminary analysis by the BWIs is correct, there is no economic justification for delaying relief further, most evidently so for countries in the 'unsustainable' category. Delay only means allowing debts to grow further, as the history of debt management in general as well as of HIPCs proves.

In April 1997, Uganda became the first country to benefit from the Initiative. Bolivia, Burkina Faso (initially categorized as 'sustainable'), Guyana, Ethiopia, Côte d'Ivoire – a country with an unusually large share of private debts still dating back to the time when it was a 'success' – and Mozambique followed. Already having a long track record with the BWIs, Uganda and Bolivia were allowed to enter the second stage earlier, which did not lead to a solution before 2000. But the first cases immediately showed that management by creditors is highly problematic and inefficient.

In the case of Uganda, the completion point, originally envisaged to be in 1997, was shifted forward owing to the creditors' unwillingness to act quickly. This shifted the period used to calculate debt (service) to export ratios considered sustainable right into the period of high coffee prices, yielding less reduction even though everyone is aware that coffee price booms are hardly the normal situation. These effects over-compensated a relatively low sustainability target near the minimum 200 per cent.

In a letter to the *Financial Times* on 10 March 1997, Ugandan Finance Minister J.S. Mayanja-Nkangi stressed his government's increasing frustration at the prospect of a further delay and reduction in debt relief, particularly as Uganda had just embarked on a major new initiative in the social sector: free primary education for four children per family – a programme with an estimated cost of $67 million. The minister argued, 'Any delay is not merely an issue of timing – a completion point in April 1998, rather than April 1997, would mean that the debt relief to be provided would be cut by half.' This completion point was a compromise between creditors, such as the UK, pushing for a 1997 completion point, and Japan, Germany, Italy and the USA demanding it in 1999. Uganda's debt relief was finally granted after further discussions in 2000. The minister confirmed that the Ugandan government was firmly committed to poverty eradication, and that any conditions linked to World Bank support in the past 'have mirrored, not driven, government policies'. Fears that debt relief may be misused were unfounded, he added, and the Ugandan government was willing to continue its practice of providing donors with full records of budget processes and expenditures on request. In spite of Uganda's efforts and its perfect track record of many years, creditors gave the impression of trying to appropriate a share of the gains themselves, thus signalling that even prolonged efforts receiving the BWIs' seal of approval do not pay.

At the Commonwealth Secretariat Debt Sustainability Workshop in London on 18–20 June 1997, a representative of the Ugandan Ministry of Finance declared that Uganda would actually have less cashflow after the implementation of the HIPC Initiative, unless donors were willing to contribute at least a further US$25 million annually to match significant relief contributions by bilateral donors to Uganda's Multilateral Debt Fund made until the completion point (EURODAD, 1997).

The bulk of Bolivia's external public and publicly guaranteed debt is multilateral (roughly two-thirds of NPV). Almost half of that is owed to the IDB, largely not to the IDB's 'soft window'. The IDB protected itself, delaying results by refusing to accept a low target for Bolivia. Thus Bolivia's target was set relatively high, at 225 per cent. Latin American states and IDB shareholders, such as Mexico and Argentina, also refused to go any lower. This shows again that the IFI preferred status must go to allow a meaningful solution.

Mozambique, a country suffering from protracted civil war, received only 67 per cent debt relief from the Paris Club in November 1996, although the BWIs had advocated going beyond 80 per cent as necessary for sustainability. Debt relief fell short of assessed needs at the very start.

Russia's stated intention of becoming a member of the Paris Club deserves mentioning. Russia's then minister of finance, Anatoli Chubais, expected that the amount of debts collected as a member would be much greater than what could have been collected without joining the Paris Club. As Mozambique has relatively large debts with Russia, dating from its relations with the Soviet Union, this does not make a real solution easier.

Mozambique posed the grave problem of being the first HIPC where crossing the 80 per cent threshold was undeniably necessary, which creditors were initially not prepared to concede. Negotiations on Mozambique were deadlocked as creditors could not agree to reduce debts to a level they – not any debtor – had defined as sustainable. NGOs monitoring the HIPC Initiative closely, such as EURODAD, Jubilee 2000 and Oxfam, appealed to creditors to find a solution. A Paris Club meeting on 21 January 1998 finally broke that deadlock. Contingent on exceptional efforts by the BWIs, Paris Club creditors agreed to go beyond 80 per cent on an 'individual basis', choosing from a 'menu' of options, which included, however, simply cancelling more. The word 'menu' recalls the 'management' of commercial debts during the 1980s.

The HIPC Initiative had dragged on even before the deadlock on Mozambique. On 16 September 1997, UK Chancellor of the Exchequer Gordon Brown presented the 'Mauritius Mandate', agreed at a Commonwealth meeting shortly before the BWI's annual meeting in Hong Kong. A White Paper on International Development published by the UK government confirmed the goals of the Mauritius mandate, calling for firm decisions on amounts and terms of debt relief for at least three-quarters of eligible countries by 2000. The chancellor's proposal was not enthusiastically received by other official creditors in Hong Kong.

The myopia of official creditors is shown by the example of the Paris Club's debt relief terms. As a matter of principle only so-called 'pre-cut-off debts' can be eligible for debt relief, such as under the *Naples Terms*. The cut-off date is when the debtor asks the Paris Club the first time for debt relief, which can be quite early. Uganda's cut-off date, for instance, is in 1981. If the cut-off date is early enough, a 100 per cent 'debt forgiveness' may mean a reduction of total debts by less than 1 per cent. Mathematically, debt relief converges to 100 per cent, while actually cancelled debts converge to zero. EURODAD (1996), an NGO campaigning for debt relief, quoted World Bank calculations for 20 countries according to which 80 per cent Paris Club debt relief would mean a mere 17 per cent actual reduction for all debts. Clinging to cut-off dates may be a short-term relief for national budgets of creditor governments, but prevents an economically meaningful solution.

Insufficient debt relief at the first try is transmitted by this principle, because debts after this cut-off date are not eligible for reductions. Therefore the share of eligible debts is likely to decrease over time. Historic errors of assessment are allowed to compromise future solutions. Since IC governments have always been reluctant to recognize the dimension of the problem and estimates of future export incomes and growth by the BWIs on which relief was based have been notoriously optimistic, a solution was foiled.

The concept of net present value (NPV) applied in the HIPC Initiative as well as in Paris Club debt relief is highly problematic. Its justification is not convincing: 'Because of concessionality, the face value of external debt relative to exports overstates the debt burden. The ratio of the present value of future debt service obligations to exports is a better indicator of these countries' debt burden' (World Bank 1997, p.42). Therefore future debt service payments are discounted with a market interest rate. This reduces debt burdens considerably on paper. The NPV of all HIPC debts was about $190 billion at the end of 1994, while their nominal debts were $241 billion (IMF, 1997, p.15), or nearly 27 per cent higher. Sustainability according to NPVs does not exclude unsustainability according to face values.

Applying NPVs is highly misleading. The concept is used for investment decisions as streams of incomes and outlays can only be compared meaningfully at the same point in time. It makes sense there because £100 today is actually equivalent to £105 in a year's time at 5 per cent interest if one invests the sum at this interest rate. Discounted values thus provide useful information for comparing expected net returns. Using discounting to calculate the grant element of ODA to compare flows makes sense too.

In the case of a debt overhang, however, discounting at market interest rates simply states that, if the debtor had the NPV today and could invest it at the discount rate, all debts would be covered. This is true but unhelpful. HIPCs qualify precisely as such because they have no spare money that could be used that way. Quite the contrary, they usually are unable to honour all financial commitments, even at prevailing concessional terms, which means that these terms are already too expensive. Arrears grow: 'In many HIPCs the negative impact of external debts seems to come more from the growing debt stock rather than from the excessive burden of debt service actually paid' (World Bank, 1997, p.44). Using NPVs is like demanding that a malnourished, burdened man run 100 metres in 13 seconds, rightly pointing out that this contains an element of concessionality of over 30 per cent compared with a world record of 9·9 seconds. Raffer's debt overhang indicator would be a better measure to estimate needed relief. It must be brought back to 1, contingent on exempting minimum outlays for social spending, such as for basic health or education of the poor.

The results of the HIPC Initiative and the rules established by creditors prove what has been known: creditors must not be allowed to decide on debt reductions. This is not allowed by insolvency procedures in any decent legal system. At the Cologne G8 summit of 1999, the major creditor governments themselves recognized HIPC's failure, demanding a new approach, now often called Enhanced HIPC or HIPC II. Analysing the performance of HIPC I, Raffer (1997c, p.364) predicted two years before Cologne that 'another round – HIPC II – might already be in the making'.

The results of the Cologne Initiative, granted under NGO pressure – supported by more than 17 million signatures collected worldwide – are arguably even more disappointing than HIPC I. Lovett (2000, p.7) sums up the harsh verdict of the NGO community: 'The betrayal of Cologne: twelve months of failure.' Comparing promises and results indeed yields a highly negative picture. In September 1999, the chairman of the International Monetary and Financial Committee, Gordon Brown, predicted that the first country would begin to benefit within weeks. In December 1999, the BWIs were still predicting that 24 countries would reach 'decision point' in 2000 (ibid., p.8), a forecast later corrected to 'up to 20 countries'. When the Okinawa summit took place in the summer of 2000, only one country, Uganda, had reached its completion point, after discussions and delays. However, on 12 September some members of the Paris Club massively arguing for less reduction are reported to have prevailed. NGOs pointed out that Uganda is now to receive $15 billion less than expected, which is 40 per cent of the resources planned for its Poverty Action Fund for 2000 and 2001. The NGO estimate that Cologne will not be fully implemented until at least 2005 is thus not unsubstantiated. Jubilee 2000 expects that no more than $90 billion will ever be cancelled, while $100 billion were promised at Cologne, as just $15 billion are likely to be cancelled by the end of 2000 (ibid.).

The BWI Conference in Prague did not produce a new impetus. During the concluding press conference on 28 September 2000, the World Bank's president answered a question on whether there were moves to simplify procedures and whether there was progress justifying high expectations for deeper debt relief for the poorest very clearly:

> There were high expectations, indeed, by some, but our expectations were to advance the implementation of the second program of the enhanced HIPC facilities. There was no indication that I'm aware of, given by Horst [Köhler, the managing director of the IMF] or myself, that we were going to get deeper or broader. That was certainly something that Jubilee 2000 and many others had been hoping for.
>
> But we have maintained a position that what we want to do between now and the end of the year is to implement, *for as many countries as possible, the enhanced*

HIPC Initiative. We are hopeful that we will reach the target of 20 countries by the end of this year, at which point debt relief can be operative. (World Bank, 2000b, p.10, emphasis added)

Even if 20 countries actually reach decision point by the end of 2000, as hoped by the World Bank, that will mean further years of the kind of delay which the World Bank itself described as so damaging to debtor economies. The record of debtors further advanced in the process corroborates such fears.

The new focus on poverty goes in the direction of one element of US Chapter 9 insolvency, debtor protection. Within an international insolvency procedure it is proposed to exempt those resources needed to finance a humane minimum of basic education, health and so on for the poorest from the reach of creditors by establishing a fund financing such measures. Focusing more on poverty (which the BWIs have claimed to have done anyway during the recent past) is thus a laudable idea. But one has to hope that it will not be used by creditors to delay further.

What happens at present largely repeats past errors. Too little is given too late, even though it may be more than in the past. By delaying a proper solution, creditors continue to make debts grow further. They increase ultimately unrecoverable amounts, which exist only on paper, thus making debt relief look more expensive than it actually is. Rather than accepting the economic fact of insolvency, let alone financial accountability for their own errors, creditors saw both HIPC I and Cologne again as acts of mercy, not as steps towards the economic solution to overindebtedness universally applied to all debtors unless they are SCs. The problems of implementing HIPC I under creditor leadership and the continued delays since Cologne show very clearly that a legal framework is needed to deal with overindebted SCs, which – in contrast to structural adjustment – protects a minimum of human dignity of vulnerable groups. Without it the goalposts for eligibility may be moved any time, and one may resort to statistical tricks to minimize actual reductions, thus prolonging the problem. Also one may go on treating countries that meet all objective economic criteria for a HIPC differently, denying them the same treatment simply because creditors are afraid that might be too costly.

Indonesia, once a 'miracle' according to the World Bank, is meanwhile qualified as a severely indebted low income country, a result of the Asian crisis. Although the Bank does not give percentages, simple division of total debts in present value terms and debt service by export revenues shows that Indonesia had a debt:exports ratio of 251·75 per cent, and a DSR of 33 per cent in 1998 (World Bank, 2000a, vol.1, p.145), both above the Cologne thresholds of 150 and 15, respectively. Economically, and judged by objective indicators (GNP/head, HIPC-relevant debt indicators), it should qualify for HIPC now. But as the amount of debts is substantial ($150·8 billion) treating Indonesia as indicated by objective criteria would be costly. Creditors thus deny this with economically unconvincing, bureaucratic reasons.

Nigeria, also a severely indebted low income country, is another interesting case. It was classified as a HIPC initially, but removed from the list in 1998 as no longer meeting the criteria (GAO, 2000). Its indicators were 250·14 and 11·22 in 1998. However, the low DSR results exclusively from the fact that Nigeria – unable to pay as due – has been accumulating huge arrears. Since 1993, debt service was a fraction of interest arrears on long term debt. Arrears of principal were always much higher than these interest arrears during that period. Simply by adding interest arrears Nigeria's DSR would have been slightly above 35 per cent in 1997. Adding all principal arrears shown by the Bank for 1997 would result in a DSR of 90·93 per cent (World Bank, 2000a, vol.2, p.418). In 1998, the situation was even more drastic. DSR obtained by dividing actual debt service plus interest arrears, as shown by the World Bank, by exports amounted to 60·4 per cent. Adding principal arrears in the numerator results in well over 160 per cent, not surprisingly, as arrears on long-term debt alone were slightly higher than export income. Recent increases in crude prices will certainly affect Nigeria positively, but it remains to be seen whether they will push ratios back sufficiently to bring DSR_d^* below the Cologne limits. Conveniently for creditors, the country's very debt overhang, producing a low DSR measured as actual payments but disregarding substantial arrears, provides a 'reason' to argue that it is not highly indebted, therefore not in need of HIPC treatment.

COMPARING THE TWO HIPC INITIATIVES WITH INTERNATIONAL CHAPTER 9 INSOLVENCY

The first HIPC Initiative was a step in the right direction and James Wolfensohn's efforts are highly commendable. By recognizing the need for IFI debt reductions, another important step forward was made. Some features of HIPC I already – though remotely – recall customary features of insolvency procedures.

The concept of debt sustainability takes the fundamental ability of the debtor to pay into account, which is very similar to the principle governing insolvency. Preparing debt sustainability analyses in cooperation between the BWIs and officials of the debtor country, on a tripartite basis, recognizes the need for debtor participation, although this appears to be reflected in theory rather than in actual practice. By contrast, the insolvent debtor is an equal partner. Finally, the World Bank made a link between the Initiative and poverty reduction, an overdue move, which again recalls debtor protection under civilized rule of law. However, poverty was not visibly reflected in sustainability indicators, or in actual creditor decisions, until Cologne. The new Poverty Reduction and Growth Facility (PRGF) has poverty in its name. Actual positive effects on the poor – some 15 months after Cologne – remain less evident. This 'process involving the active participation of civil society, NGOs, donors, and international institutions,' as the IMF's homepage describes it, is a step towards civil society participation as it was first propagated within the framework of an international Chapter 9 insolvency. Footnote 2 on 'How We Lend', however, defines the PRGF as 'Formerly the Enhanced Structural Adjustment Facility (ESAF)' (IMF, 2000b), which suggests a change in name rather than real change.

So-called 'vulnerability factors' introduced by HIPC I as well as the ranges of indicator ratios allow a more specific and tailor-made approach, as usual in insolvency cases. Finally, accepting actual data of the recent past as the basis, rather than notoriously 'optimistic' BWI projections introduced more realism. Optimism underlies HIPC II as well. In an assessment of the enhanced HIPC initiative pursuant to a congressional request, the US General Accounting Office (GAO, 2000) points out that maintaining debt sustainability will depend on assumptions of annual growth rates above 6 per cent in dollar terms – in four cases including Nicaragua and Uganda even above 9·1 per cent – over 20 years. The GAO doubts whether such growth rates can actually be maintained for that long, warning also about the volatility of commodity prices. It points out that additional money ('increased donor assistance') will be necessary. HIPC II is apparently again built on fragile, optimistic assumptions.

In practice, HIPC I fell short of the needs of debtor economies, as even creditors had to recognize, mainly because creditors remained all-powerful: judge, jury, bailiff, interested party and witness all in one. Only NGO advocacy has provided some countervailing pressure. The danger is that insufficient debt relief pressed through to keep down paper losses in the budgets of official creditors will perpetuate the situation.

One unsuccessful HIPC Initiative has created the next unsuccessful HIPC Initiative. Past record and new rhetoric about the debtor country now being in charge leads one to assume that all the blame will again be put on debtors, with the claim that they had not pursued proper policies. This blame could be corroborated by figures showing how 'generous' actually given insufficient debt relief was compared with irrelevant market conditions. According to the IMF (2000a), Poverty Reduction Strategy Papers 'have been produced by the country authorities, and not by Bank and Fund staff.' Thus blame must logically rest with the country, even though the Fund states: 'Greater ownership is the single most often cited, but also the least tangible, change in moving to PRGF-supported programs. There is no single element of program design or documentation that will signal this change' (ibid.).

An economically sensible solution with a human face is needed, an international Chapter 9. As we have presented this proposal elsewhere (Raffer & Singer, 1996, pp.203ff) only its most essential elements are briefly repeated here (for details, see also Raffer, 1990a). Designed and used for decades in the USA, as a solution to the problems of debtors vested with governmental powers – so-called 'municipalities' – it can be easily applied to sovereign lenders. Like all good insolvency laws it combines the need for a general framework with the flexibility necessary to deal fairly with individual debtors.

Under Chapter 9, US laws protect both the governmental powers of the debtor and individuals affected by the plan. Affected taxpayers as well as employees of the municipality have a right to be heard, defending their interests. Creditors are to receive what can be 'reasonably expected' from the debtor under given circumstances. The living standards of the indebted municipality's population are protected. The jurisdiction of the court depends on the city's volition, beyond which it cannot be extended. This demonstrates the appropriateness for sovereign debtors.

As courts in a creditor or debtor country are unlikely to be totally unbiased, an international court of arbitrators is necessary, as is usual in international law. Each side (creditors and debtor) nominates the same number of persons, who elect one more person to achieve an uneven number of arbitrators. People affected by the solution would be represented by organizations speaking on their behalf, such as trade unions or employees' associations, as in a US Chapter 9 case, or international organizations, such as UNICEF, religious or non-religious NGOs, or grassroots organizations of the poor.

Debt service payments have to be brought into line with the debtor's capacity to earn foreign exchange. Where the removal of protectionist barriers can be expected to lead to higher export revenues, a trade-off between more repayments and less protection or higher debt reduction without reduced protection is necessary.

It is mandatory that schemes to protect a minimum standard of living be part of every international composition plan. By analogy with the protection granted to the population of an indebted municipality by domestic Chapter 9, the money to service a country's debts must not be raised by destroying basic social services. Subsidies and transfers necessary to guarantee humane minimum standards to the poor must be maintained. Funds necessary for sustainable economic recovery must be set aside. The principle of debtor protection demands exempting resources necessary to finance minimum standards of basic health services, primary education and so on. This exemption can only be justified if that money is demonstrably used for its declared purpose. Not without reason, creditors as well as NGOs are concerned that this might not be the case.

The solution is quite simple: a transparently managed fund financed by the debtor in domestic currency. In a discussion with public servants of the G7 and representatives of the BWIs, Ann Pettifor (1999) proposed a Poverty Action Fund as a means to guarantee that the money is actually used for the poor and for expenditures necessary for a fresh start of the debtor economy. The management of such a fund could be monitored by an international board or advisory council consisting of members from the debtor country as well as members from creditor countries. They could be nominated by NGOs and by governments (including the debtor government). As this fund is a legal entity of its own, checks and discussions of its projects would not concern the government's budget, which is an important part of a country's sovereignty. Aid could also be channelled through the fund, changing its character of money just set apart from the ordinary budget towards a normal fund for the poor.

Doubtlessly, there exists a need for reform within debtor countries too. These reforms, monitored by the council of arbitrators, should adjust the debtor to the real international environment, not to a textbook illusion of 'free markets'. Realistic strategies have to drop the BWIs' predilection for one-sided liberalization by those countries that can be forced to do so. Import substitution should be encouraged where economically viable to form the basis of future economic diversification. Monitoring by the arbitrators could help to overcome the problem of petrifying protection. Temporary protection should allow domestic industries to compete with imports, and should be reduced as domestic industries become more efficient.

Finally, official creditors, including IFIs, must be treated in the same way as commercial banks during an insolvency, particularly so as they – in contrast to commercial banks – have routinely taken decisions on how their loans were to be used. It is the most basic precondition for the functioning of the market mechanism that economic decisions must be accompanied by (co)responsibility: whoever takes entrepreneurial decisions must also carry entrepreneurial risks. If this link is severed – as it was in centrally planned economies – market efficiency is severely disturbed.

For an international Chapter 9, a symmetrical treatment of all creditors follows convincingly. It is a matter of fairness to debtors as well as to other creditors. Debt reduction must be uniform; the same percentage must be deducted from all debts. Symmetrical treatment in an insolvency could be the way in which the BWIs are held financially accountable. Compensation for damages done within projects, where determining faults and errors is much easier (having nothing to do with insolvency, but being an issue in its own right) would reduce the debt burden further (Raffer & Singer, 1996). Only after removing the oppressive debt overhang can long-term plans to develop poor countries be successful. Nevertheless, creditor governments are still not prepared to realize this idea. The real reasons for the reluctance to adopt a proper solution are difficult to fathom. Clearly, moral hazard is not among them. This is proved by every insolvency case, as well as by the historical experience of present creditor countries themselves, most notably Germany, which got a de facto insolvency in 1953. As long as the big moral hazard of the present perverted incentive system allowing IFIs to gain from their own failures at the expense of the poor is tolerated by OECD governments, it is impossible to believe in their moral hazard arguments.

Like HIPC I, HIPC II is also likely to have insufficient results because of creditor power, thus prolonging the debt problem. Unfortunately, the lucid advice of a Scottish professor of moral theology held in esteem by economists as well as politicians is still not accepted:

> When it becomes necessary for a state to declare itself bankrupt, in the same manner as when it becomes necessary for an individual to do so, a fair, open, and avowed bankruptcy is always the measure which is both least dishonourable to the debtor, and least hurtful to the creditor. (Adam Smith [1776] 1979, p.930)

12. The WTO – tilting trade rules further against the South

The Uruguay Round brought about substantial changes in the framework of international trade, which are likely to increase the structural disequilibria of North–South trade to which the PST drew attention when analysing unequal gains of trade. Hence the need for financial transfers is also likely to grow. Mirroring political power and the ability to push through economic interests, the results accommodate Northern interests much better (Raffer, 1996c). Naturally, the institutionalized change brought about by the WTO regime means that any assessment at present must still be considered somewhat preliminary. Further changes in the framework of world trade emanating from the new regime have to be expected, although this built-in automaticity was at least temporarily derailed at the Third Ministerial Conference at Seattle. Many details and problems remain postponed in spite of long higgling and haggling. But all in all, the Round has strengthened the tendencies towards divergence and inequality, rather than correcting them.

Generally, the Uruguay Round liberalized where it was in the interest of ICs, while sectors important to SCs remain selectively more protected. The Agreement on Textiles and Clothing (ATC) discussed in the next chapter is the prime example of this asymmetry, showing how easily ICs are willing to infringe the very idea of liberalization when this is in their interest. The first stage of 'liberalization' in textiles and clothing and the decisions on net food importers highlight the new regime's one-sided character. The results in agricultural trade are also disappointing for the South. The chairman of the G77 saw the Uruguay Round as a further proof that the South continues to be sidelined (Peng, 1994).

Initially, however, this was not the prevailing sentiment in SCs. The Group of 15, the Summit Level Group of SCs established by the non-aligned, welcomed the conclusion of the Uruguay Round. They hoped, that 'as promised, the benefits from liberalization, increased market access and expansion of world trade for all countries, particularly for developing countries, will materialise' (G15, 1994, p.5). After the signing of the Final Act at Marrakesh, UNCTAD advocated the quick implementation of the new GATT framework and in particular of the WTO as in the interest of the South. Expectations that the WTO would contribute to a rule-based, predictable, non-discriminatory multilateral trading system, upholding the rights and interests of weaker trading partners, were voiced. Strengthening the rule of law is always in the interest of the less powerful.

The Uruguay Round was characterized by unusual Southern participation in negotiations due to the inclusion of issues such as agriculture, textiles or services, which are of massive interest to some countries, as well as because of technical assistance provided to the South by the UNDP through UNCTAD. The so-called Cairns Group, formed to defend common interests as exporters of agricultural products, comprised for the first time countries from North and South.

All estimates expected ICs to benefit most from further liberalization of world trade. Considering their large share in world trade, this is quite logical. According to UNCTAD (1995a, p.23), annual losses of $300 million to $600 million from higher food prices and the erosion of trade preferences have to be expected for LLDCs. Generally, Africa was seen as the big loser. Only the GATT itself claimed there would be no losers. Its deputy director-general, Jesús Seade (1994) saw even Africa gaining more trade and investment. Simulations by Goldin and Mensbrugghe (1995, pp.94f) indicate overall, though skewed, gains by the Round, but

> these should not mask the losses, particularly as these are concentrated in vulnerable least developed countries where the consequences of higher food prices could be particularly severe. For those countries, vigilance and the guarantee of the support of the international community is required, so that the overwhelming gains of the Uruguay Round are not tarnished by the unacceptable suffering of those unfortunate enough to suffer the marginal–negative consequences.

Real income losses were calculated for Africa, low income countries and Latin America, while upper income Asia, for instance, gained modestly. The authors predicted price increases of up to 10·3 per cent for wheat, 3·6 per cent for rice, 5·4 per cent for coarse grains and 12·1 per cent for dairy products, figures well below the significant price increases of these products in 1994, 1995 and the first half of 1996 (WTO, 1996a, p.16). Goldin and Mensbrugghe (1995, p.94f) think that factors they had been unable to incorporate into their modelling might offset 'any possible negative effects associated with higher food prices'. One of these factors is the reform of trade in textiles and clothing discussed in the next chapter. The situation of net food-importing SCs has considerably worsened.

Before discussing the provisions of the WTO trading system in more detail, one argument often used in its favour by the WTO itself should be qualified. The WTO often tries to corroborate arguments that liberalization and deregulation would increase welfare by comparing growth rates of GDPs or GNPs with growth rates of exports. It claims that 'current economic difficulties' can be solved by trade liberalization, stating trade policy to be a critical element of their solution (WTO, 1998a, p.5). This is 'corroborated' by pointing out that 'Trade growth has consistently outpaced overall economic growth for at least 250 years, except for a comparatively brief period from 1913 to 1950' (ibid., p.33; cf. also p.5). Trade has contributed to 'the enormous benefits ... from mutual inter-dependence among nations'. The comparison of growth rates looks very impressive at first sight. But the WTO fails to mention that two different concepts of measurement are compared. While GDP/GNP is measured on a net base (accumulated values added), exports are measured gross, which means import contents are not deducted. By just shipping one product around the globe from one country to another (exporting it several times) export growth is boosted. It is therefore likely to be usually above GNP/GDP growth (Raffer, 1999b). This point is particularly valid if, as the WTO (2000c, p.14) contends, '"processing trade" has gained importance and often played a crucial part in these countries' overall trade performance'.

NET FOOD-IMPORTING SCs

Some SCs had hoped to benefit from drastic reductions of Northern agrarian export subsidies destroying their export markets. However, the actual outcome remained insufficient to establish a level playing field between the South and subsidized Northern exports of agrarian surpluses. Expecting higher food prices due to reduced subsidies of agrarian exports, Article 16 of the Agreement on Agriculture demands measures in favour of net importing SCs and LLDCs, as provided for within the Decision on Measures Concerning the Possible Negative Effects of the Reform Programme on Least-Developed and Net Food-Importing Developing Countries (NFIDCs). This Decision recognizes 'negative effects in terms of the availability of adequate supplies of basic foodstuffs from external sources on reasonable terms and conditions, including short term difficulties in financing normal levels of commercial imports of basic foodstuffs'. Facing increased import bills at a time of scarce convertible currency, these countries were thought to be very adversely affected. Help had to be stipulated before signing the Agreement to allay fears of net-importing SCs. The upsurge of agrarian prices starting in the very year the Final Act was signed underlined the need for financial support.

Meanwhile, a WTO list of NFIDCs exists. However, the Committee on Agriculture (1996, para. 10) underlined that being listed does not 'confer automatic benefits since ... donors and international organizations concerned would have a role to play'. Unlike negative effects, corrective benefits do not result automatically from the treaty.

The Decision on Measures Concerning the Possible Negative Effects sees the solution for net importers experiencing difficulties financing commercial imports in getting money 'in the context of adjustment programmes'. Doing so increases the dependence of debtor countries on the BWIs. Financing expensive food imports by increased borrowing is not necessarily good advice to debt-ridden countries already unable to service debts on time and amassing huge arrears. Sub-Saharan Africa, the region expected to be most severely affected by higher food prices, paid less than one-sixth of its contractually due debt service in 1995, according to the World Bank's *World Debt Tables*. New multilateral loans for consumption, necessarily increasing the debt overhang, will certainly not alleviate this problem. They will become part of unpayable debt burdens that have to be reduced eventually, as documented by the HIPC Initiatives, which became necessary because multilateral resources did not fund economically viable – and thus self-liquidating – projects and programmes. This is another convincing reason why referring net importers to the BWIs is not economically sensible.

Implementing this Decision, the WTO approached the BWIs to discuss improved conditions of access to existing facilities, a softening of conditionality, new facilities for net food importers and 'ways in which the WTO could assist the IMF and the World Bank to be more forthcoming in these matters' (Committee on Agriculture, 1996, para. 17). Apparently, such assistance was not welcome. Although SCs expressed their disappointment regarding the accessibility of existing facilities, the BWIs denied the necessity of new, Uruguay Round-related facilities, referring to the range of available ones. Obviously, low conditionality finance is considered unnecessary.

In contrast to the Decision's wording, difficulties of most food importers will not be short-term problems, comparable to a phase of illiquidity quickly overcome. *Ceteris paribus*, higher food import prices are likely to create a permanent additional demand for foreign exchange, compounded by impacts of lopsided liberalization. This non-transitory effect calls for other measures than relatively short-term multilateral loans. Compensatory measures could be financed by donor countries from the large overall gains from trade liberalization and the reduction of expensive agrarian subsidies.

A Food Import Facility established at the WTO, as proposed by Raffer (1997a) should be envisaged, working as a contractual insurance scheme without conditionality, like the original Stabex in Lomé I. Conditionality must not creep in eventually, as it did with Stabex and the CFF. Knowing that transfers are temporary should be an incentive to use them properly. As a measure against abuse of funds, recipients themselves could monitor their use in the way the USA allowed self-monitoring by recipients under its Marshall Plan. This successful precedent should be copied (cf. Raffer & Singer, 1996, p.197f).

Furthermore, differential treatment regarding export credits and consideration by ICs to improve agricultural productivity and infrastructure through aid were agreed on. It must be questioned whether these are really going to reduce their own export outlets in net importing SCs by subsidizing competing agricultural production there. Article 10.4 of the Agreement on Agriculture meant to avoid the use of food aid to circumvent export subsidy commitments, indicates a clear concern for retaining export markets. The permission to subsidize the destruction of food ('definitive permanent disposal' of livestock) pursuant to para. 9(*b*) of Annex 2 indicates a clear interest in managing the market. SCs would thus be well advised to make good use of exemptions such as for the purpose of food security or the provision of foodstuffs at subsidized prices (the latter is considered to be in conformity with para. 4 of Annex 2 by the text). One may ask how such programmes can be implemented with 'no, or at most minimal, trade distorting effects or effects on production' (Annex 2, para. 1). Debt-ridden SCs, however, are unlikely to have the money needed to finance such schemes as safeguarding food security.

The effects of the Round on food aid depend on the evolution of surpluses. If surpluses remain stable or increase while restrictions on export subsidies reduce Northern exports, food aid may even rise in an attempt to reduce stocks. After Marrakesh both commitments and actual food aid declined. The Committee on Agriculture (1996) therefore recommended efforts to establish a level of food aid sufficient to meet the legitimate needs of SCs during the reform programme, when renegotiating the Food Aid Convention. Similarly, Singer (1994) proposed doubling the minimum commitment of food aid in the new Convention to 15 million tons a year in terms of cereals, the actual level when the Final Act was signed. Thus the quantity would not be reduced, although this would not prevent a diversion of food aid from developmental to emergency objectives. In fact, however, the minimum commitment was recently reduced. Aid for agriculture and rural development has continuously dropped, 'falling from around 25 to 30% of total ODA in the 1980s to less then 15% in the '90s', as the director general of the FAO complained to the OECD (Diouf, 2000). He compared the 'around $10 billion per annum' transferred by the OECD to rural people in the South with 'US$ 350 billion to farmers in [OECD] member countries'.

Higher food prices tend to increase the amount of food aid in value terms automatically. Simply because of higher commercial (reference) prices, subsidized exports currently too hard to qualify would become aid. Donors could appear to honour their commitments, while reducing the amount that would qualify as food aid under present circumstances. Singer (1994, p.63) advocated 'proper definitions of food aid from that point of view'. Increasing the minimum grant element would be one way to do so, agreeing that loans must not be more expensive than before. A minimum grant element of 25 per cent is equivalent to a 'non-grant' or commercial element (CE) of 75 per cent. The condition is satisfied if the new CE is 75 per cent or less of the value obtained if the transaction had taken place at the price before Uruguay Round-induced price increases (Raffer, 1998e). As the Agreement on Agriculture contains 'base periods' and 'reference prices', this would fit in perfectly. It would introduce an element of flexibility into the definition of food aid, which is absent in the definition of ODA based on a minimum grant element of 25 per cent. In the case of food aid, the OECD 'agreed on a benchmark of 25 per cent below the commercial price as an arbitrary definition of the grant element of ODA' (Shaw & Singer, 1998, p.316). As this 'commercial' price results from Northern agrarian protection and export subsidies, it is not a real market price, though. The practical relevance of this change would be limited, as most food aid has been provided in the form of grants. Furthermore, the OECD recommends a grant element of at least 86 per cent for each member's total annual ODA, a target surpassed by most OECD donors, particularly in the case of LLDCs. A higher minimum grant element would be well in line with the Agreement on Agriculture, whose Article 10(4)(c) demands food aid to be provided 'to the extent possible in grant form'.

AGRARIAN TRADE

Southern food exporters have lost substantial amounts owing to heavy subsidies, by both the EU and the USA, depressing so-called 'world market' prices. In 1985, for instance, Europe and the USA were accused of having brought the price of wheat down by 15 per cent after a fall of 40 per cent the year before. The price of maize declined by 30 per cent (Raffer, 1990b, p.852). EEC sugar exports practically annihilated world sugar prices. The initial US demands to liberalize agrarian trade radically have thus raised strong interest in the South. Although net importers feel negative effects, the outcome is a far cry from the initial US proposals SCs supported. Agreed cuts in subsidies remain very limited in scope and have been effectively postponed by the phasing mechanism allowing six to nine years for implementation.

After negotiations to continue the 'reform process' in agriculture pursuant to Article 20 of the Agreement on Agriculture had started in 2000, several SC exporters pointed out that they had agreed to the 'moderate reforms' of the Uruguay Round 'because they obtained the commitment to resume negotiations' (WTO, 2000b, p.11) on agrarian trade in return. Therefore they objected to proposals by European and some other countries to discuss agriculture only in a comprehensive round, covering a wide range of topics. Further liberalization in the interest of some SCs – and of Northern taxpayers who have to finance very costly and inefficient agrarian protection – will be dodged.

The Agreement on Agriculture (Article 6.4) states important exemptions from the calculation of the current total aggregate measurement of support. Direct payments under production-limiting programmes are exempt if based on fixed areas or yields, fixed number of head of livestock, or if these subsidies are made on not more than 85 per cent of the base level of production. Up to 5 per cent are allowed to ICs under *de minimis* as well. Furthermore, Annex 2 contains a host of subsidies for which exemption may be claimed if no price support to producers is provided and under some, not always very precise, conditions. The list includes water supply facilities (useful for heavily subsidized bananas grown by the EU on Crete), food security programmes, domestic food aid (fitting US food stamps like a glove), direct payments to producers, decoupled income support (including money for not producing anything), structural adjustment measures including investment subsidies, and payments under environmental and regional assistance programmes.

On top of these rather generous norms allowing interesting combinations of exemptions enabling governments to keep actual cuts rather small, Article 5 contains special safeguard provisions for products where non-tariff trade barriers have been converted to customs duties, so that import increases due to a 'more liberal' regime can be capped. In line with Northern interests, permitted additional duty increases with imported quantities or as the supply price of the would-be exporter decreases. If one assumes that conversions result in customs duties as restrictive as the replaced measures (which would be legally correct according to the Agreement) these additional safeguards go beyond present protection. As these additional duties may be imposed again year after year, they constitute an effective long-term instrument to limit imports. Further measures 'other than ordinary customs duties' are legal under Annex 5 and pursuant to the Understanding on Balance-of-Payments Provisions of GATT 1994.

Lower average tariffs on Southern agricultural exports were frequently implemented by granting above-average reductions for tropical products while keeping sensitive products, such as meat or milk, relatively more protected (Raffer, 1996c). Tariff reductions, a traditional result of GATT rounds, are usually of limited value to SCs because sectors of importance to them either are not subject to tariffs (raw materials) or remain selectively more protected.

Some export subsidies must be reduced, and circumvention of export subsidy commitments is explicitly prohibited. OECD countries are allowed to subsidize exports according to their own Guidelines for Officially Supported Export Credits stipulating minimum interest rates for exports to the South differentiated by country groups and currencies. Under the WTO, SCs can finance according to these conditions as well, but to what extent countries can actually do so is a financial question. As SCs are not as rich as OECD countries, and many are over-indebted, their financial possibilities are more limited than those of ICs. A solution in line with the free market principle of the WTO would have been to outlaw all export subsidies. But this would have changed price relations in favour of Southern exporters.

Export subsidies in excess of annual commitments are legal pursuant to Article 9 under certain conditions, allowing more flexibility. SCs enjoy slightly higher limits. However, cuts are insufficient to establish a level playing field for Southern exporters, as the example of Argentina illustrates. In the 1980s, President Alfonsín complained that EEC beef was offered at one-third of its production costs, thus virtually destroying Argentinian export markets, although Argentinian production costs were 50 to 60 per cent lower than Europe's (Raffer, 1990b, p.852).

Article 6 allows SCs direct and indirect measures to encourage agricultural and rural development as an integral part of their development programmes. This mirrors the provisions for structural adjustment, payments under environmental programmes and regional assistance programmes for ICs mentioned above. Investment subsidies generally available to agriculture in SCs and input subsidies generally available to low-income or resource-poor producers are exempt, as well as subsidies for diversification away from illegal drugs. Thus Colombia can subsidize its agriculture without restraint. Any SC where drugs are currently produced or people start to produce them can, of course, avail itself of this exemption. Export outlets may remain restrained, though. Roses, a major foreign exchange earner in Colombia, faced 34 per cent tariffs in the USA. As the text refers to developing members, the USA for instance, also a producer of drugs – *The Economist* (2 April 1988, *American Survey*, p.31) calls marijuana 'California's leading cash crop' – cannot subsidize under Article 6.

The GATT (1992, p.32) cites the 'reduction of the adverse effects of sanitary and phytosanitary regulations' as one main goal of the round. The Agreement on the Application of Sanitary and Phytosanitary Measures demands that restrictions be only applied to protect human, animal or plant life or health, and should not be used as non-tariff trade barriers. The practical relevance of this demand remains to be seen. Basing measures 'on international standards' means de facto on Northern standards, an advantage for ICs. Article 6 requiring members to adapt to 'regional conditions' and containing the concept of 'pest- or disease-free areas' may easily be used against SCs, where hygienic standards are, or are at least supposed to be, lower. The need for scientific justification of measures should pose no problems.

TRADE BARRIERS AND PREFERENCES

Preference margins, such as those granted under the Lomé Treaty, shrink - a fact criticized by some SCs but an inevitable result of tariff reductions. Empirical evidence suggests that actual preference systems hardly increased trade dramatically. Trade effects are thus likely to be small. However, substantial losses of preference margins by LLDCs (even higher than 25 percentage points in one case) led UNCTAD (1995a) to expect losses of market shares. An exception from the principle of equal treatment in GATT 1947 was gained by strong political pressure, enabling developing GATT members to get preference systems from ICs. These systems may be considered not very successful. Apparently, they were not intended to be. Northern markets were 'opened' in areas where little competition could be expected from SCs, leaving sectors of genuine Southern interest well protected. Empirical evidence shows that protectionist measures, especially non-tariff trade barriers, have been used asymmetrically, aimed at SCs conspicuously more often than other ICs (World Bank, 1987, p.140; Taylor, 1987). Since the South has less power to retaliate, this is not surprising, but in line with a consistent history of Northern protectionism.

In spite of the modest results of preference systems, the principle of preferential treatment as such is valuable, making it possible to take the special developmental needs of SCs into account. At the beginning of the Uruguay Round this principle was endangered. Abolishing it in favour of 'equality' was advocated. The World Bank (1987, pp.154f, 167), in line with its larger shareholders, argued strongly against preferential treatment for SCs, recommending reciprocity as fair and efficient, even advising SCs to open their markets unilaterally, if the North should become more restrictive than they already were. Compared with such views, the maintenance of the principle of preferential treatment is a small success for SCs. It can be found in many articles of the Final Act (Raffer, 1996c). Some provisions amount to mere courtesy (or lip-service), others contain substance, but substantial preferences have not been granted so far. Finally, a few norms are clear and unequivocal. Article 15.2 of the Agreement on Agriculture states that LLDCs shall not be required to undertake reduction commitments, or the higher *de minimis* percentage (10 instead of 5 per cent) regarding agricultural support reduction for SCs pursuant to Article 6.3(*b*). At the sixth session of the seminar on special and differential treatment of SCs at the WTO, one speaker stated 'that numerous provisions' for special and differential treatment in the Uruguay Agreements 'have not been applied or implemented in practice' (Akram, 2000, p.10). One must also recall that the agreements often contain non-binding commitments or best endeavour clauses.

Tariff escalation was not abolished, but the GATT claims that 'less tariff escalation' was achieved, even though its own examples quoted to support this view do not corroborate it (*GATT Focus*, March–April 1994, p.8). Protection by tariff escalation is still widely used in the North. Akram (2000, p.10) concluded:

> The failure to include measures for commodity price stabilization and the sharp tariff escalation and tariff peaks maintained against processing those commodities by developing countries have combined, over time, to erode the terms of trade of developing countries and basically bankrupting them.

As most SCs were already under pressure to open their economies unilaterally, the impact of GATT 1994 on their trade policies appears to be limited. Nevertheless, World Bank staff members found an 'alarming trend' (Low & Nash, 1994, p.59) in countries such as Brazil, Chile, Korea, Mexico and India to apply the same kind of anti-dumping and variable-levies mechanisms used by OECD countries. Practices applied by the North for decades without alarming the public, and – anti-dumping measures in particular – remaining legal under the Final Act, cause alarm if used in the South.

Voluntary export restrictions are now legal. Article 8 of the Agreement on Implementation of Article VI of GATT 1994 states that anti-dumping duties or provisional measures can be exchanged for 'satisfactory voluntary undertakings from any exporter to revise its prices or to cease exports to the area in question at dumped prices so that authorities are satisfied that the injurious effect of the dumping is eliminated'. Problems that arise in determining dumping, for instance if no like products are sold 'in the ordinary course of trade in the domestic market' (Article 2.2) may allow harassing small exporters into 'voluntary' offers.

Pursuant to the Understanding on Balance-of-Payments Provisions, members may apply 'price-based measures' for balance of payments reasons on top of duties inscribed in their schedules. If these measures cannot arrest a sharp deterioration in the balance of payments situation, new quantitative restrictions are allowed. They have to be justified, but that should not be too difficult unless a country is bound by BWI conditionality. These restrictions 'may only be applied to control the general level of imports and may not exceed what is necessary to address the balance-of-payments situation' (para. 4). Even discretionary licensing is legal 'if unavoidable' (ibid.). If a time schedule for the removal of restrictive measures has been presented, the

General Council may recommend that a member adhering to this schedule shall be deemed in compliance with its GATT 1994 obligations. Quite conspicuously, paragraph 13 avoids setting any time limit for such schedules.

PRESHIPMENT INSPECTION

The Agreement on Preshipment Inspection is of particular importance. Checks on quantity and quality of products delivered are essential for the functioning of a market system. Nevertheless, the GATT (1992, p.32) mentioned preshipment inspection under the heading *Non-Tariff Trade Barriers*, defining it as 'the use of private firms to check shipment and invoicing details where countries cannot do it adequately themselves'. This surprising attitude can be explained. Since the 1980s, some SCs have attempted to gain legitimate information on what and how much they were buying to approximate perfect market conditions with better information. This has met stiff resistance from traders. US exporters urged their government to withdraw trade privileges from SCs using international, private inspection companies to check fraud. UK exporters, too, complained bitterly about price comparisons made by these private consultants (Lapper, 1987). These reactions must be connected to the fact that SCs unable to check are routinely overcharged, as Yeats (1990) showed for African countries. During 1962–87, the period analysed by him, biennial averages of overcharging were above 70 per cent for relatively homogeneous, simple products (iron and steel). Extreme examples for shorter periods reached 120 per cent.

Thus inspection is hardly unjustified, even though it may well be that SCs are not always able to do it as quickly as might be desirable. The right to know what one is paying for should be beyond discussion. This Agreement, explicitly allowing SCs to follow a routine trading procedure, inspecting what they buy, may be seen as a small victory. SCs were able to defend both their legitimate interests and the essential market principle and right of all other buyers to information on what they buy. An Independent Entity was established to resolve disputes between exporters and inspection agencies. The WTO (2000c, p.51) reports that no application for a case was received during the period under review.

SCs applying preshipment inspection (PSI) report positive experiences. Ghana, for instance, reported that foreign exchange savings and customs revenues increased by 33 and 38 per cent, to $32 million and $110 million, respectively, in 1996 (WTO, 1997d, p.10). A number of WTO members, such as the USA, the EU and also Korea, expressed concern. The USA also complained that 'many PSI inspectors ... lacked the necessary language skills, which led to misunderstandings and confusion ' (ibid.). This deserves quoting, as the USA would rightly never dream of using any other but its own official language when processing imports, but complains when other countries do the same.

GATS: THE GENERAL AGREEMENT ON TRADE IN SERVICES

The inclusion of services was primarily due to the USA, but also the UK. Initially, the Group of 10, in particular Brazil and India, opposed it, fearing that their own evolving service firms might be nipped in the bud. Selective liberalization where ICs, notably the USA, could hope to conquer markets created resentment as well. Often the USA called for better market access, complaining about impediments in fields where Washington restricted access of foreigners most heavily (cf. Raffer, 1987c).

Nayyar (1986) argued that those countries pressing for liberalization of services opposed it in the case of labour services (migrant labour), where the South has advantages. The present outcome accommodates Northern wishes, liberalizing trade in the services of consultants, engineers, lawyers or accountants, but treating services rendered by less qualified labour differently. Noyelle (1994) explains this in part by political unease about immigration. Thus the North refused to extend the Generalized System of Preferences to services as inappropriate (UNCTAD, 1995c, p.5).

It remains to be seen to what extent Article XV *bis* (security exceptions) will be useful for SCs. When Brazil introduced legal restrictions to protect its nascent computer industry, the USA promptly intervened, irrespective of the fact that strategic reasons too were responsible for Brazil's decision (Evans, 1986, p.795). The USA, on the other hand, stretched national security in the field of communications down to fibre optics equipment (Goldstein & Krasner, 1984, p.283). Even domestic wool production was declared a matter of national security by Congress (Raffer, 1990b, p.860). A similarly generous stretching of 'strategic' would be unthinkable for any SCs.

Article V *bis* (the number indicates that it was squeezed into the text rather late) might be a trace element of Southern interests in liberalizing the services of migrant labour, which they can offer so well. It expressly allows labour markets integration agreements. But these were not illegal before.

A particular problem arises in the sector of telecommunications, called 'QWERTY-nomics' by David (1985): inferior techniques, once adopted, can freeze out more promising alternatives simply because of prohibitive costs of changing. An economy can get locked into techniques, although more efficient ones exist or come into existence. The QWERTY keyboard, for instance, froze out the Dvorak keyboard, which increases the speed of typing by 40 per cent. If the North are able to establish their techniques in the market this may bar any future alternatives by other producers, including technically more advanced SCs. Freezing out is also a potential danger with regard to complementary services in high-tech fields. Their importance is clearly illustrated by Bhagwati (1985, pp.99f), according to whom the French subsidiary of Dresser Industries was literally cut off from all relevant information within a second by order of the US president. It could thus not provide compressors for the trans-Siberian pipeline.

In contrast to textiles and clothing, where 'liberalization' cannot proceed slowly enough, information technology products were to be liberalized quickly. Starting on 1 July 1997 ('first cut'), complete elimination of duties by 1 January 2000 was stipulated (WTO, 1997b, p.3). Such speed is easily explained by the fact that Japan, the USA and the EU are the largest exporters, accounting for nearly half of global exports. Their exports were 1·5 times the amount of those by the next seven of the top ten exporters in 1995, and information technology exports have grown significantly faster than world merchandise exports. On 1 January 2000, further negotiations on trade in services started, as required by the agreement.

TRADE RELATED INVESTMENT MEASURES (TRIMs)

These rules contain substantial restrictions on SCs, enforcing the obligation of national treatment of foreign investors in the field of goods. They deprive SCs of important policy options, such as the use of national laws as bargaining chips in negotiations with transnational enterprises, or fostering their own infant industries by demanding the use of domestic inputs in production. TRIMs are not clearly defined, but the annex of this Agreement explicitly prohibits any local input requirements, restricting a transnational's access to foreign exchange in percentages of inflows attributable to it, or export restrictions. This may often make the development of domestic industries impossible. Historical evidence from successful countries, such as South Korea or Taiwan, strongly suggests that liberalization of foreign investment is not necessarily conducive to developing domestic industries. Both countries and Japan have restricted foreign investments heavily, easing their restrictions only recently. Historically, Europe and the USA have protected their new industries from foreign competition. As infant industries are by definition less efficient than experienced ones, TRIMs are likely to restrict development options seriously.

Taking the bargaining chip of domestic law away from SCs may be seen as one-sided disarmament. Without an enforceable code of conduct for transnational corporations (or international anti-cartel norms) SCs have lost their countervailing powers against transnational restrictive business practices. The old Southern demand that the power of transnationals must be checked by international norms is not part of the Agreement. Not even a general reference to restrictive business practices (as in Article IX of the Agreement on Trade in Services, where the word 'restrictive' is avoided, though) can be found in the TRIMs Agreement.

The South is deprived of important policy options still available to successful 'tiger' economies, as the World Bank (1993b, p.33) summarized in its study on the 'Asian miracle'. Noting increasing pressure on SCs to refrain from interventions violating international trading rules such as GATT, it concluded 'export subsidies and directed credits linked to exports ... are incompatible with a changing world trade environment'. Empirically successful options for development are now ruled out for 'latecomers'. The Bank supports this, arguing that the elaborate intervention systems of Japan, South Korea or Taiwan should not be copied by other SCs.

Indonesia's domestic car programme became a prominent case under TRIMs. Indonesia granted exemption from import duties and luxury tax for car parts and components contingent on local content requirements as well as to companies with 'pioneer status'. Japan and the EU argued that these measures were inconsistent with the TRIMs Agreement, the GATT 1994 and the Agreement on Subsidies and Countervailing Measures (WTO, 1997d, p.6). The USA joined later. Indonesia had to accept the obvious – local content restrictions are one of the very few explicitly outlawed measures – admitting that the TRIMs Agreement had been violated. Although it disagreed with some conclusions of the panel, Indonesia did not appeal 'in the light of its IMF commitments and the subsequent termination of its National Car Programme' (WTO, 1998b, p.8) – a good illustration of WTO–BWI cooperation. 'Japan said it understood Indonesia's desire to build its national car but believed this could be carried out in conformity with the WTO' (WTO, 1997c, p.3), a statement one might qualify as cynical.

TRADE RELATED INTELLECTUAL PROPERTY-RIGHTS (TRIPs)

ICs emphasized the need to protect firms from illegal Southern copycats. While there is doubtlessly a great deal of counterfeiting going on in SCs, *South* magazine (February 1991, p.66) claimed that 'the two hubs of the counterfeit industry ... are not Thailand and Hong Kong but Italy and America'. Be that as it may, there certainly exists a justified interest in fighting counterfeit trade. As with TRIMs, national treatment is accorded to foreigners.

But the TRIPs Agreement contains important issues. National patent laws considered to grant too little exclusivity to patent holders or to protect their rights for too short a time span have to be changed. This benefits virtually exclusively the North, holding most patents. India was seen as a prime target. Indeed, in 1996, the USA complained about 'alleged failure of India to provide interim patent protection for pharmaceutical and agricultural chemical products' (WTO, 1996c, p.6; 1996d, p.2). The EU joined in 1997. Similarly, the USA complained against Pakistan (WTO, 1997b, p.7). Article 27 allows the exclusion of inventions from patentability and the prevention of their exploitation 'to avoid serious prejudice to the environment, provided that such exclusion is not made merely because the exploitation is prohibited by their law'. Thus the Agreement overrules existing national laws.

WTO agreements do not always do so. The USA had been granted an exemption under paragraph 3 of the GATT 1994 agreement with regard to its legislation prohibiting foreign-built vessels in internal shipping. This exemption was to be reviewed five years after the entry into force of the WTO agreement. When several delegations urged the USA to modify its legislation, the USA stressed that this exemption was not a waiver or a temporary provision but an integral part of the GATT 1994. US legislation (the 'Jones Act' of 1920) 'had not been modified or amended, and thus the conditions that created the need for exemption still existed' (WTO, 1999c, p.5). Australia pointed out that all other members had been obliged to bring their previously grandfathered legislation into conformity. The USA stressed that this exemption was the result of negotiations and had not been obtained for nothing, affecting the way other elements of the WTO system had been finalized. It said 'that the exemption would vanish when the US changed the legislation or decided to end the exemption through negotiation' (ibid.)

The traditional requirements for patenting are changed by dismissing the 'inventive step' (something going beyond mere discovery) as a necessary condition for patentability. Article 27 demands an 'inventive step', but redefines it as 'non-obvious'. This makes an important difference. Applying tribal or traditional knowledge obtained in the South to problems in the North might not involve an inventive step, but it may be considered non-obvious. The case of the endod, the African soapberry plant, which kills the snails harbouring the parasites causing schistosomiasis, may serve as an illustrative example (Mooney, 1993). For centuries endod has been cultivated by innovative Ethiopian women. Attempts to get help from Northern institutes to develop endod further to obtain a preventive medicine were unsuccessful. US scientists at an Ohio university, learning about endod from an Ethiopian colleague about to receive an honorary degree, wondered whether it might kill zebra mussels, a scourge of the US shipping industry in the Great Lakes. They were told about the endod on 14 June 1990, on 15 June, they knew it worked on zebra mussels; and on 15 October, the university filed a patent application on the use of endod to kill zebra mussels. The market in the USA is estimated to be some $5 billion, while – according to Mooney – 'endod's true discoverers, the women of Ethiopia, continue their lonely war against schistosomiasis'.

The author gives further examples 'of what the South has come to call "kleptomonopoly" or "bio-piracy"' (ibid., p.11), drawing attention to US patent court decisions that 'have begun to expose the vast biological and genetic diversity of the South's fauna and flora' to patent lawyers. There is mounting evidence that intellectual property rights of people from SCs, especially tribal knowledge, have been infringed. The basic problem is simple and not without precedent. Two sets of legal systems clash. One is used by the more powerful to gain financially at the cost of the less powerful. Instead of trying to reconcile the systems, protection is only granted according to Northern (international) norms, leaving rights recognized by the other system, such as traditional knowledge, unprotected and fair game for Northern interests. Historical parallels exist. In Europe, the adoption of Roman law was used by nobility to claim peasants' land as their 'property'. Taking land and property from 'natives' under colonialism is another example. Finally, the introduction of land registers in SCs has often been used by so-called 'élites' to expropriate the real owners, who only learned that a register existed when they were driven off 'another person's' land.

Furthermore, the new possibility to patent micro-organisms and non-biological and microbiological processes harbours the danger of control of important biological resources by a few Northern firms. This would put SCs, including those able to develop their own research capacity in the foreseeable future, at a disadvantage. Plants or animals may be patented, although countries may decide not to allow it. It was stipulated that this norm should be reviewed four years after the entry into force of the WTO Agreement.

The disadvantage of Southern producers is compounded by Article 34, which shifts the burden of proof in the case of process patents onto the defendant, a highly unusual legal practice. The passage reads: 'the judicial authorities shall have the authority to order the defendant to prove that the process to obtain an identical product is different from the patented process'. If he or she is unable to do so, it will be deemed to have been obtained by the patented process. Thus it is easy to create a lot of nuisance and costs simply by accusing a competitor.

Even in 'normal' cases, SCs are likely to be at a great disadvantage, as the patent on the AIDS virus illustrates. It was awarded by the USA to Robert Gallo of the National Cancer Institute, who claimed to have identified the virus first. After six years of legal battle, he admitted in 1991 that 'the virus he "discovered" had been previously isolated by Montagnier' (*Time*, 8

November 1993, p.69). Lack of resources and political influence would simply bar most SCs from getting what is rightly theirs and from defending their legitimate interests.

Finally, calling itself WTO, the World Trade Organization itself infringed the World Tourism Organization's (WTO) intellectual property, clearly violating Article 15 of its own TRIPs Agreement, which explicitly protects letters and combinations of letters, such as WTO. This attitude of a powerful institution regarding the rights of a less powerful one bodes ill for SCs.

DISPUTE SETTLEMENT

The strengthening of multilateral decision making, mirrored in the WTO's stronger role, was seen as an advantage for SCs and small countries in general, but it is ambiguous. Installing the one country–one vote principle, WTO, like the UN General Assembly, gives SCs representing the majorities of countries and of people also the majority of votes. As the Agreement Establishing the WTO establishes majority decisions and consensus, this forms the legal base for full participation of SCs in decision making. It was often argued that the WTO's legal framework will put an end to bilateral (and GATT-violating) measures such as the US Super 301. Conducting its review on the USA in November 1996, the WTO's Trade Policy Review Body expressed 'a general dissatisfaction with the continued unilateralism inherent in "Section 301" legislation' (WTO, 1996c, p.16), questioning in particular the WTO consistency of the Helms–Burton Act (penalizing third countries for investing in Cuba) and the Iran–Lybia Trade Sanctions Act. The USA 'saw Section 301 as a means for communication of exporters' concerns' (ibid.). Apparently, the aim of replacing (Super) 301, a unilateral measure implemented in breach of international treaties, with WTO dispute settlement was not fully successful. Deciding on a complaint by the EU, the Dispute Settlement Body ruled in 2000 that 'those aspects of Sections 301–310 ... brought before us', though 'a *prima facie* violation' of WTO obligations, 'are not inconsistent with US obligations under the WTO' (WTO, 2000c, p.68). This was based on the fact that US legislation as such, not any specific action taken by the USA, was challenged, and on 'administrative statements' and 'undertakings' shedding light on how the USA has decided and bound itself to implement these sections. Briefly put, the USA had declared not to apply the law as it stands. The panel had stated that carrying a big stick without using it would itself influence markets, but this 'actual threat', to use WTO language, was finally considered all right. According to the WTO, these sections now 'provide an important avenue for the United States to enforce its rights under WTO agreements' (ibid., p.67).

In principle, the WTO's new powers should be equally strictly applied to all, not allowing big players to go on bending rules with impunity. The last resort provided to member countries invoking dispute settlement procedures is the suspension of concessions and other obligations against the violating member, subject to authorization by the Dispute Settlement Body. One may wonder whether the authorized suspension of concessions by Jamaica against the USA will be equally effective as a suspension the other way round. Suspending concessions and obligations is subject to strict rules and not always possible. Compensation for damage inflicted by breach of contract is voluntary. As in the case of voluntary export restrictions, where SCs volunteer more often, one may assume that compensation will not be forthcoming with equal eagerness from all countries either. Article 3.7 of the Understanding on Rules and Procedures Covering the Settlement of Disputes contains a subtle warning to SCs and small countries in general: 'Before bringing a case, a Member shall exercise its judgement as to whether action under these procedures would be fruitful. The aim of the dispute settlement mechanism is to secure a positive solution to the dispute.' The probability of success is explicitly established as the guiding principle of dispute settlement, more important than enforcing the Rule of Law with impartiality.

Theoretically, one could have opted for authorizing or even encouraging all members to suspend concessions and obligations against a country breaking the rules (Raffer, 1996c), an idea proposed by India in 1999. Reducing asymmetries of power, this solution would protect the interests of smaller players much better, strengthening the rule of law and the enforceability of norms agreed on by all members. But this was not wanted.

The EU's complaint against the US Helms–Burton Act (officially called 'Cuban Liberty and Democratic Solidarity Act') illustrates the WTO's limits. The USA threatened that 'the WTO panel process would not lead to a resolution of the dispute, instead it would pose serious risks for the new organization' (WTO, 1996d, p.2). Following US 'advice' to 'explore other avenues' (ibid.), the EC requested the panel to suspend its work in April 1997. While Helms–Burton is a clear violation of US obligations under the WTO, one could as well call the EU's move illegal in view of its evident unfruitfulness. The USA, by far the leading complainant with 34 per cent of cases by 19 August 1997, insists on choosing whether to comply with decisions or not. One may assume that both the EC and Japan would be equally able to assert themselves. SCs, on the other hand, are much more likely to comply with rulings, particularly if advised to do so by the WTO in cooperation with the BWIs. Rather than creating a level playing field, WTO dispute settlement is likely to provide an opportunity to exert pressure on weaker members based on or under the cloak of legal arguments. Of the first

100 cases, SCs filed 31 and were subject to 37 complaints. Quantitatively, the procedure has mostly been used between ICs.

The functioning of WTO procedures may be illustrated by two further examples. When Ecuador was allowed to start retaliations 'to encourage the EC to amend its banana regime' (WTO, 2000b, p.13) the EC said 'it recognized Ecuador's right to retaliate', a right of 'a big or a small partner' (ibid., p.14). Nevertheless, it expressed concern about the arbitrators' findings that Ecuador may cross-retaliate under the TRIPS agreement. Apparently, it would have preferred retaliation against EC banana exports to Ecuador. After a lengthy deferral of Ecuador's rights to suspend concessions to determine the appropriate level, Ecuador was left with uncompensated direct damages of $201·6 million. The country would have preferred compensation over suspension, which does not make up for any damage suffered because of a breach of obligations.

Canada, a country subsidizing its own small aircraft industry according to the WTO, complained against subsidies granted by Brazil to its aircraft producers. Brazil in turn complained against Canadian subsidies. Canada simply refused to provide information requested by the panel, in particular about the debt-financing activities of its Export Development Corporation (EDC). Declining Brazil's demand to infer that the information withheld was prejudicial to Canada's position, the panel stated that Brazil's evidence was insufficient. The Appellate Body found that Canada had violated its obligation to respond promptly and fully pursuant to Article 13.1 of the Understanding on Rules and Procedures Covering the Settlement of Disputes. It remarked that 'a party's refusal to collaborate has the potential to undermine the functioning of the dispute settlement system' (WTO, 2000c, p.59). The Appellate Body 'might well have concluded that the facts on the record did warrant the inference that the information Canada withheld ... included information prejudicial to Canada's denial that the EDC had conferred "benefit" and granted a prohibited export subsidy'. Nevertheless, the panel's finding was upheld, as Brazil had not done enough to compel it to make the inferences requested. The Body did 'not intend to suggest that Brazil was precluded from pursuing another complaint against Canada ... concerning the consistency of certain of the EDC's financing measures' with contractual obligations (ibid.). It remains unclear, however, why Canada should then provide prejudicial information it withheld successfully before.

The functioning of dispute settlement procedures has made some SC members propose modifications. Concern was voiced by several SCs about the costly nature of procedures, rendering the mechanism not as accessible to SCs as it should be. Rules were demanded to obviate the possibility of the settlement process being used as an instrument of coercion of weaker (poorer) members. The problem is precisely the same as in domestic law suits, where a rich party can outmanœuvre the poorer party financially. Among the remedies proposed was that SCs winning a case initiated by an IC should get their costs refunded, or that ICs as complainants should have to demonstrate that alleged violations by SCs cause non-negligible damages. As mentioned above, joint retaliatory action by the entire WTO membership was also suggested. It was pointed out that provisions for differential and more favourable treatment of SCs should be meaningfully implemented. Several articles in which this treatment is not articulated specifically enough should be rephrased. After long discussions, no agreement was reached and it was concluded that the review of dispute settlement had ended without a recommendation. Nor was it agreed to continue the review process. Informal discussions based on a proposal by 15 members to the Seattle Ministerial Conference continued (ibid., p.79). Those countries happy about the present functioning, dubious as it might be by any decent legal standards, were able to preserve the status quo.

In the case of textiles and clothing, complaints have to be presented to the Textiles Monitoring Body before invoking the WTO's dispute settlement mechanism. As this body is required to take all decisions by consensus (members appointed by countries involved in the unresolved issue are exempted) this is likely to prevent effective and speedy resolutions of disputes in this field. UNCTAD (1995b, p.25) rightly fears that this may result in a repetition of bilateral deals practised under the MFA and a weakening of multilateral discipline.

Considering the arrears of payments to the UN, one might also ask how enforceable Article VII.4 of the Agreement Establishing the WTO, demanding prompt payments of contributions, will be against big members. If the WTO should start to act in a way seen by big members as not in their interest – of which there is no indication – it might suffer the same financial fate as the UN, whose General Assembly has voted against the North so often.

COOPERATION WITH THE BWIs

Although cooperation with the IMF was already stipulated in Article XV of GATT 1947, the WTO Agreement's Article III.5 demanding that the WTO should cooperate, as appropriate, with the Bretton Woods institutions to achieve greater coherence in global economic policy making, fuelled fears of increased pressure on SCs by 'cross-institutional conditionality' (Peng, 1994, p.9). This means that World Bank loans or IMF drawings may be made conditional on a good report from the WTO, vouching for the country having followed its rules adequately. Such an evolution would weaken Southern members considerably. Those SCs already governed by the BWIs in all but name would lose the rest of their bargaining power.

The Declaration on the Contribution of the WTO to Achieving Greater Coherence in Economic Policy stresses trade liberalization under BWI structural adjustment programmes as an 'increasingly important component' (para. 2), reaffirming the demand to 'pursue and develop' cooperation with the Bretton Woods institutions (para. 5). It postulates that 'cross-conditionality and additional conditions' should not be imposed, but does not say how 'greater coherence in global economic policymaking' can be achieved without them. One may suppose as well that, like the BWIs, the WTO will be more successful in convincing SCs to change policies for the sake of coherence than the EU or the USA.

The Declaration on the Relationship of the WTO with the IMF reaffirms that, 'unless otherwise provided for in the Final Act, the relationship of the WTO with the International Monetary Fund ... will be based on the provisions that have governed the relationship of the contracting parties to the GATT 1947 with the International Monetary Fund'. Linguistically, this is a brilliant example of ambiguity, and it remains to be feared what it will mean in practice.

On 9 December 1996, an agreement between the WTO and the IMF was signed in Singapore as 'the basis ... to achieve greater coherence in global economic policy by cooperating with the IMF as well as with the World Bank' (WTO, 1997a, p.24). The IMF now has observer status in certain WTO bodies. The WTO expected 'that work will start soon to address issues related to better coherence in global economic policy making, an area where the WTO, the IMF and the World Bank each have a distinctive role' (ibid.). As the example of net food importers shows, the WTO's role is not necessarily the most important.

Trade Policy Reviews offer a possibility of cooperation to embed the Washington Consensus firmly in SCs: 'a virtual global consensus on the fundamentals of trade policy reinforces economic and political liberalization and lessens the risk of reversion to the old ways' (WTO, 1996d, p.6).

ENVIRONMENTAL AND SOCIAL STANDARDS

During the Uruguay Round the environment and labour standards were brought into the debate by ICs. Afraid that these issues might be abused to justify protection, SCs rejected their incorporation. The fact that the treatment of workers became an issue of concern to ICs only after some SCs became very successful exporters, while the North has too often supported dictatorships suppressing trade unions and workers, did little to alleviate fears. Thus it was agreed not to 'overburden' the Round by including these issues.

Not discussing whether this result is desirable or in the long-term interest of SCs themselves, this might be considered a small tactical but temporary 'success'. SCs were able to keep this issue more or less out of the new agreements. With few exceptions, even the word 'environment' is not found in the texts.

But on 15 December 1993, the Trade Negotiations Committee adopted a decision to elaborate a working programme on trade and the environment. The first ministerial conference in Singapore adopted a declaration calling for core labour standards as well as for further work on trade and the environment (WTO, 1997a, pp.7ff). A new set of negotiations on the environment and trade-related worker's rights is likely to be started in the future. A Ministerial Working Group on Trade and Labour Standards met for the first time at Seattle. It was set up against SC resistance to discuss proposals for creating a labour standards working group within the WTO or a body operated jointly by a number of international organizations (WTO, 2000a, p.11).

In a session of the Special Committee on Preferences, some ICs have already maintained that linking non-trade objectives such as social standards, environmental conditions or workers' rights to trade concessions is fully legitimate. The intention to provide additional advantages in the field of generalized systems of preferences in exchange for higher standards in this field was voiced, claiming that social and environmental clauses could not be considered as protectionist, being purely additional to 'normal' preferences. This argument, though, may be applied to any new preferences. Judging from 'political conditionality' (cf. Raffer & Singer, 1996), one has to assume that such arguments simply serve to veil the real reason, protectionism, with nice-sounding phrases. 'Eco-protectionism' impairing market access of SCs is certainly a possible threat. But a combination of eco-protectionism in branches where SCs threaten to become highly competitive while liberally allowing redeployment of highly polluting production to regions where human lives cost less would also be possible. In that case SCs would be in the worst of all possible worlds.

As early as 1974, Siebert cited 'comparative advantages' of SCs in polluting industries, suggesting their relocation there. Lawrence Summers, then chief economist of the World Bank, pointed out that 'the costs of forgone earnings from increased morbidity and mortality' would be lower in 'vastly *under*polluted' poor SCs, concluding: 'a given amount of health-impairing pollution should be done in the country with ... the lowest wages' (*The Economist*, 15 February 1992, p.66; emphasis in original). Although he just repeated Siebert's arguments in more colloquial English, he was severely criticized. Such relocations have remained limited so far. One reason might be that environment-friendly techniques often reduce costs as well, another that highly polluting industries usually produce rather heavy or bulky goods, where transport costs are relatively important.

On the whole, there is reason for concern that the new regime will further compound the disadvantages of SCs. They were admittedly able to defend some interests, notably the principle of preferential treatment and preshipment inspection, as well as to introduce small changes into the texts. But ICs asserted their interests and SC interests were sidelined. Concerning practice, even the WTO (1995, p.22) apparently doubts whether clauses in favour of SCs will be obeyed, warning that agreeing to strengthen multilateral rules and disciplines is not enough: 'A willingness to abide by those rule and disciplines, and to adapt them to changing circumstances is also necessary to a credible system.'

13. Textiles and apparel: double standards of adjustment and transition

Textiles and clothing provide a very telling example of selective liberalization: the slow and gradual 'adjustment' of ICs contrasts with the quick liberalization of Southern economies. But they are by no means the only sectors where ICs protect their industries against Southern exports, while pressing for liberalization and opening of markets in the South. The OECD (1992, p.37, emphasis added) contended:

> Developing countries face higher tariffs and a larger range of non-tariff barriers than developed countries reflecting the fact that, in areas of their greatest comparative advantage, *industrial countries face difficulties in implementing structural adjustment programmes* (textiles, clothing, steel, etc.). *The cost of these measures has been estimated to exceed the value of aid flows*, but such measures do not take account of the most important aspect of these restrictions, which is that they retard entry into export-oriented industries which are most accessible to developing countries – namely commodity processing, light manufactures, and textiles and clothing.
>
> While developed countries have, in principle, encouraged developing countries to diversify into these kinds of exports and, indeed, the dynamic export-oriented developing countries have benefitted dramatically from access provisions applying in developed-country markets, trade policies in the developed countries often obstruct diversification. For many commodities, tariffs escalate on processing activities. When developing country exporters, including those in the very low-income category such as Bangladesh, begin to have success, new barriers can suddenly be imposed, for example new quotas in the textiles sector, or antidumping actions and other selective trade-restricting provisions.

To understand IC protectionism properly, one has to recall that the effects of increased exports of manufactures if all SCs 'had experienced the same rapid growth rate of exports as did the Republic of Korea from 1980 to 1988' would have been negligible, '3·7 per cent of manufactured goods in all industrial country markets by 1988, instead of the 3·1 per cent they achieved' (ibid., p.46). The textile and clothing industries accounted for as little as 2·9 and 2·3 per cent of total employment in Western Europe and the USA respectively, in 1980, but profits of protected firms were 'reported to be healthy' (Koekkoek & Mennes, 1990, p.677). More than one-third of the textile firms in existence in the USA in 1982 had 'been established since 1976, and in France more than one fifth of new manufacturing firms are in textile' (Salvatore, 1990, p.63). Such information has to be seen in the light of the so-called 'Trade Pledge' by OECD governments, a declaration on the need to refrain from protectionist action (Raffer & Singer, 1996, p.37).

Generally, ICs have been much more protectionist against SCs than against one another. Discrimination against exports by the South is not at all unique to trade in textiles and apparel, and Paul Krugman (1994) even cites demands that all North–South trade be regulated according to the model of protectionism in this sector.

While denouncing List's ([1841] 1920) theory of trade interventions, ICs have nevertheless applied his teachings with at least equal fervour. Not only did they themselves once develop their infant industries under heavy protection, but they have continued to apply his ideas until this day. Analysing British trade policy, List (ibid., p.481) observed that tariff reductions followed more or less the rules of Dutch dyke-builders: high dykes where floods are likely and low ones for safe places. Fervently advocating free trade, ICs apply this very principle, subjecting sectors where SCs have gained competitive advantages to heavy protectionist restrictions. The WTO brought no change, as the prime example of textiles and apparel proves, a sector which was made and has been kept 'competitive' in the North by open intervention and protectionism.

The history of trade in textiles and clothing, usually singled out as the sectors most suitable to start industrialization, goes back quite some time. When Europeans contacted peoples on other continents, the 'discovered' mostly refused to buy European products including textiles, not least because of their inferior quality (Raffer, 1987a, pp.134ff). Threatened by a 'drain of treasure' to pay for highly competitive products from India, England decided to destroy the Indian textile and clothing industry, 'physically where necessary' (Frank, 1978, p.90; cf. also Brown, 1978, p.8; Alavi, 1980). India was forced to import British products around the turn of the 19th century. In Mahatma Ghandi's time, spinning was still prohibited by colonial law to preclude the 'competitive' advantage of English products and markets being lost. It deserves mentioning that this restriction was also applied during the period before World War I, which is usually referred to as *the* era of free trade.

When Japan started to export textiles on a larger scale, the USA forced the first 'voluntary' export quota system on Japan in 1935. Protection by tariffs of 40 to 60 per cent were considered insufficient for US textile producers. After World War II, the General Agreement on Tariffs and Trade (GATT) was signed to liberalize trade in manufactures in order to avoid the mistakes of the pre-war period, most notably its beggar-thy-neighbour policy. However, soon after GATT started to operate, ICs felt threatened by fully legal, international competition from the South.

Most people seem to have forgotten that the terms 'adjustment' or 'structural adjustment' were initially used to describe adjustment of a totally different type, namely that of ICs to increasing imports from Southern exporters. Meanwhile, the BWIs have monopolized these expressions to indicate their specific macroeconomic policies prescribed to Southern debtor countries. Long before the BWIs started their adjustment lending to SCs, Article 1 of the Long Term Arrangement Regarding International Trade in Cotton Textiles of February 1962 spoke of the desirability 'to apply, during the next few years, special practical measures of international co-operation which will assist any adjustment that may be required by changes in the pattern of world trade in cotton textiles' (Blokker, 1989, p.372). In plain English, that meant that ICs felt a need for breathing space to adjust smoothly to textile imports from SCs.

This complete change of meaning of 'adjustment' is not simply a matter of purely linguistic interest. Comparing these two types of adjustment – the very gradual 'adjustment' of ICs to trade in textiles and clothing and the quick and ruthless 'adjustment' on which the BWIs as well as ICs insist in the case of SCs – shows logically as well as economically indefensible double standards. One law for the rich and another for the poor force SCs and so-called 'countries in transition' to adjust their structures in a way that would be wholly unacceptable to ICs themselves. Even comparing the longer time periods granted to SCs under the Uruguay Round with the adjustment period for textiles and clothing shows that the North has been granted the longest adjustment period. The Agreement on Agriculture, for instance, allows six or nine years for ICs (Article 1), and up to ten years of flexible adaptation for SCs (Article 15).

PROTECTING SMOOTH ADJUSTMENT

Until 1961, GATT's Article XIX was the principal means of defence against textile-exporting SCs. It permits protection against 'unforeseen developments' affecting the obligations under GATT. In practice, ICs regarded increased imports from competitive exporters due to lower tariffs as fitting that description. Blokker (1989, pp.64ff) elaborates skilfully how Article XIX requirements were soon considered to be too strict for North–South trade, allowing too little protection for ICs. Relaxations were introduced as early as 1948, more or less on GATT's entering into force. Increases did not have to be absolute increases any longer. Article XIX could be applied in cases where imports actually decreased if they contracted less than domestic production. Soon the term 'unforeseen' was redefined in a case between the USA and

Czechoslovakia. While contending that changes in fashion are not as such unforeseen developments, it was decided that a change in consumer preferences regarding ladies' hats towards velours of the scale that had actually happened could not have been foreseen by the USA when signing the treaty. Article XIX could therefore be applied. This decision stretched the meaning of 'unforeseen' considerably. If concrete shifts in ladies' fashions are unforeseeable, one might argue that practically nothing can be foreseen. The second important point is that consumer preferences producing results disliked by one powerful IC were the reason for allowing protection: the market itself, not any government intervention.

As Article XIX was soon considered insufficient, a discussion on 'market disruption' started when IC markets became more exposed to imports as a result of the gradual elimination of post-war restrictions. When the GATT Secretariat sent out a questionnaire in December 1960 to collect information on concrete cases of market disruption, member states either could not provide the necessary information or were unwilling to do so (ibid., p.80). A clear definition of what precisely 'market disruption' is was not given, nor did this expression appear in the GATT Treaty. Opaqueness helped importing ICs to claim that they suffered from market disruption, whenever they chose to. This is at odds with the principle of the Rule of Law.

To make protectionism easier, actual market disruption was not necessary: potential increases of imports sufficed. Without any clear rules on how to assess its likelihood, potential disruption can always be claimed, even in the case of a country currently unable to export at all. Measures violating the GATT Treaty could be taken by ICs with impunity. In 1959–60 Britain, for instance, agreed to the so-called 'Lancashire Pact' affecting imports from the South, contravening both GATT and the Ottawa Agreement containing the preferential system for Commonwealth countries. Thus an industry which only came into existence because of protection and military action against more competitive Indian producers was again sheltered against imports from SCs, such as India – not a good example of an efficient and market-based allocation of resources.

But all this was considered insufficient. In 1961, the Short Term Cotton Textile Arrangement was negotiated under GATT auspices at the request of the USA, although it was a clear breach of the GATT's own most basic principle. This might have been the reason for the USA initially proposing to organize textile protectionism within the OECD framework before it was persuaded by the GATT's executive secretary, Wyndham White, to do so within GATT (ibid., p.98). The chairman of the meeting preparing the Short and Long Term Arrangements declared that 'nothing in the proposed Arrangements derogated the rights of contracting parties under GATT' (ibid., p.104), a statement clearly at odds with the facts.

It deserves special emphasis that the evolution of trade against which ICs took restrictions was not the result of any governmental intervention, but of market forces, factor endowments and of the wage levels established by ICs themselves as colonial powers, when they were interested in getting 'native' labour as cheaply as possible. Furthermore, low wages have always meant low in comparison with IC standards, not other incomes in SCs, as textile workers were often not badly paid in relation to domestic income levels. The Decision of 19 November 1960 on the Avoidance of Market Disruption explicitly referred to 'market disruption' as a situation where 'price differentials do not arise from governmental intervention in the fixing or formation of prices or from dumping practices.' (ibid., p.365). Restrictions on trade in textiles and clothing were thus explicitly introduced against the effects of the world market. The argument that trade reflected comparative advantages did not carry much weight when used by SCs (ibid., pp.72 and 76).

The Short Term Arrangement was replaced by the Long Term Arrangement Regarding International Trade in Cotton Textiles in October 1962, which ruled sectoral trade until 1974, when the first Multi-Fibre Arrangement (MFA I) replaced it. This was considered necessary by ICs because the use of synthetic fibres not covered so far had increased, and some SCs had gained progressively larger market shares. Although the MFA is again a clear contradiction of the very aim and essence of GATT – liberalizing trade in manufactures – the Textile Surveillance Body was established by GATT to supervise the implementation of this system of trade restrictions and to arbitrate disputes. The GATT provided assistance in breaking its own basic rules.

Officially, restrictions were meant to be temporary to facilitate adjustments, as Article 1 of the Long Term Arrangement states. The document on Arrangements Regarding International Trade in Cotton Textiles explicitly stipulated that the Provisional Cotton Textiles Committee was to present recommendations for long-term solutions 'not later than 30 April 1962' (ibid., p.368). These were to be based on the guiding principles of the preamble of this Arrangement, such as the 'desire' of participating countries to provide growing opportunities for SC exports. It was pointed out, however, that trade must develop in an 'orderly manner so as to avoid disruptive effects in individual import markets and on individual lines of production' (ibid., p.367). Quick liberalization of the type forced on SCs was considered unfeasible.

It must be recalled that imports from the South were not the only factor affecting jobs. Another main reason was substantially increased productivity in the textile industry, which had led to a decrease of sectoral employment in the North (World Bank, 1987, p.136). Import restrictions against SCs thus simply shifted labour-saving effects of technical progress within ICs, at least partially, onto SCs. This conclusion was corroborated by many studies years ago, such as by Schatz and Wolter (1982) for the Federal Republic of Germany, who found that job losses due to productivity changes in the case of textiles and clothing were between two and three times higher than jobs lost because of changes in imports. If one compares net import effects (job losses due to changes in imports minus job creation by export changes) productivity accounted for 44 times higher losses than foreign trade in the textile sector. For the whole economy job losses due to imports were more than outweighed by increased exports during the period 1970–78, while productivity increases cost four times as many jobs as all imports (for other studies, see Raffer, 1987a, p.225ff). Nevertheless, the going argument remained that Northern economies needed protection to adjust to Southern exports. Claiming to be a temporary measure to help ICs adjust their economic structures, each MFA was followed by another, stricter MFA. All measures have been directed against SC exporters, while exports among ICs have not been subject to the MFA. Supplying 0·22 per cent of Swedish imports, Sri Lanka was, for instance, subject to restraints necessary to protect Swedish producers, while the European Communities, accounting for nearly 40 per cent of the Swedish import market, were not (Sampson, 1990, p.712).

At the beginning of the Uruguay Round the thought surfaced to legalize the MFA within the new framework rather than phasing it out. As late as 1988, the USA refused to discuss the MFA in the Uruguay Round. In January 1989, both the EEC and the USA stonewalled in Geneva against the idea of phasing out restrictions under the Uruguay Round, seeing this as only one (but not the only) option for integrating this trade into GATT. Hence one may call the agreed phasing out after ten more years a 'success' of the South, although it remains to be seen whether the new agreement will actually be discontinued as stipulated. There is no certainty that it will happen this time, although Article 9 of the ATC states that there shall be no extension of this – once again temporary – arrangement. Even if it ends, this would mean that ICs will have enjoyed 'necessary' protection in one small part of their economies for up to about seven decades, while SCs are required to open their economies much more radically and much more quickly to trade. The continuation of the MFA means that ICs cannot adjust to 'free' trade as quickly as they want others to and, with the help of the BWIs, make SCs adjust theirs. One must recall that the USA has not been able to adjust one relatively small sector of its economy since 1935 if one evaluates the special provisions for SCs in the Final Act, such as 'longer' implementation periods in the Agreement on Agriculture.

According to the continued MFA, now called ATC and officially anointed with GATT (or rather WTO) conformity, 'not less than 16 per cent' of 1990 imports shall be liberalized on the date of the WTO Agreement's entry into force (Article 2.6). After three years at least another 17 per cent (of 1990 imports) are to be integrated into GATT 1994; after another four years a further 18 per cent; and the remaining 49 per cent after ten years.

This schedule sounds stricter than it actually is. Major restraining countries could fulfil their obligations under the Agreement in the first two stages without touching MFA quotas. UNCTAD (1995b, p.12) expected 'a modest dimension of trade opportunities' to become 'perceptible' in 2002 at best. Fully in line with the treaty, integration programmes for stage one list products that had not been subject to restrictions anyway. Statistically unclear information was provided or dubious practices were applied to boost percentage figures. Nevertheless, some ICs fell short of the 16 per cent obligation, as UNCTAD (ibid., pp.12f) pointed out. But the Textiles Monitoring Body finally found everything all right, officially declaring that at least 16 per cent of the total volume had been liberalized as agreed. It observed, however, that with one exception, one product imported by Canada, all products had not been restricted before (WTO, 1996a, p.96). The first stage did not lead to trade liberalization. As percentages are stipulated in volume terms, the USA will liberalize less than 30 per cent of the value of its 1990 imports until the end of the transition period (UNCTAD, 1995b). Nevertheless, the USA invoked Article 6 (transitional safeguards) on 24 occasions in the first half of 1995 alone (WTO, 1996a, p.96). In two instances, when the Textiles Monitoring Body found no serious damage to US industry 'but had not reached consensus on whether there was actual threat thereof, the US kept the unilateral restraints ... in place' (ibid.). Furthermore, domestic laws of some major Northern importers have linked their own liberalization measures to a further opening of Southern textile and clothing markets, something not foreseen by the Agreement. In the case of the USA, Southern importers are thus forced to remove all non-tariff trade barriers within three years (UNCTAD, 1995b, p.23) – quite a contrast to the transition period of ten years considered hard to implement by the North themselves. Even measures openly called 'GATT-inconsistent non-MFA restrictions' are allowed ten years of phasing out (UNCTAD, 1995b). Bilateral arrangements, such as on export licences or quota flexibility provisions, are fully legal (WTO, 1996a, p.97). Thus the hoped-for protection against bilateral pressure is not necessarily granted. Doubts about full liberalization by ICs therefore appear justified. India has rightly taken the logical step of linking its own tariff concessions to progress according to schedule by the North. Other SCs would be well advised to follow this lead. Those ICs most protectionist with regard to textiles did not like this move. In July and August 1997, the USA, the EU, Canada, Switzerland, Australia and New Zealand requested consultations on quantitative restrictions on imports of agricultural, textile and industrial products (WTO, 1997e, p.3).

Before the first WTO Ministerial Conference in Singapore a number of textile-exporting SCs complained about the implementation of the Agreement to the Council on Trade in Goods. Pakistan listed ten major concerns, also on behalf of the ASEAN countries, India, Hong Kong and Korea, including the following (WTO, 1996b, p.3):

- With one (!) exception [see above] the first phase covered only products that had not been subject to MFA restrictions. It was therefore commercially useless to exporters.
- Major importers had changed rules of origin to create uncertainty for trade in this sector or invoked a large number of safeguards, although they should be used sparingly according to the Agreement.
- The Textiles Monitoring Body (TMB), which supervises implementation, 'should be improved through greater transparency and ensuring impartiality in decision making' (ibid.).

These concerns were shared by a number of other SCs. In Singapore, SCs expressed concern

> that, to retain the confidence of all members, there was a particular need to make the TMB's work more transparent, notably in explaining the reasons behind its decisions, and to ensure its members really participate in their personal capacities rather than representatives of their countries so as to ensure impartiality. (WTO 1997a, p.23)

Apparently it was necessary that the Singapore Ministerial Decision admonish the TMB to 'make findings and recommendations whenever called upon to do so under the Agreement' (ibid., p.9). This does not suggest proper legal relief for all member states.

ICs see the situation differently: 'The EC [European Communities] underlined the political and economic difficulties in this sector, adding that its level of ambition would have to take into account market opportunities provided to EC exporters' (ibid.) This view is fully shared by the USA, although the Arrangement stipulates liberalization by importers without further conditions according to the agreed scheme.

SC exporters pointed out that 'their tariff schedules conformed with commitments agreed in the Uruguay Round, and that no complaint had been made in the relevant WTO bodies' (ibid., p.23). This statement was not contradicted by ICs, which can only mean that it is valid.

In the case of textiles and clothing, complaints have to be presented to the TMB before the WTO's dispute settlement mechanism can be used. As in the case of the BWIs, seats in the TMB are allocated to big countries and 'constituencies', groups of smaller countries. Japan, the EC, and the USA are their own constituencies, others have to rotate (WTO, 2000b, p.36). As this body is required to take all decisions by consensus (members appointed by countries involved in the unresolved issue are exempted) this is likely to prevent effective and speedy resolutions of disputes in this field. The principle of consensus, whose ineffectiveness was cited as a reason against the old GATT procedure by the North, was preserved in a sector where this is in its interest – although in a milder form, as affected countries cannot vote.

Textiles and clothing are not the only field where the principle of consensus has developed into an important tool of domination by powerful members and as a means to outmanœuvre majority decisions also part of the WTO's system of rules. One may assume that small and powerless members find it more difficult to stand in the way of consensus than big and powerful ones. In the case of indebted SCs, BWI advice might also play a role. According to the WTO's director general: 'Members have rightly stressed that the principle of consensus is not negotiable' (WTO, 2000a, p.4). Achieving consensus, however, does, not necessarily mean full transparency and effective participation of all members that are supposed to consent. At Seattle, the US trade representative declared that she 'much preferred a more inclusive approach in which all delegations could participate', but she 'reserved the right to hold Green Room meetings with smaller numbers of delegations' (ibid., p.9). This expression refers to the practice of backroom negotiations to which only a few countries are invited, whose results are then presented to the rest for 'consensus', sometimes under time pressure. At Seattle this practice led to strong protests. On one occasion SC delegates arriving in the morning found that the texts discussed had undergone major transformation overnight. Kwa (1999) reports that the Kenyan delegation, determined to participate in the Green Room process, was told that they were not invited to attend. They searched for the exact venue, calling around all the rooms in the convention centre, but did not find it. 'Finally, it was apparently the Swiss delegation that brought them into the meeting' (ibid.).

The ATC again contains safeguard clauses to shield IC economies from shocks by 'serious damage, or actual threat thereof' (Article 6.2). Although a lot of variables, ranging from profits and employment to investments and productivity, are enumerated in paragraph 3, no clear definition of serious damage or threat thereof is provided. Imminent – as opposed to actual – sharp and substantial increases in imports are a sufficient justification for countermeasures. Again, no clear definition of how this potential threat must be assessed is provided.

On the other hand, reimports of products exported by domestic enterprises to have them further processed in other countries are explicitly allowed more favourable treatment (Article 6.6(*d*)) when 'transitional safeguards' are applied. This is not new. The Long Term Arrangement already contained a special clause for re-exports by ICs (Blokker, 1989, p.123). Apparently, competitors exporting final products are to be kept at bay without restricting one's own possibilities to cut costs. Investment and employment seem only endangered by Southern competition, not by one's own relocation of labour-intensive processes.

ADJUSTMENT IN THE SOUTH

While ICs have been adjusting one small part of their economies for decades without yet feeling able to expose this sector to the world market, ICs and IFIs controlled by them have forced SCs and CTTs to adjust their whole economies much more quickly. Under the heading of 'Structural Adjustment' they have made debtors open their economies rapidly. Escape clauses or the breathing space necessary for adjustment in the case of ICs are not granted. Countries in transition are supposed to be able to transform themselves into modern capitalist economies immediately. When the IMF started with 'adjustment measures' (as they were initially called) in Africa after 1973, these adjustment programmes were usually planned for one year.

During the early phase of the 1970s, conditionality was lenient, as Kanesa-Thasan (1981) points out. This can be explained by the history of the IMF. Left without a raison d'être after the demise of Bretton Woods, the IMF was apparently glad to find clients to avoid discussions on its further use. In the period called the 'third phase' by Kanesa-Thasan, which started in 1979, it became stricter and supply-side policies more important. At present Structural Adjustment time frames have become longer than one year, but have still remained very short in comparison with the time for IC adjustment in the textiles and clothing sector. The IMF, now assured of being needed both in the South and in Eastern Europe, has become much stricter.

The fact that ICs have become even more protectionistic vis-à-vis the South has not been seen as a reason for less extreme liberalization forced on SCs. As quoted in Chapter 4, the World Bank (1987, p.150) even went so far as to advise SCs to open their markets unilaterally and to respond flexibly to new protectionist practices by shifting resources. The Bank fails to ask why ICs do not act according to this advice. If it were good advice it would be in their evident self-interest to do so. However, at present only SCs and CTTs are expected to practise quick and unconditional liberalization.

The IBRD is not alone in favouring one-sided action. Corden (1990, p.55), for instance, argues:

> Liberalization by developing countries would benefit the industrial countries and the world system, just as liberalization by industrial countries would benefit developing countries and the world system. It is then asked why developing countries should generate these benefits when industrial countries are failing to do

so, and, in fact are moving in the opposite direction. The answer is that liberalization by developing countries would also benefit developing countries themselves, and most debates, like the discussion in this paper, are concerned with defining these benefits.

One feels tempted to ask why 'most debates' do not choose to define the benefits of IC liberalization to ICs. Given their predominant share in global merchandise trade – well over two-thirds of all exports and imports in 1999 (WTO, 2000a, p.4), or the fact that eight of the top 15 exporters of textiles were ICs in 1998, Germany being the largest exporter (WTO, 1999a, vol.2, p.125) – this reorientation should be definitely more rewarding. Like the BWIs, Corden skirts the essential question of how SCs can be expected to increase exports under growing IC protection, which is particularly strong in branches where SCs are successful. Or in the words of the OECD (1992, p.37), when they 'begin to have success new barriers can suddenly be imposed'. ICs often sell those capital goods needed to produce exports which are then barred from IC markets.

While the BWIs tell SCs to devalue their currencies to increase their exports, IC protectionism limits possible gains of market shares and revenues considerably. In the case of exporters of textiles and clothing, this contradiction becomes particularly clear. Not only are exports over and above their quotas impossible, but even increases within the quota may be nipped in the bud. The EC introduced the so-called 'anti-surge procedure' into MFA III, which means that sharp and substantial increases of imports within previously under-utilized quotas can be prevented (Koekkoek & Mennes, 1990, p.678). Even access within the jointly agreed quota thus became not unconditional, because ICs felt unable to adjust to these limited and agreed quantities. But SCs exporting under the 'advice' of the BWIs might also fall under the concept of 'cumulative market disruption' pioneered by the EC as well. Using the argument 'if the cup is full, one more drop can cause it to overflow' (GATT, 1984, p.103), ICs have restricted imports irrespective of quantities. Even the smallest increases in imports can create market disruption and may thus trigger protectionist action. No doubt the undefined 'threat' of 'serious damage' in the present treaty will be interpreted in the light of the past evolution of sectoral protectionism and one must assume that these concepts will be applied in the future with equal fervour.

The concept of a 'minimum viable production', introduced by ICs as an instrument under the MFA to allow importing ICs to decide unilaterally what their minimum level of production of textiles and clothing should be, is not accepted as valid under SA policies. SCs are not allowed to preserve a minimum viable production of any product. As Sampson (1990, p.711) rightly points out, the concept of a minimum viable production is nonsense according to ruling economic theory. A line of production needing protection is, by force of logic, not economically viable. The question arises, though, why an argument accepted as valid for one group of adjusters is not accepted for the other. What is good for the goose must be good for the gander. If there are economic, political or social reasons why this minimum production should be maintained in one group of countries, why not in the other group as well?

The concept of market disruption, so important in the adjustment of ICs, carries no weight in the case of SCs. Sheltering against market forces or providing for any 'unforeseen development' is declared economically unsound whenever SCs are concerned. The need for an 'orderly manner' of smooth adjustment 'so as to avoid disruptive effects in individual import markets and on individual lines of production' (Blokker, 1989, p.367) is only seen in the case of ICs. Escape clauses and adjustment schemes, such as those provided for textile and clothing importing ICs in the Final Act of the Uruguay Round, are not granted in the name of market efficiency, while such clauses and special provisions are justified as necessary to allow the market to function smoothly whenever this is in the interest of ICs. Their long adjustment periods are defended as a necessity based on sound economic principles, while those SCs having Structural Adjustment programmes are expected to adjust at rapid speed, also because of sound economic principles. It goes without saying that breach of contract vis-à-vis IFIs is not accepted in the same easy-going fashion as breach of contract by ICs in the case of their 'adjustment', although 'agreements' with IFIs are virtually always made under duress.

The possibility to determine for oneself the speed of adjustment (or rather non-adjustment in the case of ICs) is ruled out in the case of Structural Adjustment programmes. SCs are not only expected to adjust more quickly and flexibly than ICs, but totally different conditions of adjustment are forced on them, which brings us to differences in so-called 'ownership'.

ICs 'own' their adjustment programmes, SCs do not. Even though attempts have been made to present Structural Adjustment as a country's 'voluntary' choice, it is easily shown that this is not so. Praising the 'comprehensiveness' of programme lending, its 'coverage in terms of both macro and sector issues of policy reform, the exclusive focus on policy and institutional reform, and the detailed articulation of the precise modifications in policy necessary to adjust to a changed economic environment', Stern (1983, p.91) explained the need for a 'firm understanding' of monitoring. Describing the mechanisms of control in some detail Stern (ibid., p.99) concludes: 'While this procedure may be called "conditionality", it is in principle no different from the relationship involved in Bank sector or project lending'. The need to claim 'ownership' by the respective SC government was not yet perceived as important as it is sometimes pretended to be nowadays.

Official IBRD publications admit frankly that the IBRD imposes economic decisions on borrowers. The Bank has frequently complained about lack of 'ownership', or lack of client interest in 'IBRD-supported' operations. The Wapenhans Report (World Bank, 1992) identified insufficient 'ownership' as one major and frequent problem in need of redress. This would be impossible if projects and programmes were indeed the client's own, and the IBRD's role were restricted to financial support and expert opinion where demanded. The IBRD's (World Bank 1989, p.26) Operations Evaluation Department concluded: 'Finally, borrower preferences are not always seen as important in supervision management, although the outcome often has a critical impact on the borrower.'

As the Fund has been less open than the IBRD – it is becoming more transparent at present under pressure – fewer statements such as those above can be found. However, as Structural Adjustment under SAF and ESAF was administered jointly by the BWIs, the problem of 'ownership' must be the same. Polak (1991), a leading theoretician of the IMF quoted in more detail in Chapter 4, made it clear that the Fund uses conditionality to ensure that those policies are pursued which the IMF wants, even if a country's own policy is not to blame for the problem. SCs are forced to adopt measures which have nothing to do with their actual urgent needs or their policies.

Unlike in the case of textiles, there exists no procedure to settle disputes between SCs undergoing SA and the IFIs, not even of the doubtful nature foreseen by the Final Act of the Uruguay Round. Furthermore, IFIs are not properly accountable for their actions. Their decisions are delinked from financial responsibilities: while the BWIs determine or at least co-determine the policies of their clients, they refuse to share the risks involved. They insist on full repayment, even if damages caused by their staffs occur. Such damages have to be paid for by their borrowers. At present, the IBRD and the IMF gain financially from their own errors by extending new loans necessary to repair damages done by prior loans. Failed projects accumulate unserviceable debts. A high rate of IFI failures is therefore likely to render Structural Adjustment necessary, which is again administered by them, just as failed Structural Adjustment programmes are likely to call for new Structural Adjustment programmes, as long as unconditional repayment to IFIs is upheld. This logical relation might be described somewhat cynically as 'IFI-flops securing IFI-jobs' (Raffer, 1993, p.158). This uniquely perverted incentive system is absolutely at odds with Western market systems and leads to inefficiencies, which are increasingly costly for SCs and the poor in the South. Not surprisingly, the BWIs cannot show any success: no debtor country following their 'advice' has been able to reach sustainable and sound economic conditions.

If adjustment is so difficult a process that the richest and economically best developed countries need decades for one small part of their economies, this is no surprise. If the social effects of liberalization in the textiles and clothing sector are unacceptable in ICs, why should the consequences of present Structural Adjustment be acceptable in SCs? If remedies against potential increases in imports and potential market disruption make sense in one part of the world, why are similar clauses not part and parcel of Structural Adjustment programmes by the BWIs as well as of policies of the countries in transition? One has to ask how IFIs can *bona fide* insist on SCs adjusting with such speed. One could easily imagine escape clauses stipulating that, say, liberalization of imports has to be stopped, contingent on defined increases in unemployment or that budget cuts of social spending have to be reduced, contingent on increases in child mortality. One would wish the PRGF to develop in this way to guarantee a minimum of human dignity to the poorest. Furthermore, the concept of 'cumulative market disruption' could be adapted, which ICs have used to restrict imports irrespective of the additional quantity actually imported. Technically, any SC facing balance of payments problems could apply this concept immediately by restricting those additional imports which are 'the last drops'. Following the example of ICs, one could think of applying restrictions only to IC exports, exempting South–South trade. The example of ICs in the first stage of liberalization in textiles and clothing pursuant to WTO obligations suggests a first stage of Structural Adjustment, where liberalization could be stipulated for sectors where no restrictions exist, or SC governments could stop intervening in branches where they have not intervened so far. While IC governments intervene heavily to protect their industries against SC imports, IFIs make SCs reduce government influence, because this is said to be harmful for sound economic development. The example of ICs apart, this view is fully contradicted by the experience of the so-called Asian 'tigers' or 'dragons' (see Chapter 9) and by Japan's history.

The BWIs claim that their recipe follows from the ruling Heckscher–Ohlin theory, a view which, as was shown in Chapter 4, was not shared by Heckscher and Ohlin. In 1923, Graham already corroborated Heckscher's and Ohlin's scepticism by showing that comparative advantage specialization may lead to disadvantages if the somewhat unrealistic assumption of constant returns is removed. This Graham-paradox combines with the PST and modern Unequal Exchange theory to explain disadvantages in trade because of specialization in products typical of many SCs (cf. Raffer, 1994a).

Even democracy was used by IC importers to justify protectionism. At the 1959 GATT ministerial meeting, the French delegate brought up this topic:

> I refer to the need (in the very interest of such countries) not to cause sudden disruptions in our economy while it is still precarious, because, in a democratic country where the Government cannot go against public opinion, such disruptions

would, I feel certain, bring about measures of safeguard which will be still more restrictive. (Blokker, 1989, p.72)

The issue of democracy was not considered of equal importance in the case of Stuctural Adjustment, when new democratic governments were forced to make the population pay for debts incurred by military dictators, who had been encouraged to borrow heavily. In such cases the predilection for autocratic reforms over democratic decisions mentioned by Rodrik (1996) asserts itself fully.

ONE LAW FOR THE RICH, ANOTHER FOR THE POOR

Contrasting these two types of 'adjustment', one sees that there is one law for the rich and another for the poor. Mechanisms considered necessary, useful and economically sound in the case of ICs adjusting their structures are denied to SCs undergoing adjustment as unnecessary, harmful and economically unsound. This shows double standards and hypocrisy. Unless one accepts different standards for the rich and the poor as the logical base of one's reasoning, one cannot explain why ICs controlling IFIs by their voting majority make SCs adopt adjustment policies they would not dream of implementing themselves, while at the same time protecting their own economies from the world market. It has to be recalled that textiles and clothing are just one example. Agriculture, iron or steel could provide similar case studies. If the mechanisms used in the textile and clothing sector are useful, it appears logical to allow SCs to shape their adjustment according to this model, precisely because of the reasons brought forward by ICs. The harmful effects of Structural Adjustment on the poor, which even the BWIs stopped denying some time ago, are a strong reason for a smoother and more IC-like adjustment of Southern economies.

So far only the Japanese government and the Directorate General VIII of the European Commission have questioned present Structural Adjustment policies. Japan's debate with the IBRD stemmed from the Japanese perception of development and is a remarkable example of a donor's intellectual honesty. Seeing the glaring differences between their own experience or the policies of successful Asian 'dragons' and the recipe of the BWIs, Japan spoke up, questioning their ideology. Although all IC governments do in fact combine market mechanisms with government interventions, none of them would even dream of applying the same liberalization and adjustment policies forced on SCs to their own countries, and all protect their industries against competitiveness resulting from market forces, ICs have always supported the BWIs and their demands for unconditional and instant liberalization in the

South. Contrasting the MFA 'needed' by the North with the demand that much less developed economies should adjust within an extremely short time 'reveals an unorthodox perception of honesty' (Raffer & Singer, 1996, p.117). As the economic policies of ICs are beyond the BWIs' reach, Japan could – like any other IC – easily have lived with the existing double standards for those controlling IFIs and those under their control. Speaking up on behalf of SCs – and indeed of the poorest people most severely affected by Structural Adjustment – the country differed from nearly all other governments. Not surprisingly, the Directorate General VIII, which also tried to work out an alternative to BWI Structural Adjustment, could not find the necessary support among the EU's member countries, which are also major BWI shareholders.

Abolishing these inequalities with regard to adjustment and establishing equal treatment of the rich and the poor is the very minimum demanded by fairness and economic reason. However, as SCs are disadvantaged by present structures, meaningful forms of special and differential treatment of SCs are necessary to halt or reverse the process of divergence. In our view there is in fact an argument for double standards, but in favour of SCs, not against them.

14. Towards a more equal world order

Because of its size, the Asian crisis of 1997 was the first real challenge to the virtually unchallenged rule of neoliberalism. The crises in Russia and Brazil that followed quickly, and possibly the crash of the LTCM hedge fund, have certainly intensified doubts. Although critically important for global economic policy, the Asian crash was nothing generically special. Liberalization and deregulation had triggered a host of crises before. Inflation-adjusted losses due to the US Savings & Loans débâcle were 'several times larger than the losses experienced in the Great Depression', as Stiglitz (1998a, p.16) pointed out. Yet, in relation to GDP, it is dwarfed by crises in SCs and formerly communist countries: 'This debacle would not make the list of the top 25 international banking crises since the early 1980s' (ibid.). This means that there was more than one such major crisis per year on average – effects of the Washington Consensus that had simply been repressed by official thinking for nearly two decades. This may be an indication of the strength of interests behind the Washington Consensus.

Joseph Stiglitz (1998a), then chief economist and a vice president of the World Bank, was the first high-ranking BWI official to draw attention to the flaws of ruling ideology and to speak about moving toward a 'Post-Washington Consensus', challenging sacred cows such as the belief that success by governments was 'at best a fluke, and at worst impossible' (ibid., p.9), that budget deficits are necessarily bad in SCs, or that moderate inflation (below 40 per cent annually) is costly. He strongly criticized the reigning ideology, concluding about East Asia:

> The more dogmatic versions of the Washington consensus fail to provide the right framework for understanding either the success of the East Asian economies or their current troubles. Responses to East Asia's crisis grounded on these views of the world are likely to be, at best, badly flawed and, at worst, counterproductive. (Ibid.)

The IMF, which had been keen on extending its mandate to capital account liberalization shortly before the crash of 1997, has meanwhile changed its unconditional advocacy of capital account liberalization, admitting that there might be scope for capital controls. Stiglitz (1998b) advocated preventing crises by controlling capital flows in a speech to the Chicago Council on Foreign Relations. The latter also accepted a financial transaction tax on international capital flows (Zee, 2000, p.4).

The Asian crisis was not the only setback for neoliberalism. Organizing via the internet civil society brought down the Multilateral Agreement on Investment (MAI) once secret negotiations had leaked. It might be an interesting footnote that the first full copy of the proposed treaty was to our knowledge made available by the Canadian Ministry of Foreign Affairs on its webpage, with the remark 'For Official Use' still on its cover page. One may ask whether Canada's experience with the first NAFTA arbitration case (see Chapter 4) could have been the trigger. In 1997, a coalition of development, environment and consumer groups from over 70 countries produced a joint NGO statement opposing MAI. Resistance also came from public entities, such as the government of British Columbia. France finally became uneasy about parts of the MAI. In 1998, MAI was shelved. In December 1998, OECD members reaffirmed the need for international rules on investment, but gave no sign of wanting to revive formal negotiations. Nevertheless, NGOs have repeatedly warned that parts of the shelved MAI might become part of other negotiations, which so far has not happened. However, the OECD (2000a, p.34) keeps demanding a 'multilateral framework for investment', without specifying whether and to what extent it would differ from MAI.

The confrontation between North and South about who should become the WTO's second director general in 1999 was another indication that some sand had found its way into neoliberal wheels. It showed a new assertiveness of SCs. In December 1999, civil society successfully resisted further liberalization and deregulation at the WTO's Third Ministerial Conference in Seattle. For the first time in years, a large coalition of wide segments of civil society, including trade unions, was formed to oppose neoliberal policies of redistribution to the rich. Differences within members and disenchantment also showed in Seattle. Many SCs expressed concern and called for changes. The non-participatory practice of decision making within the WTO, the working of the dispute settlement mechanism, or the implementation of the ATC, were targets of criticism. Speaking on behalf of LLDCs, Bangladesh complained that, while this group had been undertaking WTO commitments, their share in global trade had shrunk to less than 0·4 per cent in 1998. The EU's Trade Commissioner said that 'demonstrators are worried about "where the train is going and we should do the same"' (WTO, 2000a). President Clinton found sympathetic words for the concerns of demonstrators.

One further indication of changed perceptions is that the BWIs have come under severe attack not only by NGOs but also by their major and most influential shareholder. The Report by the Meltzer Commission (Meltzer *et al.*, 2000) recommended a substantial 'downsizing' of both institutions, transforming the World Bank into a fund disbursing grants. This reminds us that Keynes initially called what was later to become the Bank a fund. It is another sign that attitudes towards the Washington Consensus and the perceived usefulness of its main bulwarks have apparently changed within the US political establishment. At the same time, NGOs stepped up their criticism of the BWIs and their lack of success after decades of debt management.

Finally, coffee exporters accounting for three-quarters of global production have signed an agreement to push up prices. Seeing it as coming in the wake of OPEC's 'Lazarus-style return', *The Guardian* (2 June 2000) thought a resurgence of commodity power possible. The Association of Coffee Producing Countries planned to restrict output in October 2000. While it remains to be seen what coffee producers will achieve, this is the first such attempt since the collapse of the International Coffee Agreement and the demise of international commodity policy. While coffee prices reached their 'lowest for almost eight years' in July 2000, the *Financial Times* (29–30 July 2000) reported that Brazil's 'efforts to withhold stocks begin to bite. This move is part of the international deal to restrict exports, agreed under the Association of Coffee Producing Countries ... to bolster prices'.

These evolutions corroborate the impression that we may witness yet another cycle in the history of (development) economics, even though neoliberalism is still strong. The ratchet effects of international treaties, such as the WTO framework or Maastricht, will certainly be felt for some time to come. At the beginning of the third millennium, the pendulum seems to have started swinging back. This encourages us to think of a new era of North–South cooperation, and to propose ideas to strengthen the forces of convergence and for a world where people seem again to matter. We are aware that some of our proposals may look Utopian at present, but we want to encourage a debate that takes long-term goals into account. These ideas may be grouped as follows:

- new international financial architecture,
- development cooperation,
- global public goods,
- changes in the framework of international trade,
- reforms of the UN.

TOWARDS A NEW AND BETTER INTERNATIONAL FINANCIAL ARCHITECTURE

Liberalizing capital markets has been the most prominent feature of neoliberal policies. We therefore start with ideas on how to put these markets again under appropriate control. Under OECD (ed., 1998) auspices working groups were formed to propose reforms of the international financial architecture after the Asian shock. The BIS thought the Russian crisis 'can be seen as part of a series of mutually reinforcing events which have highlighted a number of deficiencies in the world financial system' (quoted from UNCTAD, 1999, p.68). The Hong Kong Monetary Authority, one of the least interventionist institutions in financial markets, saw itself forced to intervene to limit speculative strain on its currency. Among the measures taken were margin surcharges on large positions in the stock futures market and a temporary moratorium on short selling of three shares (ibid., p.55). Nevertheless, most governments and central banks are still reluctant to put capital markets under appropriate control. Tobin's proposal in particular has remained anathema, possibly because the idea of taxing capital transactions like many other activities still goes against the very grain of politicians.

The Tobin Tax

Tobin (1974, p.89) proposed his currency transactions tax, lecturing in honour of Joseph Alois Schumpeter at Princeton in 1972, as a measure to enhance the efficacy of macroeconomic policy. He explicitly advocated (ibid., pp.87f) the tax as a means 'to preserve some autonomy in national and continental monetary policies and to defend them against the growing internationalization of money markets'. A few years later he drew attention to the revenue potential of the proposed tax, which he saw as a by-product. For decades his proposal was generally ignored. In the 1990s, the Tobin tax became part of a surge of thoughts about new international governance. These proposals included strengthening the role of the UN, an Economic Security Council, the supervision of international banking and tradable pollution permits, as well as other international taxes, such as on energy consumption (for example, a carbon tax) or air travel. A brief but broad discussion followed when the UNDP (1994) advocated this idea, and James Tobin reformulated it briefly. The main arguments and counter-arguments were set out in a book edited by ul Haq, *et al.* (1996), but this discussion was soon stopped by political censorship.

As a rule, proposals by great economists do not trigger laws against discussing them in Western democracies. Tobin's idea is the famous exception said to confirm the rule. Senator Bob Dole and three other politicians introduced a bill in the Senate to stop UN officials and agencies developing and promoting Tobin's proposal or any other international taxation scheme. The short title of this act was 'Prohibition on United Nations Taxation Act of 1996'. Senator Dole's bill is remarkable since its aim was to limit the freedom of thinking and researching by government action. The group of people that kept the discussion on international taxes going were silenced by legislators. In spite of a long record of non-payment by the USA, this initiative successfully stopped the propagation of the Tobin tax by the UNDP. Dole's bill itself did not become law, but its content did. Public Law 106-113 of 29 November 1999 (H.R. 3194), an Act making consolidated appropriations to the fiscal year ending 30 September 2000, and for other purposes, has taken up Dole's initiative. Pursuant to Section 561, the president has to certify to Congress 15 days in advance of any voluntary contribution to the UN (expressly including the UNDP) that 'the UN is not engaged in any effort to implement or impose any taxation on United States persons in order to raise revenue for the United Nations or any of its specialized agencies'.

This formulation comes straight from Dole's bill, whose Section 4 had demanded under the title 'Prohibition on Continued Development and Promotion of Global Taxation Proposals' that the USA withhold any voluntary or assessed contribution to the UN or any of its specialized and affiliated agencies (including the UNDP) unless the president certifies 15 days in advance that the UN 'is not engaged in any effort to develop, advocate, promote, or publicize any proposal concerning taxation or fees' on US persons. Compared with Dole's intention to censor discussion by explicitly prohibiting attempts to publicize, the Act sounds *prima facie* less rigorous. However, as the UN does not even have the administrative infrastructure to actually levy any taxes and will never be able to establish a tax administration, 'engaged in' must mean activities the UN is actually capable of. What it can do is develop, advocate, promote or publicize proposals – which brings us back to Dole's bill. Publishing a proposal is no doubt covered by 'effort to implement'. As the UNDP is financed by voluntary contributions, this Act is sufficient to stop the member of the UN family that had publicized the Tobin tax quite efficiently. When the USA agreed to pay $926 million of the $1·8 billion owed, one string attached for the first $100 million paid in 1999 was, incidentally, that President Clinton had to certify 'that the U.N. had not imposed any taxes on Americans' (*Time*, 4 September 2000, p.45). As it is generally known that the UN had not imposed any taxes at all, this must be interpreted in connection with the history of Dole's bill.

It is surprising that Tobin's idea met such exceptionally strong political resistance, although proposals to increase government influence are not welcome at a time when this influence is deliberately reduced by international agreements. Various ideas of international taxation have been published over the years (cf. Thirlwall, 1999, p.399), both by individuals and by institutions such as the Brandt Commission. Even proposals to tax speculative transactions were made occasionally, for instance by Joseph Stiglitz in 1989.

The origins of Tobin's proposal go back to Keynes, who 'pointed out that a transaction tax could strengthen the weight of long-range fundamentals' (Tobin, 1994). Proposing the tax, Tobin (1974, pp.88ff) closely followed Keynes's ([1930] 1971, pp.286ff) reasoning in the *Treatise on Money* that risk and cost would reduce short-term international flows without harming long-term investment. Keynes ([1936] 1967, p.160) also argued that 'a substantial government transfer tax' to 'mitigate the predominance of speculation over enterprise in the United States' might 'prove the most serviceable reform available'. In an era when Keynesianism was held in disrepute, this idea was not politically welcome. Indications exist that the pendulum may swing back, bringing the anti-Keynesian cycle to an end. Regarding the South, poverty reduction might take the place of full employment.

Owing to limitations of space, the discussion on the Tobin tax cannot be reproduced. Interested readers are referred to ul Haq *et al.* (1996), Michalos (1997) and Raffer (1998d) where it is shown that this tax can be implemented easily, not least because all relevant accounting exists, provided there is the political will to do so. The tax is a good means to prevent short-term interest rate arbitrage. It would have been a strong disincentive to 'carry trade' in Asia that boomed prior to the crash, and thus a stabilizing factor. Creating larger margins by which interest rates can differ between two currencies, it re-establishes some freedom of manoeuvre for central banks. Without the Tobin tax other methods to increase costs are used, such as exchange controls or compulsory deposit requirements. The Tobin tax cannot serve as a disincentive to large-scale speculation against a currency, as can be illustrated with the example of the speculators against the European Exchange Rate Mechanism, who sought and got returns in excess of what any likely Tobin tax could counteract. However, one cannot expect one measure to correct everything – reality does not know panaceas. The Tobin tax would reduce interest arbitrage and the attractiveness of small exchange rate changes, and it would produce revenue. It might have prevented the Asian crisis. In 1994–5, a transaction tax would have raised funds from foreign investors and should, *ceteris paribus*, have reduced their exposure in Mexico unless all investors behaved cost-inelastically. Reduced exposure would mean lower sums in the case of a bail-out. Speculators attracted by interest rate differentials would pay a percentage of the bail-out themselves. It would thus be an economically efficient way of bailing-in private investors.

Looking into the matter for the IMF, Spahn (1996) elaborated Tobin's idea further, advocating a two-tier tax, following Keynes's ([1930] 1971) idea of differentiating transaction costs within pre-set rules according to national policy choices. A low underlying transaction tax should combine with an exchange surcharge severely taxing excessive volatility. The possibility of increasing the tax quickly and substantially if needed could be a powerful instrument against speculative attacks on currencies such as in the case of the pound in the early 1990s. This stabilizing device against speculation would provide official income in contrast to regular bail-outs by central banks: 'Instead of depleting public assets it would generate revenues' (Spahn, 1996, p.27). Like Tobin's own, Spahn's variant would be a possible way to tame capital flows. However, the low rate during 'normal' times should not be too low to generate finance for international purposes. Furthermore, capital controls during and because of crises must be possible.

The paucity of counter-arguments is proved by Stotsky (1996). In her 'Counterpoint' against Spahn, she finally argues that monetary and fiscal authorities cannot cooperate sufficiently well, and doubts that 'monetary authorities would have the ability and independence to administer such a tax wisely'. It is unclear whether she means the 'normal' Tobin tax or Spahn's two-tier version. Logically, this would raise the question of what simple task monetary authorities can fulfil sensibly at all. Such arguments highlight the apparent lack of convincing counter-arguments. If such reasoning were taken seriously, one would have to argue against the principle of taxation as such, as well as against any activity by governments or monetary authorities.

Meanwhile, an international capital transaction tax is even proposed by an IMF Working Paper (Zee, 2000). As the disclaimer states, the views expressed in this paper are not necessarily the IMF's. But a working paper describes 'research in progress' and is 'published to elicit comments and further debate'. By publishing it, the IMF has taken a step towards renewing the debate and seems to have changed its position on this issue considerably. Zee (ibid., p.10) qualifies the 'argument that volatile capital movements could have a destabilizing impact on the domestic economy of a country' as 'uncontroversial'. Therefore he recommends a withholding tax on all private capital inflows with a credit and refund provision operating within the administrative framework of the existing domestic tax system. The tax would be refunded on export receipts and the sale of assets abroad, credited against income tax in the case of any income (interest, dividends, repatriated profits). Thus only 'financial inflows of a capital nature' (ibid., p.7), or taxpayers deciding not to declare income from abroad, would have to bear the tax. It might be difficult to tell sales of assets from speculative capital movements, but this problem is not tackled. Recalling that Malaysia's capital controls also exempted dividends, interest earned or rental income, one might wonder whether this relatively successful practical example influenced research within the IMF. The recommended rate of 'rarely' more than 1 per cent is higher than the rates usually proposed at present by advocates of the Tobin tax. This tax is seen as the better alternative to non-remunerated reserve requirements. Although a national measure, this comes very close to Tobin's proposal if many countries introduce it with the same rate. Its economic effects would then be equivalent.

Zee (ibid., p.4) argues that, while the Tobin tax 'is aimed at reducing global destabilizing speculative movements', his own goal is 'more modest', namely 'to merely moderate the impact of volatile world capital flows on a country's domestic economy'. This distinction is not logically convincing because Zee (ibid., p.7) rightly points out that his variant would be 'equivalent to a prohibitive income tax rate' on short-term movements. How rates can be prohibitive without reducing volumes goes unexplained.

Like some Tobin tax critics, Zee takes up the point whether governments would remain virtuous with large revenues generated by such a tax. He sees huge problems about their disposal by governments, recommending that 'part or all' of revenues should go to the financial institutions charged with withholding the tax. Very much along neoliberal lines, a tax could thus be transformed into a banking fee. Apparently, the idea that governments might raise money by new taxes *and* use it – for instance, to finance social expenditures – is still anathema within the Fund.

Zee rightly points out that his proposal could be implemented easily, as administrative structures exist and financial institutions are well equipped technically to collect the tax. This is not a distinctive feature vis-à-vis the Tobin tax, as Zee claims. Collecting the Tobin tax by those national governments that have agreed to introduce it was proposed as the simplest way to levy it by many authors, including James Tobin (cf. Raffer, 1998d). Zee is right in pointing out that his withholding mechanism makes collecting easy, but there is no reason why it could not be applied in the case of a Tobin tax. All in all, the author seems somewhat too eager to find differences. He even repeats arguments against the Tobin variant that have already been proved wrong, such as the need to apply it universally. Nevertheless, this publication is much less inimical towards taxing transactions than the Fund used to be, and one may hope that it actually elicits further discussion.

International Insolvency Procedures

An international insolvency procedure for states – as recommended by us some years ago (Raffer & Singer, 1996) and described briefly in Chapter 11 – is a necessary part of a meaningful international financial architecture. Under the code, 'Orderly Workouts for Sovereign Debtors', improvements of present debt management, unsuccessful since 1982, have been sought. After the Asian crisis adequate insolvency procedures for firms were seen as essential for avoiding future crises. The Reports on the International Financial Architecture published by the OECD (ed., 1998) recommend it strongly, but avoid 'insolvency' with regard to sovereign debtors. The Working Group on International Financial Crises proposed an insolvency procedure in all but name, demanding that the international community provide 'in exceptional and extreme circumstances ... a sovereign debtor with legal "breathing space" so as to facilitate an orderly, cooperative and negotiated restructuring' (ibid., p.37). It is even admitted that 'a purely voluntary approach' might not be feasible because 'the government may not have the bargaining power to obtain sustainable terms' (ibid., p.30), for instance if creditors demand destabilizingly high interest rates. It remains to be asked why the working group shied away from the obvious conclusion – the need of an independent entity empowered to decide in such cases – and why all the advantages praised by the working group in the case of firms should not be equally advantageous in the case of sovereign debtors, as already advised by Adam Smith ([1776] 1979). Why emulate features of insolvency instead of simply using the existing model, which can be adapted so easily?

Although tendencies towards some form of international insolvency can be discerned, decision makers still shy away from a proper international insolvency modelled on the US Chapter 9 as recommended by Raffer (1990a) and Raffer & Singer (1996). Recently, this idea has been taken up by NGOs, such as the Jubilee 2000 movement, sometimes under the formulation 'fair and transparent process of arbitration', or by the secretary general of the UN, Kofi Annan. The OECD (1999c, p.191) accepted it as a useful part of a new international financial architecture: 'Moreover, an international lender of last resort and an international bankruptcy court could help to prevent financial panics altogether.' Even the last head of the IMF, Michel Camdessus, suggested 'some sort of Super Chapter 11 for countries' in an interview with the *Financial Times* (17 September 1998), qualifying the need for international bankruptcy procedures as 'already' (after decades of debt management) an 'obvious lesson'. As the US Chapter 11 (insolvency of firms) does not demand the open and transparent procedure of Chapter 9 conferring a right to be heard on affected people, one might be tempted to ask whether it is mere happenstance that Camdessus suggested some kind of international Super Chapter 11 for countries instead of Chapter 9, in spite of the fact that the problem of sovereignty is not solved by Chapter 11. But, unlike Chapter 9, it would accommodate the IMF's well documented desire for secrecy.

The basic function of any insolvency procedure is the resolution of a conflict between two fundamental legal principles. In a situation of overindebtedness, the right of creditors to interest and repayments collides with the principle recognized generally (not only in the case of loans) by all civilized legal systems that no one must be forced to fulfil contracts if that leads to inhumane distress, endangers one's life or health, or violates human dignity. Briefly put, debtors cannot be forced to starve themselves or starve their children to be able to pay. Although their claims are recognized as legitimate, insolvency exempts resources from being seized by bona fide creditors. Human rights and human dignity of debtors are given priority over unconditional repayment. It is important to emphasize that insolvency only deals with claims based on a solid and proper legal foundation. In the case of odious debts, no insolvency is needed, as these are null and void. Demands for cancelling apartheid debts (the debts incurred by the former South African regime) are therefore based on the odious debts doctrine.

Debtor protection is one of the two essential features of insolvency. The other is the most fundamental principle of the Rule of Law: that one must not be judge in one's own cause. Civilized insolvency laws applicable to all debtors except SCs demand a neutral institution assuring fair settlements. Like all legal procedures, insolvency must comply with the minimal demand that creditors must not decide on their own claims. Even at the time of debtor prisons, creditors were not allowed to do so, in contrast to present international practice violating this very minimum required by the Rule of Law. Creditors have been judge, jury, experts, bailiff, even the debtor's lawyers, all in one. This unrestricted creditor domination is not only an open breach of the Rule of Law, a principle currently preached to SCs by OECD governments, but also inefficient from a purely economic perspective. Creditors tend to grant too small reductions too late, thus prolonging the crisis rather than solving it.

Without such an orderly and fair procedure, crises are prolonged and damage is inflicted unnecessarily, mostly to the poorest, so-called 'vulnerable groups'. History shows that protracted manoeuvring does not make unpayable debts paid. Sometimes countries, most of them nowadays themselves creditors, simply refused to pay. Occasionally, de facto insolvency was granted, Germany in 1953 being one prominent case. Comparing Germany's debt indicators with those considered generous for the poorest countries by the Cologne Summit of 1999 shows an inexplicable difference regarding the treatment of debtors. During the years before the London Accord, Germany had a debt service ratio of less than 4 per cent (Hersel, 1998), which was considered unsustainable, though well below the 15 per cent of HIPCs after Cologne. The successful economic policies Germany was allowed to pursue, characterized by the term 'social market economy' (*Soziale Marktwirtschaft*) were the very opposite of BWI-type structural adjustment. Disagreements between Germany and its creditors were to be settled by arbitration, not by creditor decisions. Present unrestricted creditor domination denies debtors the basic human right of debtor protection. Insolvency protection for the last unprotected type of debtors is demanded by the Rule of Law as well as by the concept of debtor protection granted to anyone except people in SCs. It is an issue of equity and human rights for all human beings.

PROPOSALS CONCERNING DEVELOPMENT COOPERATION

Although OECD countries have moved further away from the famous target that 0·7 per cent of the OECD's GSP be given as ODA, and all discernible signs show that ODA is likely to fall further, one should remind DAC member governments that nearly all of them have voluntarily stipulated that this target be reached. Few have done so. To ensure that increases in ODA are actually help, not ODA that is not help, changes in present practices are necessary. Raffer & Singer (1996) made several relevant proposals, from linking emergency and development aid – an approach the EU Commission (2000a, p.22) is considering to address the particular difficulties of post-conflict countries – to financing institutional reforms by grants.

The new convention between the EU and African, Caribbean, Pacific (ACP) countries would have provided an excellent opportunity to introduce and test important changes, such as the proposal of self-monitoring of recipients, which worked so successfully in the case of the Marshall Plan. This framework would have been ideal since the amount of money is determined in advance, and donors need not fear unforeseeable financial consequences. The process of self-monitoring and joint requests to the EU could have been further enhanced by integrating NGOs. Present institutional contacts between the EU and NGOs could have served as a starting point. Public discussions including affected people, open information policies and thus strong transparency could have been encouraged. But this opportunity of fundamentally changing development cooperation was not taken.

Financial Accountability

One main shortcoming of present development cooperation is that aid recipients are denied any form of protection usual in all other cases. Thus damage done by grave negligence has to be compensated in all cases unless this is done in the context of development cooperation. Therefore Raffer & Singer (1996) and Raffer (1993) recommended holding donors and IFIs financially accountable for grave negligence. In essence, this means simply making the public sector with regard to development cooperation accountable in the same way as anyone else already is, bringing the most essential principles of law to development cooperation. Consultants are liable to pay damage compensation if/when negligence on their part causes damage. Within OECD countries, governments are financially accountable if they create damages by negligence or violating laws. By contrast, victims of development cooperation remain unprotected. IFIs may and sometimes do even gain financially from their errors and failures. It is of utmost importance to bring development cooperation finally into the realm of the Rule of Law and to improve its economic efficiency. As was shown, this could be easily done. Apparently, this was also seen as the proper way of doing business for the World Bank at Bretton Woods.

The World Bank's (1999b, VII.3) Articles of Agreement allow actions against the Bank except by members or persons acting for or deriving claims from members. Members are not supposed to sue, as the Bank's *General Conditions* (Section 10.04) foresee arbitration as the means to settle disagreements with borrowers. Pursuant to Article VII, property and assets are 'immune from all forms of seizure, attachment or execution *before* [emphasis added] the delivery of final judgment against the Bank'. Actions may be brought against the Bank in courts of competent jurisdiction in the territories of members in which the Bank has offices, appointed agents for the purpose of accepting service or notice of process, or issued or guaranteed securities. The Bank's founders had no intention to exempt and protect it from all legal and economic consequences of failures. Accountability was not initially meant to be removed. Suing the Bank in national courts was therefore considered technically feasible. One might argue, though, that a specialized panel, more familiar with development work, would be a better choice (Raffer, 1999c).

Regarding programmes, there is an easy way of holding the Bank financially accountable. Instead of attempting to determine precise shares in failed programmes, the Bank – and all IFIs in general – should lose the same percentage of claims as other creditors once a country becomes unable to repay. Instead of present 'preferred creditor' status, the Bank should be treated symmetrically. Projects and programmes actually financed under conditions of accountability would have much better rates of success and much better developmental impacts. Totally lacking any form of financial accountability, IFIs and sometimes donors have neglected appropriate care: a textbook-type moral hazard problem that must not be allowed to go on.

Addressing only the results of donor/IFI negligence currently shouldered by the poor, our proposal is much less radical than a proposal by the OECD (2000a, p.13) to focus 'on shared risks, and the search for ways to limit those risks should be conducted jointly'. Our proposal leaves the risk of failure of a well and properly designed project wholly with the recipient. This risk – risk in the proper sense – would not be shared. We do second the idea of a contractual right of compensation by NGOs or persons employed by donors to implement projects if costs are caused by mismanagement and delay by the donor (cf. Chapter 7).

Reforming Political Conditionality

After the Cold War, all donors have increasingly shifted towards demanding political rather than economic conditions. An immediate connection between these conditions and projects and programmes often does not exist. The point which raises most concern, though, is that donors alone determine whether political conditionality, such as democracy, transparency, good governance or participation, was observed or not. The opaqueness of these principles is a further problem, opening up possibilities of arbitrary decisions. Combined with the tendency towards greater flexibility of donors with regard to continuing or discontinuing aid, this makes SCs extremely dependent.

To practise what they preach, donors would have to be prepared to introduce a fair and transparent mechanism to decide whether conditionality, or an essential element clause in the case of EU–ACP relations, was violated, and whether such breach would justify reductions of ODA, particularly if that aid has already been stipulated. As in many other cases, the solution is again an independent panel of arbitrators. Introducing this form of dispute settlement is another opportunity missed by the EU and the ACP group when formulating the Cotonou Convention. Ideally – but this may be Utopian – donors should also be subject to checks, obliging themselves to pay money to international organizations for financing development agenda or global public goods if found guilty of breaching their own principles. This would prove beyond doubt that OECD countries are sincere.

Independent Reviews of ODA

ODA statistics produced by the DAC suffer from inconsistencies, and too often activities are recorded as ODA that do not even satisfy the DAC's own criteria for inclusion. As Raffer (1998a) showed, the DAC has always been prepared to allow doctoring of aid statistics within limits, presumably as long as this remained within proportions considered acceptable by the donor community.

To improve aid statistics, their consistency and comparability, some form of independent auditing would have to replace present peer reviews. Ideally, this should be done by a group of independent experts from both donor and recipient countries. This new form of reviewing would not mean large additional costs since it would replace present peer reviews. These also cost money that could be used to cover the expenses of independent auditing instead. Independent auditing would secure a minimum of statistical correctness. Although it cannot be expected to correct all the numerous problems of present ODA, it would be an important improvement. It would constitute a barrier against reporting and including flows that are not ODA by the DAC's own definition. The quality of aid and aid statistics would improve.

GLOBAL PUBLIC GOODS

Increasingly, global challenges and problems, such as concern for sustainability, global environmental policies, peace keeping, or controlling AIDS, have been addressed by donors. The North has done so with a paradigm shift of its ODA, discussed in Chapter 6, increasingly focusing on new tasks, less developmental in the strict and traditional sense, but rather tasks of common global interest, remedial action against international externalities. The OECD's paradigm shift proves that donors themselves see a need for global activities other than traditional aid and are prepared to finance them, although, deplorably, at the cost of ODA as defined by donors themselves. GPGs are likely to become more important in a globalized world (cf. Kaul *et al.*, 1999). While usually not ODA in the DAC's sense, because their main objective is not promoting development and welfare of any SC, such activities have increasingly been recorded as ODA. Admittedly, these activities are still insufficiently developed and underfunded. Cross-border spillovers documenting a close link between national, regional and global public goods, such as the spread of diseases, migration or the ripple effects of financial crises, are examples showing that a better developed international framework is necessary.

Unlike ODA, non-ODA expenditures are not recorded centrally. Therefore totals are not available. From the perspective of international burden sharing, this is a severe shortcoming. As non-ODA expenditures show, sums used for GPGs can be quite substantial. But they still remain to be recorded consistently.

From the perspective of global housekeeping peace keeping is very important. Some peace keeping expenditures are included under ODA. The USA, for instance, spent $6·6 billion for peace keeping during 1992–5, but 'Less than half was reportable as aid' (OECD, 1997, p.121). A year later the OECD (1998a, p.59) remarked that a further $3 billion of peace keeping costs were not counted as ODA. Peace keeping costs have in fact soared between 1990 and 1995, mainly owing to the problems of the former Yugoslavia. The OECD (1997, p.98) correctly pointed out that military expenditure on peace keeping does not count as ODA, but 'represents an additional contribution to the international peace and security which is essential for development'. Peace keeping is in fact an important task and countries prepared to participate are doing the global community and affected people a great service. The idea of burden sharing suggests that it be recorded, and the OECD started to provide data on post-conflict peace operations on its homepage, including non-ODA flows.

The growing importance of GPG financing suggests that these activities should be reported and recorded separately, in the same way as ODA. Recording could be done by the DAC Secretariat, currently responsible for aid statistics, which handles the data it gets quite efficiently. The correct solution would be to book all GPG expenditures separately, in their own right, not as ODA. Although this would not change facts, official aid flows would look smaller if those GPGs at present subsumed under ODA and boosting aid figures were no longer recorded as aid. Therefore strong resistance by donors – with a well documented predilection for 'broadening' ODA – can be expected to prevent it. As long as donors themselves produce aid data without participation of recipients or independent experts, the desire to 'broaden' ODA must be expected to prevail.

As shown by the example of the global environment, one could argue that both the high income elasticity of environmental protection above a certain income threshold, earlier environmental destruction by OECD countries during historical phases of their own development paths, and the idea of financing common goals within countries by progressive taxation suggest that the North should carry a significantly higher share of the financial burden. One way of raising money would be by international taxation, for instance a Tobin tax. As the incidence of such taxes would be higher on the North, they would also imply an element of redistribution. New international sources of liquidity are needed, both to finance GPGs and for traditional ODA activities, to close the widening gap. Many years ago Keynes wanted similar measures, for instance taxing balance of payments surpluses in order to increase productive employment globally. There would also be a new/old role for a totally reformed IMF: providing liquidity along the lines initially proposed by Keynes, acting as an institution stabilizing global effective demand rather than as a bailiff for the North. A return to the spirit of Bretton Woods, especially by the BWIs, would allow addressing global issues much better.

REFORMS OF THE GLOBAL FRAMEWORK OF TRADE

The present globalization process is tailored to suit the wishes of the North and to increase profit opportunities of transnational firms. The new trading environment has been shaped accordingly. To move towards convergence, reforms of world trade are necessary. A reform of the WTO as well as measures regarding commodity exporters are proposed.

Reforming the WTO

The new WTO framework denies SCs important policy options to foster development. The protection of nascent industries along the lines indicated by List, Heckscher and the PST, which was successfully practised by the Asian tigers and ICs themselves in the course of their own development, is now prohibited. Invoking the free trade dogma when it suits them, the North does not practise what is preached to others. While pressing for liberalization and opening of Southern markets, ICs keep their own markets protected. The OECD (1992, p.37) stated with the utmost clarity that SCs face higher tariffs and more non-tariff barriers (NTBs), which cost them more than all development aid received. In addition, entry into export-oriented industries most accessible to SCs is retarded. The OECD did not fail to point out that, while ICs have encouraged SC diversification, IC trade policies often obstruct it with tariff escalation, suddenly imposed new trade barriers, anti-dumping actions and other selective trade restricting provisions, when SC exports start to take off successfully.

This picture has not changed. The OECD (2000a, p.31) quotes a study according to which 'rich countries' average tariffs on manufactured imports from poor countries are four times higher than those on imports from other developed countries'. Tariff escalation hinders Southern exports: 'OECD tariffs on finished industrial products are about eight times higher than on raw materials ... These barriers delay entry into the export-oriented industries, which are most accessible to developing countries – namely commodity processing, light manufactures, and textiles and clothing' (ibid., pp.31f). The OECD also mentions the pivotal role of agriculture in development and the damaging effects of Northern agrarian policies that 'impair the role of agriculture as an engine for ... overall growth'. Non-tariff measures, certain 'behind-the-border' regulations and practices greatly impede trade.

Differentiated and preferential treatment

As a first step this discriminatory trading system described by the OECD must be abolished. Market access must be equal irrespective of whether the exporting country is Northern or Southern. Non-discriminatory barriers, particularly equal tariffs for all imports in OECD countries, could easily have been negotiated into the relevant WTO agreements, but the North apparently chose not to do so. The economic doctrines which OECD countries use to advocate liberalization are forgotten when it comes to discriminating against Southern suppliers. Abolishing discrimination is therefore an important demand.

But to encourage development, trade policy should go further. To allow SCs to develop their economic structures, they should have the right to protect their economies at least as strongly as the North. Preferences for the South, an exception from the principle of equal treatment in GATT 1947, were gained by strong political pressure. Even though actual results remained sobering, the principle of preferential treatment as such is valuable, allowing the special developmental needs of SCs to be taken into account. The Uruguay Round pushed this principle further back, containing as it did clauses that can be used to dismantle valuable preferences for some Southern exporters. To allow SCs to develop their economic structures, their right to protect their economies at least as strongly as the North must be built into the WTO agreements. This system could be differentiated by a country's stage of development (for instance, by using GDP/head as an indicator). Poorer countries should be allowed more protection, and one should incorporate some form of graduation, as well as provisions for an eventual phasing out – or, rather, phasing down to the Northern level. However, as proved by the case of textiles and clothing, where the North has been protecting its industry over decades, and still drags its feet today, claiming that too 'quick' liberalization would be unrealistic, this phasing out should not be too quick either. Sequencing liberalization would be necessary, a process already established within the WTO in favour of the North by the ATC. It would be a matter of discussion whether this right to developmental protection should be extended to all investments or limited to domestically controlled firms. The former solution would have the advantage of forming an additional incentive to foreign direct investment in SCs.

One possible way of integrating infant industry protection into the WTO framework would be to establish a right of any SC to obtain a given number of waivers for industries the country specifies, and for a specified time, depending on the country's stage of development. One would have to apply Prebisch's proposals against petrification by calculating protection in such a way that differences in productivities between SCs and the global market are equalized. This means that protection will be reduced over time, either because SC producers have reduced their productivity gaps or because they have failed to improve their productivity within a reasonable period of time. Furthermore, we propose a measure that can be easily combined with it, which would raise funds for development. Rather than lowering tariffs in line with productivity changes, SC governments could keep tariffs constant but levy taxes that increase slowly in line with productivity, thus abolishing incentives to producers to establish themselves comfortably behind high protectionist walls. The money obtained would have to be used to finance diversification, but also for redistributive measures in favour of the poor.

The WTO's arbitration process
This must be changed. At present the possibility of suspending the application of concessions and other obligations vis-à-vis the other member country, subject to authorization by the Dispute Settlement Body, is the only means a country has to take action against an offender. Suspending concessions and obligations is subject to strict rules and not always possible. As discussed in Chapter 12, one could have opted for authorizing or even encouraging all members to suspend concessions and obligations vis-à-vis a country breaking the rules. Financial problems faced by SCs trying to defend their rights should be solved (cf. Chapter 12). Provisions for differential and more favourable treatment of SCs should be implemented in a meaningful way. Reducing asymmetries of power, this solution would protect the interests of smaller players much better, strengthening the rule of law and the enforceability of the

norms, which were agreed by all members. The fact that the transparency and impartiality of the TMB has come under heavy criticism corroborates the view that it would be better not to have this two-tier procedure.

WTO and net food importers

Higher food prices expected as a consequence of reduced export subsidies prompted ICs to promise relief to net food-importing SCs that did not materialize once the agreements were signed. A Food Import Facility should be established at the WTO, as proposed by Raffer (1997a), working as a contractual insurance scheme without conditionality, like the original Stabex in Lomé I. Conditionality must not creep in eventually, as it did with Stabex and the IMF's Compensatory Financing Facility. The knowledge that transfers are temporary should be an incentive to use them properly. As a measure against abuse of funds, recipients themselves could monitor their use in the way the USA allowed self-monitoring by recipients under its Marshall Plan. This successful precedent should be copied (Raffer & Singer, 1996, pp.197f) in this case as well as for development cooperation in general.

Protecting indigenous knowledge as the intellectual property of people in the South

This is an important issue. Rules must be enacted to stop 'bio-piracy' by the North. Article 34 of the TRIPS Agreement, which shifts the burden of proof in the case of process patents onto the defendant, should be abolished, at least for SCs. Those claiming infringement of their intellectual property must have to prove it. Furthermore, possibilities to patent micro-organisms and non-biological and microbiological processes should be limited. Plants or animals must be exempt from patenting.

Compensatory and Stabilization Schemes for Commodity Exporters

Compensatory and stabilization schemes for commodities must be revived. The currently existing but not operating Common Fund could be invested with sufficient financial resources to stabilize prices. As price stabilization may destabilize earnings, a safety net stabilizing revenues should be established, too. Parts of the gains from commodity price stabilization should be used by the exporting countries to finance diversification. Diversification measures could be elaborated by the recipient country choosing freely which projects to finance. If the proposal of copying the Marshall Plan's feature of regional cooperation among recipients were adopted, such measures could be elaborated by joint assessments of needs within the respective country groups. As this emulation of Marshall aid would also mean introducing the principle of self-monitoring by recipients, a body checking the use of money would automatically be established. Countries would have to notify what they have done with money received for that purpose. Failure to use it according to contract could lead to fines. Both failures and fines would have to be determined by an independent body. This arrangement would avoid petrification of production structures, not least because actual producers would not be sheltered from market price movements – as by the EU's Common Agricultural Policy. The obligation to report internationally would create transparency. This would contribute to avoiding the problem of domestic commodity boards operating without such international scrutiny, where money was often not used in an economically sensible way.

REFORMS OF THE UN

Many proposals for reforming the UN have been made, among others by the UNDP (1994), as well as by a special edition of the *IDS Bulletin* edited by Singer and Jolly in October 1995. We would like to draw attention to some of these proposals by seconding them. For reasons of space, we have to limit ourselves.

Reforming the Voting System

Arguing that the difference between the voting rules of the UN and the BWIs is the reason for unequal support and resources, Singer (1995) proposed introducing the same voting system for both. Double majorities, both of member countries and of financial contributions, should be required. In the case of the BWIs, this principle was realized to some extent, when they were founded: even today, each member's quota consists of two parts, the first is an equal amount of votes given to all alike, the second depends on capital shares. Repeated capital increases have diminished the egalitarian part of votes. Re-establishing the initial relation between the egalitarian and the capital components of votes as it was at Bretton Woods would thus not even be a radically new proposal. In the General Assembly double majorities would mean majorities of both Northern and Southern Countries. This is a slightly different double majority from the one above, an exception justified by the different structures and purposes of the UN compared with IFIs.

Linking the BWIs to the UN

In the original pre-Bretton Woods proposals, global management was assumed to be in the UN. Although the UN did not yet exist (being created a year later at San Francisco) its creation had been announced and the outlines of its organization were under negotiation. As its specialized agencies, the BWIs should be brought under real guidance by the UN, as opposed to the purely theoretical guidance currently existing. They should have to report to the General Assembly and ECOSOC, or to a new Economic Security Council (see Chapter 1 and also below). Their guidelines should include the original aims of their founders, fighting poverty and unemployment, rather than creating them. They could be responsible to the Economic Security Council as the major world economic decision body (cf. Stewart, 1995, p.32).

Economic Security Council

One of the advantages of setting up such a new ESC is that its composition can reflect the changes since 1945, as ul Haq (1995, p.26) points out. It should be larger than the present Security Council, comprising about 20 countries, ten from the South, ten from the North. All large countries should be members. It would be ideal if it could replace the G7/G8, because this forum, which decides on global policies, represents only a small minority of the world's population. In particular, no Southern nation is represented.

Independent Monitoring Body

An independent body should be set up within the UN to monitor divergence and propose appropriate measures to the Economic Security Council. It should be composed of independent experts selected by the UN General Assembly. It could use indices such as the Human Development Index as the basis on which to judge whether divergence has increased. It could dispose of funds raised by international taxation to finance measures against poverty. These measures would have to be planned and carried out by UN agencies or other suitable organizations. Regarding Africa, where neoliberalism has at least contributed to the breakdown of statehood, a special action of Marshall Plan dimensions for the continent – as once proposed by Bruno Kreisky – appears necessary to stop further divergence and marginalization.

This (or a similar) body could also serve to monitor the implementation of UN summit meetings, such as Copenhagen with its 20:20 target or the commitment to reduce extreme poverty and malnutrition by half by the year 2015.

We repeat that we realize these proposals sound Utopian at present, but that is intended. We are also aware that these proposals will create many problems of implementation, which we have deliberately disregarded at this stage.

At a moment when the 'number of people living in poverty has reached a historic high' (OECD, 2000a, p.123) it is particularly important to change North–South relations in such a way as to reduce the effects of inequalizing forces, and to improve the foundations of development. We are also in agreement with the OECD (ibid., p.9) that 'Partnership is no longer an option. It is a necessity.' The proposals we made or seconded above all aim at creating a real partnership, where everyone 'abides by the same rules ... applied across the board' (ibid., p.10). It is precisely our point that there must not be one law for the rich and another law for the poor, but a globally level playing field. Therefore we propose the removal of any negative discrimination against SCs, but also measures to allow them to progress from the present status of dependence and patronage towards the status of a real partner. To overcome present disadvantages of the South, positive discrimination is also necessary to level the playing field, for instance in the case of unequal conditions in North–South trade. As we have shown with the example of financial accountability and risk sharing, the proposals we made or seconded are not always as radical as they might look at first glance. They combine rather well with official declarations of OECD members and IFIs about partnership, transparency, the Rule of Law and policy coherence. This gives us hope that – in the end – these ideas might not be as Utopian as we have feared at the outset.

Bibliography

Abbott, George C. (1972), 'Aid and Indebtedness – A Proposal', *National Westminster Bank Review* (May), pp.55ff.

Adler, John H. (1952), 'The Fiscal and Monetary Implementation of Development Programs', *American Economic Review, P&P*, **42** (2), pp.584ff.

Agarwala, A.N. and S.P. Singh (eds) (1968), *The Economics of Underdevelopment*, London and New York: Oxford UP.

Aghion, Philippe and Peter Howitt (1994),'Endogenous Technical Change: The Schumpeterian Perspective', in Luigi L. Pasinetti and Robert M. Solow (eds), *Economic Growth and the Structure of Long-term Development*, London and Basingstoke and New York: Macmillan and St Martin's Press (in association with the International Economic Association), pp.118ff.

Ahmed, M. and L. Summers (1992), 'Zehn Jahre Schuldenkrise – eine Bilanz', *Finanzierung & Entwicklung*, **29** (3), pp.2ff.

Akram, Munir (2000), 'Special and Differential Treatment for Developing Countries', *South Letter*, No. 35, pp.10ff.

Akyüz, Yilmaz (1998), 'The East Asian Financial Crisis: Back to the Future?', mimeo.

Alavi, Hamza (1980), 'The Colonial Transformation of India', *The Journal of Social Studies*, 8, pp.32ff.

Amin, Samir (1974), 'Verso una nuova crisi strutturale del sistema capitalistico', *Terzo Mondo*, 24–5, pp.8ff.

Arellano, J.P. and J. Ramos (1987), 'Chile', in D.R. Lessard and J. Williamson (eds), *Capital Flight and Third World Debt*, Washington, DC: Institute of International Economics, pp.153ff.

Ariyoshi, Akira *et al.* (1999), 'Country Experiences with the Use and Liberalization of Capital Controls' (advance copy, downloaded from the IMF's homepage).

Auty, Richard M. and John Toye (eds) (1996), *Challenging the Orthodoxies*, London and Basingstoke and New York: Macmillan and St. Martin's Press.

Avramovic, Dragoslav (1987), 'Conditionality: Facts, Theory and Policy – Contribution to the Reconstruction of the International Financial System', *Development & South–South Co-operation*, **III** (4), pp.110ff.

Bairoch, Paul (1993), *Economics and World History: Myths and Paradoxes*, Chicago: University of Chicago Press.

Balogh, Thomas (1963), *Unequal Partners*, Vol. I: *The Theoretical Framework*, Oxford: Blackwell.

Baran, Paul A. (1968), 'On the Political Economy of Backwardness', in A.N. Agarwala and S.P. Singh (eds), pp.74ff (first published in *The Manchester School of Economic and Social Studies*, January 1952).

Bauer, P.T. (1976), *Dissent on Development*, London and Cambridge (Mass.): Weidenfeld and Nicolson/Harvard UP.

Balassa, Bela (1988), 'The Lesson of East Asian Development: An Overview', *Economic Development and Cultural Change*, **36** (3 Supplement), pp.S273ff.

Bernstein, Henry (ed.) (1978), *Underdevelopment and Development, The Third World Today*, 3rd edn, Harmondsworth: Penguin.

Bhagwati, J.N. (1985), *Wealth and Poverty*, Oxford: Blackwell.

Bhagwati, Jagdish (1997), 'Wall Street, not economics, dictates the agenda', interview in *The Times of India*, 31 December (downloaded from its website, 18 January 1998).

Blackwell, M. and S. Nocera (1988), 'Developing Countries Develop Debt-Equity Swap Programs to Manage External Debt', *IMF Survey*, 11 July, pp.226ff.

Blokker, Niels (1989), *International Regulation of World Trade in Textiles - Lessons for Practice, A Contribution to Theory*, Dordrecht: M. Nijhoff.

Blomström, M. and B. Hettne (1984), *Development Theory in Transition, The Dependency Debate and Beyond: Third World Responses*, London: Zed.

Boote, Anthony R. and Kamau Thugge (1997), *Debt Relief for Low-Income Countries, The HIPC Initiative* (IMF Pamphlet Series no. 51), Washington, DC: IMF.

Bossuyt, J., G. Laporte and G. Brigaldino (1993), *European Development Policy After the Treaty of Maastricht - The Mid-Term Review of Lomé and the Complementary Debate*, Maastricht: European Centre for Development Policy Management.

Bransilver, E. and E.T. Patrikis (1984), 'Lending Limits and Regulatory Constraints under US Law', in M. Grueson and R. Reissner (eds), pp.1ff.

Braun, Oscar (1977), *Comercio internacional e imperialismo*, 3rd edn, Mexico: SXXI (Eng. tr.: ISS, The Hague 1977, rev. edn 1980).

Bräutigam, Deborah A. (1994), 'What Can Africa Learn from Taiwan? Political Economy, Industrial Policy, and Adjustment', *The Journal of Modern African Studies*, **32** (1), pp.111ff.

Brookfield, Harold (1979), *Interdependent Development*, 2nd edn, London: Methuen.

Brown, Richard (1978), 'The Theory of Unequal Exchange: The End of A Debate?', *ISS Occassional Paper*, no. 65, The Hague.

Bruton, Henry J. (1968), 'Growth Models and Underdeveloped Economies', in Agarwala and Singh (eds), pp.219ff (first published in *The Journal of Political Economy*, August 1955).

Cardoso, F.H. (1972), 'Dependency and Development in Latin America', *New Left Review*, 74, pp.83ff.

Cassen, Robert *et al.* (1986), *Does Aid Work? Report to an Intergovernmental Task Force*, Oxford: Clarendon Press.

Cataquet, Harold (1989), 'Country Risk Management: How to Juggle with Your Arms in a Straitjacket?', in H.W. Singer and S. Sharma (eds), pp.337ff.

Chakravarty, Sukhamoy (1989), 'Mahalanobis, Prasanta Chandra', in J. Eatwell *et al.* (eds), pp.222ff.

Chang, Ha-Joon (2000), 'The Hazard of Moral Hazard: Untangling the Asian Crisis', *World Development*, **28** (4), pp.775ff.

Chang, Ha-Joon, Hong-Jae Park and Chul Gyue Yoo (1998), 'Interpreting the Korean crisis: financial liberalisation, industrial policy and corporate governance', *Cambridge Journal of Economics*, **22** (6), pp.735ff.

Chen, John-ren and Herbert Stocker (1993), 'The experience of the "Gang of Four"', in S. Mansoob Murshed and Kunibert Raffer (eds), pp.67ff.

Chenery, Hollis (1989), 'Foreign Aid', in J. Eatwell *et al.* (eds), pp.137ff.

Chenery, Hollis, Montek S. Ahluwalia, C.L.G. Bell, John H. Duloy and Richard Jolly (1974), *Redistribution with Growth*, Oxford and New York: Oxford UP.

Christoffersen, Leif E. (1978), 'The Bank and Rural Poverty', *Finance & Development*, **15** (4), pp.18ff.

Clark, Colin (1968), 'Population Growth and Living Standards', in A.N. Agarwala and S.P. Singh (eds), pp.32ff (first published in *International Labour Review*, August 1953).

Cline, William R. (1985), 'International Debt: From Crisis to Recovery?', *American Economic Review, Papers & Proceedings*, **LXXV** (2), pp.185ff.

Commission (of the EU) (1992), *The role of the Commission in supporting structural adjustment in ACP states*, DG Development, Brussels/ Luxembourg.

Commission (of the EU) (1996), *Green Paper on relations between the European Union and the ACP countries on the eve of the 21st century* (draft), Brussels (14 November).

Commission (of the EU) (1998a), 'Analyse du projet des directives de négociations, Accord du partenariat CE-ACP', document du travail des services de la Commission (January).

Commission (of the EU) (1998b), 'Projet de communication de la Commission au Conseil, Recommendations de décision du Conseil autorisant la Commission à négocier un accord du partenariat pour le développement avec les ACP' (28 January).

Commission (of the EU) (2000a), *Communication to the Commission on the Reform of the Management of External Assistance*, Brussels (16 May).

Commission (of the EU) (2000b), *Communication from the Commission to the Council and the European Parliament, The European Community's Development Policy*, COM(2000) 212 final, Brussels (26 April).

Committee on Agriculture (1996), 'Report by the Committee on Agriculture on the Marrakesh Ministerial Decision on Measures Concerning the Possible Negative Effects of the Reform Programme on Least-Developed and Net Food-Importing Developing Countries, Report for the Singapore Ministerial Conference adopted by the Committee on Agriculture on 24 October 1996', WTO, Geneva (G/L/125).

Committee on Foreign Relations (of the US Senate) (1977), *Bretton Woods Agreements Amendments Act of 1977*, United States Senate, 95th Congress, 1st Session, Report No. 95-603, Washington, DC: Government Printing Office.

Cook, John (2000), 'Statement of John Cook, Director Petroleum Division Energy Information Administration, before the Committee on Energy and Natural Resources, United States Senate, July 13, 2000' (downloaded from *http://www.eia.doe.gov/pub/oil_gas on* 16 August 2000).

Corden, W. Max (1990), 'Protection, Liberalization and Macroeconomic Policy', in H.W. Singer, N. Hatti and R. Tandon (eds), pp.39ff.

Cornia, G.A., R. Jolly and F. Stewart (eds) (1987), *Adjustment with a Human Face*, 2 vols, Oxford and New York: Oxford UP.

Crockett, Andrew (1982), 'Issues in the use of Fund resources', *Finance & Development*, **19** (2), pp.10ff.

David, P.A. (1985), 'Clio and the Economics of QWERTY', *American Economic Review (Papers & Proceedings)*, pp.332ff.

Dearden, Stephen J.H. (1999), 'Immigration Policy in the European Union', in Marjorie Lister (ed.), pp.59ff.

Diouf, Jacques (2000), 'Poverty Reduction and Food Security', Statement to the Development Assistance Committee of the Organisation for Economic Cooperation and Development, Paris, 9 June (downloaded from *http://www.fao.org/dg/oecd00-3.htm*).

Dobbs, Michael and Paul Blustein (1999), 'Lost Illusions about Russia' (downloaded from the *Washington Post*'s homepage *http://search.washingtonpost.com/wp-srv/WPlate/1999-09/121861-091299-idx.html* on 14 September 1999).

Dos Santos, Theotonio (1978), 'The Crisis of Development Theory and the Problem of Dependence in Latin America', in H. Bernstein (ed.), pp.57ff (Spanish version in Jaguaribe *et al.*, 1978).

Eatwell, J., M. Milgate and P. Newman (eds) (1989), *Economic Development – The New Palgrave*, London and Basingstoke: Macmillan.

ECA (UN Economic Commission for Africa) (1989), *African Alternative Framework to Structural Adjustment Programmes for Socio-Economic Recovery and Transformation* (E/ECA/CM.15/6/Rev.3), New York: UN.

EIA (US Energy Information Administration) (2000a), 'World Oil Market and Oil Price Chronologies 1970-1999 – January 2000 (downloaded from *http://www.eia.doe.gov/emeu/cabs/chron.html* on 21 June).

EIA (2000b), 'Monthly Energy Chronology – 2000 (September 2000)' (downloaded from *http://www.eia.doe.gov/emeu/cabs/monchron.html* on 23 September 2000).

Emmanuel, Arghiri (1972), *Unequal Exchange, A Study in the Imperialism of Trade*, New York and London: Monthly Review Press (original publication *L'échange inégal*, Paris: Maspéro 1969).

Emmanuel, Arghiri (1980), 'Le "prix rémunérateur", epilogue à l'échange inégal', *Revue Tiers-Monde*, January/March, pp.21ff.

EURODAD (1996), 'Multilateral Debt Update', 30 September (received by e-mail from *eurodad@knooppunt.be*).

EURODAD (1997), 'Eurodad Analysis', 18 September (received by e-mail from *eurodad@agoranet.be*).

Evans, Peter B. (1986), 'State, Capital, and the Transformation of Dependence: The Brazilian Computer Case', *World Development*, **14** (7), pp.791ff.

Federal Chancellery (of Austria) (1983), *Dreijahresprogramm der österreichischen Entwicklungshilfe 1984-1986 (Fortschreibung)*, Vienna.

Federal Chancellery (of Austria) (1994), *Dreijahresprogramm der österreichischen Entwicklungshilfe 1995 bis 1997 (Fortschreibung)*, Vienna.

Fishlow, Albert *et al.* (1994), *Miracle or Design? Lessons from the East Asian Experience*, Washington, DC: Overseas Development Council.

Frank, A.G. (1972), *Lumpenbourgeoisie, Lumpendevelopment, Dependence, Class and Politics*, New York: Monthly Review Press (Spanish original: Santiago: editorial PLA 1972).

Frank, A.G. (1978), *Dependent Accumulation and Underdevelopment*, London and Basingstoke: Macmillan.

Freeman, Christopher and Luc Soete (1997), *The Economics of Industrial Innovation*, 3rd edn, London: Pinter.

Friedman, Milton (1970), 'Foreign Economic Aid: Means and Objectives', in J. Bhagwati and R.S. Eckaus (eds), *Foreign Aid*, Harmondsworth: Penguin, pp.63ff (first published in *Yale Review* (1958), vol. 47, pp.24ff).

Frisch, Dieter (1996), 'Die Zukunft des Lomé-Abkommens, Erste Überlegungen zur europäischen Afrika-Politik nach dem Jahr 2000', *Afrika spectrum*, **31** (1), pp.57ff.

Furtado, Celso (1976), *El desarrollo económico – un mito*, 2nd edn, Mexico:

SXXI.

Furtado, Celso (1978), 'Elements of a Theory of Underdevelopment – The Underdeveloped Structures', in H. Bernstein (ed.), pp.33ff (excerpt from his book *Development and Underdevelopment*, Berkeley: University of California Press, 1964).

G15 (Group of 15) (1994), *The Summit Level Group of Developing Countries*, Geneva.

Galbraith, John Kenneth (1979), 'Oil: A Solution', *The New York Review*, 27 September.

GAO (General Accounting Office) (2000), 'Developing Countries: Debt Relief Initiative for Poor Countries Faces Challenges' (Chapter Report, 06/29/2000, GAO/NSIAD-00-161, downloaded from its homepage *http://www.gao.gov.*).

GATT (1980), *International Trade 1979/80*, Geneva: GATT.

GATT (1984), *Textiles and Clothing in the World Economy*, Geneva: GATT.

GATT (1986), *International Trade 1985–86*, Geneva: GATT.

GATT (1987), *International Trade 1986–87*, Geneva: GATT.

GATT (1992), *GATT – What it is, What it Does*, Geneva: GATT.

George, Susan (1976), *How the Other Half Dies, The Real Reasons of World Hunger*, Harmondsworth: Penguin.

Georgescu-Roegen, N. (1960), 'Economic Theory and Agrarian Economics', *Oxford Economic Papers,* **12** (1), pp.1ff.

Ghilarducci, Teresa and Patricia Ledesma Liébana (2000), 'Unions' Role in Argentine and Chilean Pension Reform', *World Development*, **28** (4), pp.753ff.

Goldin, Ian and Dominique van der Mensbrugghe (1995), 'The Uruguay Round: An Assessment of Economywide and Agricultural Reforms', in Fritz Breuss (ed.) *The World Economy after the Uruguay Round*, Vienna: Service Fachverlag, pp. 67ff.

Goldman, Marshall I. (1967), *Soviet Foreign Aid*, New York and London: Praeger.

Goldstein J.L. and S.D. Krasner (1984), 'Unfair Trade Practices: The Case of Differential Response', *American Economic Review (Papers & Proceedings)*, pp.282ff.

Gotur, Padma (1983), 'Interest rates and the developing world', *Finance & Development*, **20** (4), pp.33ff.

Graham, Frank D. (1923), 'Some Aspects of Protection Further Considered', *Quarterly Journal of Economics*, **37,** pp.193ff.

Greenidge, Carl B. (1999) 'Return to Colonialism? The New Orientation of European Development Assistance', in Lister (ed.) (1999), pp.103ff

Grueson, M. and R. Reissner (eds) (1984), *Sovereign Lending – Assessing Legal Risk*, London: Euromoney Publications.

Hardy, Chandra S. (1979), 'Commercial Bank Lending to Developing Countries: Supply Constraints', *World Development*, **7** (2), pp.189ff.

Harrod, R.F. (1951), *The Life of John Maynard Keynes*, New York: Harcourt, Brace and Company.

Hayter, Teresa and Catherin Watson (1985), *Aid: Rhetoric and Reality*, London and Sydney: Pluto Press.

Heckscher, Eli (1950), 'The Effect of Foreign Trade on the Distribution of Income', in H. Ellis and L. Metzler (eds), *Readings in the Theory of International Trade*, London: Allen and Unwin, pp.272ff (slightly abbreviated version of the original, published in *Ekonomisk Tidskrift*, XXI, 1919, pp.497ff).

Helleiner, G.K. (1979), 'Relief and Reform in Third World Debt', *World Development*, **7** (2), pp.113ff.

Hersel, Philipp (1998), 'The London Debt Agreement of 1953 on German External Debt: Lessons for the HIPC Initiative', in EURODAD (ed.) *Taking Stock of Debt, Creditor Policy in the Face of Debtor Poverty*, Brussels: EURODAD, pp.15ff.

Hirschman, Albert O. (1958), *The Strategy of Economic Development*, New Haven: Yale UP.

Hirschman, Albert O. (1981), *Essays in Trespassing, Economics to Politics and Beyond*, Cambridge and New York: Cambridge UP.

Hirschman, Albert O. (1989), 'Linkages', in Eatwell *et al.* (eds), pp.210ff.

Husain, Ishrat (1994), 'Anpassungsergebnisse in Afrika: Ausgewählte Fälle', *Finanzierung & Entwicklung*, **31**(2), pp.6ff.

IDB (1991), *Economic and Social Progress in Latin America, 1991 Report*, Washington, DC: IDB.

IDB (1992), *Economic and Social Progress in Latin America, 1992 Report*, Washington, DC: IDB.

IDC (International Development Committee, House of Commons) (2000), *The Effectiveness of EC Development Assistance* (Session 1999–2000, Ninth Report), London: Stationery Office.

IMF (1997), *IWF-Nachrichten – Beilage über den IWF* (September).

IMF (1998), 'The IMF's Response to the Asian Crisis' (April), *http://www.imf.org/External/np/exr/facts/asia.HTM*.

IMF (1999), 'The IMF's Response to the Asian Crisis' (17 January), *http://www.imf.org/External/np/exr/facts/asia.HTM*.

IMF (2000a), 'Key Features of IMF Poverty Reduction and Growth Facility (PRGF) Supported Programs', Prepared by the Policy Development and Review Department downloaded from (*http://www.imf.org/external/np/prgf/2000/eng/key.htm#P31_2132* on 8 September 2000).

IMF (2000b), 'How We Lend' (downloaded on 7 September 2000 from *http:www.imf.org/external/np/exr/facts/howlend.htm*).

Ingham, Barbara (1995), *Economics and Development*, London and New York: McGraw-Hill.

IPE (1999), 'OPEC's future: survival with dramatic changes', in International Petroleum Institute (ed.), *International Petroleum Encyclopedia 1999*, Tulsa, OK, pp.213ff.

Jaguaribe, H., A. Ferrer, M. Wionczek and Th. Dos Santos (1978), *La dependencia politico-económica de América Latina*, 10th edn, Mexico: SXXI.

Jolly, Richard (1998), 'Redistribution without Growth', in David Sapsford and John-ren Chen (eds), *Development Economics and Policy, The Conference Volume to Celebrate the 85th Birthday of Professor Sir Hans Singer*, London and Basingstoke: Macmillan, pp.172ff.

Jones, Charles I. (1997), 'On the Evolution of the World Income Distribution', *The Journal of Economic Perspectives*, **1** (3), Summer, pp.19ff.

Jones, Chr. and M.A. Kiguel (1994), 'Afrikas Streben nach Wohlstand: Haben die Anpassungsmaßnahmen geholfen?', *Finanzierung & Entwicklung*, **31** (2), pp.2ff.

Kaiser, Walter (1986), 'Die Entwicklungshilfe-Leistungen der Sowjetunion in den OECD-Publikationen', *Journal für Entwicklungspolitik (JEP)*, **2** (2), pp.32ff.

Kalecki, Michał (1971), 'Political Aspects of Full Employment', *Selected Essays on the Dynamics of the Capitalist Economy, 1933–1970*, Cambridge: Cambridge UP, pp.138ff (paper first published in 1943).

Kanesa-Thasan, S. (1981), 'The Fund and adjustment policies in Africa', *Finance & Development*, **18** (3), pp.20ff.

Kaul, Inge, Isabelle Grunberg and Marc A. Stern (eds) (1999), *Global Public Goods, International Cooperation in the 21st Century*, Oxford and New York: Oxford UP.

Kay, Cristóbal (1989), *Latin American Theories of Development and Underdevelopment*, London and New York: Routledge.

Keynes, John Maynard (1930), 'The Economic Possibilities of our Grandchildren', *Nation* (11–18 October).

Keynes, John Maynard ([1930] 1971), *A Treatise on Money – The Applied Theory of Money*, London and Basingstoke: Macmillan.

Keynes, John Maynard ([1936] 1967), *The General Theory of Employment, Interest and Money*, London and Basingstoke: Macmillan.

Keynes, John Maynard (1938), 'The Policy of Government Storage of Food-Stuffs and Raw Materials', *The Economic Journal*, **XLVIII**, pp.449ff.

Keynes, John Maynard (1974), 'The International Control of Raw Materials', *Journal of International Economics*, **4** (3), pp.299ff.

Keynes, John Maynard (1980), *The Collected Writings of John Maynard*

Keynes, vol. XXV: *Shaping the Post-War World: The Clearing Union, Activities 1940-1944*, edited by Donald Moggridge, London and Basingstoke and Cambridge: Macmillan and Cambridge UP for the Royal Economic Society.

Kindleberger, Charles P. (1978), *Manias, Panics, and Crashes: A History of Financial Crises*, New York: Basic Books.

Koekkoek, K.A. and L.B.M. Mennes (1990), 'Liberalizing the Multi-Fibre Arrangement: Some Aspects for the Netherlands, the EC and LDCs', in H.W. Singer, N. Hatti and R. Tandon (eds), pp.673ff.

Krause, Lawrence B. (1988), 'Hong Kong and Singapore: Twins or Kissing Cousins?', *Economic Development and Cultural Change*, **36** (3, Supplement), pp.S45ff.

Krause, Lawrence B. (2000), 'The Aftermath of the Asian Financial Crisis for South Korea', *The Journal of the Korean Economy*, **1** (1), pp.1ff.

Krueger, Ann O. (1997), 'Trade Policy and Economic Development – How We Learn', *American Economic Review*, **87** (1), pp.1ff.

Krugman, Paul (1988), 'Financing vs. Forgiving a Debt Overhang', *Journal of Development Economics*, **29** (3), pp.253ff.

Krugman, Paul (1994), 'Does Third World Growth Hurt First World Prosperity?', *Harvard Business Review*, July–August, pp.113ff.

Krugman, Paul (1996), *Pop Internationalism*, Cambridge (Mass.) and London: MIT Press.

Kuznets, Paul (1988), 'An East Asian Model of Economic Development: Japan, Taiwan and South Korea', *Economic Development and Cultural Change*, **36** (3, Supplement), pp.S11ff.

Kuznets, S. (1955), 'Economic Growth and Income Inequality', *American Economic Review,* **45** (1), pp.1ff.

Kwa, Aileen (1999), 'From Crisis to Victory for Developing Countries', *Focus on Trade*, no. 42 (December), Chulalongkorn University Social Research Institute, Bangkok.

Lal, Deepak (1984), *The Poverty of 'Development Economics'*, London: Institute of Economic Affairs.

Lapper, Richard (1987), 'Fraud – Policing the Fast Trade Lines', *South*, (October), pp.16f.

Laughland, John (1997), *The Tainted Source, The Undemocratic Origins of the European Idea*, London: Little, Brown and Company.

Leibenstein, Harvey (1957), *Economic Backwardness and Economic Growth, Studies in the Theory of Economic Development*, New York and London: J. Wiley and Sons and Chapman and Hall.

Leontief, Wassily (1953), 'Domestic Production and Foreign Trade, The American Capital Position Re-examined', *Proceedings of the American Philosophical Society*, vol. **97**, pp.332ff; (reprinted in J. Bhagwati (ed.)

(1969), *International Trade*, Harmondsworth: Penguin).

Lewis, W. Arthur (1954), 'Economic Development with Unlimited Supplies of Labour', *The Manchester School of Economic and Social Studies*, **22** (May), pp.139ff (reprinted in A.N. Agarwala and S.P. Singh (eds) (1968), pp.400ff).

Linder, Staffan Burenstam (1985), 'Pacific Protagonist – Implications of the Rising Role of the Pacific', *American Economic Review*, **LXXV**(2), pp.279ff.

Lipton, M. and A. Shakow (1982), 'Die Weltbank und die Armut', *Finanzierung & Entwicklung*, **19** (2), pp.16ff.

Lipton, Michael and John F.J. Toye (1990), *Does Aid Work in India? A Country Study of the Impact of Official Development Assistance*, London: Routledge.

List, Friedrich ([1841] 1920), *Das nationale System der politischen Ökonomie*, Jena: G. Fischer.

Lister, Marjorie (1999a), 'The European Union's Relations with the African, Caribbean and Pacific Countries', in Marjorie Lister (ed.), pp.143ff.

Lister, Marjorie (ed.) (1999b), *New Perspectives on European Union Development Cooperation*, Boulder, Colorado and Oxford: Westview.

Litan, Robert E. (1992), 'Savings and loan crisis', in J. Eatwell, M. Milgate and P. Newman (eds), *The New Palgrave: Dictionary of Money and Finance*, vol. 3, London and Basingstoke: Macmillan, pp.389ff.

Louven, Erhard (1983), 'Taiwan', in Dieter Nohlen and Franz Nuscheler (eds), pp.152ff.

Lovett, Adrian (2000), *The Okinawa Summit and the Failure of Leadership*, London: Jubilee 2000 UK.

Low, Patrick and John Nash (1994), 'Der schwierige Weg zu einem freieren Welthandel', *Finanzierung & Entwicklung*, **31** (3), pp.58ff.

Luther, Hans U. (1983), 'Republik Korea (Südkorea)', in Dieter Nohlen and Franz Nuscheler (eds), pp.115ff.

Maddison, Angus (1985), *Two Crises: Latin America and Asia in 1929–38 and 1973–83*, Paris: OECD.

Mahalanobis, C.P. (1953), 'Some Observations on the Process of Growth of National Income', *Sankhya* (The Indian Journal of Statistics), **12**, pp.307ff.

Mahalanobis, C.P. (1955), 'The Approach of Operational Research to Planning in India', *Sankhya*, **16** (1&2), pp.3ff.

Mariategui, J.C. ([1928] 1955), *Siete ensayos de interpretación de la realidad peruana*, Santiago: Editorial Universitaria.

Marin, Manuel (1989), 'Lomé IV – the scope of a new Convention', *The Courier*, no.120 (March–April), pp.12ff.

Mathews, John A. (1998), 'Fashioning a new Korean model out of the crisis: the rebuilding of institutional capabilities', *Cambridge Journal of*

Economics, **22** (6), pp.747ff.

McKinnon, Ronald I. (1999), 'Exchange Rate Co-ordination for Surmounting the East Asian Currency Crisis', *Journal of International Development*, **11** (1), pp.95ff.

McQueen, Matthew (1997), 'Book Review' (of Raffer and Singer 1996), *The Economic Journal*, **107** (444), pp.1638f.

Meier, Gerald M. (1964), *Leading Issues in Development Economics*, New York and London: Oxford UP.

Meltzer, Allan H. (chair) *et al.* (2000), *Report of the Meltzer Commission* (downloaded from *http://phantom-x.gsia.cmu.edu/IFIAC/Report.html* on 9 March 2000).

Michalos, Alex C. (1997), *Good Taxes, The Case for Taxing Foreign Currency Exchange and Other Financial Transactions* (Science for Peace Series), Toronto and Oxford: Dundurn Press.

Mooney, Pat Roy (1993), 'Profiteering from the Wisdom of the South', *Choices*, **2** (4), pp.10ff.

Morrissey, Oliver and Howard White (1996), 'Evaluating the Concessionality of Tied Aid', *The Manchester School of Economic and Social Studies*, **LXIV** (2), pp.208ff.

Mosley, P., J. Harrigan and J. Toye (1991), *Aid and Power, the World Bank and Policy Based Lending*, 2 vols. London: Routledge.

Murshed, S.M. and Kunibert Raffer (eds) (1993), *Trade, Transfers and Development, Problems and Prospects for the Twenty-first Century*, Aldershot (UK) and Brookfield (US): Edward Elgar.

Myrdal, Gunnar (1944), *An American Dilemma, The Negro Problem and Modern Democracy*, New York: Harper's.

Myrdal, Gunnar (1957), *Economic Theory and Underdeveloped Regions*, London: Duckworth.

Myrdal, Gunnar (1970), *The Challenge of World Poverty, A World Anti-Poverty Program in Outline*, London: Allan Lane, The Penguin Press.

Myrdal, Gunnar (1985), 'Relief instead of Development Aid', *Journal für Entwicklungspolitik (JEP)*, **1** (1), pp.4ff (Swedish original in *Ekonomisk Debatt*, 8/1980).

NACLA (North American Council on Latin America) (1976), *Weizen als Waffe, Die neue Getreidestrategie der amerikanischen Außenpolitik*, Reinbeck: rororo aktuell.

Navarrete, J.E. (1988), 'Talking Points on Practicable Solutions', All Party Parliamentary Group on Overseas Development:'Growing out of Debt', Conference at the House of Commons Grand Committee Room, 6th December 1988 (mimeo).

Nayyar, D. (1986), *International Trade in Services*, Bombay: Exim Bank of India.

New Economics Foundation (1996), *'More isn't always better', a special briefing on growth and quality of life in the UK*, London: New Economics Foundation.

Nicholson, Walter (1992), *Microeconomic Theory, Basic Principles and Extensions*, 5th edn, Forth Worth and London: Dryden.

Nohlen, Dieter and Franz Nuscheler (eds) (1983), *Handbuch der Dritten Welt, Ostasien und Ozeanien*, vol. 8, Hamburg: Hoffmann und Campe.

Nowzad, Bahram (1982), 'Debt in developing countries: some issues for the 1980s', *Finance & Development*, **19** (1), pp.13ff.

Noyelle, Thierry (1994), 'Revamping World Trade: What's in it for the South?', *Choices*, **3** (2), pp.27ff.

Nurkse, Ragnar (1952), 'Some International Aspects of the Problem of Economic Development', *American Economic Review, P&P,* **42**, pp.571ff (reprinted in A.N. Agarwala and S.P. Singh (eds) (1968), pp.256ff).

Nurkse, Ragnar (1953), *Problems of Capital Formation in Underdeveloped Countries*, Oxford: Blackwell.

Odell, Peter R. (1983), *Oil and World Power*, Harmondsworth and New York: Penguin.

OECD (1967), *The Flow of Financial Resources to Less-Developed Countries 1961-1965*, Paris: OECD.

OECD (1983a), *Aid from OPEC Countries*, Paris: OECD.

OECD (1983b), *Development Co-operation, Efforts and Policies of the Members of the Development Assistance Committee, 1983 Review*, Paris: OECD.

OECD (1985), *Twenty-Five Years of Development Co-operation – A Review, Efforts and Policies of the Members of the Development Assistance Committee, 1985 Report*, Paris: OECD.

OECD (1992), *Development Co-operation, Efforts and Policies of the Members of the Development Assistance Committee, 1992 Report*, Paris: OECD.

OECD (1994), *Development Co-operation, Efforts and Policies of the Members of the Development Assistance Committee*, 1993 Report, Paris: OECD

OECD (1995), *Development Co-operation, Efforts and Policies of the Members of the Development Assistance Committee*, 1994 Report, Paris: OECD

OECD (1996a), *Development Co-operation, Efforts and Policies of the Members of the Development Assistance Committee, 1995 Report*, Paris: OECD.

OECD (1996b), *Shaping the 21st Century: The Contribution of Development Co-operation*, Paris: OECD.

OECD (1996c), *Development Co-operation Review Series: Austria*, no.15,

Paris: OECD.

OECD (1997), *Development Co-operation, Efforts and Policies of the Members of the Development Assistance Committee, 1996 Report*, Paris: OECD.

OECD (1998a), *Development Co-operation, Efforts and Policies of the Members of the Development Assistance Committee, 1997 Report*, Paris: OECD.

OECD (1998b), *Geographical Distribution of Flows to Developing Countries*, Paris, OECD.

OECD (1999a), *Development Co-operation, Efforts and Policies of the Members of the Development Assistance Committee, 1998 Report*, Paris: OECD.

OECD (1999b), 'Financial Flows to Developing Countries in 1998: Rise in Aid; Sharp Fall in Private Flows', *News Release* (10 June), *http://www.oecd.org/news_and__events/release/nw99-60a.htm*.

OECD (1999c), *OECD Economic Outlook*, no. 65 (June).

OECD (2000a), *Development Co-operation, Efforts and Policies of the Members of the Development Assistance Committee, 1999 Report* (*The DAC Journal 1(1)*) Paris: OECD.

OECD (2000b), 'Attachment 2 from Press Statement by the DAC Chairman, DAC High Level Meeting, 11–12 May 2000' (statistics, downloaded on 19 September 2000, *http://www.oecd.org/dac/htm/HLM2000sttats.htm*).

OECD (2000c), *Prüfbericht über die Entwicklungszusammenarbeit – Österreich*, Paris: OECD.

OECD (ed.) (1998), *Reports on the International Financial Architecture: Report of the Working Group on International Financial Crises* (*http://www.oecd.org/subject/fin_architecture*).

OED (of the World Bank) (1989), *Project Performance Results for 1987*, Washington, DC: IBRD.

Ohlin, Bertil ([1933] 1967), *Interregional and International Trade*, Cambridge (Mass.): Harvard UP.

Ohlin, Göran (1966), *Foreign Aid Policies Reconsidered*, Paris, OECD.

OPEC (1999), *Annual Statistical Bulletin 1998*, Vienna: OPEC.

OPEC (2000a), 'Speculation cause of oil market volatility', *Press Release* (17 July).

OPEC (2000b), 'OPEC makes announcement on oil market situation', *Press Release* (14 September).

OPEC (2000c), 'Why you pay so much for gasoline and other oil products' (downloaded from *http://www.opec.org* on 23 September 2000).

Oppenheim, V.H. (1975), 'Why Oil Prices Go Up (1): The Past, We Pushed Them', *Foreign Policy*, 25, pp.24ff.

Palma, Gabriel (1998), 'Three and a half cycles of "mania, panic, and (asymmetric) crash": East Asia and Latin America compared', *Cambridge Journal of Economics*, **22** (6), pp.789ff.

Palma, J.G. (1989), 'Dependency', in Eatwell *et al.* (eds), pp.91ff.

Park, Yung Chul (1996), 'The Republic of Korea's Experience with Managing Foreign Capital Flows', in M. ul Haq, I. Kaul and I. Grunberg (eds), *The Tobin Tax, Coping with Financial Volatility*, New York and Oxford: Oxford UP, pp.193ff.

Pearson, Lester B. *et al.* (1969), *Partners in Development: Report of the Commission on International Development*, New York: Praeger.

Peng, Martin Khor Kok (1994), 'The End of the Uruguay Round and Third World Interests', *South Letter*, no. 19 (Winter 1993/Spring 1994), pp.6ff.

Perroux, François (1950), 'Economic Space: Theory and Applications', *Quarterly Journal of Economics*, **64**, pp.89ff.

Perroux, François (1955), 'Note sur la notion de pôle de croissance', *Economie Appliquée*, **8**, pp.307ff (English trans. in I. Livingstone (ed.) (1971), *Economic Policy for Development: Selected Readings*, Harmondsworth: Penguin, pp. 278ff).

Pettifor, Ann (1999), 'Concordats for debt cancellation, a contribution to the debate', Jubilee 2000 Coalition UK, 18 March (mimeo).

Pincus, Jonathan and Rizal Ramli (1998), 'Indonesia: from showcase to basket case', *Cambridge Journal of Economics*, **22** (6), pp.723ff.

Polak, Jaques J. (1991), *The Changing Nature of Conditionality*, Essays in International Finance No.184, International Finance Section, Department of Economics, Princeton University, NJ.

Prebisch, Raúl (1949), 'El desarrollo económico de la América Latina y algunos de sus principales problemas', *El Trimestre Económico*, **63**, pp.347ff (English translation New York: UN 1950; reprinted in *Economic Bulletin for Latin America*, **7**(1), 1962).

Prebisch, Raúl (1959), 'Commercial Policy in the Underdeveloped Countries', *American Economic Review*, **XLIX** (2), pp.251ff.

Prebisch, Raúl (1976), 'A Critique of Peripheral Capitalism', *CEPAL Review*, first semester, pp.9ff.

Prebisch, Raúl (1984), 'Five Stages in My Thinking on Development', in G.M. Meier and D. Seers (eds), *Pioneers in Development*, Oxford and New York: Oxford UP, pp.175ff.

Prebisch, Raúl (1988), 'Dependence, Development, and Interdependence', in G. Ranis and T.P. Schultz (eds), pp.31ff.

Price Waterhouse (1992), *Study on the Causes of Delay in the Implementation of Financial and Technical Cooperation – Final Report*, November (ACP.RPR.472) (mimeo).

Pritchett, L. (1997), 'Divergence, Big Time', *The Journal of Economic Perspectives*, **1** (3), pp.3ff.

Radelet, Steven and Jeffrey Sachs (1998), 'The East Asian Financial Crisis: Diagnosis, Remedies, Prospects', Harvard Institute for International Development, 20 April (mimeo).

Raffer, Kunibert (1986), 'Siphoning Off Resources from the Periphery: The Relevance of Raúl Prebisch's Thinking for the Eighties', *Development & South-South Cooperation*, **II**(3), Special Issue: Homage to Raul Prebisch, pp.101ff (reprinted in H.W. Singer, N. Hatti and R. Tandon (eds), 1991 *Aid and External Financing in the 1990s* (*New World Order Series*, vol. 9), New Dehli: Indus, pp. 583ff).

Raffer, Kunibert (1987a), *Unequal Exchange and the Evolution of the World System, Reconsidering the Impact of Trade on North–South Relations*, London and Basingstoke: Macmillan

Raffer, Kunibert (1987b), 'Tendencies Towards a "Neo Listian" World Economy', *Journal für Entwicklungspolitik (JEP)*, **3** (3), pp.45ff.

Raffer, Kunibert (1987c), '"Invisible" Dependence – A Critical Contribution to the Discussion of Liberalising Trade in Services', *Scandinavian Journal of Development Alternatives*, **VI** (2&3), pp.138ff.

Raffer, Kunibert (1989), 'International Debts: A Crisis for Whom?', in H.W. Singer and S. Sharma (eds), pp.51ff.

Raffer, Kunibert (1990a), 'Applying Chapter 9 Insolvency to International Debts: An Economically Efficient Solution with a Human Face', *World Development*, **18** (2), pp.301ff.

Raffer, Kunibert (1990b), 'Trade in Agrarian Products and Services: How Free Should it Be?', in H.W. Singer, N. Hatti and R. Tandon (eds), pp. 851ff.

Raffer, Kunibert (1991), 'Tax-Deductible Loan Loss Reserves and International Banking: An Economist's Unbiased Analysis', *Working Papers in Commerce WPC 91/19*, Birmingham University, Department of Commerce, The Birmingham Business School.

Raffer, Kunibert (1992), 'The Effects of Oil Prices on Peripheral Net Importers: A Crude Estimate with Special Reference to LDACs', in K. Raffer and M.A.M. Salih (eds), *The Least Developed and the Oil-Rich Arab Countries, Dependence, Interdependence or Patronage?*, London and Basingstoke: Macmillan, pp.13ff.

Raffer, Kunibert (1993), 'International financial institutions and accountability: The need for drastic change', in S.M. Murshed and K. Raffer (eds), pp.151ff.

Raffer, Kunibert (1994a), '"Structural Adjustment", Liberalisation, and Poverty', *Journal für Entwicklungspolitik (JEP)*, **X** (4), pp.431ff.

Raffer, Kunibert (1994b), 'Disadvantaging Comparative Advantages: The Problem of Decreasing Returns', in Renée Prendergast and Frances Stewart (eds), *Market Forces and World Development*, London and Basingstoke and New York: Macmillan and St Martin's Press, pp.75ff.

Raffer, Kunibert (1995), 'Österreichs Entwicklungshilfe: Ein trauriges Kapitel', in Österreichische Gesellschaft für Außenpolitik und Internationale Beziehungen (ed.), *Österreichisches Jahrbuch für Internationale Politik 1995*, Vienna: Böhlau, pp.21ff.

Raffer, Kunibert (1996a), 'Is the Debt Crisis Largely Over? – A Critical Look at the Data of International Financial Institutions', in Richard M. Auty and John Toye (eds), pp.23ff (paper initially presented at the DSA Conference, Lancaster, 7–9 September 1994).

Raffer, Kunibert (1996b), 'Exportorientierte Entwicklung und Weltmarkt – Das Beispiel der asiatischen "Tiger"', in E. Binderhofer, I. Getreuer-Kargl and H. Lukas (eds) *Das pazifische Jahrhundert?*, Frankfurt a.M. and Vienna: Brandes and Apsel and Südwind, pp.41ff.

Raffer, Kunibert (1996c), 'The Uruguay Round: Tilting Trade Rules Further in Favour of the North', in G. Köhler, Ch. Gore, U.-P. Reich and T. Ziesemer (eds), *Questioning Development, Essays in the Theory, Policies and Practice of Development Interventions*, Marburg: Metropolis, pp.329ff.

Raffer, Kunibert (1997a), 'Helping Southern Net Food Importers after the Uruguay Round: A Proposal', *World Development*, **25** (11) pp.1901ff.

Raffer, Kunibert (1997b), 'Debt Management and Structural Adjustment: Neglected Issues', in Satya Dev Gupta (ed.), *The Political Economy of Globalization* (Recent Economic Thought Series), Boston and Dordrecht: Kluwer, pp.269ff.

Raffer, Kunibert (1997c), 'Controlling Donors: On the Reform of Development Assistance', *Internationale Politik und Gesellschaft/ International Politics and Society*, 4/1997, pp.357ff.

Raffer, Kunibert (1998a), 'Looking a Gift Horse in the Mouth: Analysing Donors' Aid Statistics', *Zagreb International Review of Economics and Business*, **1** (2), pp.1ff.

Raffer, Kunibert (1998b), 'Is a Revival of Keynes's Ideas Likely? (Some Comments on Chapters by Gerald M. Meier and Sir Hans W. Singer)', in Soumitra Sharma (ed.), *John Maynard Keynes – Keynesianism into the Twenty-First Century*, Cheltenham (UK) and Lyme (US): Edward Elgar, pp.116ff.

Raffer, Kunibert (1998c), 'Rolling Back Partnership: An Analysis of the Commission's Green Paper on the Future of Lomé', *DSA European Development Policy Study Group Discussion Paper,* no. 9 (also available on *http://www.oneworld.org/euforic/dsa/dp9.htm).*

Raffer, Kunibert (1998d), 'The Tobin Tax: Reviving a Discussion', *World Development*, **26** (3), pp.529ff.

Raffer, Kunibert (1998e), 'Food Aid, North–South Trade, and the Prebisch– Singer Thesis', in David Sapsford and John-ren Chen (eds), *Development*

Economics and Policy, The Conference Volume to Celebrate the 85th Birthday of Professor Sir Hans Singer, London and Basingstoke: Macmillan, pp.230ff.

Raffer, Kunibert (1999a), 'Lomé or Not Lomé – The Future of European–ACP Cooperation', in Marjorie Lister (ed.), pp.125ff.

Raffer, Kunibert (1999b), 'The WTO's First Years – The New Regime's Effects on the South', *Journal für Entwicklungspolitik (JEP)*, **XV** (1), pp.9ff.

Raffer, Kunibert (1999c), 'Introducing Financial Accountability at the IBRD: An Overdue and Necessary Reform', paper presented at the conference *Reinventing the World Bank* at Northwestern University, Evanston (Ill.) (14–16 May 1999), available at the Conference's site: *http://www.worldbank.nwu.edu*, forthcoming in the Conference volume, ed. Jonathan Pincus and Jeffrey Winters, Cornell UP.

Raffer, Kunibert (2000), ' New Forms of Dependence in the World System", in Andreas Müller, Arno Tausch and Paul M. Zulehner (eds), *Global Capitalism, Liberation Theology and the Social Sciences*, Huntington (NY): Nova Science, pp.169ff.

Raffer, Kunibert and H.W. Singer (1996), *The Foreign Aid Business, Economic Assistance and Development Co-operation*, Cheltenham (UK) and Brookfield (US): Edward Elgar (paperback: 1997).

Ranis, G. and J.C.H. Fei (1988), 'Development Economics: What Next?', in G. Ranis and T.P. Schultz (eds), pp.100ff.

Ranis, G. and T.P. Schultz (eds) (1988), *The State of Development Economics, Progress and Perspectives*, London: Blackwell.

Reichmann, Wilhelm (1988), *Die Verschuldung der Dritten Welt 1970–1983, Entwicklung und Ursachen der Krise in den Finanzbeziehungen zwischen Norden und Süden*, Frankfurt a.M. and New York: P. Lang.

Rhee, Yung Whee, Bruce Ross-Larson and Garry Pursell (1984), *Korea's Competitive Edge – Managing the Entry into World Markets* (A World Bank Research Publication), Baltimore and London: Johns Hopkins UP.

Robinson, Sherman (1976), 'A Note on the U Hypothesis Relating Income Inequality and Economic Development', *American Economic Review*, **66** (June), pp.437ff.

Rodrik, Dani (1996), 'Understanding Policy Reform', *Journal of Economic Literature*, **XXXIV**(1), pp.9ff.

Rosenstein-Rodan, P.N. (1943), 'Problems of Industrialisation of Eastern and South-Eastern Europe', *The Economic Journal*, **53** (June–September), pp.202ff (reprinted in A.N. Agarwala and S.P. Singh (eds) (1968), pp.245ff).

Rosenthal, Gert (1997), 'Social Development in Latin America and the Caribbean', *Social Development Review*, **1** (4), pp 4ff.

Rostow, W.W. (1960), *The Stages of Economic Growth, A Non-Communist Manifesto*, Cambridge: Cambridge UP.

Ruttan, Vernon W. (1996), *United States Development Assistance Policy – The Domestic Policies of Foreign Aid*, Baltimore and London, Johns Hopkins UP.

Sachs, Jeffrey (1988a), 'Comprehensive Debt Retirement: The Bolivian Experience', *Brookings Papers on Economic Activity*, no. 2, pp.705ff.

Sachs, Jeffrey (1988b), 'New Approaches to the Latin American Debt Crisis', paper prepared for the Harvard Symposion on New Approaches to the Debt Crisis (mimeo).

Sachs, Jeffrey (1997), 'IMF is a power unto itself', *Financial Times* (11 December).

Sachs, Jeffrey (1998), 'The IMF and the Asian Flu', *American Prospect*, March–April, pp.16ff.

Salvatore, D. (1990), 'Voluntary Export Restraints, Escape Clause Protectionism and Economic Development', in H.W. Singer, N. Hatti and R. Tandon (eds), pp.59ff.

Sampson, Gary P. (1990), 'The Pseudo-Economics of the Multi-Fibre Arrangement: A Proposal for Reform', in H.W. Singer, N. Hatti and R. Tandon (eds), pp.701ff.

Schatz, Klaus W. and Frank Wolter (1982), 'International Trade, Employment and Structural Adjustment: The Case Study of the Federal Republic of Germany', *ILO-Working Paper*, 2-36/WP 19 WEP (October).

Schulmeister, Stephan (1998), 'Globalization without Global Money, The Double Role of the Dollar as National Currency and as World Currency and its Consequences', *WIFO Working Papers*, 106/1998, Vienna: Österreichisches Institut für Wirtschaftsforschung.

Schultz, T. Paul (1988), 'Economic Demography and Development: New Directions in an Old Field', in G. Ranis and T.P. Schultz (eds), pp.416ff.

Scitovsky, Tibor (1989), *Essays on the Frontiers of Economics*, New York: New York UP.

Scitovsky, Tibor (1995), *Economic Theory and Reality: Selected Essays on Their Disparities and Reconciliation*, Cheltenham (UK) and Brookfield (US): Edward Elgar.

Seade, Jesús (1994), 'Africa to gain more trade and investments from Round', *Focus – GATT Newsletter*, no. 106 (March–April).

Seers, Dudley (1963), 'The Limitations of the Special Case', *Bulletin of the Oxford University Institute of Economics and Statistics*, **25** (May), pp.77ff.

Seers, Dudley (1979), 'Introduction: The Congruence of Marxism and Other Neoclassical Doctrines', in A.O. Hirschman *et al.*, *Toward a New Strategy of Development. A Rothko Chapel Colloquium*, New York and Oxford: Pergamon, pp.1ff.

Serfas, Alexander (1987), *An der Schwelle zum Industrieland: Die wirtschaftliche Entwicklung Südkoreas 1963–1983*, Frankfurt a.M. and New York: P. Lang.

Shaw, John and H.W. Singer (1998), 'A Future Food Aid Regime: Implications of the Final Act of the Uruguay Round', in Helen O'Neill and John Toy (eds), *A World Without Famine? New Approaches to Aid and Development*, London and Basingstoke: Macmillan, pp.305ff.

Siebert, Horst (1974), 'Environmental Protection and Industrial Specialization', *Weltwirtschaftliches Archiv*, **110** (3), pp.494ff.

Singer, H.W. (1950), 'The Distribution of Gains between Investing and Borrowing Countries', *American Economic Review, P&P*, **40**, pp.478ff.

Singer, H.W. (1964), *International Development: Growth and Change*, New York and London: McGraw-Hill.

Singer, H.W. (1984), 'The Terms of Trade Controversy and the Evolution of Soft Financing': Early Years in the U.N.', in Gerald M. Meier and Dudley Seers (eds), *Pioneers in Development*, Oxford and New York: Oxford UP, pp.275ff.

Singer, H.W. (1986), 'Raúl Prebisch and His Advocacy of Import Substitution', *Development & South–South Cooperation*, **II** (3), (Special Issue: 'Hommage to Raúl Prebisch'), pp.1ff.

Singer, H.W. (1989), 'Lessons of Post-War Development Experience: 1945–1988', *IDS Discussion Paper*, no. 260 (April).

Singer, H.W. (1994), 'Problems and Future of Food Aid in the Post-GATT Era', *Newsletter, Bruno Kreisky Dialogue Series*, no. 10, pp.42ff.

Singer, H.W. (1995), 'Revitalizing the United Nations: Five Proposals', *IDS Bulletin*, **26** (4), pp.35ff.

Singer, H.W. and Sumit Roy (1993), *Economic Progress and Prospects in the Third World*, Cheltenham (UK) and Brookfield (US): Edward Elgar.

Singer, H.W. and S. Sharma (eds) (1989), *Economic Development and World Debt*, London and Basingstoke: Macmillan.

Singer, H.W. *et al.* (1938), *Men Without Work: A Report Made to the Pilgrim Trust*, Cambridge: Cambridge UP.

Singer, H.W., N. Hatti and R. Tandon (eds) (1990), *Trade Liberalization in the 1990s* (*New World Order Series*, 8), New Delhi: Indus.

Smith, Adam ([1776] 1979), *An Inquiry into the Nature and Causes of the Wealth of Nations*; reprinted in R.H. Campell, A.S. Skinner and W.B. Todd (eds) (1979), *Glasgow Edition of the Works and Correspondence of Adam Smith* vol. II, Oxford: Oxford UP.

Spahn, Paul Bernd (1996), 'The Tobin Tax and Echange Rate Stability', *Finance & Development*, **33** (2), pp.24ff.

Spraos, John (1986), *IMF-Conditionality: Ineffectual, Inefficient, Mistargeted*, Essays in International Finance, no. 166, International Finance Section,

Department of Economics, Princeton University.

Stern, Ernest (1983), 'World Bank Financing and Structural Adjustment', in John Williamson (ed.), *IMF Conditionality*, Washington, DC: Institute of International Finance and MIT Press, pp.87ff.

Stevens, Paul (1993), 'OPEC and oil revenues', in S.M. Murshed and Kunibert Raffer (eds), pp.82ff.

Stewart, Frances (1995), 'The Governance and Mandates of the International Financial Institutions', *IDS Bulletin*, **26** (4), pp.28ff.

Stiglitz, Joseph (1989), 'Using Tax Policy to Curb Speculative Short Term Trading', *Journal of Financial Services Research*, **3** (2–3), pp.101ff.

Stiglitz, Joseph (1998a), 'More Instruments and Broader Goals: Moving toward the "Post-Washington Consensus"', WIDER Annual Lectures 2, UN University (downloaded from *http://www.wider.unu.edu/stiglitz.htm* on 17 September 1999).

Stiglitz, Joseph (1998b), 'The Role of International Financial Institutions in the Current Global Economy', address to the Chicago Council on Foreign Relations, February 27 (downloaded from *http://www.worldbank.org/html/extdr/extme/jssp022798.htm* on 11 February 1999).

Stiglitz, Joseph (2000), 'Democratic Development as the Fruits of Labor', Keynote Address, Industrial Relations Research Association, Boston, January (mimeo).

Stotsky, Janet G. (1996), 'Why a Two-Tier Tobin Tax Won't Work', *Finance & Development*, **33** (2), pp.28f.

Streeten, Paul (1993), 'From growth via basic needs, to human development: the individual in the process of development', in S.M. Murshed and Kunibert Raffer (eds), pp.16ff.

Streeten, Paul (1994), 'Markets and States: Against Minimalism', *Journal für Entwicklungspolitik (JEP)*, **X** (4), pp.413ff.

Streeten, Paul, Louis Emmerij and Carlos Fortin (1992), *International Governance*, Sussex: IDS (with an introduction by H.W. Singer).

Sunkel, Osvaldo (1973), 'Transnational Capitalism and National Disintegration in Latin America', *Social and Economic Studies*, **22** (1), pp.132ff.

Sunkel, Osvaldo (1979), 'The Development of Development Thinking', in J.J. Villamil (ed.), *Transnational Capitalism and National Development*, Hassocks (Sussex): Harvester, pp.19ff.

Svendsen, K.E. (1987), *The Failure of the International Debt Strategy*, CDR-Report no.13, Copenhagen: Centre for Development Research.

Swenarchuk, Michelle (1999), 'Liberalized Investment and Investor–State Suits: Threats to Governmental Power', Canadian Environmental Law Association, 20 April, (mimeo).

Taylor, Judith (1987), 'Non-Tariff Protection and Exports of Developing Countries', *Journal für Entwicklungspolitik (JEP)*, **3** (3), pp.57ff.

Tetzlaff, Rainer (1980), *Die Weltbank: Machtinstrument der USA oder Hilfe für die Entwicklungsländer?*, Munich and London: Weltforum Verlag.

Thirlwall, A.P. (1999), *Growth and Development*, 6th edn, London and Basingstoke: Macmillan.

Thurow, Lester C. (1983), *Dangerous Currents: The State of Economics*, New York: Random House.

Tobin, James (1974), *The New Economics One Decade Older*, Princeton, NJ: Princeton UP.

Tobin, James (1994), 'A tax on international currency transactions', in UNDP (1994), p.70.

de la Torre, Augusto and Margaret R. Kelly (1992), *Regional Trade Arrangements*, IMF Occasional Paper no. 93, Washington, DC.

Toye, John (1995), 'Evaluation of EC/EU–Ethiopia Cooperation, Sectoral Report on Programme Aid', in Simon Maxwell (ed.), *An Evaluation of Development Cooperation between the European Union and Ethiopia 1976-1994*, Institute of Development Studies, Brighton and Addis Ababa University.

ul Haq, Mahbub (1995), 'An Economic Security Council', *IDS Bulletin*, **26** (4), pp.20ff.

ul Haq, Mahbub, Inge Kaul and Isabelle Grunberg (eds) (1996), *The Tobin Tax, Coping with Financial Volatility*, New York and Oxford: Oxford UP.

UN Secretariat (1949), *Methods of Financing Economic Development in Underdeveloped Countries*, New York: UN (E/1333/Rev.1, no. 1949.II).

UNCTAD (1995a), *Analysis of the Modalities to Give Effect to the Decisions on Special Provisions for the Least Developed Countries as Contained in the Final Act of the Uruguay Round* (21 June 1995), Geneva: UN (TD/B/WG.83).

UNCTAD (1995b), *Preliminary Analysis of Opportunities and Challenges Resulting from the Uruguay Round Agreement on Textiles and Clothing* (6 October 1995), Geneva: UN (UNCTAD/ITD/17).

UNCTAD (1995c), *Review of the Implementation, Maintenance, Improvement and Utilization of the Generalized System of Preferences, Rules of Origin and Technical Assistance, Chairman's Summary* (27 October 1995), Geneva: UN (TD/B/SCP/L.9).

UNCTAD (1999), *Trade and Development Report, 1999*, Geneva: UN.

UNDP (1992), *Human Development Report 1992*, Oxford and New York: Oxford UP.

UNDP (1994), *Human Development Report 1994*, Oxford and New York: Oxford UP.

UNDP (1998), *Human Development Report 1998*, Oxford and New York:

Oxford UP.

UNDP (1999), *Human Development Report 1999*, Oxford and New York: Oxford UP.

van der Laar, Aart (1980), *The World Bank and the Poor*, Boston, Dordrecht: M. Nijhof.

Veblen, Thorstein (1899), *The Theory of the Leisure Class*, New York and London: Macmillan.

Versluysen, Eugene L. (1982), 'Der Kapitaltransfer in Entwicklungsländer zu Marktbedingungen', *Finanzierung & Entwicklung*, **19** (4), pp.33ff.

Wade, Robert (1990), *Governing the Market*, Princeton, NJ: Princeton UP.

Wade, Robert (1994), 'Selective Industrial Policies in East Asia: Is The East Asian Miracle Right?', in Albert Fishlow *et al.*, pp.55ff.

Wade, Robert (1998a), 'The Asian Debt-and-development Crisis of 1997-?: Causes and Consequences', *World Development*, **26** (8), pp.1535ff.

Wade, Robert (1998b), 'From Miracle to Meltdown: Vulnerabilities, Moral Hazard, Panic and Debt Deflation in the Asian Crisis', paper presented at a seminar at the IDS (*http://www.ids.ac.uk/ids/research/wade.pdf*).

Wade, Robert (1998c), 'From "miracle" to "cronyism": explaining the Great Asian Slump', *Cambridge Journal of Economics*, **22** (6), pp.693ff.

Wade, Robert and Devesh Kapur (1998), 'Paying for privilege', *Financial Times*, 29 September.

Wallerstein, Immanuel (1974), *The Modern World-System, Capitalist Agriculture and the Origins of the European World Economy in the 16th Century*, New York: Academic Press.

WDT (*World Debt Tables*) (various years), IBRD, Washington, DC (WDT 1993–94 quoted, for instance, WDT, 1993, vol. 1 unless otherwise specified).

White, Howard (1993), 'Aid, investment and growth: what prospects in the 1990s?', in S.M. Murshed and K. Raffer (eds), pp.99ff.

Williams, Bob (1999), 'Seeds for change seen in profile of tomorrow's petroleum company', in International Petroleum Institute (ed.), *International Petroleum Encyclopedia 1999*, Tulsa, OK, pp.5ff.

Williamson, John (1983a), 'The Lending Policies of the International Monetary Fund', in John Williamson (ed.), pp.605ff.

Williamson, John (ed.) (1983b), *IMF Conditionality*, Washington, London: Institute for International Economics and MIT Press.

Williamson, John (1985), 'Four Lessons of the Debt Crisis', *Development & South–South Co-operation*, **I** (1), pp.24ff.

Williamson, John (1996), 'Lowest Common Denominator or Neoliberal Manifesto? The Polemics of the Washington Consensus', in Richard M. Auty and John Toye (eds), pp.13ff.

Wionczek, Miguel S. (1978), 'El endeudamiento público externo y los cambios sectoriales en la inversión privada extranjera de América Latina', in H. Jaguaribe, A. Ferrer, M.S. Wionczek, and T. Dos Santos, *La dependencia político-económica de América Latina*, 10th edn, Mexico: SXXI.

Wionczek, Miguel S. (1979), 'Editor's Introduction', *World Development*, **7** (2), pp.91ff.

Wood, Adrian (1994), *North-South Trade, Employment and Inequality: Changing Fortunes in Skill-Driven World*, Oxford: Clarendon Press.

Wood, Adrian and Cristóbal Cano (1996), 'Trade and International Inequality, *IDS Working Paper*, no. 47.

Wood, Adrian and Jörg Mayer (forthcoming), 'Africa's Export Structure in a Comparative Perspective', in *Cambridge Journal of Economics*.

World Bank (1979), *World Development Report 1979*, Washington, DC: IBRD.

World Bank (1980), *World Development Report 1980*, Washington, DC: IBRD.

World Bank (1985), *World Development Report 1985*, New York and Oxford: Oxford UP.

World Bank (1987), *World Development Report 1987*, Oxford and New York: Oxford UP.

World Bank (1988), *World Development Report 1988*, New York and Oxford: Oxford UP.

World Bank (1989), *Sub-Saharan Africa - From Crisis to Sustainable Growth*, Washington, DC: IBRD.

World Bank (1990), *World Development Report 1990*, Oxford and New York: Oxford UP.

World Bank (1992), *Effective Implementation: Key to Development Impact, Report of the World Bank's Portfolio Management Task Force*, (Wapenhans Report), Washington, DC.

World Bank (1993a), *The East Asian Miracle, Economic Growth and Public Policy*, Oxford and New York: Oxford UP.

World Bank (1993b), *The Asian Miracle, Economic Growth and Public Policy - Summary*, Washington, DC: IBRD.

World Bank (1994), *World Development Report 1994*, Oxford & New York: Oxford UP.

World Bank (1997), *Global Development Finance 1977*, Washington, DC: IBRD.

World Bank (1998), *Global Development Finance 1998*, Washington, DC: IBRD.

World Bank (1999a), *1998 Annual Review of Development Effectiveness* (OED, Task Manager: Robert Buckley), Washington, DC: IBRD.

World Bank (1999b), 'Articles of Agreement (As amended effective

February 16, 1989)', *http://www.worldbank.org/html/extdr/backgrd/ World Bank/arttoc/htm*.

World Bank (2000a), *Global Development Finance 2000*, Washington, DC: IBRD.

World Bank (2000b) 'Joint Press Conference with Horst Köhler, Managing Director of the IMF, James D. Wolfensohn, President of the World Bank, and Trevor Manuel, Chairman of the Board of Governors, Transcripts, Prague, 28 September 2000 (downloaded from *http://www.worldbank.org*).

World Bank and UNDP (1989), *Africa's Adjustment with Growth in the 1980s*, Washington, DC: IBRD.

WTO (1995), *International Trade 1995 - Trends and Statistics*, Geneva: WTO.

WTO (1996a), *Annual Report 1996*, vol. 1, Geneva: WTO.

WTO (1996b), *WTO Focus*, no. 12, August-September.

WTO (1996c), *WTO Focus*, no. 13, October-November .

WTO (1996d), *WTO Focus*, no. 14, December.

WTO (1997a), *WTO Focus*, no. 15, January.

WTO (1997b), *WTO Focus*, no. 17, March.

WTO (1997c), *WTO Focus*, no. 19, May.

WTO (1997d), *WTO Focus*, no. 20, June-July.

WTO (1997e), *WTO Focus*, no. 21, August.

WTO (1997f), *WTO Focus*, no. 25, December.

WTO (1998a), *Annual Report 1998*, vol. 1, Geneva: WTO.

WTO (1998b), *WTO Focus*, no. 33, August-September.

WTO (1999a), *Annual Report 1999*, Geneva: WTO.

WTO (1999b), *WTO Focus*, no. 39, April.

WTO (1999c), *WTO Focus*, no. 41, July-August.

WTO (2000a), *WTO Focus*, no. 44, January-February.

WTO (2000b), *WTO Focus*, no. 45, March-April.

WTO (2000c), *Annual Report 2000*, Geneva: WTO.

Yeats, Alexander J. (1990), 'Do African Countries Pay More for Imports?', *Finance & Development*, **27**(2), pp.38ff.

Zee, Howell H. (2000), 'Retarding Short-Term Capital Inflows Through Withholding Tax', *IMF Working Paper*, WP/00/40 (March).

Index

commercial banks 3, 13-14, 136-7, 149,
    151-4, 158-63, 165-72, 175, 179,
    182, 195
commodity
    agreements 5, 34-5
    price(s) 4-5, 8-9, 24-5, 32, 100, 102,
        129, 133, 160, 193, 206, 253
        stabilization 5, 8, 34, 38, 100, 111,
            206, 253
    power 100, 126, 238
    primary 4-5, 16-19, 24-6
    reserve currency 8
Common
    Agricultural Policy (of EU) 108, 116,
        254
    Fund 34-5, 253, 256
Commonwealth 67, 99, 187-8, 223
communism 44, 64-5, 67, 76, 90, 142
communist countries 67-8, 70, 84
    former 77-8, 81, 83, 236
comparative advantages (theory of) 21,
    25, 49, 220, 224, 233
    dynamic 25
    in polluting industries 218
compensation(s) 51, 60, 72, 100,
        106-107, 111-12, 145, 174, 195,
        200, 246-7, 253
    and WTO 214-15
Compensatory Financing Facility (of
    IMF) 9, 51, 112, 200, 253
composite barrel 131-2
Comprehensive Development
    Framework 96
concerted lending 167, 169
concessionality 6, 65, 73-4, 80-81,
    83-4, 111, 165, 184-5, 189
conditionality 3, 14, 51, 54, 95, 100,
    102-104, 118, 156-7, 164, 200,
    206, 229, 231-2, 253
    cross-institutional 216-17
    political 55, 93, 105
    reform proposals 247-8
consensus (at WTO) 58, 213, 216, 226,
    228
conspicuous consumption 25, 29-30,
    42
convergence 9, 15-23, 25-6, 48, 52, 59,
    160, 238, 250
corruption 33, 107, 139, 161
Cotonou 22, 102, 113-14, 248

Council of Mutual Economic Assistance
    (CMEA) 68
counterpart funds 65
Countries and Territories in Transition
    (CTTs) 79-81, 90, 229
country-a-vote system 9-10, 66
creative destruction 16, 19, 26-7
creditor(s)
    domination 166, 245
    symmetrical treatment of 171, 195
    unequal treatment of 171
crisis prevention 115
critical minimum effort 43
crony capitalism 139, 148, 150
cross-retaliation 215
crude (oil) 120-35, 192
    domestic US production of 124,
        128-9
    see also oil; Gulf-plus: marker crude
Cuba 438, 66, 68-9, 104-105, 213-14
currency transaction tax(es) (CTT) 239
    see also Tobin Tax; Spahn; Zee
current account deficits 39, 133, 177
cut-off date 188-9

DAC (Development Assistance
    Committee) 67-75, 78-95, 97, 114,
    135-6, 246, 248-9
debt
    crisis 6,14, 50, 55, 61, 93, 101, 120,
        149, 151, 158, 163, 165, 168,
        173-80
        underlying structural causes 158,
            163
    changes in structure of 179
        equity swaps 167-8
        equity ratios 149, 156-7
        exports ratio 166, 186
    forgiveness 84, 87, 91, 110, 188
    indicators
        conventional 175-7, 180-81, 189,
            191-3
        proposed 176-7, 181, 189
    management 54, 109, 158, 164,
        166-7, 172-3, 176, 184, 186,
        188, 238, 243-4
    overhang 109, 118, 172-3, 175-6,
        183, 189 ,192, 195, 200
        index proposed by Raffer 176-7,
            189

Generalized System of Preferences
  (GSP) 208
globalization 24, 26, 60–61, 108, 115,
  153, 157, 250
gold 4–5, 8, 64, 185–6
governance
  global 9–10, 12
  good 55–6, 94–6, 118, 247
government take (oil products) 130–32
graduation 80–81, 252
Graham-paradox 233
grant(s) 65, 68, 92, 103, 107, 112, 114,
  136, 142, 183, 185, 202, 237, 246
  element 72, 74–5, 92, 97, 189,
  201–202
Great Depression 1, 5, 36, 60, 173,
  236
Greece 21, 64, 80
Green
  Revolution 15
  Room meetings 228
Greenidge, Carl B 102, 104, 106,
  109–110, 117
gross capital formation, fall of 173
Guidelines for Officially Supported
  Export Credits 204
Gulf
  War 91–2, 135–6
  plus pricing system (of crude) 123

Harrod-Domar growth model 2, 38–40
Heckscher, Eli 56, 250
  full accordance with List 49
  Ohlin theory 49, 56, 233
hedge fund(s) 63, 150
  see also Long Term Capital
  Management Fund
Helms-Burton Act 213–14
Highly Indebted Countries (HICs) 166,
  169, 173
HIPC (Highly Indebted Poor Country)
  Initiative 118, 183–93, 196, 200
  Enhanced (HIPC II) 111, 190, 192–3,
  196, 245
  Trust Fund 184–5
Hong Kong 140, 143, 145, 147, 188,
  210, 227, 239
human
  capital *see* capital
  Development Index 255

Development Report (of UNDP) 15,
  21, 42
rights 11, 55, 87, 94–6, 98, 104, 118,
  244–5, 256
hunger 11, 118

ICOR (incremental capital output ratio)
  19, 39
IDA (International Development
  Association) 6, 38, 66, 171–2,
  184–5
IDB (Inter-American Development
  Bank) 175, 187
IFIs (International Financial Institutions)
  56–7, 87, 97, 118, 163, 166,
  169–72, 174, 179–83, 185, 187,
  192, 195, 229, 231–5, 246–7, 254,
  256
  non-accountability of *see*
  accountability
illiquidity (theory, as opposed to
  insolvency) 137, 163, 166, 172,
  179, 182, 200
ILO (International Labour Organization)
  10, 75
IMF 2–3, 6, 8, 9, 12–14, 50–51, 56, 62,
  64, 102, 104, 112, 114, 133, 142,
  147–9, 151, 153–7, 160–62, 164–6,
  169–71, 174, 180–83, 185–6,
  189–90, 193, 200, 210, 216–17,
  229, 232, 236, 241–2, 244, 250, 253
  gold sales by 185–6
immigration 74, 118, 135, 208
immunity (of World Bank) 247
import
  permissions 145
  substitution 16, 34, 44, 50, 195
income concentration 41
indentured labour 22, 113
Index of Sustainable Economic Welfare
  (ISEW) 26
India 3–4, 10, 22–3, 40, 67, 113, 135,
  160, 206, 208, 211, 214, 221, 223,
  226–7
indigenous knowledge 253
Indonesia 55, 74, 148, 152–5, 159,
  161–2, 191, 210
  as success of IBRD 148, 153
industrialization 16–17, 23, 34, 37, 39,
  44, 111–12, 127, 144, 221